SYNTAX AND SEMANTICS

VOLUME 21

SYNTAX and SEMANTICS

VOLUME 21
Thematic Relations

Edited by

Wendy Wilkins

Department of English
Arizona State University
Tempe, Arizona

ACADEMIC PRESS, INC.
Harcourt Brace Jovanovich, Publishers
San Diego   New York   Berkeley   Boston
London   Sydney   Tokyo   Toronto

ACADEMIC PRESS, INC.
1250 Sixth Avenue
San Diego, California 92101

United Kingdom Edition published by
ACADEMIC PRESS INC. (LONDON) LTD.
24-28 Oval Road, London NW1 7DX

Library of Congress Cataloging-in-Publication Data

Thematic relations / edited by Wendy Wilkins.
     p. cm. — (Syntax and semantics ; v. 21)
   Includes index.
   ISBN 0-12-613521-5 (hardcover)(alk. paper)
   ISBN 0-12-606102-5 (paperback)(alk. paper)
    1. Grammar, Comparative and general—Syntax. 2. Semantics.
   I. Wilkins, Wendy K. II. Series.
   P1.S9 vol. 21
   [P291]
   415—dc19

PRINTED IN THE UNITED STATES OF AMERICA
88 89 90 91   9 8 7 6 5 4 3 2 1

For Ben B.-W.

CONTENTS

Preface   xi

Introduction
WENDY WILKINS

1. Background   1
2. Issues Addressed by Contributors   2

What to Do with θ-Roles
MALKA RAPPAPORT AND BETH LEVIN

1. Introduction   7
2. The Motivations for PASs   10
3. Syntactically Relevant Lexical Representations   13
4. Where Do θ-Roles Come From?   16
5. The Locative Alternation   18
6. A Predicate Decomposition Approach to the
   Locative Alternation   24
7. The *With* Phrase   28
8. Lexical Decomposition versus Features   31
9. Predicate Argument Structures Once Again   33
10. Conclusion   36

Autonomy, Predication, and Thematic Relations
PETER W. CULICOVER

1. Introduction   37
2. Autonomy   38
3. Predication   40
4. R-Structure   44
5. Control   46
6. Nonthematic Predication   53
7. Summary   60

Toward a Nongrammatical Account of Thematic Roles
WILLIAM A. LADUSAW AND DAVID R. DOWTY

1. The Diacritic Use of θ-Roles   62
2. Are Thematic Roles in the World or the Grammar?   62
3. Nishigauchi's Hierarchy of Relations in Control   64
4. Cases of Obligatory Control   69
5. Conclusion   73

Thematic Relations in Control
CHARLES JONES

1. Introduction   75
2. Thematic Roles as Verb Entailments   77
3. *CP versus θCP   77
4. Syntax in Control   79
5. Thematic Relations in the Grammar   88

Complex Predicates and θ-Theory
K. A. JAYASEELAN

1. Introduction   91
2. θ-Marking in Complex Predicates: Three Problems   92
3. The Phrasal Node θ-Frame and Promotion   97
4. Restrictions on Promotion   102
5. Double Object Constructions   107

Multiple θ-Role Assignment in Choctaw
GEORGE AARON BROADWELL

1. Introduction   113
2. The Choctaw Agreement System   114
3. Verbal Suppletion   121
4. Auxiliary Selection   123
5. Multiple θ-Roles and the θ-Criterion   124
6. Conclusion   126

Inheritance
JANET H. RANDALL

1. Introduction   129
2. Lexical Levels: An Inadequate Solution   130
3. The θ-Hierarchy and the Inheritance Principle   136
4. Uniformity   141
5. Absorption   143
6. Summary   145

Thematic Restrictions on Derived Nominals
BOŻENA ROZWADOWSKA

1. Introduction   147
2. English Transitive Nominals   148
3. Single-Argument Transitive Nominals   157
4. Feature Approach to Thematic Relations   158
5. Polish Derived Nominals   161
6. Conclusions   164

Thematic Relations and Case Linking in Russian
LINDA SCHWARTZ

1. Introduction   167
2. Russian Reflexive Controllers   168
3. -sja Constructions   174
4. Conclusion   189

Thematic Structure and Reflexivization
WENDY WILKINS

1. Introduction   191
2. R-Structure   192
3. Role Assignment and Conditions on R-Structure   195
4. External Arguments   203
5. The Thematic Hierarchy   206
6. Conclusion   212

Toward a Lexical Representation of Warlpiri Verbs
MARY LAUGHREN

1. Introduction   215
2. Grammatical Functions   219
3. Case Marking: NPs and Person–Number AUX Clitics   221
4. Semantic Decomposition and Lexical Conceptual Structure   226
5. Relation between LCS and PAS   234
6. Relation between PAS and Syntactic Component   235
7. Conclusion   240

The Feature +Affected and the Formation of the Passive
DAVID LEBEAUX

1. Introduction   243
2. The Possibilities   244
3. Semantic Bootstrapping and the Feature +Affected   248
4. The Grammaticalization of Passives   256
5. Passives, Analytic Priority, and the
   Structure of the Grammar   258
6. Conclusion   260

Thematic Roles and Language Comprehension
GREG N. CARLSON AND MICHAEL K. TANENHAUS

1. Introduction   263
2. Background and Motivation   264
3. Representational Assumptions   266
4. Empirical Predictions   273
5. Concluding Remarks   283

References   289

Index   301

PREFACE

Grammarians have long recognized the importance of grammatical relations in the description and explanation of linguistic phenomena. These relations, for example, "subject of the sentence" or "object of the verb," are not relevant, however, for expressing the recognizable relation exemplified by *the ice cream* in both (1) and (2).

(1) *The sun melted **the ice cream**.*
(2) ***The ice cream** melted.*

Any speaker of English knows that in some basic sense the relationship between *ice cream* and *melt* is the same in these two sentences. In both cases the resulting state is identical for *ice cream*. This is true in spite of the fact that in sentence (1) the noun phrase *ice cream* is the object and in sentence (2) it is the subject. The grammatical system that expresses the English speaker's sense of some shared meaning in (1) and (2) is the system of THEMATIC RELATIONS. The semantic role played by *ice cream* is the same in both sentences even though the grammatical relation differs. In both sentences *ice cream* bears the same thematic relation to the verb.

The studies of thematic relations in this volume focus both on what semantic roles are expressible in the grammar and on how these roles come to be associated with noun phrases in particular grammatical relations with their verbs. Many theoretical viewpoints are represented here, and the themes discussed are diverse. Nevertheless, because accepted syntactic mechanisms are not sufficient to explain many identifiable language phenomena traditionally viewed as syntactic, each of the contributors addresses, more or less directly, the central issue of the status of the system of thematic relations in the theory of grammar.

This volume will be important for all linguists, syntacticians, and semanticists with an active interest in research on natural language. It will also be relevant for researchers in related disciplines who are interested in the interaction of components of the language faculty and other aspects of cognition. Research on thematic relations may well provide vital insights about the interface between grammar and other cognitive systems. It may also provide a readily adaptable system for computer scientists who recognize the importance of semantic representations in computational linguistic theories. Additionally, the volume's multifaceted approach to its topic makes it particularly appropriate for students of linguistics, as well as of cognitive science more generally.

The motivation for a book on thematic relations grew out of the successful symposium on the same topic at the 1985 meeting of the Linguistic Society of America in Seattle, Washington. Although few of the original symposium members collaborated in the present volume, I would like to express my thanks to them all for their lively and informative participation at that time. Joe Emonds was the coorganizer, with me, of the symposium. The other participants were Stephen Anderson, Hagit Borer, Ray Jackendoff, Paul Kiparsky, Beth Levin, Fritz Newmeyer, Janet Randall, Leonard Talmy, Hanna Walinska de Hackbeil, and Annie Zaenen.

I thank Stephen Anderson for his interest in this project since its conception and for his support of it in his role as *Syntax and Semantics* Series Editor. All of the authors deserve my thanks, gratefully extended, for their willing response to editorial comments and suggestions. It was a pleasure to collaborate with each of them, especially since it provided me with the opportunity to get to know each one, not only professionally, but also personally.

Thanks are due to my linguistics colleagues at Arizona State University, especially Dan Brink and Karen Adams, who helpfully responded to many of my queries about both linguistic issues and book editing. I am grateful for the generally supportive and collegial atmosphere, thanks in large part to Nicholas Salerno, Chairman of the Department of English, where linguistics flourishes even without (yet) having its own administrative unit. This project was begun while I was a Visitor in the Department of Linguistics of the University of Washington. I gratefully acknowledge the support, both professional and personal, that I received there.

Finally, I happily thank Jay Rodman, linguist and friend, for all his help. That help, in many ways, made this whole project possible.

INTRODUCTION

WENDY WILKINS

Department of English
Arizona State University
Tempe, Arizona 85287

1. BACKGROUND

At least since Gruber's (1965, 1967) initial examination of the set of semantic relations involved in interpreting the NP arguments of certain verbs,
linguists have taken these relations into some account in discussing syntactic
phenomena. Variations on this set of semantic relations have been used over
the years in a number of different models, including Fillmore-type (1968)
roles in terms of lexical cases, Jackendoff's (1972) well-known system of thematic relations, Talmy's (1972) work on the categories underlying surface
roles, and the almost completely syntactic θ-criterion in current versions of
government–binding theory (Chomsky, 1981).

Given the enduring interest in, and focus on, the semantic relations involved
in verb–argument structure, it is appropriate to bring together current work
on this topic in a single collection. Evidence of the high level of interest in the
issue of thematic relations was provided by the enthusiasm shown during the
symposium on thematic relations at the 1985 Linguistic Society of America
annual meeting. It was this enthusiasm, on the part of both the symposium
participants and the audience, which inspired this collection of articles on
the linguistic relevance of thematic relations.

1

Because of the many divergent approaches to thematic relations in the current literature, a volume of articles by a number of researchers could not pretend to present a coherent approach, nor even a consensus about directions for continuing research. However, all analyses (including those collected here) which incorporate a system of thematic roles, even the most syntactically oriented ones, recognize that the head–argument relation must be based on some limited set of semantic roles. Some analyses have concentrated on the inventory of specific thematic roles to the exclusion of the mechanisms for assigning these roles to particular syntactic positions. Other work has discussed the interaction of syntactic positions with thematic relations without insisting on specific semantic roles. Government–binding theory has attempted to explain the conditions which allow the (well-formed) assignment of the roles in general (whatever those roles may happen to be). Until recently, few linguists have focused either on the exact formal representation of thematic roles or on the relation between syntactic and morphological configurations and corresponding constraints on the assignment of particular thematic roles. The articles collected in this volume address precisely these interrelated issues.

2. ISSUES ADDRESSED BY CONTRIBUTORS

While the themes discussed in the present volume are diverse, each of the contributions addresses, to a significant extent, one central issue: What role, if any, should representations in terms of thematic relations play in the theory of grammar? Each author is brought to confront this question by the recognition that standard syntactic mechanisms (e.g., grammatical relations, hierarchical configuration) are not sufficient to explain certain language phenomena that might, from a more traditional perspective, seem to be syntactic in nature.

As to the central issue, two distinct points of view are discernible among the contributors. Some of the authors conclude that while semantic roles operate in the grammar, they do not take the form of thematic relations as generally (or historically) conceived, for example, in the early work of Gruber and Jackendoff. They argue for the separation of thematic relations from the domain of syntactic or lexical rules. The most extreme representation of this view is presented by Ladusaw and Dowty, who grant thematic relations no independent status whatsoever in linguistic theory. They suggest that, to the extent that they are recognizable entities, thematic roles are notions derived from verb entailments and "reasoning from general principles of human action."

Rappaport and Levin also directly address the general question of whether thematic relations play a role in the grammar. They distinguish predicate–argument structure from lexical–conceptual structure and argue that in the former it is the manner of role assignment, but not the (contentful) role labels as such, that is represented. At lexical–conceptual structure, where predicate decomposition is relevant, the thematic relations are derived nonprimitives identified with variables in the semantic substructures. The thematic roles are directly relevant only for the mapping between the two distinct levels of lexical representation. This conception of θ-roles is exemplified by an analysis of the locative alternation verbs. Laughren shares many of the basic assumptions of the view presented by Rappaport and Levin and proposes, at least for Warlpiri, that the predicate–argument structure for each verb (that is, its syntactic properties) must be derived from its semantic structure. This allows for the explanation of certain morphosyntactic differences in Warlpiri AUX clitics. They correspond to semantic contrasts determined by the lexicosemantic properties of the verb.

Both Culicover and Wilkins take the view that the thematic relations comprise a component of linguistic semantics without precluding the possibility that they are derived from some more-general aspect either of cognition or of the representation of meaning. Both authors, however, argue that thematic roles exist neither in the syntax nor at lexical structure. Rather, thematic relations belong at the level of semantics, in a representation comprised of roles and formally represented individuals and domains. The separation of the thematic relations from the syntax in Culicover's account of control and Wilkin's account of reflexives is supported by a strong interpretation of the autonomy thesis.

Schwartz finds evidence for a linguistic level of thematic relations, distinct from the syntax, in the analysis of Russian -*sja* constructions. Without directly addressing where thematic roles belong in the theory, she shows how the use of a thematic level, along with case theory and certain linking principles, permits a syntactically monostratal theory of reflexives and related phenomena.

In contrast to the authors who propose a clear separation of the thematic relations from either the syntactic component or the application of lexical or syntactic rules, there are those who propose to constrain syntactic and/or lexical processes by the use of thematic roles as more traditionally conceived. Jones directly confronts the issue of whether thematic relations are a part of grammar, and his view is to be contrasted with that expressed by Ladusaw and Dowty. He focuses on the choice of controller for syntactically empty categories in purpose clauses, infinitival relatives, and subcategorized infinitive complements, and argues for the relevance of a thematic constraint on the controller.

The articles by Jayaseelan and Broadwell both address the distribution of thematic roles in the syntax and with respect to certain syntactic criteria.

Broadwell presents a revision of the well-known θ-criterion to accommodate complex thematic roles resulting from the multiple role assignment of lexically decomposed items. He argues that this is necessary using evidence from morphological processes in Choctaw that identify certain arguments as both Agent and Theme. Jayaseelan discusses the distribution of thematic roles in complex predicates in English and Malayalam (of the form *give . . . permission*) and also resultatives and double-object constructions. He considers θ-marking that extends outside the maximal projection of the head and the θ-marking of arguments by both the host verb and the nominal. He suggests a rule of θ-role promotion to account for indirect (compositional) θ-marking which involves the amalgamation of certain distinct roles. This syntax-based theory of compositional role assignment contrasts with the semantic-based theory presented by Culicover.

Randall and Rozwadowska both suggest thematic restrictions on lexical processes. Randall discusses the systematicity of argument alterations in lexical rules that affect argument structure. She proposes a thematic inheritance principle based on whether a particular rule changes the category of its input item and whether it blocks the assignment of a θ-role. Rozwadowska, in examining derived nominals in English and Polish, argues that thematic, rather than syntactic, restrictions are relevant in determining the distribution of arguments in the nominals. She presents evidence that militates against NP movement in NP for passive nominalizations and suggests a general feature system for thematic relations.

Lebeaux, using the thematic feature [+ affected] in the syntax, explains the acquisition delay for nonactional passives. He argues that in the theory of acquisition the primitives of θ-theory are analytically prior to those of case theory. An analysis involving this thematic feature allows Lebeaux to explain the postulation of NP-trace by the language learner and the later grammaticalization of NP movement for passivization. It also provides the basis for explaining the restrictive domain for so-called passive nominals.

The article by Carlson and Tanenhaus, while viewing the thematic roles themselves in rather traditional terms (in the sense of Gruber or Jackendoff), extends their domain into the new arena of language comprehension. They explore the idea that thematic roles are central to language comprehension, allowing early, but correctable, semantic commitments on the part of the parser. They also suggest that thematic roles facilitate interaction among the processor, the discourse model, and knowledge of the world, and are important for coherence in local discourse structure. The article focuses on the parsing of sentences with potentially ambiguous verbs and, assuming that thematic roles are assigned on-line, suggests a mechanism in which lexical structures, in terms of thematic roles, help guide the syntactic parser.

The research reported on in this volume has been informed by a variety of different theoretical approaches. Even so, a number of themes and topics of common interest emerge. Interestingly, although perhaps not surprisingly, the present collection of articles would seem to corroborate many of the seminal insights with respect to thematic relations.

Gruber, Jackendoff, and Talmy recognized the value of the semantic decomposition of lexical items in terms of certain predicates and roles. This view remains central in the work of Rappaport and Levin, Broadwell, and Laughren. It is inherent in the feature-based analyses of Rozwadowska and Lebeaux, as well as in the work of Wilkins and Culicover, who distinguish distinct sets of roles, and Schwartz, who locates roles along a hierarchy defined by macro-role labels.

Fillmore discovered the importance of restricting the pairing of semantic roles with the NP arguments of predicators. This currently takes the form of some version of the θ-criterion and the projection principle and plays a prominent role in the work of Culicover and Wilkins at the semantic level, in the work of Jayaseelan, Broadwell, and Lebeaux at the syntactic level, and in the work of Randall on the lexicon. A version of Fillmore's restriction also underlies the parsing assumptions of Carlson and Tanenhaus.

Even in his earliest work, Jackendoff claimed that thematic relations were relevant to a number of apparently syntactic phenomena. The current volume returns to several of these phenomena. The influence of thematic relations on control is recognized by Jones and Jayaseelan. Culicover removes control from the syntactic component entirely, moving it into an exclusively thematic domain. Ladusaw and Dowty move it out of the grammar proper and into the realm of meaning and knowledge of the world. Following Jackendoff, Lebeaux recognizes thematic influence on passivization. Both Schwartz and Wilkins, like Jackendoff, explore the thematic restrictions on reflexivization, Schwartz admitting syntactic influences and Wilkins permitting only thematic constraints.

Too rarely have research results obtained by linguists from differing theoretical backgrounds led to extensive interaction. In many cases there is little knowledge of what is being done by colleagues who work within different frameworks, even when the focus of the investigations is very similar. Mutual influence among several differing lines of research is often, at best, indirect. By bringing together work by a number of researchers on a topic they all consider central, this volume, ideally, will stimulate a sharing of information and knowledge. This could result in a small number of comparable, competing frameworks for discussing the issue of thematic roles. Or perhaps there will emerge a common framework in which to assess recent results.

The lack of ready comparability among theories, evident in the work on semantic roles is, unfortunately, only symptomatic of the difficulty of comparing theoretical linguistic frameworks more generally. By showing that divergent approaches to the investigation of a common theme can benefit a wide range of readers when presented in a common and structured context, this volume could foster more endeavors of a similar nature, on other topics, in the future.

WHAT TO DO WITH θ-ROLES

*MALKA RAPPAPORT**
BETH LEVIN[†]

*Department of English
Bar-Ilan University
52 100 Ramat-Gan, Israel

†Department of Linguistics
Northwestern University
Evanston, Illinois 60201

1. INTRODUCTION

Predicate-argument representations have come to figure prominently in all current generative theories of syntax. Within the government–binding (GB) framework (Chomsky, 1981), this representation, frequently called a θ-GRID following Stowell (1981), often takes a form similar to (1).

(1)   PUT: ⟨Agent, Theme, Location⟩

The θ-grid of a verb or other predicator indicates its adicity, with the number of elements in this list corresponding to the number of places in the function the verb names.[1] The places in this representation are usually referred to by

---

[1] We use the term PREDICATOR to refer to any argument-taking lexical head. This term is to be distinguished from PREDICATE, which is a maximal projection of a lexical category and necessarily takes a subject as its argument. We nonetheless retain the traditional term PREDICATE-ARGUMENT

Syntax and Semantics, Volume 21
Thematic Relations

labels, drawn from the lexical semantics literature, which identify the thematic (θ)-roles borne by the arguments in the syntax which are associated with them.

Two general approaches to the use of θ-role labels may be discerned within the generative literature. On the one hand, θ-role labels have been implicated in numerous grammatical rules and principles. Over the years, various researchers have suggested that reference to θ-role labels is involved in the description of linguistic phenomena, including the distribution of reflexive anaphors (Jackendoff, 1972), the choice of controllers (Jackendoff, 1972; Růžička 1983; Nishigauchi, 1984; Melvold, 1985; Culicover and Wilkins, 1986), adjectival passive formation (Wasow, 1980; Williams, 1981; Bresnan, 1982b), and the expression of arguments in syntax (Ostler, 1979; Marantz, 1984; Zaenan and Maling, 1984; Kiparsky, 1985a).

On the other hand, the use of θ-role labels has been criticized by researchers, primarily because of the lack of consensus concerning the appropriate set of θ-roles and the criteria for determining what θ-role any given argument bears. The definitions given for θ-roles are typically vague, and as a result they either cannot be applied easily outside the core classes of verbs which have been used to motivate the θ-roles or are extended in unprincipled ways to new cases. These difficulties have led some to conclude that θ-roles have no grammatical import and no status in syntactic theory (e.g., Zubizaretta, 1987).

This article represents an attempt to reconcile the two general approaches just sketched by focusing attention on the following set of questions:

1. What is the nature of θ-roles?
2. Are θ-roles syntactically relevant?
3. What rules and principles may make reference to θ-roles?
4. What criteria determine whether an NP argument of a verb bears a θ-role with a particular label?

Before answering these questions directly, we argue in Section 2 that the term θ-ROLE is used ambiguously in the literature. At times it is treated as a synonym

---

STRUCTURES or representations when referring to the argument-taking properties of predicators, recognizing that they should more accurately be called PREDICATOR-ARGUMENT STRUCTURES.

Words of other lexical categories may be predicators as well, although their θ-role-assigning properties may be different from those of verbs (see Levin and Rappaport, 1986; Zubizarreta, 1987). Also, languages may vary with respect to whether words of a particular category may function as predicators. Verbs, however, are the prototypical predicators and are the main focus of this study. Bearing these comments in mind, we continue to refer chiefly to verbs in the exposition which follows.

of the term ARGUMENT; on this use the particular semantic relation which the argument bears to its predicator is irrelevant. The term is also sometimes used to name a specific semantic relation which an argument may bear to its predicator.

A major claim of this article is that the two uses of the term θ-ROLE are a reflection of two distinct lexical representations. The first use of the term is relevant to a lexical–syntactic representation, which we call the PREDICATE-ARGUMENT STRUCTURE (PAS), while the second is relevant to a lexical–semantic representation, which we call the LEXICAL CONCEPTUAL STRUCTURE (LCS), following Hale and Laughren (1983) and Hale and Keyser (1986, 1987), who in turn draw much from the work of Jackendoff (1976, 1983) and Carter (1976a,b). We argue further that a lexical representation which consists of a list of θ-roles, as illustrated in (1), does not exist.

In Section 3, we propose that PASs do not contain θ-role labels. Rather, they provide an explicit representation of hierarchical relations between the verb and its arguments. These relations are reflected in the d-structure grammatical functions ultimately borne by the NPs corresponding to the arguments. The PAS contains variables which serve as placeholders for arguments, and these placeholders can be distinguished only in terms of the manner of θ-role assignment to their corresponding NPs. The principles and rules which effect the mapping between the PAS and syntactic structure do not make reference to θ-role labels, nor do syntactic or productive morphological processes. They may distinguish among arguments of a predicate only in terms of the manner of θ-role assignment.

Although PASs do not directly reflect θ-roles, it is clear that the properties encoded in particular PASs are to a large extent predictable from some representation of the meaning of verbs. As we review in Section 4, it is often assumed that a list (or hierarchy) of θ-role labels serves as such a representation of meaning and that PASs may be derived from such lists via linking rules of the sort described by Carter (1976a,b) and Ostler (1979).

In Section 5, we demonstrate some of the problems with a lexical–semantic representation consisting solely of a list of θ-roles by examining one class of verbs—the LOCATIVE ALTERNATION verbs—whose members participate in an alteration in the syntactic expression of their arguments. In Section 6, we show that these problems may be overcome with the adoption of lexical conceptual structures as lexical-semantic representations. These representations encode certain aspects of a verb's meaning through predicate decomposition and indicate the arguments of a verb through variables in the substructures of the decomposition. Linking rules refer to variables in substructures common to the LCSs of many verbs. These substructures serve to define semantically coherent classes of verbs, whose members express their arguments in similar ways. On this approach, θ-roles are derived, not primitive, notions, identified with variables in recurring substructures of LCSs.[2]

The LCSs of verbs do not interact directly with the syntax. We claim that the mapping between LCS and d-structure is mediated by the PAS. The PAS, by encoding the compositional relations between the verb and its arguments, determines the basic syntax of a sentence, in conjunction with the projection principle and the θ-criterion (Chomsky, 1981). The linking rules, which derive the PAS from the LCS, ultimately result in the association of variables in the LCS with particular syntactic relations via the PAS. But it is the PAS, and not the LCS, which is syntactically relevant. As we discuss in Section 6, θ-roles, even as derived notions, have a restricted role in the grammar, as they are relevant only for the rules which effect the mapping between PAS and LCS.

2. THE MOTIVATIONS FOR PASs

The role of the categorial component of the grammar has been greatly diminished within the GB framework, and concomitantly lexical structure has assumed a more-central role in syntactic description. As Chomsky (1981) notes, there is an undesirable redundancy between the lexicon, as conceived of in the *Aspects* model (Chomsky, 1965), and the categorical component. The lexicon and the categorical component both specify the range of possible complement structures in a language. Moreover, viewing the phrase structure rules as lexical redundancy rules does not allow for the simplification of individual lexical entries, because each lexical item will still have to specify the complements it selects. The elimination of that redundancy is permitted by the introduction of the projection principle, which requires that each level of syntactic representation be a projection of lexical representation in observing the subcategorization properties of lexical items. The projection principle ensures that many aspects of the syntax of a clause are determined by the syntactic complement-taking properties of the predicator which heads it. The phrase structure rules need not duplicate information contained in sub-categorization frames and can then be reduced to the principles of X-bar theory.

The increased reliance on general principles which constrain the form of grammatical representations indicates that subcategorization frames are not the appropriate representation for encoding the syntactic complement-taking properties of verbs. A considerable amount of the information contained in

---

[2] This point is also made forcefully in Jackendoff (1987). In fact, it has been reiterated through all his work on conceptual structures, dating back to Jackendoff (1972).

the subcategorization frames, such as facts about linear order and case marking, follows from universal principles and from language-particular generalizations (see the discussion in Section 3). These principles and generalizations are taken to operate on an appropriate predicate–argument representation, a representation which has traditionally been assumed to play an important part in semantic description. Predicate–argument representations, then, serve as the lexical representation from which crucial aspects of d-structure are projected. These ideas are further elaborated in Stowell (1981), Pesetsky (1982), and Marantz (1984), among others.

The types of predicate–argument representations adopted in current work in syntax share properties with the representations that have been developed by lexical semanticists, and the labels used to identify the places in the predicate–argument representations are usually drawn from their work. Researchers in lexical semantics independently motivated predicate–argument representations in order to overcome what they saw to be a deficiency of syntactic representations: the obscuring of semantic relations between predicators and their arguments. A syntactic phrase structure representation of pairs of sentences such as those in (2) and (3) fails to bring out the near-paraphrase relation between the members of each pair.

(2) a. *We emptied water from the tank.*
     b. *We emptied the tank of water.*

(3) a. *Jacob bought his birthright from Esau.*
     b. *Esau sold his birthright to Jacob.*

Such a representation does not make explicit intuitive assessments that certain NPs bearing different GRAMMATICAL relations may bear the same SEMANTIC relations either to a single verb, as in (2), or to different semantically related verbs, as in (3). A representation that allows the NPs in the sentences to be identified in terms of the semantic relations they bear is preferable for these purposes.[3]

Independent support for such representations comes from systematic meaning–form correspondences which suggest that various syntactic properties of verbs, as argument-taking lexical items, are predictable from aspects of their meaning: verbs selecting the same types of arguments and adjuncts tend to express them in similar ways. For example, the alternation illustrated with the verb *empty* in (2) is displayed by other verbs that describe bringing about a change of state by means of removing some substance from a location, including *clean*, *cleanse*, and *drain*.

---

[3] It is possible to capture the near-paraphrase relation transformationally, but it has long been recognized that transformations, as currently conceived, are the wrong mechanisms for expressing these kinds of lexical relations (see, for example, Oehrle, 1976, on the dative alternation).

Systems of predicate–argument relations such as Fillmore's (1968) case relations, Gruber's (1965) and Jackendoff's (1972, 1976, 1983) thematic relations, and Talmy's 1972, 1985) Figure and Ground are intended to provide a level of representation where arguments are identified according to the semantic, rather than the syntactic, relation they bear to a predicator. One of the goals of all these systems is to find a small number of appropriate semantic relations (i.e., θ-roles) that would permit the statement of generalizations describing the syntactically relevant semantic regularities. This set of semantic relations, each identified with a natural class of relations of arguments to predicators, then forms the basis of a lexical-semantic representation of the argument-taking properties of verbs.

Although a representation of the argument-taking properties of verbs is relevant for the purpose of both syntax and lexical semantics, it does not follow that the same representation of argument-taking properties is appropriate for both concerns. An examination of the predicate–argument representations which have been used in recent studies reveals two ways of identifying arguments: (a) by means of the θ-role borne by the argument; (b) by means of the grammatical function borne by the corresponding NP in syntax.[4]

θ-grids, as described by Stowell (1981), have no internal structure, and the arguments are distinguished only by the θ-roles they bear.

(4)   PUT: $\langle$Agent, Theme, Location$\rangle$($= (1)$)

We can then consider a θ-grid of the type in (4) to be a purely lexical-semantic representation. The representations in studies that have followed have become increasingly elaborated, with the arguments in the θ-grid annotated to indicate the grammatical function the corresponding NP will bear in the syntax. Williams (1981), for example, introduces the distinction between EXTERNAL and INTERNAL ARGUMENTS. The internal arguments are those which are realized internal to the maximal projection which the verb heads, while the external argument is the argument realized outside this maximal projection.[5] Marantz (1984) makes a further distinction between DIRECT and INDIRECT

---

[4] Note the confusion in the literature surrounding the term ARGUMENT. Traditionally, the term refers to an element in a logical function. In recent generative studies, the term has been used to refer to a syntactic constituent in an argument position (i.e., a position where a θ-role may be assigned; see below), as opposed to a syntactic constituent which is not in such a position. To avoid confusion, we refer to elements in the PASs as ARGUMENTS, and elements in argument positions in the syntax as NP ARGUMENTS, or NPs IN ARGUMENT POSITIONS, or CORRESPONDING NPs IN THE SYNTAX. Note too that other syntactic categories may be associated with variables in a PAS; however, we are concerned here only with NP arguments.

[5] The fact that a verb may have only one external argument follows from the principles of predication theory (Williams, 1980; Rothstein, 1983).

internal arguments of a verb, which is also relevant to the structural realization of these arguments. In (5), we illustrate a mixed predicate–argument representation, taken from Levin and Rappaport (1986), in which arguments are distinguished both by θ-role labels and by annotations encoding information about grammatical functions.

(5)   PUT: Agent ⟨Theme, Location⟩

This representation encodes the fact that *put* takes arguments bearing the θ-roles Agent, Theme, and Location, and that the agent is the external argument and the theme is the direct internal argument.

Although the annotations are associated with θ-role labels, the annotations, rather than the labels themselves, are relevant for the purposes of determining the syntactic dependents of a verb. For this reason some linguists represent the arguments of verbs simply by means of annotated variables (Zubizarreta, 1987) or numbers (Higginbotham, 1985). The representation in (6), which is a purely syntactic predicate–argument representation, is taken from Zubizarreta (1987).

(6) $\widehat{\text{put } y}$, x; loc $\overset{\frown}{\text{P}z}$

This representation contains information necessary to ensure the proper realization of the arguments of the verb in the syntax.

3. SYNTACTICALLY RELEVANT LEXICAL REPRESENTATIONS

To stress the idea that the syntactically relevant lexical representation does not contain a list of θ-role labels, we employ the more traditional term PREDICATE–ARGUMENT STRUCTURE, instead of the currently commonly used—but perhaps misleading—term θ-GRID, to refer to this representation. The PAS of a verb indicates the number of arguments it takes, with a variable corresponding to each argument. The θ-criterion (Chomsky, 1981) requires that each variable in the PAS be evaluated (or SATURATED in the terminology of Rothstein, 1983, and Higginbotham, 1985) by corresponding to a syntactic constituent of the appropriate sort (e.g, an NP).[6] It is the process of θ-ROLE ASSIGNMENT which establishes the association between NPs occupying the argument positions of a verb in the syntax and the variables in the

---

[6] As mentioned earlier, although other syntactic categories may be associated with variables in a PAS, we are concerned here only with NP arguments.

verb's PAS.[7] Thus the predicate *is assigned a θ-role*, commonly found in
the literature, can be interpreted as "is associated with a variable in the
verb's PAS."

We follow the general assumptions made in the literature that there are
primarily three basic modes of θ-role assignment: (a) by the verb, (b) by a
preposition, and (c) by a VP via predication. Furthermore, a verb itself may
normally assign a θ-role to at most one argument.[8] It now becomes possible to
distinguish among the NP arguments of a verb in the syntax according to the
manner in which they are assigned a θ-role. The NP argument assigned its
θ-role by the VP via predication must be outside the maximal projection of
the verb as required by predication theory (Williams 1980; Rothstein, 1983).
Hence it is referred to as the EXTERNAL NP argument of the verb (Williams
(1981)). The remaining arguments are realized internal to the maximal
projection of the verb, and are referred to as INTERNAL NP arguments. The NP
argument assigned its θ-role directly by the verb is referred to as the DIRECT NP
argument, while any NP arguments assigned their θ-role by a preposition are
referred to as INDIRECT NP arguments (Marantz, 1984).

The syntactic relations between the syntactic dependents of a verb are
determined by the information concerning manner of θ-role assignment, in
conjunction with universal and language-specific principles of grammar. In
order to be assigned a θ-role, each NP argument must be in a structurally
appropriate position with respect to the constituent which assigns it its θ-role.
All internal NP arguments are assigned their θ-roles in the syntax under
government, so each internal NP argument must be governed by its θ-role
assigner. The direct NP argument must be governed by the verb which assigns
it its θ-role, and, since in English the other θ-role assigners are usually
prepositions, indirect NP arguments are the objects of prepositions. Both
direct and indirect NP arguments, being internal, are realized internal to the
maximal projection of the verb. In contrast, the external NP argument must
be in a relation of mutual c-command with the maximal projection of the verb,
as required by predication theory.

Since the properties of a verb relating to manner of θ-role assignment are
lexical properties, the lexical representation of a verb must include, besides the
number of its arguments, a specification of how each corresponding NP
argument is assigned its θ-role. An illustration of our conception of PASs is
provided by the following PAS for *put*.

---

[7] This is reminiscent of other discussions of θ-role assignment, for example, Stowell (1981),
where this process is indicated by co-indexing the NPs in the syntax with the appropriate slot in
the PAS, and Culicover and Wilkins (1984), where r-structure is a mapping from deep structure
sensitive to lexical requirements.

[8] Here we follow Marantz (1984), although there is some disagreement about the validity of
this assumption. See Baker (1988) for another point of view.

(7)   PUT: $x\langle \underline{y}, P_{loc}z\rangle$

The three variables in this structure indicate that *put* is a triadic verb. The structure also encodes how the NP arguments in the syntax that correspond to each variable will be assigned their θ-roles. The variable outside the brackets represents the external argument, and it is associated with an NP in the syntax external to the maximal projection of the verb. The variables inside the brackets represent the internal arguments and are associated with NPs internal to the verb's maximal projection. One internal argument (corresponding to the underlined variable) is a direct argument and one is an indirect argument assigned its role by a locative preposition (represented in (7) as P_{loc}).[9] We refer to the variables in the PAS as direct, indirect, internal, or external argument variables according to how the NP corresponding to the variable in the syntax is assigned its θ-role.

The difference between our lexical-syntactic representation and traditional subcategorization frames should be emphasized. First, our representations are explicitly taken to be projections from the more fully elaborated lexical semantic structure (see Section 6). This assumption helps constrain the correspondence between the semantic representation of a predicator and its syntactic representation. Second, to the extent that information concerning linear order, case, and categorial selection are predictable, this information, which is encoded in traditional subcategorization frames, is absent from our PASs.

The assumption that the lexical-syntactic representation does not contain a list of substantive θ-roles is generally implicit in current work within the GB framework, and it is made explicit in the work of Burzio (1986) and Zubizarreta (1987).[10] The concerns of θ-theory as it figures in this framework are primarily with the process of θ-role assignment, i.e., the establishment of correspondences between positions in PAS and positions in syntax, and not

---

[9] We do not address the important question of whether prepositions may be only case assigners, both case and simple θ-role assigners, or case and compositional θ-role assigners. It may be, for example, that *put* selects the whole locative phrase and the NP within the locative phrase is an argument of the preposition and not of the verb. See Baker (1988) for some discussion of these issues. In addition, the PAS must indicate whether each argument is optionally or obligatorily realized. As this aspect of the lexical representation has no bearing on the issues addressed in this article, we have not specified the status of each argument with respect to this property in our lexical representations (see Levin and Rappaport, 1986, for lexical representations which include this information and for an illustration of the relevance of this information to the syntax).

[10] A somewhat similar position has been adopted within the LFG framework by L. Levin (1985) in a departure from earlier work in LFG (Bresnan, 1982a). She introduces a new level of representation, the level of ARGUMENT CLASSIFICATION, which has the function of our PAS. This allows her to divorce the syntactically relevant representation of the argument-taking properties of a verb from the lexical-semantic representation, which for her takes the form of a θ-role list.

with the content of θ-roles. D-structure is a "pure representation of the thematically relevant grammatical functions (GF-theta)" (Chomsky, 1982, p. 9) in the sense that it must contain a structurally appropriate position for each variable in the PAS, as required by the projection principle (and no position which does not correspond to a variable in the PAS). The particular θ-role label attached to the variable does not have an immediate bearing on this. For the purposes of the syntax, each NP argument must be in a structural relation with its θ-role assigner, and θ-theory ensures that the appropriate conditions for θ-role assignment are met.

The syntactic realization of the grammatical relations encoded in the PASs are constrained by language-particular parameters concerning the position of heads and the direction of θ-role and case assignment (Koopman, 1984; Travis, 1984). These parameters, however, are also not sensitive to θ-role labels. We would indeed be surprised to encounter a language in which the direction of θ-role assignment is contingent upon the particular θ-role assigned to the NP argument. The θ-criterion too, is to be interpreted as ensuring a proper correspondence between variables in the PAS and the NPs occupying argument positions in the syntax. But once again the θ-criterion need not concern itself with the substance of θ-roles.[11]

Given a level of PAS which does not have access to θ-role labels, it may turn out that some of the more problematic rules which have been purported to make reference to θ-role labels must be reanalyzed. In Levin and Rappaport (1986), we demonstrate that although a rule of adjectival passive formation, formulated so as to single out an argument bearing the Theme role, may achieve the correct results in most instances, in a number of crucial cases this formulation leads to the wrong results. The desired results can be shown to derive from a combination of general rules and principles which are only sensitive to manner of θ-role assignment.

4. WHERE DO θ-ROLES COME FROM?

While the PASs of verbs determine the syntactic expression of their arguments, it is clear that these structures are often themselves predictable. Pervasive generalizations concerning the expression of arguments have been described in the lexical semantics literature by various authors (Fillmore,

---

[11] Chomsky (1981, p. 139) suggests that the θ-Criterion does refer to the substantive nature of θ-role labels, but it is clear that it is not this interpretation of the θ-criterion which is put to use throughout the book or in most subsequent literature. See Jackendoff (1987) for additional discussion.

1968; Carter, 1976a,b; Ostler, 1979, among others) and are referred to as LINKING RULES following Carter and Ostler. Few disagree, for example, that when in English a verb selects an Agent argument and a Patient or Theme argument, the verb will be transitive, and, moreover, the Agent role is associated with the external argument variable and the Patient or Theme role is associated with the direct argument variable in the verb's PAS. These generalizations raise the question of the status of θ-role labels.

As mentioned earlier, a problem with the use of θ-role labels is the lack of criteria for determining whether an argument bears a particular θ-role. For example, there appears to be no single definition for what qualifies as Theme or Patient. While some researchers have tried to apply these terms with care, they often mean nothing more than "the NP which is assigned its θ-role directly by the verb." This usage reflects a desire to simplify the linking rules by finding a small set of broadly defined θ-roles which cover arguments of a wide range of verbs. The result is the near identification of θ-roles with grammatical functions. The value of positing the θ-roles involved is decreased by such efforts, since the characterization of a given θ-role often breaks down as it is extended to larger classes of verbs. As the classes are broadened, they are more likely to include verbs that have no common semantic characterization, even if all the verbs in the class do express their arguments in the same way. It is not at all clear that there is a single all-encompassing semantic characterization which applies to all NPs that are assigned their θ-roles directly (cf. *I shattered the glass, I memorized the list, I adopted the suggestion,* and *I refused the offer*).

Nonetheless, we are still confronted with the numerous generalizations concerning the expression of arguments in which θ-role labels do appear to be implicated. We think that many of the problems associated with the use of θ-role labels stem from the practice of representing those aspects of a verb's meaning which determine its PAS as a simple list of θ-roles. The most successful attempts at dealing with phenomena in which θ-roles have been implicated recognize the predicate-centered nature of θ-roles. θ-roles are inherently relational notions; they label relations of arguments to predicators and, therefore, have no existence independent of predicators. A list of θ-role labels proves to be inadequate as a lexical-semantic representation since it obscures the complex cross-classification of verbs according to shared components of meaning, which is manifested in various syntactic properties related to the expression of arguments. As we discuss in Section 6, more-articulated lexical-semantic representations, involving predicate decomposition of the sort described in Carter (1976a,b), Jackendoff (1976, 1983), Hale and Laughren (1983), and Hale and Keyser (1986, 1987) provide a basis for isolating such recurring subcomponents of meaning, allowing for the characterization of the rich system of cross-classification that exists among verbs.

Before elaborating on the structure of the lexical–semantic representations we adopt and their relationship to PASs, we illustrate the shortcomings of θ-role lists as lexical–semantic representations.[12] We consider the problems facing any attempt to formulate linking rules for the class of locative alternation verbs, whose members exhibit two alternate syntactic realizations of their arguments. When the lexical-semantic representation of these verbs takes the form of a list of θ-roles, no satisfying account of the possible syntactic expressions of the verbs' arguments is available. Given a lexical-semantic representation which involves predicate decomposition, however, a more explanatory account of the locative alternation is provided. This approach enables us to capture certain aspects of a verb's meaning which, while relevant to the syntactic expression of its arguments, are not perspicuously captured by a simple list of arguments identified by the traditional θ-role labels.

5. THE LOCATIVE ALTERNATION

The locative alternation verbs[13] have been described as verbs that display an alternation in the expression of their arguments because they occur in two syntactic frames, giving rise to pairs of sentences which appear to be paraphrases.[14]

(8)   a.   *Jack sprayed paint on the wall.* (locative variant)
      b.   *Jack sprayed the wall with paint.* (*with* variant)

(9)   a.   *Bill loaded cartons onto the truck.*
      b.   *Bill loaded the truck with cartons.*

The (a) and (b) sentences in each pair seem to describe the same event, as they each involve an entity or a substance coming to be at a particular location

[12] Some of the problems we describe can be overcome through the use of more elaborated θ-role list representations, such as those which provide for the definition of θ-roles in terms of a set of features (cf. Ostler, 1979). For purposes of exposition, we postpone the discussion of such approaches to Section 8.

[13] Much of the discussion in Sections 5 and 6 draws on our ongoing study of the locative alternation verbs, which is reported in a more extensive but preliminary form in Rappaport and Levin (1985). Here we concentrate on one subclass of the locative alternation verbs, which we term the *spray/load* class, after two of its prototypical members. We intend to present a fuller analysis of the *spray/load* verbs, as well as the two other subclasses of the locative alternation verbs, in a future work. One of these two subclasses, the *clear* verbs, is discussed briefly later in this section.

[14] This view takes the two variants of a locative alternation verb to have a single lexical-semantic structure. The alternation arises from two mappings from the lexical-semantic structure to the syntactic structure. See below for another possible view.

through the action of an Agent. We refer to their arguments as AGENT, LOCATUM and GOAL.[15] In (9), the NP *Bill* bears the Agent role, the NP *cartons* bear the Locatum role. and the NP *the truck* bears the Goal role.

Another aspect of locative alternation has drawn the attention of various researchers (Anderson, 1971, 1977; Schwartz-Norman, 1976; Jeffries and Willis, 1984, among others). The pairs of sentences in (8) and (9) are only near-paraphrases: A change in interpretation accompanies the alternation in the expression of the arguments. When the Goal argument is realized as direct object, it is understood to be wholly affected by the action denoted by the verb. When this argument is realized as the object of a preposition, a partially affected interpretation is also possible. In (9b), the truck is full of cartons, but this is not necessarily so in (9a).[16]

An adequate lexical semantic representation of the locative alternation verbs ought to meet the following requirements:

(10) a. The near-paraphrase relation between the two variants must be captured.
      b. The linking of the arguments should be predictable in terms of their θ-roles.
      c. The affected interpretation of the goal as direct argument must be accounted for.

In the remainder of this section we show that it is difficult to simultaneously meet all three requirements using a lexical-semantic representation which consists of a list of θ-roles.

[15] The term LOCATUM is taken from Clark and Clark (1979). The term GOAL here is probably to be understood as a PATH of the form $[_{path}$ TO($[_{place}\cdots]$)$]$ in the notation developed by Jackendoff (1983). In particular, this argument should be distinguished from the Goal argument of verbs of change of possession (e.g., *give, sell, send, lend*), which denotes the generally animate potential possessor and can appear only with *to* and not with the range of prepositions which the Goal of the *spray/load* verbs appears with. The use of the term GOAL rather than PATH permits us to distinguish these verbs from verbs such as *clear, empty,* and *wipe*, which take Agent, Locatum, and Source arguments.

[16] A more refined description of the effect is presented below, but its exact characterization is a matter of much debate; for example, see the discussion in Anderson (1977), Carter (1984), and Jeffries and Willis (1984). We believe that the elusive nature of this effect arises from the interaction of its pragmatic and linguistic components, which have not been adequately distinguished.

This effect is to be distinguished from the effect that is observed when the Locatum argument specifies a delimited quantity. When the Locatum NP is definite, for example, as in (i), it is interpreted as denoting all the hay present, as noted, for example, by Schwartz-Norman (1976).

(i)   *Bill loaded the hay onto the truck.*

The effect involving the interpretation of the Locatum argument is independent of syntactic position. It is also achieved when this argument is expressed in the prepositional phrase.

(ii)   *Bill loaded the truck with the hay.*

Assuming that a list of unanalyzed θ-role labels constitutes a lexical-semantic representation, the paraphrase relation between the two variants of a locative alternation verb such as *load* can be captured by attributing a single shared θ-role list to the two variants.

(11)   LOAD: $\langle$Agent, Locatum, Goal$\rangle$

It is clear from the presence of the two variants in (8) and (9) that each locative alternation verb is associated with two distinct PASs, one for each variant:

(12)   a. LOAD: $x\langle \underline{y}, P_{loc}z \rangle$
       b. LOAD: $x\langle \underline{y}, P_{with}z \rangle$

The question remains why, given a single lexical-semantic representation, each of these verbs is associated with more than one PAS. Since we claim that PASs are derivable from the lexical-semantic representation by means of linking rules, we turn to an examination of the linking rules, as they may shed light on the alternation. In (13) we recast linking rules representative of those found in the literature in terms of the linking of θ-role labels with variables in PASs (rather than grammatical relations, for example). We identify these variables according to the manner of θ-role assignment of the corresponding NP in the syntax.[17]

(13)   LINKING RULES:
    Link the Agent role with the external argument variable in the PAS.
    Link the Theme or Patient role with the direct argument variable in the PAS.
    Link each remaining θ-role to an indirect argument variable in the PAS which is associated with an appropriate preposition.

These linking rules could be trivially applied to the locative alternation verbs to give rise to the PAS of the locative variant if we acknowledge that the Locatum argument, as the argument denoting the entity that undergoes the movement described by the verb, qualifies as Theme in the sense of Gruber (1965) and Jackendoff (1972, 1976, 1983). That is, the θ-role list in (11) could be reinterpreted as in (14).

(14)   LOAD: $\langle$Agent, Theme, Goal$\rangle$

---

[17] Some researchers propose that linking rules do not refer to θ-role labels directly (see Kiparsky, 1985a). Instead, they propose that θ-roles are arranged in a hierarchy and state linking rules that refer to relative positions on the hierarchy. But it is still necessary to identify the θ-roles of the arguments in order to determine the appropriate hierarchical arrangement of the θ-roles. This task faces problems analogous to those described below concerning the statement of linking rules that apply to locative alternation verbs.

On the basis of this revised list, the Theme (originally, Locatum) role is linked to the direct argument variable in the PAS. The Goal role is linked to an indirect argument variable associated with an appropriate locative preposition.

We now turn to the syntactic expression of the arguments in the *with* variant. Leaving aside the question of whether *with* is a preposition which may assign the Theme (Locatum) role, this variant involves the linking of the Goal role to the direct argument variable in the PAS. This situation requires positing what appears to be an additional linking rule specific to these verbs.[18]

Furthermore, we must posit a rule of interpretation, which assigns an affected (also known as 'holistic') reading to a direct object NP bearing the Goal role. But such a rule would provide no principled connection between the direct argument variable and an affected interpretation. There is no reason why a rule that assigns an affected interpretation to an NP bearing the Goal role when it corresponds to an indirect argument variable could not just as easily have been formulated. Yet the affected reading is not manifested on this realization of the Goal argument. Furthermore, in other languages where the locative alternation has been reported [for example, Berber (Guerssel, 1986), French (Boons, 1973), Hungarian (Moravcsik 1978), Japanese (Fukui *et al.* 1985); Kannada, (Bhat 1977); Russian (Veyrenc, 1976)] the effect is again found when the Goal role is associated with the direct argument variable, regardless of the language-specific devices employed to realize a direct argument. Finally, the affected interpretation observed in the *with* variant is not associated with all direct arguments, so that the affected interpretation cannot be simply seen as a consequence of the linking rule.

One way of dispensing with the rule of interpretation is to reject the assumption that the two variants share a single lexical-semantic representation. We could propose that the two variants are associated with distinct θ-role lists and ascribe the subtle difference in interpretation between them to their different thematic analyses. That is, the θ-role list in (14) would be retained for the locative variant, and a second θ-role list would be introduced for the *with* variant. In taking this approach, we can take advantage of a second notion of Theme found in the literature. Besides the Gruber/Jackendoff notion of Theme, the term Theme has been used by Anderson (1977) in a sense similar to "affected entity." Drawing on Anderson's discussion, we might propose that in the *with* variant, the NP we have described as bearing the Goal role, actually bears the Theme role in the affected entity sense. On this analysis, this NP would receive an affected

---

[18] A similar rule is needed for dative verbs in order to deal with the linking found in the double object construction. With dative verbs, unlike locative alternation verbs, the Goal is interpreted as a (potential) possessor, so that somewhat different θ-roles, and hence, somewhat different linking rules, are involved.

interpretation, which is then simply a reflex of the θ-role of Theme borne by the NP. The linking rules in (13) would then apply, yielding the appropriate PAS.

We are still left with the question of what θ-role to attribute to the NP which we originally described as bearing the Locatum role (see the θ-role list in (11)). One option is to take the label LOCATUM seriously and provide the *with* variant with the θ-role list in (15), even though this θ-role list has not been independently attested in the lexical-semantics literature.

(15)   LOAD: ⟨Agent, Theme, Locatum⟩

In order to give some content to this assignment of θ-roles, we would have to distinguish the θ-role of an entity that undergoes a change of state from that of an entity that undergoes a change of location, calling the former a THEME and the latter a LOCATUM. We could then interpret the term THEME in the affected entity sense as referring to an entity that undergoes a change of state, following a move made by Hale and Keyser (1987).[19]

Any account of the *spray/load* alternation which relies on two different θ-role lists, one for each variant, is problematic. In the absence of a clear definition of Theme, the two lists might be regarded as just another way of encoding the fact that either the Goad or Locatum role may be associated with the direct argument variable. Worse, when the two variants are given different thematic analyses, the ability of the analysis to capture the near-paraphrase relation between them is lost. The θ-role lists provide no indication that the variants are related. Finally, as we now discuss in more detail, the θ-role lists also hide the relation between the *spray/load* verbs and another subclass of the locative alternation verbs, the *clear* verbs.

Like the *spray/load* verbs, the *clear* verbs allow two alternative realizations of their arguments. The form of this alternation is illustrated with two verbs selected from this subclass:

(16)   a. *Doug cleared dishes from the table.* (locative variant)
        b. *Doug cleared the table of dishes.* (*with/of* variant)

(17)   a. *Mary emptied water from the tub.*
        b. *Mary emptied the tub of water.*

---

[19] This distinction is incompatible with the Gruber/Jackendoff notion of Theme. In the Gruber/Jackendoff system, the θ-role of an entity that undergoes a change of state and the θ-role of an entity that undergoes a change of location are both tokens of a single θ-role Theme, manifested with verbs from two different semantic fields. This system makes no accommodation for a single verb with one argument that qualifies as a Theme of change of location and a second argument that simultaneously qualifies as a Theme of change of state. In recent work, Jackendoff (1987), like Culicover and Wilkins (1984), deals with the notion of affectedness by introducing a second representation, the ACTION TIER.

The members of this subclass are in some sense the semantic inverses of the *spray/load* verbs since they denote the removal of a substance or entity from a location by an agent. Their lexical semantic representation would be expected to bring out this difference, for example, by attributing to them the θ-role list in (18).

(18)   CLEAR: ⟨Agent, Theme, Source⟩

This θ-role list differs from that of the *spray/load* verbs only in the specification of a Source, rather than a Goal, role.

The affected interpretation is again manifested in the *with/of* variants of the *clear* verbs, represented in the (b) examples in (16) and (17). If the affected interpretation were a consequence of a second thematic analysis in which the direct NP argument is analyzed as Theme, then the *clear* verbs in the *with/of* variant would also be associated with the θ-role list (15), repeated here.

(19)   CLEAR: ⟨Agent, Theme, Locatum⟩

The θ-role lists of the two subclasses are no longer distinct on the *with/of* variant. Yet the Theme in this θ-role list is also interpreted as a Goal with a verb like *load* but as a Source with a verb like *clear*. This very obvious difference is no longer reflected in the lexical-semantic representation, a serious drawback, since lexical-semantic representations are supposed to capture precisely such differences in interpretation. Furthermore, in order for the linking rules to apply successfully, the Locatum argument must receive a different preposition in the *with/of* variant of the two subclasses. On a θ-role list approach, the choice of preposition has to be explained by attributing different θ-roles to the Locatum argument in the *with/of* variant of the two types of verbs. But it seems odd that, on the proposed thematic analysis, the distinction between Source and Goal is lost, only to have another distinction surface that needs to be encoded in the Locatum argument. A θ-role list representation loses crucial information about a verb's meaning unless it encodes it by proliferating θ-roles. The problem here appears to be that one argument must be specified both as Theme and as Source for the *clear* verbs and as Theme and as Goal for the *spray/load* verbs.

An analysis which makes use of a single θ-role list gives a simple account of the near-paraphrase relation but fails with respect to the linking rules and affected interpretation. An account based on two θ-role lists is more successful at dealing with the affected interpretation and the linking rules but is unable to capture the near-paraphrase relation. Thus, each of the analyses handles separate facets of the alternation. We take this as a reflection of the fact that θ-role lists abstract away from the meaning of a verb in such a way that they can provide only a partial meaning representation. What is necessary is a more complex and structured lexical-semantic representation that will permit an analysis of the locative alternation verbs satisfying all the requirements set out in (10).

6. A PREDICATE DECOMPOSITION APPROACH TO THE LOCATIVE ALTERNATION

In this section we consider the way in which a lexical-semantic representation which takes the form of a predicate decomposition meets the requirements in (10). The assumption behind predicate decomposition is that at some level of representation the meanings of verbs have internal structure. They are composed of a number of primitive elements that recur in the definitions of many verbs. Similarities in the meanings of verbs can be captured by attributing shared elements to their decompositions. Verbs fall into classes and are therefore expected to have shared properties by virtue of these common elements.[20]

To make explicit the aspects of meaning relevant to our concerns, we employ lexical conceptual structures (LCSs) similar to those used by Hale and Laughren (1983) and Hale and Keyser (1986, 1987), which in turn are motivated by Jackendoff's (1976, 1983) conceptual structures. These structures provide specifications of the verb's meaning, where the arguments are indicated in the definitions through the use of variables. For example, the LCS of *put* might take the form in (20).

(20)   PUT: $[x$ cause $[y$ come to be at $z]]$

The definition in (20) is intended to capture the fact that *put* is used to describe an Agent (represented by the x variable in the LCS) bringing about a change in the location of an entity (the y variable); the z variable indicates the Goal of this change of location. The three distinct variables in the LCS indicate that *put* is a triadic predicate. Presumably, a limited set of predicates is found in the meaning decompositions; see Jackendoff (1983) for one proposal. The identification of a comprehensive set of predicates is a matter requiring extensive further study.

The linking rules must be able to identify the different participants in the actions denoted by the locative alternation verbs. On the decomposition approach, these participants are not identified by θ-role labels, but rather in terms of variables occurring in substructures of LCSs. Consider, for example,

[20] The decomposition of θ-role labels into feature complexes or the use of a two-tier representation also allows for the description of cross-classification. There is good reason, we feel, for favoring the predicate decomposition approach over these approaches. See Section 8.

the counterpart on this approach to the linking rule that determined the direct argument variable in a verb's PAS. On the θ-role list approach, this rule referred to the term "THEME" (see (13)), which, to the extent that it can be defined, is usually associated with arguments denoting entities which either undergo a change of location or a change of state. On the LCS approach, the relevant linking rule can be restated as in (21), so that it refers to the appropriate LCS substructures, given in (22).[21]

(21)   When the LCS of a verb includes one of the substructures in (22), link the variable represented by x in either substructure to the direct argument variable in the verb's PAS.

(22)   a. ... [x come to be at LOCATION] ...
        b. ... [x come to be in STATE] ...

This linking rule, for example, would apply to the verb *put*, since its LCS subsumes the structure in (22a).

Certain substructures recur in the LCSs of many verbs, serving to define semantically coherent classes of verbs. These substructures figure prominently in linking rules, as these rules dictate particular associations of variables in LCSs with variables in PASs. θ-roles are defined on this approach with respect to variables occurring in particular recurrent substructures of LCSs. For instance, instead of trying to find a single all-encompassing definition of Theme, this notion may be identified with the x variable that occurs in the substructures in (22).[22]

In the framework we have been developing, θ-role labels are not primitives of any level of representation. They are defined notions, which may be convenient for referring to particular arguments. We continue to refer to variables in LCSs by θ-role labels, but the labels are to be understood as referring to variables in particular LCS substructures, such as those in (22).

The formulation of the LCSs for the two variants of the locative alternation verbs requires the identification of the components of meaning involved. We assume that the verb in the locative variant denotes a simple change of location, just as *put* does, and has the LCS appropriate to such verbs. Whatever linking rules derive the PAS of *put* from its LCS will derive the PAS associated with the locative variant of *load* from its LCS. As a consequence, the arguments are expressed like those of a change of location verb such as *put*.

---

[21] In (22) we are using LOCATION and STATE as placeholders for either variables or constants of the appropriate type.

[22] We are not committed to any specific proposal about the form that linking rules should take. Linking rules stated over a hierarchy of θ-roles (see footnote 17) may be integrated into our approach, if the labels used in the hierarchies are derived from more elaborately decomposed representations.

The verb in the *with* variant requires a more-complex meaning representation. Taking the affected interpretation as a guide, we propose that the *with* variant has a component of meaning that the locative variant lacks, and that the affected interpretation can be ascribed to it. As evidence for the proposal's plausibility, note that while both variants in (23) entail (24a), only the *with* variant, (23b), entails (24b).

(23) a. *Henry loaded hay onto the wagon.*
      b. *Henry loaded the wagon with hay.*

(24) a. *Hay was loaded on the wagon.*
      b. *The wagon was loaded with hay.*

This entailment suggests that the verb in the *with* variant, but not in the locative variant, denotes the bringing about of a change in the state of the goal argument.[23] The affected interpretation of the goal argument can be attributed to the change of state that is entailed. Yet the representation must capture the near-paraphrase relation between the two variants. A more careful look at this relation shows that it also might be more precisely characterized as a consequence of an entailment relation, but this time a relation holding between the two variants. Note that (23b) entails (23a) but not vice versa. A representation of the meaning of the two variants of *load* should indicate that the meaning of the locative variant is properly included in that of the *with* variant. This requirement is compatible with the suggestion that the verb in this variant involves an additional component of meaning.

Drawing together these observations, we propose the following LCSs for the two variants of *load*.

(25) a. LOAD: $[x$ cause $[y$ to come to be at $z]/$LOAD$]$
      b. LOAD: $[[x$ cause $[z$ to come to be in STATE$]]$
                 BY MEANS OF $[x$ cause $[y$ to come to be at $z]]/$LOAD$]$

The representation in (25a) indicates that *load* names an event which involves a change of location (the locative variant). The representation in (25b) indicates that *load* names an event in which a change of state is brought about by means

---

[23] In fact, not all the locative alternation verbs in the *with* variant can be said to be verbs of *change* of state. (i) for example, could be used felicitously even if the plants were still wet from a previous spraying.

(i) *Linda sprayed the plants with water.*

The relevant notion here seems to be achievement of state. In (i) the state that is achieved is the state of being sprayed. We plan to treat these issues in depth in future work. Here we simplify matters and continue to talk about all the verbs in the class as if they were verbs of change of state. However, the alternate characterization of some of the locative alternation verbs does not affect the force of the argument.

of a change of location (the *with* variant). Thus the LCS in (25b) subsumes that in (25a). The locative variant's representation is embedded in a MEANS clause within the *with* variant's representation in order to capture the paraphrase relation. The /LOAD in the representations in (25) is intended to indicate the manner in which the action came about; it represents the component of meaning that sets *load* apart from the other *spray/load* verbs. The presence of this component of meaning sets the locative alternation verbs apart from verbs of pure change of state, such as *break*, or verbs of pure change of location, such as *put*.[24]

The use of the same set of variables (x, y, z) in both the main and the subordinated MEANS clauses in (25b) is meant to indicate that the participants of the embedded clause are to be identified with those of the main clause. In this way, the analysis is able to capture the fact that the entity denoted by the z variable both undergoes a change of state (the occurrence in the main clause) and serves as the goal of the change of location of the entity denoted by the y variable (the occurrence in the embedded clause). This dual relation poses a problem for a representation which consists solely of a list of θ-role labels, because each label can only single out a particular semantic relation.

This duality was also the source of difficulty in formulating the linking rules within a θ-role list approach. The statement of these rules requires determining which argument qualifies as Theme. On the *with* variant, one argument undergoes a change of location and another undergoes a change of state, so that both arguments meet common criteria for Theme. There is no principled way to choose which of these arguments should be analyzed as Theme for the purposes of the linking rules. To put this another way, it is not possible to decide whether it is the change of state or the change of location which is relevant to the application of the linking rules.

The predicate decomposition approach does provide a way of making this choice. In this representation, the change of location is embedded under the change of state in a MEANS clause. We may assume that, as a general convention, the main clause of the decomposition determines the basic class membership of the verb and determines the linking of variables (see also Laughren, 1986, and this volume, for a similar proposal in Warlpiri). Given this assumption, the verb in the *with* variant is basically a verb of change of state, so it follows that the z variable in (25b), which corresponds to the argument denoting the entity which undergoes the change of state, will be associated with the direct argument variable.

On this view, the locative alternation is not the result of an alternation in the syntactic expression of the arguments of a verb with a single lexical-semantic

---

[24] We believe that only verbs whose meaning involves a manner component undergo the locative alternation. Lacking this component, the English verb *put* does not display the alternation.

representation, be it an LCS or a θ-role list. Rather it reflects the existence of two distinct but related LCSs named by a single verb, each realizing its arguments in accordance with independently necessary linking rules. Furthermore, instead of choosing a single all-encompassing definition of Theme, we have identified this label with the variable in a particular LCS substructure which normally dictates the association of that variable with the direct argument variable of the PAS. By providing a decomposition, the LCS allows the expression of the fact that in the *with* variant a single argument may be interpreted both as Theme of a change of state and Goal of a change of position. Our analysis of the locative alternation meets the requirements for an account of the alternation set out in (10): (a) the representations capture the near-paraphrase relation between the variants; (b) the observed realizations of the arguments in the two variants is predicted on the basis of the lexical-semantic representation, obviating the need for idiosyncratic linking rules; and (c) the affected reading associated with the *with* variant need not be stipulated as it is a direct reflection of the meaning of the verbs in that variant.

7. THE *WITH* PHRASE

A question that remains to be addressed is whether the syntactic realization of the Locatum argument in the *with* variant is predictable. In Rappaport and Levin (1985) we suggest that the preposition *with* is used to case mark any Theme of a change of location that is not assigned structural case by virtue of qualifying as the direct argument of the verb. Consider the proposed LCS of the *with* variant for *load* in (25b), where the Locatum argument is represented by the variable z. The entity that this variable denotes undergoes the change of location that is the means of bringing about the change of state in the Goal (represented by the y variable). But in this LCS, it is the Goal that qualifies as the direct argument, since it appears in the main clause of the LCS (see the previous section). We propose that *with* is introduced as a θ-role and case assigner for the Locatum. For this reason, in that paper, we called the *with* variant the DISPLACED THEME VARIANT. *With* has the same function with three other types of alternating verbs: verbs of inscribing, verbs of presenting, and verbs of forceful contact. The alternations characteristic of the members of these three classes are illustrated with the verbs *inscribe*, *present*, and *hit*.

(26)   a. *The jeweler inscribed a motto on the ring.*
       b. *The jeweler inscribed the ring with a motto.*

(27)   a. *The judge presented a prize to the winner.*
       b. *The judge presented the winner with a prize.*

(28) a. *Kevin hit the stick against the wall.*
      b. *Kevin hit the wall with the stick.*

These verbs share some, but not all, of the properties of the locative alternation verbs. Therefore, although they appear to participate in the same alternation as the locative alternation verbs, they have not been included in this class (see Rappaport and Levin, 1985). While we do not want to propose LCSs here for each of these classes, note that the arguments expressed in the *with* phrase all qualify as Themes in the Gruber/Jackendoff sense, since they denote entities which undergo actual or abstract movement.

There is, additionally, a more subtle point to be made. The displaced Theme is expressed in the same way that an instrument is, through the use of a *with* phrase.

(29) *I broke the window with a hammer.*

The fact that across languages the two tend to be realized in the same way[25] suggests that the choice of a single preposition is not fortuitous. Ideally, our goal is to determine on the one hand what displaced themes and instruments have in common in order to explain why they are both marked by *with*, and, on the other, to find how they differ in order to account for the syntactic differences between them (see Rappaport and Levin, 1985, for illustration of the differences between the two types of *with* phrases). The answer probably lies in recognizing that both are themes of change of location found in MEANS clauses. In general, instruments are entities manipulated by an agent in order to bring about an action. For example, when a verb of change of state such as *break* takes an instrumental adjunct as in (29), the instrument is the Theme of the action (a change of location) which brings about the change of state that the verb *break* denotes; the instrument is the entity handled by the Agent and brought into contact with the entity that changes state.

Furthermore, a Theme of change of state, unlike a Theme of change of location, cannot be expressed as the object of *with*, as the contrast between the syntactically parallel examples in (30) and (31) illustrates.

(30) a. *I hit the stick against the wall.*
      b. *I hit the wall with the stick.*

(31) a. *I broke the stick against the table.*
      b.*I broke the table with the stick.* (ungrammatical on a reading where the stick breaks)

---

[25] See Hook (1983) for a discussion of Old English, Latin, and Sanskrit, Bhat (1977) for Kannada, and Veyrenc (1976) for Russian.

In both sentences of (30), the NP *the stick* is interpreted as an entity that changes location, despite the different syntactic relations it bears (the object of the verb, as in (a), or the object of *with*, as in (b)). Although both sentences in (31) describe a change in the state of some entity, this entity is never expressed as the object of the preposition *with*. The object of the verb denotes this entity in both, even though the object is the NP *the stick* in (31a) and the NP *the table* in (31b). While in (31a) the NP *the stick*, the object of the verb, denotes an entity that undergoes both a change of state and a change of location, (31b) is only grammatical on a reading where this NP, now the object of *with*, denotes an entity that undergoes a change of location and not a change of state. The interpretation of (31b) is consistent with the proposed *with* generalization. More important, this generalization is sensitive to the two types of Theme— Themes of change of state and Themes of change of location.

Once the basic components of LCSs are identified, the constraints, both universal and language specific, on combining these elements may be studied. In fact, it appears that the MEANS relation, in which an event or process serves as the means of bringing about a second state, event, or process, frequently licenses extended uses of verbs in English and in other languages. This relation is implicated in what Talmy (1985) calls LEXICALIZATION PATTERNS. The MEANS relation allows the primary meaning of a verb *V* to become a subordinate clause in a new LCS associated with an extended use of the verb. The new use does not denote an arbitrary action, but rather it denotes an action that is typically brought about by means of *V*ing. For instance, in the *with* variant, a locative alternation verb takes on an extended meaning as a change-of-state verb, since a change of location could be the means of bringing about a change of state in the goal of the change of location. Other examples of MEANS extension include the extended use of contact-effect verbs such as *cut* or *chop* as verbs of obtaining or verbs of creating.

(32)   a. *Molly cut the paper.* (simple use of the contact-effect verb *cut*)
       b. *Molly cut a piece of bread off the loaf.* (obtain use: obtain by means of cutting)
       c. *Molly cut a flower out of the paper.* (create use: create by means of cutting)

In the extended uses in (32b,c), the action of cutting is the means of creating or obtaining something.

The systematic investigation of the ways in which the components of LCSs may combine, giving rise to such lexical extensions, is essential. Particularly important is the identification of any constraints on the possible LCSs that may be constructed. Furthermore, cross-linguistic investigations must also form a central part of these studies. It appears that certain cross-linguistic differences in the possible predicates of a language can be reduced to dif-

ferences in the lexicalization possibilities between languages (Talmy 1985);
Green, 1973). Furthermore, such studies provide the basis for predicting and
explaining properties of lexical items such as systematic and accidental gaps in
possible predicators (see Carter, 1976b; Talmy, 1985).

8. LEXICAL DECOMPOSITION VERSUS FEATURES

We have posited predicate decomposition as a more-articulated lexical–
semantic representation that overcomes the deficiencies of representations
that consist of a list of unanalyzed θ-roles. It may be suggested that a feature analysis of θ-roles would allow these problems to be surmounted without recourse to predicate decomposition (see, for example, Rozwadowska,
this volume).[26] In this section we discuss the problems with adopting this
approach.

A possible feature analysis of the two variants of locative alternation verbs
is illustrated in (33).

(33)   a. LOAD: $\langle$[+ Agent], [+ Theme], [+ Goal]$\rangle$ (locative variant)
      b. LOAD: $\langle$[+ Agent], [+ Goal, + affected, + Theme],
             [+ Theme]$\rangle$ (*with* variant)

In these lists, the θ-roles of the arguments of the verb are each identified by a
set of features. The multiple features associated with the goal argument are
intended to capture the various semantic relations that this argument bears on
this variant. These same relations were expressed on the predicate decomposition approach by attributing to the *with* variant a biclausal LCS. The
following ordered linking rules could then be employed to derive the appropriate PASs from the representations in (33).[27]

(34)   a. Link [+ Agent] to the external argument variable.
      b. Link [+ affected] to the direct argument variable.
      c. Link [+ Theme] to the direct argument variable.
      d. Link all other roles to indirect argument variables.

[26] Another alternative to simple θ-role lists is the simultaneous use of multiple (usually two) θ-
role lists, often called TIERS (see Culicover and Wilkins, 1984, 1986; Jackendoff, 1987). The use of
tiers allows a more articulated and fine-grained representation than a simple θ-role list, and it can
even be used to duplicate certain aspects of predicate decomposition. We do not discuss this
approach in detail since we feel that the tiered approach faces problems comparable to those
facing a feature approach.

[27] Instead of ordering the rules, the features may be arranged in a hierarchy reminiscent of the
θ-role hierarchies used in Jackendoff (1972), Belletti and Rizzi (1986), and Kiparsky (1985a),
among others, so that the θ-role highest in the hierarchy link to the grammatical function highest
in a hierarchy of grammatical functions.

This analysis of the locative alternation allows a successful formulation of the linking rules, but it does not precisely characterize the near-paraphrase relation between the two variants. Although the list in (33b) expresses the fact that a single argument is both [+ Goal] and [+ affected], the decomposed representation in (25b) above indicates, as the feature representation in (33b) does not, that the change of state in the *with* variant is brought about by means of a change of position. To the extent that the additional structure that a predicate decomposition approach provides through the use of embedding is relevant to the statement of linguistic generalizations, such as that governing the distribution of *with*, a representation that encodes the information is to be preferred over one that does not.

Several more general considerations also argue against a feature analysis. First, it is unable to characterize natural sets of θ-roles. Certain lists of θ-roles, corresponding roughly to the case frames of case grammarians, are "natural", in that verbs of particular semantic types take sets of arguments bearing these particular θ-roles. The list in (35a), for example, is intuitively natural, whereas the one in (35b) is not.

(35) a. $\langle$[+ Agent], [+ Goal, + affected, + Theme], [+ Theme]$\rangle$
          (= (33b))
      b. $\langle$[+ Agent], [+ Location], [+ Experiencer], [+ Instrument]$\rangle$

To constrain combinations of features and combinations of roles, the feature approach would have to resort to encoding information about verb classes within the set of features defining each role. Yet this same information is an integral part of the representation in a predicate decomposition approach. When θ-roles are defined structurally over the variables of well-motivated primitive predicates in a decomposition, there is a way to study natural sets of roles and possible combinations of features. Possible combinations of roles are determined by the sets of argument positions of the particular predicates that are found in decompositions. Attested combinations of θ-roles are determined by the options available to languages for combining simple LCSs to form more complex ones, for example, through the use of the MEANS relation.

Furthermore, when θ-roles are decomposed into features, a small set of features can be combined in many ways, often allowing for the definition of many more roles than are attested. Ostler (1979), for example, develops a feature analysis of θ-roles intended to facilitate the statement of linking rules. But as noted by Kisala (1985), although Ostler makes use of 48 roles, he introduces 8 features to describe these roles. Yet, these are enough features to distinguish 256 roles. This leaves a large discrepancy between the number of roles that could potentially be described and the number of roles actually described. Considering the care that Ostler takes in motivating this set of features and the wide range of phenomena he attempts to deal with, it is doubtful that other attempts at defining comprehensive feature systems will meet with much more success.

9. PREDICATE ARGUMENT STRUCTURES ONCE AGAIN

We have developed a theory of lexical representation with two distinct levels of structure. The question, of course, is whether a lexical-semantic representation that takes the form of predicate decomposition is sufficient alone, obviating the need to postulate an additional lexical-syntactic representation such as PAS. The introduction of a level of representation is justified if there are generalizations which are most economically stated at that level and cannot be stated at other levels of representation. In this last section, then, we demonstrate that the PAS is indeed a linguistic entity, since there are principles and rules that can be shown to apply to this structure.

The PAS, as we have defined it, does not consist of a series of variables alone. Rather, it represents the compositional properties of verbs by explicitly indicating the relation between θ-role assigners and their dependents. By referring to PAS it is possible, for example, to distinguish between internal and external arguments or between arguments assigned their θ-roles directly and those assigned their roles indirectly. The classes of arguments defined by manner of θ-role assignment cannot necessarily be characterized as natural classes at the level of predicate decomposition due to the many-to-one relation between argument type and manner of θ-role assignment. Once again, this may be demonstrated by the impossibility of finding a single semantic characterization for all arguments that are assigned their θ-roles directly by a verb. Therefore, if there are rules which distinguish among arguments in terms of manner of θ-role assignment, the postulation of an additional level of representation is justified.

Consider the rule of Adjectival Passive Formation (APF), which has often been cited as a process that requires reference to the notion of Theme. Williams's (1981) formulation of the rule, for example, is Externalize(theme), where externalization is one of the operations that morphological rules can perform on argument structure in Williams's theory of morphology. Bresnan (1982b) formulates a condition on the output of the rule of APF in terms of the label Theme. The reference to the θ-role label in both accounts is intended to ensure that the appropriate argument of the verb becomes the derived subject of the adjectival passive. The restriction cannot be stated solely in terms of the syntactic position of the argument to be externalized, as Wasow (1977) was the first to show systematically. In Levin and Rappaport (1986) we show that not only is reference to the label Theme unnecessary in describing APF, it is also untenable. Our account of APF involves no explicit rule of externalization; APF is reduced to a simple rule of category conversion. In effect, the result of category conversion is the externalization of a single argument of the verb from which the adjectival passive is derived. The result is grammatical so long as all well-formedness conditions of grammar are met by the output. In this way we show that the effect achieved by the various Theme analyses can be derived by appeal to well-motivated principles of grammar, such as the projection principle and the θ-criterion. We leave aside the details of the analysis and simply show that the principles involved in the derivation of adjectival passive participles discriminate between internal and external arguments and between direct and indirect arguments.

We show that if adjectival passive participles have the same argument structure as their base verbs, then in order for an adjectival passive to be well formed, all the obligatory arguments of the base verb must be realized. Therefore, if an adjectival passive participle has a single argument expressed, it must be capable of being the sole complement of the base verb. For example, we attribute the ungrammaticality of *the unsold customer to the fact that the obligatory Theme argument of the verb sell is not expressed (cf. I sold the car (to the customer) vs. I sold the customer *(the car)). Notice, however, that with a verb such as read, the ungrammaticality of *the unread children (on the interpretation where the children is Goal) cannot be attributed to an unexpressed obligatory Theme argument, since I read to the children, with the Theme argument unexpressed, is perfectly acceptable. The ungrammaticality appears to stem from the fact that the goal argument is sole complement only when it is expressed as an indirect argument (cf. *I read the children), but only a direct, and not an indirect, argument of a verb can become the external argument of the related adjectival passive. Notice that the generalization is stated simply in terms of PAS configurations. Restating the generalization in terms of LCS configurations would probably be very difficult, as arguments bearing a wide variety of semantic relations to their predicates may become external arguments of the related adjectival passives.

The distinction between internal and external arguments of the base verb is also relevant for the proper functioning of the process of APF. Bresnan (1982b) has drawn attention to the fact that -ed participles of certain intransitive verbs can also be converted to adjectives. An examination of the intransitive verbs which may undergo this process reveals that they are unaccusative verbs (in the sense of Perlmutter, 1978)[28] Compare the participles in (36), which are derived from unaccusative verbs, with those in (37), which are derived from unergative verbs.

(36)   *wilted lettuce, a fallen leaf, a collapsed tent, burst pipes, rotted railings, swollen feet, vanished civilizations*

(37)   **a run man*, *a coughed patient*, *a swum contestant*, *a flown pilot*, *a cried child*, *an exercised athlete*, *a laughed clown**

Leaving aside the reason why this process distinguishes among the two verb classes, it is clear that the relevant distinction can easily be captured in terms of PAS configurations. Unergative verbs have a single external argument and no direct internal argument; unaccusative verbs have a single direct internal argument but no external argument. Due to the many-to-one nature of the LCS-to-PAS mapping, there is probably no single semantic characterization that will distinguish all external arguments from all internal ones, just as there is no single semantic characterization of all direct arguments. Without a representation of PAS, the generalization cannot be concisely stated.

A variety of grammatical processes that systematically distinguish unaccusative verbs from unergative verbs is now well documented in a wide range of languages. The existence of such processes provides support for PAS since the two classes of verbs are easily differentiated at this level of representation. Although it appears that a verb's membership in either of these classes is more often than not predictable from its meaning, it is difficult to give a unified semantic characterization of either class (Rosen, 1984). For example, the class of unergative verbs includes verbs of manner of motion, communication, bodily processes, gestures and signs, and involuntary emission of stimuli, while the class of unaccusative verbs includes verbs of inherently directed motion, change of location, change of state, and appearance and existence. Thus, restating certain generalizations in terms of lexical-semantic representation, while possible, is not very revealing.

It is true that certain linguistic processes single out particular subclasses either of the unaccusative class or the unergative class, but several characteristics of these processes should be pointed out. First, we do not know of any process that requires reference to members of subclasses of both the unergative verbs and the unaccusative verbs. This fact is more significant than it might appear to be, since verbs that come under the rubric of verbs of

---

[28] Following Perlmutter (1978) and Burzio (1986), we assume that intransitive verbs fall into two classes: unaccusative and unergative verbs. The single argument of an unaccusative verb is an underlying (d-structure) object, or direct argument in the terms we use here, while the single argument of an unergative verb is an underlying (d-structure) subject, or external argument.

motion on the broadest construal of this class are found among both the unaccusative verbs (verbs of inherently directed motion and pure change of location) and the unergative verbs (verbs of manner of motion). Second, those processes that do refer to some subclass of either the unaccusative or unergative verbs are not productive morphological processes but rather involve diathesis alternations. For example, *there* insertion is limited to those unaccusative verbs that are verbs of existence and appearance (L. Levin, 1985), while the ability to participate in causative/inchoative pairs (ergative, in the sense of Keyser and Roeper, 1984) characterizes verbs of change of state and verbs of change of location (Guerssel *et al.*, 1985). Such diathesis alternations, we feel, are best stated at the level of LCS. And since this is the level of lexical-semantic representation, reference to such classes is natural. See Laughren (1986) for more discussion.

10. CONCLUSION

In this article we have examined the notion of θ-role, which figures prominently in many current descriptions of the argument-taking properties of verbs. The term is used ambiguously to refer to both the notions of argument and semantic relation. This ambiguity, we suggest, stems from a failure to distinguish between the levels lexical-syntactic and lexical-semantic representation. We have sketched our conceptions of these two levels of representation and clarified which sense of the term θ-ROLE is relevant to each. The argument sense is important to PAS, the lexical-syntactic representation, while the semantic-relation sense is relevant to the LCS, the lexical-semantic representation. Neither of these representations takes the form of a θ-role list. θ-roles may be defined over substructures in the predicate decompositions that constitute the LCS. Thus θ-roles in our framework have a status similar to grammatical relations in some syntactic theories; they are useful labels, but they are not primitive elements at any level of lexical representation.

ACKNOWLEDGMENTS

This study has benefited from many discussions with Ken Hale and Mary Laughren. We also thank Jay Keyser, David Pesetsky, Wendy Wilkins, Annie Zaenen, Maria Luisa Zubizarreta, and the participants of the MIT Lexicon Seminar for their questions and comments. This work was conducted as part of the Lexicon Project of the MIT Center for Cognitive Science. Support for the project was provided by a grant from the System Development Foundation.

AUTONOMY, PREDICATION, AND THEMATIC RELATIONS

PETER W. CULICOVER

Department of Linguistics
The Ohio State University
Columbus, Ohio, 43210

1. INTRODUCTION

Thematic relations are grounded in the elements that constitute our mental representation of events.[1] I take it as given that there is a correspondence between our mental representation of events and the meanings of sentences used to express them.

Concerning the thematic relations such as Agent and Patient, we may distinguish two views. On one view, thematic relations are components of the linguistic representation of meaning. On the other view, they are not components of the linguistic representation of meaning, but are derivable from it (Jackendoff, 1987). The view that I adopt here is the first one, without excluding the possibility that the second may ultimately prove to be correct.[2]

---

[1] Throughout I construe the term EVENT as broadly as possible, so as to include states and actions.

[2] See, for example, Ladusaw and Dowty (this volume) and Culicover (1987). In the latter paper I argue that there are properties of the representation of complex events that cannot be captured by mapping syntactic structures decompositionally into representations such as Culicover and Wilkins's (1984) r-structure or Jackendoff's (1983) conceptual structure. In the current article, however, I assume r-structure because of its notational tractability.

Syntax and Semantics, Volume 21
Thematic Relations

What is somewhat more controversial is the notion that there is a corresponding representation of these components in syntax, in the form of θ-roles. In this acticle I pursue some of the consequences of the view that syntactic θ-roles per se do not exist. I arrive at this position through a consideration of a strong form of the autonomy thesis and a consideration of whether generalizations about thematic relations are most insightfully captured at the level of syntax or at the level of semantics. Some consequences for the analysis of control and predication are also explored.

2. AUTONOMY

2.1. The Autonomy Thesis

I take seriously a strong form of the autonomous systems view (Hale *et al.*, 1977; Culicover and Rochemont, 1983) as a methodological principle of linguistic research.[3] The extension of the autonomous systems view that I entertain here is most clearly articulated by Jackendoff (1983). According to this view, a grammar consists of a set of components, each of which characterizes a set of well-formed representations at one or more levels. Each component of the grammar has its own primitives, rules of combination, and well-formedness conditions. Moreover, there are correspondence rules that map representations at one level into representations at another. On this view, the primitives of one component are not the primitives of any other, and the well-formedness conditions at one level do not make reference to aspects of representations at any other level.

As can be seen, the autonomous systems view stands in direct contrast to approaches such as generative semantics (see Newmeyer, 1983, for discussion and criticism), in which no distinction is made between syntactic and semantic rules, and where syntactic well formedness is expressed in terms of semantic primitives. Much earlier work in generative grammar even outside of generative semantics shows occasional departures from a strict observance of autonomy. For example, application of the syntactic rule of EQUI required coreference of NPs. But reference per se is a semantic or pragmatic phenomenon, and so the derivative notion of coreference is defined in semantic or pragmatic terms (see Jackendoff, 1972, for discussion). While syntactic rules may take into account the syntactic category of a phrase (e.g., NP) we would not expect a syntactic rule to take into account the fact that the phrase refers to a human being ("move α where referent of α is human") or to a member

---

[3] The autonomous systems view bears a close relationship to the autonomy thesis of Chomsky (1975), which holds that semantics plays a limited or nonexistent role in formal grammar (i.e., syntax).

of the set of minerals occurring in nature, or that two NPs are in fact coreferential.[4] It is of course possible to assign indices to NPs in some formal representation and to define coreference as "same index," but this approach would appear to be somewhat of a metaphor. It is not without empirical problems, either, as Farmer (1987) shows.

There is no question, of course, that there can be strong correspondences, even near isomorphisms, between two levels of representation. Montague grammar (and other versions of categorial grammar) assumes an isomorphism between the syntactic categories and the semantic categories.[5] The function/argument structure of a semantic representation may provide explanations for distributions of phrases in syntactic structure (see, for example, Chierchia, 1984). Generally, in any theory, a syntactic structure determines in large part the formal representation of the meaning associated with it. Thus generalizations over one level often have their counterparts in another.

The appearance of such correlated generalizations at several levels of representation allows for a situation in which a generalization that is properly represented at one level can be formally expressed at another. Autonomy does not explicitly rule out the possibility of such a situation. It does brand such a situation as methodologically unsound, though it may prove to be notationally convenient. For example, the use of θ-roles and referential indices in syntactic representations is notationally convenient. But syntactic θ-roles should be ruled out if we adhere strictly to autonomy, assuming that thematic roles are properties of interpretations.[6] More generally, purely notational indices should be suspect, no matter what the level of representation at which they are employed.

As is clear from work in government-binding theory, generalizations such as the θ-criterion can be stated, perhaps observationally adequately, in terms of syntactic structures.[7] However, it is argued here that a natural account of

---

[4] Obviously this methodological restriction limits one's options severely in cases where there are surface-order constraints on noun phrases in terms of features like [animate] or [human]. If the methodology is well founded, these limitations should prove to be productive. For discussion see Hale *et al.* (1977).

[5] See Montague (1973), and for an exposition, Dowty *et al.* (1981). See also Gazdar *et al.* (1985) for a related approach in generalized phrase structure grammar.

[6] The position taken here is one advocated by Jackendoff (1983, and elsewhere). In earlier work Jackendoff took thematic roles to be primitives of the semantic representation (see Jackendoff, 1972); in more recent work he has articulated the view that they are relations defined over representations at conceptual structure.

[7] The θ-criterion is formulated by Chomsky (1981, p. 36) as follows: "Each argument bears one and only one θ-role, and each θ-role is assigned to one and only one argument." A somewhat different and ambiguous version is given in terms of chains elsewhere in the same work (1981, p. 335). For some suggestions that the θ-criterion is not a correct generalization, regardless of whether it is stated at the correct level, see Culicover and Wilkins (1986) and Jackendoff (1987).

control and predication can be formulated without reference to syntactic relations in the interpretation.

2.2. θ-Roles Are Interpretive

The resolution of whether or not θ-roles are syntactic is not a directly empirical matter, given that it is possible to map syntactic θ-roles into the corresponding semantic elements, thereby allowing generalizations to be expressed at either level. Rather, the question appears to be one of theoretical simplicity and naturalness.

Culicover and Wilkins (1984), referring to the usual interpretation that requires one-to-one mapping between θ-roles and arguments, argue that a syntactically formulated θ-criterion fails to capture generalizations about the assignment of thematic roles to representations of individuals. These generalizations do not reduce one-to-one to syntactic generalizations, suggesting that the syntactic θ-criterion is not doing the real work (see Chierchia, 1984; Jackendoff, 1987). The representation of a noun phrase in the interpretation may have more than one thematic relation, drawn from distinct classes.[8] Moreover, the same interpretation may be associated with a number of predicates, and it thereby is assigned thematic relations by each such predicate. For example, in the sentence *Bill left angry*, *Bill* has a thematic function with respect to both *left* and *angry*. Syntactically, the θ-role of *angry* cannot be assigned to the NP *Bill*; rather, there must be a dummy element PRO that is co-indexed with *Bill* to which this θ-role is assigned, as in *Bill$_i$ left* [PRO$_i$ *angry*]. This syntactic analysis is unmotivated outside of the problem induced by the syntactically expressed θ-criterion.[9]

3. PREDICATION

3.1. Co-index

Culicover and Wilkins (1986) show that Predication is a rule that is sensitive to locality as defined over r-structure. R-structure is a level, distinct from d-structure and s-structure, at which thematic roles are associated with

---

[8] Or as Jackendoff (1987) calls them, TIERS. Chomsky (1981) has a version of the θ-criterion that can be read as allowing more than one θ-role to be assigned to a given NP, but most work involving the θ-criterion has assumed a more restrictive view (see, for example, Safir, 1985, p. 18).

[9] For arguments that there is no syntactic reality to PRO, see Culicover and Wilkins (1984, Chapter 2). The arguments are briefly summarized in Culicover and Wilkins (1986). As is discussed later in this article, the empty-subject argument of an infinitive does exist, but at a nonsyntactic level of representation (called R-STRUCTURE by Culicover and Wilkins, 1984).

representations of entities that can bear these roles. I do not repeat the analysis here, except to restate the coindex rule as it appears there. R(X) refers to the representation of the constituent X in r-structure.

CO-INDEX:
(i)   Co-index R(NP) and R(X) where X is a predicate.
      THEMATIC CONDITION ON R-STRUCTURE:
        a. If R(X) bears no thematic role, then R(NP) must be a Theme or a Source.
        b. If R(X) is a Goal, then R(NP) must be a Theme.
        c. If R(X) is a Theme, then R(NP) must be a Source.
      LOCALITY CONDITIONS:
        a. If R(NP) and R(X) both bear thematic roles, they must do so within the same domain (i.e., with respect to the same role-assigning element) at r-structure.
        b. If R(NP) or R(X) bears no thematic role, then X must be bijacent to NP in syntactic structure.
      DEFINITION:
      X is bijacent to NP iff:
        a. X is a sister to NP, or
        b. X is immediately dominated by a sister of NP.
(ii)   Assign [arb] to R(X) if it lacks an index.

In what follows, the case where R(X) has no thematic role is called NONTHEMATIC PREDICATION.

In earlier work along the same lines (Culicover and Wilkins, 1984) predication was characterized as a co-indexing relation on syntactic structures. Such an approach is impossible under the autonomy thesis. The approach expressed in Co-index as stated here is somewhat more satisfactory, in that the level of representation relevant to predication is taken to be r-structure. But this formulation does not yet make use entirely of essential primitives of this level of representation, and still incorporates the syntactic relation of bijacency. As we see below, syntactic structure does play a role in determining predication possibilities, even though syntactic relations are not available at the level of r-structure.

The correct modification of the account of predication under the autonomy thesis is one in which only primitives of the interpretation are available as a means of relating distinct constituents of a sentence. These are θ-roles and referential indices. If a θ-role governed by constituent X is assigned to the representation of constituent Y, then we have, in effect, a co-indexing relation between X and Y. Similarly, if X were to be assigned in some way the referential index of Y, a different, and more explicit, co-indexing relation would be established.

3.2. θ-Assignment

I rule out the possibility that predication involves the assignment of referential indices on the grounds that predicates are not referential expressions. We are thus left with θ-roles as the only means by which distinct constituents can be related to one another in r-structure. As an initial hypothesis, suppose that all cases in which a nonreferential expression, i.e., a predicate, is linked to an antecedent are characterized by the assignment to the antecedent of an external θ-role governed by the predicate. Consider, for example, the case of control. In a sentence such as (1), the infinitive *to leave* governs the θ-role Agent. Assignment of Agent(*leave*) to the subject NP effectively co-indexes the infinitive and its antecedent without the use of arbitrary indices.

(1)   *John tries to leave.*

However, there is superficial evidence that not all types of predication function like control. That there are two types of predication (at least) is captured in the rule of Co-index above. Here are the main points of difference.

1. An infinitive, if it lacks a controller, will be assigned an [arb] interpretation. A noninfinitival predicate will not be. Thus we have contrasts such as the following.

(2)   *To swim nude is fun.*

(3)   **It is important nude.*

(4)   **The bed was slept in nude.*

(5)   **Nude is fun.*[10]

2. As indicated in the rule Co-index, controlled predicates, including arb predicates, are those that have θ-roles, while uncontrolled predicates lack θ-roles.

3. The interpretation of a predication relation is dependent on the matrix verb. Compare the following examples.

(6)   a. *John drinks coffee hot.*
        b. *John considers coffee dangerous.*
        c. *John pushed the door open.*

---

[10] An example like **John wants rich* is ruled out on other grounds. While there is a predication relationship between *rich* and *John*, *wants* must assign a θ-role to a complement. Either this θ-role is not assigned, in which case the interpretation is incomplete, or it is misassigned to *rich*. In general, APs cannot take θ-roles because they do not denote things, and so the sentence is ungrammatical one way or the other. To the extent to which an AP can be interpreted as denoting a thing, of course, the sentence will be good.

In each of these cases, the adjectival predicate has the direct object as its antecedent. But as the paraphrases in (7) suggest, there is more to the interpretation than simply specifying the antecedent.

(7) a. *John drinks coffee (while the coffee is hot).*
     b. *John considers (that coffee is dangerous).*
     c. *John pushed the door (so that the door was open).*

Only the first and third type of interpretation occur when the antecedent is the subject of an active sentence, as shown in (8), while passives in (9) show the full distribution exemplified in (6).

(8) a. *John swims nude.*
     b.**John considers lucky.*
     c. *The door fell open.*

(9) a. *The coffee is drunk hot.*
     b. *Coffee is considered dangerous.*
     c. *The door was pushed open.*

The ungrammaticality of (8b) is presumably due to the fact that *consider* subcategorizes a referential complement. A plausible account would take *coffee dangerous* in (6b) to be such a complement, while *lucky* in (8b) is not. On such an account, (8b) could not be analyzed as [PRO *lucky*], of course.

I assume here that the differences in interpretation exemplified above are orthogonal to the predication relation, which I take to be uniform. That is, in general, predication will be characterized in terms of the assignment of a θ-role to some antecedent in r-structure.

As background to the remainder of this discussion, let us establish a number of assumptions concerning the mechanism by which θ-roles are assigned in the construction of r-structure. It is natural to assume that a verb governs a set of θ-roles that are assigned to particular grammatical arguments. Let us call this LEXICAL- or L-GOVERNMENT. In a particular syntactic structure, a given verb governs in a different sense a set of grammatical arguments. Let us call this sense GOVERNMENT. The construction of r-structure involves the association of each l-governed θ-role with the semantic representation of a specified governed argument that appears in the syntactic structure.

The preceding is of course a schematic characterization of θ-role assignment. There are a number of central empirical questions that are left open. One such question is what constitutes government. Another is how the appropriate argument is specified for each θ-role. The familiar approach, exemplified in Chomsky (1981), is to assume that θ-assignment proceeds strictly on the basis of syntactic configuration. Government is defined in terms of configuration, and θ-roles are assigned in terms of government. For such an approach to work it is necessary to assume that all languages are sufficiently close configurationally that a single definition of government can be formulated. An example of such a definition is the following from May (1985, pp. 33–34), where government is defined in terms of the configurational notion C-COMMAND.

> **C-command**: α c-commands β if every maximal projection that dominates α dominates β, and α does not dominate β.
> **Government**: α governs β if α c-commands β, β c-commands α, and there are no maximal projection boundaries between α and β.

For the purpose of this article I assume these definitions.

The function of θ-role assignment is to get the right θ-role on the right argument. θ-role assignment yields a structure in which θ-roles are assigned to representations of the grammatical arguments. Depending on our assumptions about syntactic structure, it is possible that not all θ-roles are assigned in this way. Specifically, external θ-roles that are l-governed by predicates such as *nude* in *John swims nude* are not assigned directly, since such predicates lack governed grammatical antecedents. Moreover, if we do not assume syntactic PRO (see Culicover and Wilkins, 1984), the "subject" θ-role of an infinitival complement is not assigned directly either, but must be assigned by a rule applying at the level of r-structure, as discussed in Section 5.

4. R-STRUCTURE

In order to be precise about the properties of predication, let us first fix some assumptions about the representations over which it operates. In Culicover and Wilkins (1984) a view of interpretation is laid out that bears a resemblance to modern phonological theory in the following respect. Rather than there being a single level of semantic representation, there are several levels of representation, not necessarily strictly ordered with respect to one another, which express generalizations about the interpretation of sentences and relate these generalizations to levels of syntactic representation. In part, the problem of representing the interpretation is that of specifying precisely what these interpretive levels are, and what their properties are.

A crucial component of the account is the interpretive level of r-structure, that is, the level at which the θ-roles are represented. It is plausible to suppose that r-structure, in some appropriate formulation, contributes to what is called LOGICAL FORM. R-structure is a collection of representations of entities with θ-roles assigned to them. Given a lexical entry, an r-structure representation for a phrasal projection of some head is constructed by assigning θ-roles l-governed by that head to the appropriate representations of the syntactic arguments.

On the view of the construction of r-structure articulated in Culicover and Wilkins (1984, 1986), certain θ-roles are assigned directly, under government. Others are assigned indirectly, through predication.

Let us consider how r-structure is to be constructed from s-structure (the discussion applies to d-structure as well). I represent a θ-role as a pair $\langle \theta, \alpha \rangle$, where θ is the type (e.g., Agent, Patient) and α the relevant θ-assigner. α functions essentially as an index to distinguish different θ-roles of the same type within a single sentence. An r-structure is a pairing of sets of θ-roles with representations of individuals or sets of individuals, φ, corresponding to referring expressions. For perspicuity it is convenient to use the corresponding linguistic expressions to represent the θ-assigners and individuals in r-structure. Moreover, a simple list of the form in (10) enhances readability as compared with a complex bracketed expression.

(10) $\langle \theta, \alpha \rangle \; \varphi$
        $\langle \theta', \alpha \rangle$
        $\langle \theta, \beta \rangle$
        $\overline{\langle \theta, \alpha' \rangle \; \varphi'}$
        $\bullet \bullet \bullet$

To construct an r-structure, let us assume an algorithm, similar to that of Higginbotham (1985), that systematically traverses s-structure, picking out each θ-assigner α that governs θ-roles $\{\theta, \theta', \ldots\}$. Assume that these θ-roles are independently strictly ordered in a hierarchy. Suppose that α appears in a syntactic structure like (11).

(11)

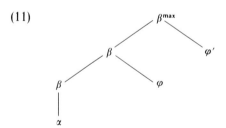

In (11), lexical item α is a member of syntactic category β, and appears in a phrasal projection of type β^{max}.

Beginning with the first θ-role l-governed by α, optionally assign this θ-role to the minimal expression that α governs (e.g., φ). If φ is not assigned a θ-role, ill formedness will result.[11] Ill formedness will also result if φ is not a referring expression, but is assigned a θ-role.

Moving up through the syntactic structure, continue assigning the l-governed θ-roles until the maximal projection is reached. Any unassigned

---

[11] This is essentially the completeness condition of Culicover and Wilkins (1984).

θ-role is associated with the maximal projection; it is in effect an external θ-role. This is illustrated by the s-structure in (12).

(12)

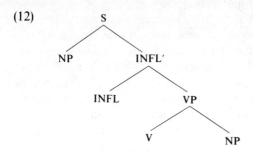

Suppose that V is a transitive verb that governs two θ-roles, θ and θ'. Suppose that θ' is assigned to the representation of the direct object. Then θ is an external θ-role and is formally associated with the VP. While V does not govern the subject NP, VP does. By taking the external θ-role to be in effect l-governed by the VP, we ensure that the external θ-role can be assigned to an antecedent NP under government.

The relation of predication here is the assignment of an external θ-role, as Williams (1980) suggests. The difference between predication as in (12) and nonthematic predication, as in *John swims nude*, is that in the latter case the antecedent is not governed by the predicate. Thus the relation between grammatical subject and its VP-predicate may be thought of as syntactic predication, while nonthematic predication and control will prove to be otherwise.

With these preliminaries out of the way, I consider in the remainder of this article the two main cases of nonsyntactic predication: control and nonthematic predication.

5. CONTROL

In the construction of r-structure, an infinitive may be assigned a θ-role. This will yield a representation along the lines of (13).

(13)   *John wants to leave.*
         $\langle\theta,want\rangle$ *John*
         $\langle\theta',want\rangle$ [*to leave*]
         $\langle\theta,leave\rangle$

In other words, the infinitive *to leave* bears a θ-role θ' with respect to *want*, and *leave* governs the unassigned θ-role θ. This latter θ-role is unassigned because *to leave* does not govern *John* or any other NP. Crucially, the role $\langle\theta,leave\rangle$ must be represented in r-structure because of the fact that *to leave* is assigned a θ-role under government and therefore appears in r-structure.

In r-structure, *John* and *to leave* fall within the same domain, defined as the set of expressions assigned θ-roles by the same element, in this case *want*. In order to express the fact that *John* is the antecedent of *to leave* in this sentence, we may simply assign $\langle\theta,leave\rangle$ to *John*, yielding (14). Note that there is no formal co-indexing involved in this process, which I refer to as θ-LINKING.

(14) $\langle\theta,want\rangle$ *John*
       $\langle\theta,leave\rangle$
       ———————————
       $\langle\theta',want\rangle$ [*to leave*]

Consider now the case in which the infinitive is the only argument in a domain.

(15)   *To leave would be fun.*
       $\langle\theta,fun\rangle$ [*to leave*]
       ———————————
       $\langle\theta,leave\rangle$

Here, θ-linking cannot apply, since *to leave* has no coarguments. I adopt the convention that a representation such as (15) is an expression of the arbitrary PRO interpretation. The introduction of a PRO argument into an r-structure such as (15) is an automatic consequence of the formal structure of the representation (see footnote 9).

Verbs, nouns, and adjectives are θ-assigners that define domains.[12] It follows that an infinitive is "free" when it appears within an S, NP, or AP that does not contain a suitable antecedent. The examples in (16) show that this is a correct prediction of the theory.[13]

---

[12] Prepositions may define domains but need not, even though they assign θ-roles. See Culicover and Wilkins (1984, chapter 2) for some relevant discussion with regard to sentences like *The bed / *Washington was slept in.* For further discussion, see section 6.2 below and Wilkins (this volume).

[13] I do not give examples involving AP. In general, all APs that allow for infinitives also allow for PPs. Such PPs are *for* phrases and have particular semantic properties. Consider, for example, the following.

(i)   *John is eager* $\left\{ \begin{array}{l} \textit{for a miracle.} \\ \textit{(*for) to shave himself.} \\ \textit{for Bill to shave himself.} \end{array} \right\}$

I do not completely understand the properties of *for*, but suspect that the control properties of these adjectives follow from them. Other prepositions do not in general allow for the infinitive, so that it is not easy to determine whether the determining factor is in fact *for* or whether there is some alternative explanation.

(16)   a. *John thinks* [$_S$ *that it is fun to shave* $\begin{Bmatrix} himself \\ oneself \end{Bmatrix}$].

     b. *Mary asked John* [$_{NP}$ *how to make* $\begin{Bmatrix} herself \\ oneself \end{Bmatrix}$ *rich*].

     c. *Fred will discourage any attempts to shave* $\begin{Bmatrix} *himself \\ oneself \end{Bmatrix}$.

     d. *John wants to shave* $\begin{Bmatrix} himself \\ *oneself \end{Bmatrix}$.

The distribution of *oneself* is possible only when there is no control relation between the infinitive and an antecedent. The fact that one can get a coreferential reflexive in (16a,b) might be taken as evidence that control is optional in these cases and obligatory in others. However, on a nonsyntactic theory of reflexives there is no particular need to extend the domain of control phenomena this widely (see Culicover and Wilkins, 1984; Wilkins, this volume). It is in fact possible to characterize control as obligatory wherever it occurs.

The general view of control in terms of representations at r-structure follows quite naturally from the autonomy thesis. The identification of the antecedents in terms of the argument domain, and moreover in terms of θ-roles, is in fact the only sort of control theory that can be formulated, given a strict interpretation of the autonomy thesis.[14] Specifically, a theory involving co-indexing of PRO and an antecedent NP is ruled out, if coreference by co-indexing is not allowed.

Another theory of control, involving a thematic hierarchy, has been proposed by Nishigauchi (1984), but he draws different distinctions within the data. Nishigauchi's view is that within S there is obligatory control. Thematic control operates over the domain of an NP and the S that contains it. Other cases of control are "pragmatic" control. Space does not permit a detailed consideration of his views here. The crucial difference is that in the theory espoused in this article, the local domain for control does not extend into NPs (or other θ-marked constituents) that contain their own θ-assigning heads. The domain for control (so-called obligatory control) is the θ-domain of the head of the predicate, and nothing else. Thus, it should in general be possible to have arbitrary infinitives within NP, but certain contexts will rule out this interpretation:

---

[14] This last statement must be modified slightly to be completely accurate. A theory of syntactic control can be given in terms of empty categories and syntactic co-indexing that makes no claims about reference. Such a theory is an artifact, however, given that an interpretation exists for the empty categories and the indices in terms of another level of representation such as r-structure.

(17)   a. *John made an attempt to shave* $\begin{Bmatrix} himself \\ *oneself \end{Bmatrix}$.

     b. *John discouraged any attempt to shave* $\begin{Bmatrix} *himself \\ oneself \end{Bmatrix}$.

     c. *John regrets all attempts to shave* $\begin{Bmatrix} himself \\ oneself \end{Bmatrix}$.

The different distributions of reflexive are not, I presume, indicative of different syntactic structures in these three sentences; in fact there is no independent evidence to suggest that syntactic differences exist. Rather, they appear to be explained by the relationship between John and the actions *shaving himself* and *shaving oneself* that are expressed by the main verbs. An inferential account of control is possible in these cases along lines similar to those suggested by Ladusaw and Dowty (this volume). In (17a), making an attempt is semantically (thematically) equivalent to attempting, and therefore the interpretation 'John attempts to shave oneself' is ruled out. In (17b), discouraging an action implies strongly that the action is taken by someone else, and hence the interpretation where John shaves John is ruled out. In (17c), John expresses an attitude toward an event, which entails nothing about the actor. Hence either interpretation is possible.

There is one case, however, where obligatory control into an NP might occur. Suppose that the subject is an infinitive, and suppose that there is also a direct object. Then the two are assigned θ-roles l-governed by the same element. Consider example (18).

(18)   *To leave would bother me.*

$\langle \theta, bother \rangle$	*me*
$\langle \theta', bother \rangle$	*[to leave]*
$\langle \theta, leave \rangle$	

Formally, there is nothing to distinguish this case from that of *John wants to leave*, discussed earlier. θ-linking should occur, yielding (19).

(19)

$\langle \theta, bother \rangle$	*me*
$\langle \theta, leave \rangle$	
$\langle \theta', leave \rangle$	*[to leave]*

This analysis presumes that the subject θ-role is assigned directly to the infinitive. It is plausible, however, that there is a syntactic difference between subject infinitives and the majority of the infinitives that are verbal complements. The latter, it appears, are not NPs, while there is good evidence that subject infinitives are NPs. Before considering the evidence, let us note that if this distinction holds, we would expect subject infinitives not to display obligatory control, because obligatory control cannot hold across an NP boundary.

To test whether there is in fact obligatory control in these subject cases, we attempt to use the arbitrary *oneself* in the subject infinitive.

(20)   *To shave oneself* $\begin{Bmatrix} *would\ bother\ me \\ *would\ offend\ me \\ *hurts\ my\ pride \\ *would\ exhaust\ me \\ *would\ make\ me\ nervous \end{Bmatrix}$.

(21)   *To shave oneself* $\begin{Bmatrix} would\ confuse\ everyone \\ would\ suggest\ ignorance\ of\ the\ rules \\ speaks\ volumes \\ says\ that\ one\ is\ unrefined \end{Bmatrix}$.

(22)   *To shave oneself* $\begin{Bmatrix} carries\ no\ weight\ around\ here \\ means\ nothing \\ would\ raise\ a\ suspicion \\ requires\ considerable\ toughness \end{Bmatrix}$.

The best cases, those in (21) and (22), occur when there is no direct relationship between the action expressed by the infinitive and the direct object. The difference that we see here is reminiscent of the difference illustrated in (17) in connection with *attempt*. As in (17), the evidence here suggests that control of subject infinitives is inferentially determined, as is control of infinitives within NP. Thus it is plausible that the subject infinitive is also within an NP.

There is some evidence that subject infinitives are in fact NPs. While it is possible to develop an analysis in which all infinitives are S' (see Koster and May, 1982), certain differences appear to hold between subject infinitives and nonsubject infinitives.

1. Nonsubject infinitives cannot in general conjoin with nominals, but subject infinitives can, albeit marginally.

(23)   a. *John attempted to read the letter and to answer at once.*
        b. *John attempted a reading of the letter and an immediate response.*
        c. **John attempted a reading of the letter and to answer at once.*
        d. **John attempted to read the letter and an immediate response.*

(24)   a. *Mary wants to run and to win.*
        b. *Mary wants an election and a victory.*
        c. **Mary wants to run and a victory.*
        d. **Mary wants an election and to win.*

(25) a. ⎡*To read the letter and to answer at once* ⎤ *would be nice.*
     b. ⎢*A reading of the letter and an immediate response* ⎥
     c. ⎢*A reading of the letter and to answer at once* ⎥
     d. ⎣*To read the letter and an immediate response* ⎦

2. Subject infinitives can topicalize, while nonsubject infinitival complements cannot.

(26) a. *Bill believes that to read the letter would be a big mistake.*
     b. *Bill believes that Mary wants to read the letter.*
     c. *Bill believes that it would be a big mistake to read the letter.*

(27) a. *To read the letter, Bill believes t would be a big mistake.*
     b.**To read the letter, Bill believes that Mary wants t.*
     c.**To read the letter, Bill believes that it would be a big mistake t.*

(27b,c) show that topicalization is ruled out whether or not the infinitive is in an argument position, if it is not a subject.

On the view that subject infinitives are NPs, the actual r-structure for a sentence like *to leave would bother me* would not be (18), but (28). There is an extra set of brackets around *to leave*, indicating that the infinitive is a constituent of the subject and not the subject itself.

(28)   *To leave would bother me.*

$\langle \theta,bother \rangle$	*me*
$\langle \theta',bother \rangle$	[[*to leave*]]
$\langle \theta,leave \rangle$	

In summary, cases of control into subject infinitives are only apparent cases of obligatory control, a conclusion that correlates well with the NP-like behavior of subject infinitives in other respects.

Let us next consider cases in which an infinitive is a constituent of another constituent. The representation that I have developed here extends naturally to such cases, as shown in (29).

(29)   *Mary wants to try to leave.*

$\langle \theta,want \rangle$	*Mary*
$\langle \theta',want \rangle$	[*to try to leave*]
$\langle \theta,try \rangle$	
$\langle \theta',try \rangle$	[*to leave*]
$\langle \theta,leave \rangle$	

The first step is to link $\langle \theta,leave \rangle$ to the antecedent of *try*. Even when the antecedent of *try* is unspecified, as it is in (29), θ-linking applies straightforwardly.

(30) $\langle\theta,want\rangle$ *Mary*
        $\langle\theta',want\rangle$ *[to try to leave]*
        $\langle\theta,try\rangle$
        $\langle\theta,leave\rangle$
        $\langle\theta',try\rangle$ *[to leave]*

The next step is to link the set $\{\langle\theta,try\rangle, \langle\theta,leave\rangle\}$ to *Mary*.

(31) $\langle\theta,want\rangle$ *Mary*
        $\langle\theta,try\rangle$
        $\langle\theta,leave\rangle$
        $\langle\theta',want\rangle$ *[to try to leave]*
        $\langle\theta',try\rangle$ *[to leave]*

In order to achieve this result, it is not necessary to apply θ-linking from the bottom up. Suppose that we linked $\langle\theta,try\rangle$ with *Mary* first.

(32) $\langle\theta,want\rangle$ *Mary*
        $\langle\theta,try\rangle$
        $\langle\theta',want\rangle$ *[to try to leave]*
        $\langle\theta',try\rangle$ *[to leave]*
        $\langle\theta,leave\rangle$

In order to link $\langle\theta,leave\rangle$, we must assign it to a coargument. Since *to leave* is an argument of *try*, the only available coargument is *Mary*. Hence we will derive (31) once again.

Finally I note the stipulations in the rule of Co-index (Section 3.1) concerning the thematic properties of antecedents. As before, these are well-formedness conditions on linked r-structures like (31). I repeat them here for reference.

THEMATIC CONDITION ON R-STRUCTURE:
    a. If R(X) bears no thematic role, then R(NP) must be a Theme or a Source.
    b. If R(X) is a Goal, then R(NP) must be a Theme.
    c. If R(X) is a Theme, then R(NP) must be a Source.
A violation will occur when there is a possible antecedent that does not bear the correct θ-role. For example, consider (33).

(33)   *John promised Mary to leave.*
        $\langle Source,promise\rangle$ *John*
        $\langle Goal,promise\rangle$ *Mary*
        $\langle Theme,promise\rangle$ *[to leave]*
        $\langle Theme,leave\rangle$

To leave has two coarguments, *John* and *Mary*. Suppose that we link ⟨Theme,*leave*⟩ to *Mary*.

(34)   ⟨Source,*promise*⟩   *John*
        ─────────────────────────────────
        ⟨Goal,*promise*⟩   *Mary*
        ⟨Theme,*leave*⟩
        ─────────────────────────────────
        ⟨Theme,*promise*⟩   [*to leave*]

In (34) we have a violation of condition c. The antecedent of *to leave* is a Goal, not a Source.

In this section we have seen how obligatory control is a strictly local phenomenon, defined in terms of thematic domains. Since verbs, nouns, and adjectives are θ-assigners that define domains, we correctly predict that an infinitive is "free" when it appears within an NP that lacks a subject. Control in these latter cases is determined by inferential rules.

6. NONTHEMATIC PREDICATION

6.1. θ-Linking

I turn now to predicates that are not thematic arguments. From the point of view of logical form, such adjunct predicates may be represented in much the same way as adverbials, as suggested by their paraphrases.

(35)   a. *John drank the coffee hot.*
        b. *Mary swims nude.*
        c. *Fred pushed the door open.*

(36)   a. *John drank the coffee while it was hot.*
        b. *Mary swims while she is nude.*
        c. *Fred pushed the door so that it was open.*

Ignoring for now the formal representation of the details of the relation between an adjunct and its head, the r-structure for a sentence like (35b) is as in (37).

(37)   *Mary swims nude.*
        ⟨θ,*swim*⟩   *Mary*
        ⟨θ,*nude*⟩

The goal here is to capture the relationship between the adjunct predicate and its antecedent.

To begin, I repeat the relevant portions of the rule of Co-index from Section 3.1.

CO-INDEX

Co-index R(NP) and R(X) where X is a predicate.
   a. If R(X) bears no thematic role, then R(NP) must be a Theme or a Source;
   b. If R(NP) or R(X) bears no thematic role, then X must be bijacent to NP in syntactic structure.

DEFINITION:

X is bijacent to NP iff:
   (a) X is a sister to NP, or
   (b) X is immediately dominated by a sister of NP.

The formal relationship here between predicate and antecedent is the same in the case of nonthematic predication as it is in the case of control. Recasting the matter in terms of θ-role assignment, the claim is that nonthematic predication is the assignment of an external θ-role to an antecedent.

The conditions are radically different from the two cases of predication, however. For control we were able to formulate the conditions strictly in terms of θ-linking between arguments of the same θ-assigner at the level of r-structure. But in the case of nonthematic predication, there is a syntactic condition on the predication relation.

On the assumption of strict autonomy of components, we would expect to be able to eliminate this syntactic condition on predication. I turn to this problem in the next section. To complete this section, let us review the extent to which nonthematic predication falls under the rule of θ-linking.

I continue to assume that all θ-roles are expressed in r-structure, even those governed by adjuncts. Like controlled predicates that are assigned θ-roles, nonthematic predicates will be introduced into r-structure without antecedents. Suppose that the θ-roles governed by the nonthematic predicate are simply listed in r-structure. An illustration is given in (38).

(38)   *Mary swims nude.*
$$\frac{\langle \theta, swim \rangle \qquad Mary}{\langle \theta, nude \rangle}$$

Comparing (38) with (37), we see that the trick is to link the θ-role of *nude* with *Mary*. In a simple case such as this there is no problem, since there is only one possible antecedent. If there were two possible antecedents, then an ambiguity would be predicted, as illustrated in (39).

(39)   *Mary drank the coffee cold.*

$\langle\theta,drink\rangle$	Mary
$\langle\theta',drink\rangle$	coffee
$\langle\theta,cold\rangle$	

The predicted ambiguity in fact occurs.

A problem arises in more complex structures. The predicate must be local with respect to its antecedent, in a sense that is captured by the bijacency requirement. There are two sorts of cases where locality becomes an issue. If the antecedent is in a prepositional phrase, at least in some clear examples it cannot be the antecedent of a nearby predicate.

(40)   a. *I presented it$_i$ to John dead$_i$.*
        b.*I presented John with it$_i$ dead$_i$.*
        c. ?*I presented John$_i$ with it dead$_i$.*

The other case is where the antecedent is in a different clause from the predicate.

(41)   *John$_i$ said [that it would rain angry$_i$ tomorrow].*

These cases indicate that there is a problem with simply listing the non-thematic predicates in r-structure and then applying θ-linking to them. It would appear that reference to the syntactic structure is necessary in order to ensure the appropriate locality for these cases. But strict adherence to autonomy rules out reference in r-structure to such syntactic relations as bijacency. The type of solution that we must seek is one in which the syntactic structure imposes restrictions on r-structure from which the locality property will follow directly. I explore such a solution in Section 6.2.

6.2. θ-Merging

In order to incorporate the syntactic structure into the analysis of nonthematic predication without explicitly mentioning it in r-structure, I introduce a formal mechanism by which θ-roles of diverse θ-assigners are composed and assigned as a unit. The notion that composition applies to predicates is a natural one, but the particular form that this composition must take is somewhat exotic, for empirical reasons.

A naive view of composition might take the following form. Consider a complex predicate such as *swim nude*. Suppose that *swim* assigns θ-role $\langle\theta,swim\rangle$, while *nude* assigns θ-role $\langle\theta,nude\rangle$. I have already established that a θ-role unassigned within the predicate becomes the external θ-role of the predicate. A natural extension of this approach would be to take the external θ-role to be a set consisting of the unassigned θ-role of the head and the unassigned θ-role of any governed predicate. The situation for *swim nude* is illustrated in (42).

(42)

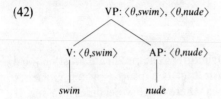

Carrying out this composition has a number of consequences. First, if the main predicate has an arbitrary antecedent, then the nonthematic predicate linked to it will have an arbitrary antecedent. Moreover, the two will, correctly, be "bound together", so that they cannot have different, but arbitrary, antecedents. Thus, *to swim nude* does not mean "to swim while someone is nude."

Second, if the main predicate has a definite antecedent, the nonthematic predicate cannot have an arbitrary antecedent. Thus, *Mary swims nude* cannot mean "Mary swims while someone is nude."

Conversely, if a nonthematic predicate has an arbitrary antecedent, it will be the same arbitrary antecedent as the higher predicate. If the composition is obligatory, there is no way that the external θ-role of the predicate can be unassigned while the external θ-role of the higher predicate is assigned to some antecedent.

The difficulty with this version of compositionality turns out to be an empirical one. Composition of the external θ-role of the predicate with the external θ-role of the higher predicate is not obligatory, as we can see from the numerous cases of object predication (e.g., *John drank the coffee cold*). Either object predication is a completely different phenomenon, or this view of composition requires some elaboration.

Let us take the latter route. Let α be a θ-assigner and let P be a governed nonthematic predicate. Suppose that composition consists of a merger, which I call θ-MERGING, between the external θ-role of P and any θ-role l-governed by α. If θ-merging occurs in the course of θ-role assignment, then the locality requirement on predication will be preserved.

Consider *John drank the coffee cold*. *Drink* l-governs the θ-roles θ and θ', while *cold* l-governs the θ-role θ. Merging $\langle \theta, cold \rangle$ with $\langle \theta', drink \rangle$ yields (43), while merging $\langle \theta, cold \rangle$ with $\langle \theta, drink \rangle$ yields (44).

(43)   *John drank the coffee cold.*
         $\langle \theta', drink \rangle$ *coffee*
         $\langle \theta, cold \rangle$
         _____
         $\langle \theta, drink \rangle$ *John*

(44)   *John drank the coffee cold.*

$$\frac{\langle \theta',drink \rangle \qquad coffee}{\langle \theta,drink \rangle \qquad John}$$
$$\langle \theta,cold \rangle$$

The effect of merging θ-roles is, in the end, formally the same as that of linking an unassigned θ-role to an antecedent in r-structure. θ-merging is part of θ-role assignment, while θ-linking follows it. Distinguishing the two processes in this way allows us to capture the fact that control is not subject to any particular syntactic configurational conditions, while nonthematic predication appears to be.[15]

Let us consider again the bijacency condition. θ-merging clearly eliminates assignment of a nonthematic predicate to an argument of a different clause. However, such a result could be achieved by a range of locality conditions, all of which require that the antecedent and the predicate be constituents of the same sentence. The more specific motivation for a bijacency condition is the fact that a predicate does not appear to allow an antecedent in a PP, as illustrated in Section 6.1, example (40b), repeated here as (45).

(45)   *I presented John with it$_i$ dead$_i$.

I assume that the structure is that of (46).

(46)

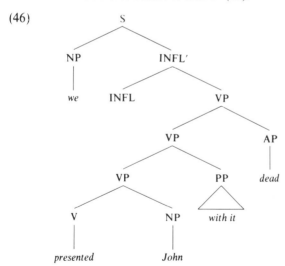

---

[15] θ-merging does not constitute an illegitimate use of θ-roles in the syntax, since it is not assignment of a θ-role to an NP. Rather, θ-merging is an extension of the association of external θ-roles with predicates, which determines the assignment of θ-roles to representations of NPs in r-structure.

The predicate and the object of the preposition are not within the same phrase. The predicate is therefore not bijacent to it. The predicate is in fact governed by the verb *presented* and not by the preposition *with*. Thus we do not require the bijacency condition for this type of example if we can ensure that the relevant θ-assigner for *it* is not *presented*, but *with*.

While verbs assign θ-roles to arguments, they also govern PPs that actually express the arguments. A verb like *present* in fact subcategorizes the prepositional phrase *with* NP while it associates some θ-role with the NP. The obvious way of expressing this is to associate both the θ-role and the subcategorized preposition with the verb in the lexical entry, as in (47).

(47)   *present*: θ,θ' (*with*)

What (47) expresses is that while *present* l-governs θ', *with* is the θ-assigner. θ-merging of the predicate *dead* with *present* in (45) may only involve θ, and not θ', given that θ-merging is constrained by government. Hence, for examples such as these, we derive the bijacency condition without making a formal stipulation.

When the verb directly assigns the θ-role, there is a violation of bijacency. This is an important point, since it demonstrates that the crucial factor in determining the antecedent of a predicate is not the branching structure of the syntactic representation per se, but the thematic structure associated with it. The violation is explained in the current approach, since the θ-role is associated with the verb and is merged with the predicate. (48) illustrates. Note that the syntactic structure is in essential respects the same as that in (46).

(48)   a. *John slept in the bed$_i$ unmade$_i$.*

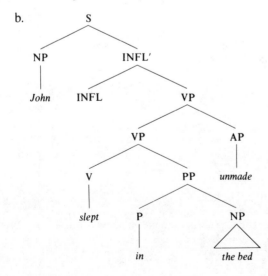

b.

The possibility of the passive in these cases shows that the θ-role is assigned directly to the object of the preposition by the verb: *The bed was slept in (unmade).* (For discussion, see Culicover and Wilkins, 1984.)

Eliminating the bijacency condition on predication has another significant consequence. For β to be bijacent to α, it is necessary that either β or the node that immediately dominates β be a sister of α. If α and β are not adjacent, then all nodes between them must also be sisters of α, yielding multiple branching structures. Consider, for example, (49), where *still wet* is predicated of *the lettuce.*

(49)   *John put the lettuce on the counter last night still wet.*

For *still wet* to be bijacent to *the lettuce*, they must be sisters. Then so must *on the counter* and *last night* be sisters of *the lettuce*. This structure is illustrated in (50).

(50)

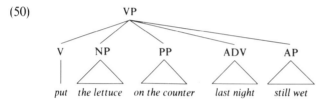

There is no evidence, however, that more than binary branching structure is necessary for syntax.[16] On the other hand, if the requirement is that *put* governs *still wet*, a binary branching structure will be sufficient for nonthematic predication, given θ-merging, as illustrated in (51).[17]

(51)

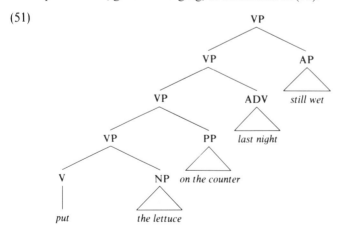

[16] See Kayne (1984), where binary branching is explicitly assumed as the only possible structure.

[17] In order for the definition of government to work correctly for (51), it must be the case that only the highest VP is a maximal projection, in contrast to May's (1985) assumptions.

To show that binary branching is necessary, at least for the relevant cases, consider an example such as (52).

(52)   *John put the lettuce on the counter last night and Mary did this morning.*

Because *did* must correspond to a constituent, (52) shows that *put the lettuce on the counter* must be a constituent. This is correctly represented in (51), but not in (50).

7. SUMMARY

Summarizing, we find that Co-index as a syntactic rule would constitute a violation of strict autonomy, since it would require arbitrary syntactic indices that serve no other function. The translation of Co-index into a rule of θ-role assignment in r-structure is still a violation of strict autonomy, because non-thematic predication, but not control, would require a syntactic condition of bijacency. The solution is to separate the two cases of predication, which are formally distinct in any case. Control is achieved by θ-linking in r-structure, while nonthematic predication involves composition of θ-roles in the course of θ-role assignment from s-structure. The effects of the bijacency requirement follow automatically from the requirement that θ-merging involve a θ-assigner and a predicate governed by that θ-assigner. What results is the framework of a theory of control and predication that is sufficiently sensitive to syntactic structure, but that preserves the strict autonomy of components.

ACKNOWLEDGMENT

This work has developed out of a long and stimulating collaboration with Wendy Wilkins on questions of predication and control, as well as other problems in linguistic theory. I would like to acknowledge that much of what appears here probably is due to her, although after all these years it is hard to sort out exactly what. The responsibility for any errors is mine alone, of course.

TOWARD A NONGRAMMATICAL ACCOUNT
OF THEMATIC ROLES

*WILLIAM A. LADUSAW**
DAVID R. DOWTY[†]

Department of Linguistics
University of California
Santa Cruz, California 95064

[†]*Department of Linguistics*
The Ohio State University
Columbus, Ohio 43210

There has been a renaissance in work on the sensitivity of grammatical generalizations to such as Agent, Theme, Goal, and Source, referred to here as THEMATIC ROLES. Our concern in this discussion is to present an approach to such phenomena which is based on formal semantics and contrast it with some of the ongoing work on thematic roles. Much of what we have to say about the particular data we discuss is implicit or explicit in Bach's (1982) work in so-called English metaphysics. We claim that arguments that some grammatical phenomenon requires the assumption that thematic roles have an independent status in linguistic theory, comparable to categories or grammatical functions, must be examined carefully. Often the phenomenon so analyzed may be better explained by generalizations about the entailments and presuppositions of verbs and reasoning from general principles of human action.

We begin with some comments about some of the different positions being taken on thematic roles as a preparation for the presentation of our

Syntax and Semantics, Volume 21
Thematic Relations

position. The body of this article is a discussion of some of the data in
Nishigauchi (1984).

1. THE DIACRITIC USE OF θ-ROLES

It is not too controversial to claim that the rise of interest in thematic
roles in the government-binding (GB) community is due to the introduction
(Chomsky, 1981) of the θ-theory, which is not claimed to be a substantive
theory of thematic relations. Despite Chomsky's (p. 35) invocation of the
work of Gruber, Jackendoff, Fillmore, and Davidson and the suggestive use
of the θ, the θ-criterion and θ-roles themselves are a principally diacritic
theory: What is crucial in their use in the core of GB is whether an argument
is assigned a θ-role or not, which limits possible structures and thereby constrains the application of rules.

The theory assumes that individual verbs have a θ-grid, a list of θ-roles all
of which must be assigned to argument positions, one-to-one in accordance
with the θ-criterion. As Chomsky (1981, p. 139) notes, the θ-Criterion construed as restricting assignment of substantive thematic roles is not obviously
correct. It is possible to use the criterion in this diacritical way, but it seems
to us that in any serious attempt to bring the range of phenomena discussed
in the literature under the general topic of thematic roles or relations, the
θ-criterion and θ-grids must be revised.[1]

These comments are not the preface to a longer critique of the θ-theory of
GB, though that would be an interesting debate, but rather are intended to
emphasize the word *thematic* in the title in contrast to *theta*. We are interested
in generalizations which are claimed to require reference to particular thematic roles and not those which can be stated in terms of whether or not
some role is assigned. In particular, we are concerned with the semantic
content of such roles.

2. ARE THEMATIC ROLES IN THE WORLD OR THE GRAMMAR?

Our position on this question is that the phenomena which purport to show
that thematic roles are relevant to the grammar have their ultimate etiology
in facts about the world. As an illustration of this consider the sentences in (1).

---

[1] Culicover and Wilkins (1986, p. 123) discuss one way of revising it under a theory which
makes substantive use of thematic roles.

(1) a. *Fido chased Felix.*
     b. *Felix was chased by Fido.*

It is a commonplace that (1a) and (1b) have different subjects, *Fido* in (1a) and *Felix* in (1b), but the two sentences have the same agent: Fido. What is usually glossed over is the use/mention difference here. The only sense in which it is reasonable to think of the subject NP of (1a) as the Agent is the sense in which it is a shorthand for saying that the object (in the world) referred to by the subject is the Agent in the action described by the sentence. What makes Fido an Agent in the event described by (1a) and (1b) is information about Fido and his role in the event, not about the grammatical category or function of anything in the sentence. The lexical meaning of the verb *chase* is such that in order for a situation to be described by it, certain things must be true of Fido. That is, the meaning of the verb *chase* is such that certain things are entailed or presupposed about Fido qua dog. For an event to count as an event of Fido chasing Felix, Fido must be moving with an intention of catching Felix and Felix must be moving away from Fido. If one wishes to associate the term AGENT with one of the two participants, it is reasonable that it be with Fido rather than Felix, because it is Fido's intentions that are crucial to the event's being a chase (rather than, say, a fleeing-from). It is our view that the thematic role associated with Fido is the set of entailments concerning Fido which the lexical meaning of the verb *chase* enforce, and that role names like AGENT, PATIENT, SOURCE, GOAL, and THEME are used as names for types of such sets of entailments.

This view of thematic roles does not commit us to the idea that they are discrete, in that there is a limited set of thematic roles which can be defined so as to hold consistently across verbs. It is possible that if one were to catalog all of the entailments associated with the arguments of predicates and then to consider the intersection of those entailments for all of the arguments which are called "Agents," some nonempty set of entailments would result.[2] We doubt that such a fixed set of roles could be defined in this way.

This issue is important in clarifying the question of whether thematic roles are to be accorded theoretical significance in linguistic theory independent of grammatical relations and lexical semantics. If there is such a fixed set of roles, it can be added to the vocabulary for stating grammatical generalizations. Principles which make reference to these roles lose their generality when further distinctions among role types must be drawn, calling into question their theoretical independence of the lexical semantics of individual verbs.

For example, consider the generalization about the control of the empty NP of a purpose clause proposed in Jones (1985a, p. 114):[3]

---

[2] In the terms of Dowty (1988), this is the question of whether there is a set of l-thematic role types to which grammatical generalizations make reference.

[3] Jones (this volume) addresses this issue more directly.

(2)   S[ubject-gap] P[urpose] C[lauses] must be controlled by a
        (subsequently) possible Agent.
        O[bject-gap] PC must be controlled by a *(subsequently) possible
        Patient.* [Emphasis added]

Assume that (2) represents a true generalization which constrains the construal of the gap in a purpose clause. Does it provide support for according
to Agent and Patient some theoretical status independent of the semantics of
the purpose clause construction and the verbs which allow it? It might, if the
italicized parts of (2) could be replaced by the unqualified use of the role
name without altering role assignments made by matrix or embedded predicates. But, as Jones takes pains to point out, only the qualified version in
(2) is possibly true.

Our suspicion is that in fact proposed grammatical generalizations which
mention thematic roles, when taken together, do not produce a small set of
consistently applicable role names.[4] To establish this point in detail would
require more than we can put into this brief article; hence the words *Toward
a* in the title. Here we discuss some of the data dealt with in Nishigauchi
(1984), the burden of which is that control of the empty category PRO is
established in some cases by reference to a hierarchy of thematic roles in the
sense of Jackendoff (1972, p. 43).

3. NISHIGAUCHI'S HIERARCHY OF RELATIONS IN CONTROL

We begin by developing Nishigauchi's analysis of thematic control cases
(infinitival relatives, purpose clauses, and infinitival indirect questions) step
by step, showing at each stage how we believe the control generalizations in
question follow from a theory of human action and the semantics of the verbs
involved, and also pointing out additional data in some cases which seem
consistent with our view of thematic roles but not with his.

Nishigauchi's starting point is the hypothesis, proposed in Jackendoff
(1972) and Grimshaw (1975), that the controller of the null subject in these
constructions is always the NP bearing the Goal role. As (3) (= Nishigauchi's
(4a,b)) shows, the structural position of the controller is not constant, but the
Goal role often is; Susan is Goal in the event described by (3a), and John is
Goal in the event described by (3b).

(3)   a. *Bill bought for Susan$_i$ a large flashy car [PRO$_i$ to drive].*
        b. *John$_i$ received from Susan a book [PRO$_i$ to read].*

---

[4] This suspicion seems to be shared by Culicover and Wilkins (1986, note 11), despite their use
of the classical set of roles as elements of the vocabulary of grammatical theory.

We suggest that this first fact follows from three things: (a) The semantics of the purpose construction entails that the action described by the infinitive is the purpose for which the action of the main clause was performed. (b) Bach's observation (1982, p. 54) that "a necessary condition for you to do something with an object, or use it to some end ..., is that you have it available, or in your control, or that it be in your 'control space.'" (c) The semantics of the purpose construction is future oriented, i.e., to be performed later than the action of the main clause. Given these three facts, it is only reasonable that the bearer of the Goal role (and only this bearer) can be understood as the missing subject of the purpose clause, as the Goal is, by definition, the person in whose possession the Theme resides when the actions entailed by the main clause are over, and therefore the person in whose possession the referent of the Theme will be at the later time that the purpose clause refers to.

Nishigauchi's first qualification of the Jackendoff–Grimshaw hypothesis is that in cases like (4) (= his (8)), the controller of the null subject is not Goal, but Location, and in fact there is no Goal here (because these sentences are stative, not active).

(4)   a.   *John$_i$ owns a car [PRO$_i$ to carry his belongings in].*
      b.   *Man$_i$ retains [the ability [PRO$_i$ to deceive himself]].*

Our explanation for (4a) is the same as for (3): it is who has the car (and therefore who can use it to some end) that is relevant here; the fact that the object undergoes no change here but does in (3) is of no consequence. For (4b), our explanation is an equally common sense one: It is asserted that man has the ability in question, and one's abilities can only be characterized in terms of what one can do oneself, not in terms of what others can do. For such cases, Nishigauchi modifies his principle to say that either Goal or Location must be the controller. He assumes that the subjects of *own* and *retain* are not Goals but Locations, and further that every sentence will have either a Goal or a Location, but not both of these thematic roles.

Nishigauchi's second supplemental condition is prompted by cases like (5) (= Nishigauchi's (10)–(12)).

(5)   a.   *They deprived Mary$_i$ of the money [PRO$_i$ to pay her rent with].*
      b.   *We soon forgot that defiance cost us$_i$ the ability [PRO$_i$ to speak the language of animals].*
      c.   *They freed Mary$_i$ of an obligation [PRO$_i$ to fulfill for herself].*
      d.   *It cured Mary$_i$ of the desire [PRO$_i$ to kill herself].*

In these cases (all infinitival relatives), the controller is not Goal but Source; in fact there is no Goal role specified by the sentence (it is not specified what happens to the money, ability, obligation, and desire after Mary ceases to have them). Therefore Nishigauchi adds Source as one of the roles that can exercise thematic control. It must be specified, however, that Source may be chosen only if there is no Goal specified in the sentence, because examples like (3) have a Source as well as a Goal.

The notion of using an object is still the determining factor of control in the first of these examples, though it is entailed or presupposed in a more indirect way than before. Part of the semantics of *deprive* is that the object removed from the purview of its possessor is one to which the possessor attaches some value, i.e., it can be put to some desirable use. It is hard to make sense of the assertion that someone deprived Mary of the empty milk carton she threw in her trash can, or of her hopelessly irreparable can opener, because it is difficult to imagine what purpose or value such objects could have had for her. The infinitival relative in (5a), by its semantic nature, must characterize a purpose to which the money is, at some point, to be put, and Mary is both mentioned in the sentence and entailed to be someone who would have a purpose for it (before it was taken from her). In the remaining three cases, the infinitives are noun complements (to *ability, obligation,* and *desire*), and the semantics of *cost, free,* and *cure* is such as to presuppose that Mary (or us in (5b)) had these properties at one time. But to characterize an ability as "to do something" is only intelligibly understood as saying that if one has that ability, one can do it oneself, not that someone else can do it, and similarly for *obligation* and *desire*. Given that someone is asserted to have had these qualities, it is this former possessor of them that must be understood as subject of the infinitive, and no one else.

Though Nishigauchi assumed that no verb could ambiguously allow either Source or Goal as controller, we note that *rob* permits just this ambiguity:

(6)   *The administration's tax plan robbed people of money to pay the interest with.*

This ambiguity is brought out by modifying (6) as in (7a) or (7b).

(7) a. *The administration's tax plan robbed people of money to pay the interest on their home mortgages with.*
     b. *The administration's tax plan robbed people of money to pay the interest on the national debt with.*

The reason that the appearance of this ambiguity is in accord with our position is that the semantics of *rob* entails both that the former owner attached some value to the object stolen (i.e., would have been able to put it to some purpose) and that the thief would now do so as well. It is for this reason that it is difficult to understand the assertion that someone robbed Mary of the empty milk carton she put in her trash can; how could either Mary or the thief care about an empty milk carton? As the existence of some purpose for the stolen object is implied on the part of both participants, both are reasonable controllers for the infinitive's subject.

Note, on the other hand, the difficulty that such an ambiguity presents for Nishigauchi's analysis in terms of thematic role assignments, since, as he points out, it is a consequence of his general theory that any verb will uniquely assign each of its thematic roles to some NP.

Another condition which Nishigauchi adds is necessary because of cases like (8).

(8) ?*John received a book from a man* [PRO$_i$ *to talk to*].

As he observes, this is difficult to interpret, and if interpretable at all, must have a generic interpretation for the missing subject. Yet his analysis, at this point, would predict *John* to be the controller, because John bears the role of Goal. He concludes that the relevant fact here is that the NP of which the infinitive is a part (on the infinitival relative analysis), namely *a man*, is not the Theme of the sentence, whereas the corresponding NP is the Theme in all cases discussed up to this point. So for control of a subjectless infinitive to be thematically determined, the infinitival must either be part of the theme constituent or else be predicated of it (in the sense of Williams, 1980). Noun complements and infinitival relatives are instances of the former; purpose clauses are instances of the latter.

We believe that this new condition also is consistent with our position. The NP bearing the Theme role is, by definition, the object whose ownership (or location in a general sense) is at issue. It is asserted or presupposed to be changed from the Source or to the Goal, or else to stay in the ownership of the Location in the case of a stative sentence. A purpose clause, by definition, modifies the NP denoting the object which is used, rather than an NP which might name the person who owns, acquires, or loses this object. An infinitival relative, likewise, restricts the reference of its head via a purpose it can serve or goal it can satisfy (*The man to see is John, A book to read is on the table*), and, as a matter of human action, the referents of such NPs are not Goals or Sources.

To summarize Nishigauchi's analysis to this point, he says that an argument β can control a PRO α in a certain domain if (a) α is the Theme or else is predicated of the Theme in that domain, and (b) β bears the highest thematic relation on the primary location hierarchy in that domain, where this hierarchy is one that orders Goal above Source and Location.

A final complication for Nishigauchi is provided by (9a,b).

(9) a. *John$_i$ bought a mirror* [PRO$_i$ *to look at himself in*].
  b. *John bought Mary$_i$ a mirror* [PRO$_i$ *to look at herself / *himself in*].

The NP *John* is Goal in (9a), and does, as expected, control the PRO. But if this were the correct analysis, we would expect that same NP to remain the Goal in (9b). Yet not it but rather the NP *Mary* controls the PRO there. Nishigauchi suggests that there are really two transitions in (9b), first a transition of the mirror from the seller to John (with *John* as Goal), and then a transition of the mirror from John to Mary (with *Mary* then as Goal); he concludes that it is the final location of the Theme that determines the controller in such cases. We note, however, that this position about (9b) seems to depart radically from Nishigauchi's basic view that thematic role assignment (as defined in the GB theory) determines controller, since, as already mentioned above, it is a basic tenet of that theory that only one NP may be given a particular thematic role in one sentence; Nishigauchi does not offer any way of resolving his apparently contradictory claims that both *John* and *Mary* are assigned the Goal roles in (9b).

On the other hand, (9b) is, we feel, perfectly consistent with our belief that the verb's entailments and facts about human actions always determine the controller: If John bought Mary the mirror, then Mary, not John, is to end up in possession of it, so only she will be in a position to use it for some purpose. To interpret the sentence (with *himself* substituted for *herself*) as saying that he intends the mirror for Mary as well as for the purpose of viewing himself in it is to ascribe contradictory purposes to John, and this is apparently not consistent with the uniqueness of purpose implied by all these constructions, a fact which presumably also rules out *John bought a sponge to take a bath with to wash the car with.*

Furthermore, there appear to be at least a few examples in which the intended possession of the Theme by one person is not inconsistent with its use by a different person, but rather, this use indirectly benefits the person who possesses it. One such case would be (10b), when used in the special context established by (10a):

(10) a. *In recent weeks, John has been spending the night at Mary's house quite regularly, and every time he has done this he has used Mary's toothbrush to brush his teeth. This annoyed Mary a great deal.*
      b. *So to satisfy Mary, John bought her a second toothbrush to brush his teeth with when he stayed at her house.*

The reading of (10b) we are interested in is the one in which John uses the toothbrush to brush his own teeth (i.e., not one in which Mary brushes John's teeth), and we find this reading quite natural for (10b). We believe that it is our common understanding of how the use of an instrument by one person can benefit a different person who owns it that saves this interpretation from the inconsistency that prevents the subject-controlled reading of (9b). On the other hand, this reading of (10b) contradicts Nishigauchi's claim that it is always the final possessor (location) of the theme that controls the PRO in a purpose clause or infinitival relative.

4. CASES OF OBLIGATORY CONTROL

We next turn to some examples of obligatory control, i.e., the subcategorized infinitival arguments of verbs like *promise* and *persuade*. While we argue that the control pattern of these infinitives complies with the same principles of rational actions and verb entailments as do the Nishigauchi thematic control cases already discussed, we believe that, in addition, these control relations have been "grammaticized." That is, they have become a learned part of the grammar (more exactly, of the semantic interpretation of lexical items and/or compositional interpretive principles).[5] This is similar to the analysis given to Neg Raising in Horn (1978) and Horn and Bayer (1984). They argue that Neg Raising, while having its origin in conversational implicature, has nevertheless acquired the status of a grammaticized process. It is therefore interesting to ask the following questions: Can the intra- and extrasentential context be manipulated in these grammaticized cases in such a way that a controller different from the normal obligatory controller of the infinitive becomes the more natural controller according to these principles of action and verb entailments? If so, what interpretation(s) are possible when this happens? It turns out that the rational principles of control can override the grammatical determination of control in some cases, though varying degrees of reduced acceptability result from this conflict.

Let us first consider some entailments and presuppositions that are constant across all the subcategorization frames for *promise* (and some related verbs); purely for expository convenience (and without any analytical significance), we label the arguments A, B, and C.

(11)   **A**   **B**   **C**

     a. *Mary* $\begin{Bmatrix} \textit{offered} \\ \textit{gave} \end{Bmatrix}$ *John*   *a book.*

     b. *Mary*   *promised*   *John*   *a book.*

     c. *Mary*   *promised*   *John*   *to leave.*

     d. *Mary*   *promised*   *John*   *that she would leave at 10* P.M.

     e. *Mary*   *promised*   *John*   *that he would leave at 10* P.M.

---

[5] As the final revisions to this article were being made, Comrie (1985) came to our attention. This paper arrives at a similar conclusion about these cases and contains much additional interesting data which may further support the conclusion.

In each case, we suggest, the referent of A is entailed (or presupposed) to have have some control (in a nonlinguistic sense) over C. That is, Mary cannot offer, give, or promise John a book unless she has (or eventually will have, in the case of *promise*) a book at her disposal. But in (11c), by the same token, the possibility of leaving must be available to Mary; it is this fact which makes examples like (12) anomalous.

(12)   ??*Mary promised John to be five feet tall.*

Thus, we propose, the fact that the subject of *promise* controls its infinitive complement (rather than its object) is virtually inevitable, given the basic meaning of *promise* and the facts of human action. We can further see this entailment of *promise* in examples (11d,e), where no control in the grammatical sense is involved: (11d) meets this condition in an almost trivial way, since whether Mary leaves at 10 P.M. is, normal circumstances, under Mary's control. But (11e) reveals this entailment of *promise* in a more striking way, as we must imagine a more unusual circumstance in which Mary is in a position to determine whether John leaves at 10 P.M. or not, in order to understand (11e) as describing a felicitous promise. A second entailment common to all these examples is that the referent of B has some interest—positive or negative—in C, is not affectively neutral with respect to it. (In the case of *promise*, we would say "positively disposed toward C," except that *promise* is also used in colloquial speech to describe a kind of threat, as in (13a).

(13)   a. *I promise you that if you do that one more time, you'll stay*
           in your room until I tell you you can leave it.
        b. *I promised John that he would be 5 feet tall.*

Moreover, it is entailed that B would not ordinarily have C without A's intervention (and for this reason it would be odd to say (13b) in the case where he IS 5 feet tall.) In the case of (11a,b) of course, the nonneutral disposition of B is toward possessing the object C. In (11c–e), there is a nonneutral disposition toward making the state of affairs described by C true.

Let us turn our attention now to the much-discussed (Hust and Brame, 1976, p. 255; Bresnan, 1982d, pp. 403–405) example (14b) and its (slightly less acceptable) active counterpart (14a).[6]

(14)   a. ?*Someone promised John to be allowed to leave.*
        b. *John was promised to be allowed to leave.*

---

[6] The explanation given in Bresnan (1982d) is very similar to the one given here, though we believe that there are some potential differences. The LFG explanation depends upon the distinction between closed COMPs and XCOMPs and a particular linguistic theory of control. The account given here makes use only of a nongrammatical notion of consistency of entailments.

These examples, of course, are noteworthy because the only sensible interpretation we can assign to them is one in which the complement of *promise* is controlled by its object (in (14a), or by its subject in the passive (14b)), rather than by its subject (in (14a), or by its unmentioned agent in (14b)). We propose that the unexpected acceptability of such examples is due to the fact that the thematic entailment relations for *promise* discussed above are preserved in (14), even though the grammaticized control relation is not. That is, in (14a), the A-argument of *promise* is understood as the agent of the situation described by the complement *to be allowed to leave*, and therefore A can be understood to have control (in the nonlinguistic sense) of C, i.e., of the state of affairs in which John has permission to leave. Also, we can understand that B would not have C without A's intervention, and that C is a state toward which B might reasonably be favorably or unfavorably disposed, rather than neutral.

It is less clear why (14b) should be more acceptable than (14a). We hypothesize that the object-controlled reading of (14b) has, in addition to its sensibleness in terms of generalizations about human action, a grammatical factor in favor of it, namely, whatever is responsible for Visser's generalization: "A passive transform is only possible when the complement relates to the immediately preceding (pro)noun" (Visser, 1973, 3.2:2118). Given that (14b) obviously is passive, Visser's generalization implies that we are dealing with an object-control verb (whereas active sentences with infinitive complements are sometimes object controlled, sometimes not). (14a) does not benefit from the effect of Visser's generalization and is thus less palatable. Another factor that contributes to the acceptability of (14) is the passive verb *be allowed* in the complement, as is witnessed by the lesser acceptability of (15) vis-a-vis (14).

(15) a.??*Someone promised John$_i$ [PRO$_i$ to be given a ride].
      b. ?*John$_i$ was promised [PRO$_i$ to be given a ride].

We suspect that *be allowed* in the complement of (14) stresses the responsibility of the unmentioned giver of this permission for the truth of *John is allowed to leave*. There is clearly an entailment that argument A has control over C, in spite of the fact that A is not its syntactic controller.

Another verb that (for some speakers, at least) vacillates between subject and object control is *ask*. In addition to its familiar object-controlled interpretation (16a), some speakers allow the subject-controlled interpretation (16b).

(16) a. *Mary asked John$_i$ [PRO$_i$ to shave himself]*.
      b. *Johnny$_i$ asked his mother [PRO$_i$ to go to the movies]*.

Note that there is a parallel between the entailment relations in (16) and (17).

(17)   a. *Johnny asked his mother for permission to go to the movies.*
       b. *Johnny asked his mother for a chocolate cookie.*

In all these cases, the B argument is entailed to have (nonlinguistic) control over the C argument, and in all these cases, A stands to benefit from C if the request is fulfilled. But in (16b) there is syntactic control of C by A, while in (16a) there is syntactic control of C by B. The difference in the two meanings of *ask* responsible for this is between requesting permission to do something yourself, (16a), and requesting that someone else do something which benefits you, (16b).

We now ask whether Visser's generalization and other manipulations of the examples will affect the acceptability of these two interpretations in a way parallel, *mutatis mutandis*, to *promise*. If we passivize (16b), we should expect the interpretation in which Johnny goes to the movies to vanish, and indeed it does.

(18)   a.*$Johnny_i$'s $mother_j$ was asked [PRO_i to go to the movies].
       b. $Johnny_i$'s $mother_j$ was asked [PRO_j to go to the movies].

If we change the complement of (16b) to one where it is implausible that B would have (nonlinguistic) control over it, the sentence is anomalous.

(19)   *$Johnny_i$ asked his mother [PRO_i to behave himself].

Note that this is so even though *himself* prejudices the reading in favor of subject control. As we saw in the case of *promise* (in (14)), when entailments and human action principles come in conflict with grammatical principles, it is the former that win out. Thus (19) is bad, and (14) is good.

As a final experiment in the interaction of grammatical control and non-linguistic thematic control, it is natural to ask whether this kind of reversal of grammatical control can be produced with classic object-control verbs, such as *persuade* and *convince*. Indeed it can, as (20b) indicates, given the context (20a).

(20)   a. *John, a prisoner, was reviewed today by the parole board to determine whether he was eligible for an early parole. A number of behavior problems on his record argued against his release.*
       b. *However, he made such a favorable impression in his interview that he finally convinced the parole board to be allowed to take an early parole after all.*

Here, the passive *to be allowed* again permits the complement to be understood as describing a state of affairs that is in the nonlinguistic control of the parole board, though the syntactic controller is thereby made to be the subject, contrary to the normal behavior of *convince*. The example sounds fairly acceptable to us, at least as acceptable as (14b). As Visser's generalization predicts, such a subject-controlled interpretation is impossible in the passive:

(21)   *He made such a favorable impression that the parole board was
        convinced by him_i [PRO_i to be allowed to take an early parole].

It is possible, of course, if we replace the passive complement with active one:

(22)   He made such a favorable impression that the parole board_i was
        convinced [PRO_i to allow him to take an early parole].

5. CONCLUSION

To reiterate our main point, we believe that principles of control of subjectless infinitives are ultimately determined by entailments of verbs together with principles of human action that exist quite apart from language. This is so both of Nishigauchi's cases of so-called thematic control, and, to a certain extent, of obligatory control as well. Since thematic roles are properly understood, in our view, as merely labels for clusters of verb entailments and presuppositions, it is not surprising that principles of control appear to be describable to a significant extent in terms of discrete θ-roles viewed as a part of grammatical theory. However, closer inspection shows that these correlations of thematic roles with grammar break down in certain cases, while the explanation of control in terms of verb entailments and human action theory continues to describe them correctly. This implies to us that a theory of grammar—and the compositional semantic rules that interpret grammatical structures—does not really miss any important generalizations by failing to include θ-roles as grammatical notions, for the true locus of these generalizations lies elsewhere.

ACKNOWLEDGMENTS

This article is a revised version of a paper read at the Southern California Conference on General Linguistics in April 1985 under the title "Towards a Formal Semantic Account of Thematic Roles." That paper was written while Dowty was at the Center for Advanced Studies in the Behavioral Sciences in Stanford, California. The comments and suggestions received since the initial circulation of the paper have not all been addressed in this version. This work is continued in Dowty (1988, in press) and Ladusaw (1987). Ladusaw gratefully acknowledges the support of university grants to the Syntax Research Center, University of California, Santa Cruz.

THEMATIC RELATIONS IN CONTROL

CHARLES JONES

Department of English
George Mason University
Fairfax, Virginia 22030

1. INTRODUCTION

Consider the problems for control theory along broad lines. Arguments in certain syntactic constructions are allowed to be phonetically unrealized, yet nevertheless they are considered to be (more or less) referentially dependent on other, phonetically realized, arguments elsewhere in the construction. Control theory has to be concerned with, at least, (a) characterizing the syntactic mechanisms that allow the phonetically empty arguments which I designate simply as *e*, (b) determining the circumstances under which *e* must be referentially dependent on another argument, and (c) picking out that phonetically realized argument, the CONTROLLER, on which *e* is to be referentially dependent. Let us restrict our attention to the third problem, which we refer to as the "controller problem" (CP).

There are several kinds of proposals concerning the characterization of the controller. Among them are the structural characterizations of Rosenbaum (1967), Chomsky (1980), and, following them, Huang (1984); the lexical–functional grammar characterization in terms of grammatical relations of Bresnan (1982d); the semantic, Montague grammar, characterization of Bach (1979, 1982) and the generalized phrase structure grammar of Gazdar *et al.*

75

(1985); and, of particular interest to the present article, the characterizations in terms of thematic relations of Jackendoff (1972), (to some extent) Williams (1980), Chierchia (1984), Nishigauchi (1984), Jones (1985a,b), and Culicover and Wilkins (1986). All the above proposals have in common the assumption that CP is a grammatical problem. That is, in all of the above proposals, the characterization of the controller is in terms of primitives or mechanisms that are at work in the particular grammatical theory adopted in the proposal.

In their article, "Toward a Nongrammatical Account of Thematic Roles," Ladusaw and Dowty (this volume) take issue with the notion that thematic relations must be primitives or mechanisms at work in a particular grammar. Ladusaw and Dowty argue that the true nature of thematic roles, and, by extension, the proper account of CP, may not be found in the grammar, in the above sense, at all, but rather in "the entailments and presuppositions of verbs and reasoning from general principles of human action." In this article I point out certain aspects of control in general, and CP in particular, that suggest that CP, and, by extension, thematic relations, should not be completely outside the grammar.

In order to focus clearly on the issue raised by Ladusaw and Dowty's article, I contrast a theory like one of those mentioned above, one that takes CP to be a grammatical problem to be characterized with thematic relations (which I refer to as THEMATIC CP or θCP), with a radical version of Ladusaw and Dowty's proposal, a version I refer to as the NONGRAMMATICAL THEORY OF CP, or *CP. The *CP theory I discuss may not in fact be the kind of theory Ladusaw and Dowty themselves would ultimately endorse; it is difficult to assess the strength of the qualification that the *Toward* in the title of their article is intended to convey. However, I think *CP will serve as a sharp formulation of a kind of theory that Ladusaw and Dowty's proposal anticipates, and it is the consequences of such a theory that I am interested in in this article.

Much of Ladusaw and Dowty's discussion concerns the θCP theory of Nishigauchi (1984). The important points they make about Nishigauchi's theory can be generalized to cover θCP theories in general. Hence, in what follows, the discussion is in terms of θCP and *CP, although much of the data, and many of the theoretical arguments, come from either Nishigauchi or Ladusaw and Dowty.

In Section 2 I point out an important matter concerning the nature of thematic roles, a matter that is not at issue, in this article at least; Section 3 is a brief, general discussion of the nature of a *CP theory, contrasting it with a θCP theory. In Section 4 I discuss in detail a few specific apparent difficulties for a θCP theory and point out their syntactic dimensions. Section 5 contains concluding remarks.

2. THEMATIC ROLES AS VERB ENTAILMENTS

What is not at issue here is Ladusaw and Dowty's claim that thematic roles, like Theme or Agent, are names we give to clusters of verb entailments and presuppositions. I think this is the right idea. Indeed, insofar as these names have any intuitive appeal, it would be difficult to think of a more likely origin for these intuitions than in what we know about the actions or events these thematic roles are relative to.

This conception of thematic roles allows for the possibility of there being several, distinguishable, clusters of verb entailments and presuppositions around a certain argument. Jackendoff (1972) apparently had such a conception of thematic roles in mind when he characterized the subject argument of the *buy* relation illustrated in (1) as Agent (of the action), Goal (of the pig), and Secondary Source (of the money).

(1)   *Harriet bought a pig from Zelda for $5.98.*

In what follows I contrast *CP with this kind of thematic theory, a θCP theory in which thematic relations can be characterized as sets of clusters of verb entailments and presuppositions.

The issue in this article is the question of whether these intuitions about thematic roles, these nameable, characterizable clusters of verb entailments and presuppositions, are ever put to work in the grammar.

3. *CP VERSUS θCP

Consider a thematic relations theory of CP, θCP, that has the following characteristics.

(2) θCP: a. Given a relation α along with its arguments, $\langle \alpha, x_1, \ldots, x_n \rangle$, every $x_i, 1 \leq i \leq n$, bears a thematic relation (or set of thematic relations) $\theta_i(\{\theta_{i,1}, \ldots, \theta_{i,n}\})$, to a.[1]

---

[1] We leave open the possibility that the thematic relation(s) of θ_1 can be determined independently of α, as, for instance, with the temporal adverbial in (i), in which the preposition *after* presumably determines, independently of α (= *hit*) the thematic relation *the party* bears to the matrix α-relation denoted by *hit*.

(i)   *John hit Mary [after the party].*

   b. If x_i contains an e to be controlled, the controller of e is
   characterized as an argument, $x_j, 1 \leq j \leq n$, of α,
   bearing some thematic relation $\theta_j(\{\ldots \theta_{j,k} \ldots\})$ to α in
   $\langle \alpha, x_1, \ldots, x_j, \ldots, x_n \rangle$.

If a theory like that in (2) is to have any interest, the characterization of the
controller called for in (2b) must be predictable by either (a) general principles;
(b) lexical properties of α, (c) the thematic status of the argument containing e,
or (d) orderly interactions among any subset of the factors in (a)–(c). All of the
thematic theories mentioned in the introduction are theories that seek to
characterize the controller in just these ways.

A *CP objection to such θCP theories of control is not so much that they
cannot get all the relevant facts straight (they may not, but we return to this
matter in Section 4), but rather that any account along the lines of (2) does not
illuminate in any interesting way what happens when e gets a controller. Let us
consider in general the kind of illumination that *CP casts on the problem.
The examples in (3) are from Nishigauchi (1984).

(3)   a. *Bill bought for Susan$_i$ a large flashy car [e$_i$ to drive].*
      b. *John$_i$ received from Susan a book [e$_i$ to read].*

A θCP theory could get the facts presented in (3) by requiring the Goal
argument in each of the constructions in (3), regardless of structural position
or grammatical relation, to control the phonetically empty subject argument
of the infinitival.

In a *CP theory, on the other hand, the Goal arguments would not be
selected as controllers by virtue of their thematic roles per se, but rather by
virtue of what we know about (human) actions and events: verb entailments
and presuppositions. In a *CP theory, the Goal arguments in (3) control the
infinitives (a) because the infinitives in (3) characterize the purpose the
arguments of which they are predicates are supposed to serve, and (b) because
Goal arguments of the relations in (3) are the arguments that we understand
are the most likely to end up able to exploit that purpose. The point made by
the *CP theory is that there are nongrammatical reasons why what we
consider the Goal argument in the sentences in (3) is the most salient choice of
the controller, and it is these reasons that make up a more interesting, and
enlightening, story about the control that we find in (3) than any account in
which a thematic relation is simply named.

The general objection *CP has to θCP is that being able to pick out some
thematic relation or other as the controller does not reveal much about what is
actually going on in a control construction. This objection would be
interesting even if it were an objection to a theory that always managed to pick

out the appropriate controller, and we return to consider the general point of this objection in Sections 4.1.2.4 and 5. Ladusaw and Dowty, however, note several cases in which a θCP theory has difficulty picking out the appropriate controller, and they demonstrate the superiority of a *CP kind of account by showing how it handles the problem cases. It is to a detailed examination of these cases that we now turn.

4. SYNTAX IN CONTROL

We first consider infinitives that exhibit what has been called NONOBLIG-ATORY CONTROL (NOC). Actually these infinitives exhibit different kinds of referential dependence. These differences are clarified in the discussion. We then discuss obligatory control (OC) of subcategorized infinitive complements in terms of *CP and θCP.

4.1. Nonobligatory Control Infinitives

The examples of NOC we discuss here involve finding an antecedent for the phonetically empty subject arguments of infinitival relatives (IR) and purpose clauses (PC).[2] These two constructions differ syntactically, and this difference is pertinent to the discussion, so I briefly point out the difference between IR and PC before considering the difference between *CP and θCP.

4.1.1. INFINITIVAL RELATIVES AND PURPOSE CLAUSES

Differences between IR and PC were discussed first in Faraci (1974) and have been subsequently recapitulated and expanded on in Bach (1982), Kirkpatrick (1982), and Jones (1984, 1985b). In this article, I consider IR to be predicated, indicated by co-indexing à la Williams (1980), of a head N', as in (4a), and the object gap in PC to be (obligatorily) controlled, indicated by co-indexing e, by a matrix NP, as in (4b).

(4)   a. IR $\ldots [_{NP} \ldots [_{N'} N'_i [IR]_i]] \ldots$
      b. PC $\ldots NP_i \ldots [_{PC} \ldots e_i \ldots] \ldots$

---

[2] Throughout this article, except where I explicitly state otherwise (especially in 4.1.2.1), I refer to purpose clauses featuring an obligatorily controlled object gap, as opposed to purpose clauses featuring an obligatorily controlled subject gap, simply as PURPOSE CLAUSE, or PC. See Faraci (1974). Jones (1985a,b) for details and discussion.

Consistent with the syntax in (4) is the fact, which we use as a diagnostic between IR and PC, that IR cannot occur with a full NP or pronominal head, and PC can.

(5) a. IR   i. *[A[man_i [to talk to]_i]] came along.*
                 ii.**John to talk to came along.*
                 iii.**He to talk to came along.*
     b. PC   i. *They brought [a man]_i along [to talk to e_i].*
                 ii. *They brought John along to talk to.*
                 iii. *They brought him along to talk to.*

4.1.2. PARTICULARS

Ladusaw and Dowty point out three kinds of problems that a θCP theory like Nishigauchi's runs into. While their points hold against Nishigauchi's particular theory, they do not necessarily argue against thematic relations figuring in a significant way in a theory of θCP. In fact, they show just the opposite.

4.1.2.1. Restriction to Theme.   Cases like (6) force Nishigauchi to limit his theory of CP to only the subjects of those infinitives that are associated with (by being predicated of, or modifying) the matrix Theme argument.

(6)   *?John received a book from a man [to talk to].*

Nishigauchi attributes the marginal status of (6) to the fact that the infinitive is not associated with the matrix Theme. Ladusaw and Dowty, noting that IR and PC are semantically similar in characterizing the purpose to which something is to be put, state that this restriction to Theme is consistent with the *CP position, since it is Theme after all, "whose ownership (or location in a general sense) is . . . asserted or presupposed" in a particular sentence. It is the Theme about which we know the most concerning the possibilities of future use.

Only PC, however, is absolutely restricted to Theme. Note how much worse (6) becomes when a PC reading is forced by the pronominal antecedent in (7).

(7)   **John received a book from him [to talk to].*

The contrast between IR and PC with respect to dependence on Theme is much clearer in (8), where the infinitives are more appropriate to the context. The IR in (8a) simply modifies its head, regardless of thematic role, while PC is impossible with an antecedent that is not Theme.

(8)   a. IR   *I steered John over to [some [books$_i$ [to read]$_i$]].*
      b. PC   **I steered John over to them$_i$ [to read e$_i$].*[3]

The fact that PC is restricted to Theme is a problem for *CP. A dis-
criminating look at the different kinds of purposes characterized by IR and
PC might indeed suggest a likely story about why only PC is restricted
absolutely to that argument around which cluster entailments and presuppositions we associated with the name "Theme," but would leave unexplained
why a "thematic" control enters into the theory at all. That is, if a likely story
about the entailments and presuppositions of the verbs that PC associates
with invariably involve Theme, while a similar story about IR is independent
of thematic relations, then an obvious place to locate that difference between
IR and PC would be in a theory containing explicit thematic relations that
work in the grammar. *CP is not such a theory.

To put the point of this section a bit differently, while it may be the case that
the most appropriate characterization of thematic relations is that they are
clusters of verb entailments and presuppositions, *CP claims that these clusters themselves play no significant role in the grammar. The dependence of
PC on the argument that can be consistently characterized as Theme must be
accidental in a *CP theory.

Actually, things may be worse than that for *CP. As is pointed out in Faraci
(1974), Bach (1982), and Jones (1985a,b), it is not simply Theme status that
characterizes the controller of purpose clauses in general. The explicit
proposal in Jones (1985a) is that the Theme of the matrix relation α that
controls PC must have additional connotations of "possible Agent" or
"possible Patient," in the resultant state α′ of α, and these "resultant possible
Agent/Patient" connotations, which we refer to as "Agent′" and "Patient′,"
correlate directly to the surface-syntactic Subject/Object status of *e* that must
be obligatorily controlled in the purpose clause.

On one hand, such a characterization of the controller of the two kinds of
purpose clause is right at home in the part of Ladusaw and Dowty's theory
that is not at issue here, the part that holds that thematic relations have their
"ultimate etiology in facts about the world." The kinds of Agent′/Patient′
connotations requisite for purpose clause control are not mutually exclusive,
and thus it comes as no surprise that a single Theme argument could have

---

[3] There is a reading of (8b) that is good. It involves a subject-gap purpose clause, with an
intransitive *read* in the infinitive.

(i)   *I steered John$_i$ over to them [e$_i$ to read].*

Note that in (i) the subject-gap purpose clause is dependent on the Theme, as is characteristic of
purpose clauses in general.

connotations of both kinds, given a suitable verb, and thus serve as either kind of controller for either kind of purpose clause, as in (9).

(9)   a. *They brought John$_i$ along [e$_i$ to talk to the children].*
      b. *They brought John$_i$ along [to talk to e$_i$].*

On the other hand, this syntactically related thematic generalization about the character of the controller becomes an accidental coincidence in a theory in which thematic relations like Theme (or Agent, Patient, etc.) have no grammatical status.

4.1.2.2. One Relation, Two Controllers.   Ladusaw and Dowty note that a verb like *rob* permits an ambiguity in the antecedent for the subject of the infinitive in (10), which they illustrate with (11a,b).

(10)   *The administration's tax plan robbed people of money to pay the interest with.*

(11)   a. *The administration's tax plan robbed people of money to pay the interest on their home mortgages with.*
       b. *The administration's tax plan robbed people of money to pay the interest on the national debt with.*

The ambiguity of referential dependence in (10) is a problem for θCP, since such a theory usually predicts a particular antecedent for each particular construction. However, (10) hides a distinction that gives further evidence for an independent status for some types of thematic relations.

Since *money* in (10) is neither pronominal nor necessarily a full NP, the infinitive could be either IR or PC. A *CP explanation offered by Ladusaw and Dowty of the ambiguity exhibited in (10) rests on the property of *rob* that implies that both the robber and the person robbed consider the money to have some value, some possible use. Hence either is an appropriate candidate for the controller of the subject of the infinitive. Such an explanation is complicated, however, when the example is disambiguated with a pronominal antecedent, as in (12), forcing a PC reading.

(12)   *The administration's tax plan robbed people of it to pay the interest with.*

In (12), only the (11b) reading is allowed, in which what we characterize as the Location of the Theme in the resultant state α', or Location', is the antecedent for the subject of PC.[4] I have discussed at some length in Jones (1985b) this thematic characterization of the controller (if one wishes to call

---

[4] I consider Location' to have the same essential thematic content as the "eventual possessor" of Jones (1985b, II:4.2.3).

it that) of the subject of object-gap PC.[5] I have yet to see an exception
to it.

Confirmation that the (11b) reading is in fact a PC reading comes from the
fact that the two infinitives can be stacked, but only in the IR–PC order, as one
would expect if IR is in construction with its head.

(13)   a. *The administration's tax plan robbed people of money to pay the
           interest on their home mortgages with to pay the interest on the
           national debt with.*

     b.* *The administration's tax plan robbed people of money to pay the
           interest on the national debt with to pay the interest on their home
           mortgages with.*

Once again we have seen a general tendency, this time of a certain kind of
NOC, about which a likely story can be offered from the *CP position, turn
out to be a thematically invariant story for PC, while remaining merely a
tendency for IR. The *CP position is perhaps appropriate for characterizing
the NOC of IR. PC, which calls for a treatment separate from IR, finds its most
appropriate treatment in a theory in which thematic relations have content
and can be referred to.

4.1.2.3. Close Relations and Their Controllers.   Ladusaw and Dowty note
that sentences like those in (14) (which differ from their particular examples in
that a PC reading is forced in (14) by the pronominal Theme argument in each)
are particularly troublesome for a certain kind of θCP theory.

(14)   a. *John$_i$ bought it [e$_i$ to look at himself in].*
     b. *John bought it for Mary$_i$ [e$_i$ to look at herself / *himself in].*

Why does one argument of the *buy* relation control PRO in (14a) and
another do the controlling in (14b)?

The problem for a thematic theory of CP that (14) poses is, however, only a
problem for a thematic theory that requires biunique assignments of thematic
relations. We have already seen how a conception of thematic relations as sets
of clusters of verb entailments and presuppositions could be appropriate for
characterizing certain thematic properties of PC. Consistent with the verb
entailment and presupposition view of thematic roles is the possibility that
verbs in relations containing different types of arguments would assign, or
entail, thematic roles according to each particular relation.[6]

---

[5] Note that the Location' PC antecedent, *the administration*, does not c-command the infinitive.
It would depend on a particular theory of control whether this non-c-command disqualifies the
relation between the two from being characterized as control.

[6] There would be two different *buy* relations in (14a,b), for example, within a theory of
adverbial modification like that of McConnell-Ginet (1982).

(14) does not have much of a bearing on the question of whether thematic relations should have an independent status in the grammar. From where I sit, it could not be a coincidence that my intuitions tell me that *John* in (14a) and *Mary* in (14b) control the subject of the infinitive. *John* in (14a) and *Mary* in (14b) are the Locations' of their respective relations; and Location', if anything, invariably controls the subject of PC. A generalization about the controller of the subject of PC needs a vocabulary of thematic relations in which to be stated.

4.1.2.4. Conclusion. A good deal of Ladusaw and Dowty's case against a θCP theory of NOC rests on their demonstrations that, when thematic predictions come up against verb entailments and presuppositions, the thematic predictions lose. We have seen that this is true only of infinitival relatives. Purpose clauses, on the other hand, apparently are licensed under certain specific conditions, and these conditions can be stated succinctly using the vocabulary of thematic relations.

Specifically, the gap of PC that must be obligatorily controlled is controlled by a Theme carrying certain connotations along Agent'/Patient' lines. The nonobligatorily controlled subject of the object-gap PC is controlled by an argument that can be characterized as Location' (by virtue of its own connotations of "possible Agent"), or by nothing.[7]

The obligatorily bound object gap in IR, on the other hand, is bound, I presume, independently of the theory of control. Whatever mechanism handles the relation of relative clauses to their heads in general will extend to include IR as well. As for controlling the empty subject of an object-gap IR, there may in fact be no reliable, invariant thematic story about the controller. Something like *CP may be the appropriate kind of account of what happens to these *e*. This either means that control itself cannot in general be characterized by a θCP theory, or, more likely, that there is a distinguishable subpart of the control problem that is not to be thematically characterized, but rather is more closely related to something like pronominal coreference.[8]

To put the same point a bit differently, I suggest that simply because the IR presents an empty (subject) argument for which an antecedent can frequently be found is not sufficient justification for equating those mechanisms at work

---

[7] Bach's (1982) discussion of the nonobligatoriness of the control of PC is relevant here, as is that of Williams (1980). As Bach puts it, "Suppose I hand my host a bottle of wine and say *I brought this miserable Morgon to enjoy with our dinner*; I'm surely not suggesting that I alone enjoy the wine" (p. 41). The point here is that when the subject of PC does find an antecedent, it is invariably a Location'.

[8] The difficulties with IR may be similar to the problems of characterizing the relation of empty categories in Chinese to their antecedents, problems that figure prominently in the exchange of

in IR with those identifiably thematic mechanisms at work in PC. It may be reasonable to adopt a nongrammatical *CP account of the antecedent of the subject to IR, without assuming that such nongrammatical control, or coreference, generalizes to all cases of control.

Thus, while the properties of IR do not make a persuasive case for a thematic account of control, those of PC still do. We might perhaps wonder how two things that look so much alike, and have the same sort of purposeful semantics, could bear so differently on the question of thematic control. I suggest that, in spite of the semantics, the looks are deceiving. IR and PC have significant, syntactically characterizable, differences; their significance resides in the fact that these differences can be characterized in the grammar. Control of PC can be characterized by thematic generalizations, hence only PC has any bearing on the question of whether there is to be some independent notion of thematic control at work in the grammar.

4.2. Obligatory Control

The *CP account Ladusaw and Dowty give of the several cases of obligatory control (OC) of subcategorized infinitive complements is, to me at least, so intuitively natural and comprehensive that it is difficult to see how it could be wrong. However, there are different ways of being right about something, and I briefly discuss here how *CP does it, and a way in which it might be done better.

All of the *CP accounts of OC have a similar form. They go something like this: We have an intuition, from the verb entailments and presuppositions, about which argument in the relation has some kind of nonlinguistic control

---

views between Huang (1982, 1984, 1987) and Xu (1986). We can illustrate this controversy with the following example from Xu (1986).

(i)   *xiaotou yiwei mei ren kanjian e.*
       thief   think no man see
       'The thief thought nobody saw (him).'

Two positions taken on the possible reference of (*him*) in (i) are that it is a matter for something like simple pronominal coreference (Xu), as in (ii), or that it involves a pragmatically inferred referential dependence of a kind of operator-variable structure (Huang), which I presume is related to something like the structure in (iii).

(ii)   *John lost his₇ book.*

(iii)   *[Me/myself]ᵢ, I don't think anybody likes eᵢ.*

The differences in the two positions have various consequences, the correct account is of course not an obvious choice, and this is hardly the place to try to resolve the matter.

over the outcome of the relation denoted in the infinitive. Hence it is only natural that we take this argument to be the controller of the infinitive. For example, consider the Ladusaw and Dowty examples in (15).

(15)   a. *Mary asked John$_i$ [PRO$_i$ to shave himself].*
      b. *Johny$_i$ asked his mother [PRO$_i$ to go to the movies].*

In both these cases, the object of *ask* is considered to have some kind of non-linguistic control over the infinitive. Thus it is unremarkable, from the *CP point of view, that the object controls the subject of the infinitive in (15a). The subject-controlled interpretation in (15b), on the other hand, is possible only if we understand Johnny to be asking for some kind of permission, something we understand that his mother, as the object of *ask*, has nonlinguistic control over.

What is significant about the *CP story for OC is that it is, after all, always essentially the same story. This, I think, is unexpected in a *CP theory. That is, if the criterion for explanation is the possibility of there being a likely story about the relation between an argument and an infinitive subject, then one might reasonably expect there to be all kinds of stories, not just one. For example, assume, contrary to fact, that the examples in (16) or, for that matter, those in (17), illustrate the only grammatical OC possibilities for *ask*.

(16)   a. *John$_i$ asked Mary [e$_i$ to send the package].*
      b. *Mary asked John$_i$ [e$_i$ to receive the package].*

(17)   a. *John asked Mary$_i$ [e$_i$ to send the package].*
      b. *Mary$_i$ asked John [e$_i$ to receive the package].*

If (16) illustrated a fact about control, *CP could account for it along these lines: In (16a), since *John* is considered to be Source, "where the request comes from," it is only to be expected that he should also be considered to be associated with the embedded Source, "where the package comes from." Likewise, but with Goal/Goal connotations, in (16b).

If, instead, (17) illustrated a fact about control, *CP could account for it along these lines: In (17a), since *Mary* is considered to be Goal, "where the request goes to," she is also considered to be associated with the embedded Source, "where the package comes from." Likewise, but with Source/Goal connotations, in (17b).

Of course, the foregoing are not explanations of any facts about English OC. The kinds of explanations that do, in fact, seem to be appropriate for English OC constructions are the kinds of explanations that Ladusaw and Dowty indeed provide in their article. All of their explanations have to do with the possible nonlinguistic, but essentially Agentive, control some argument is considered to have, as entailed or presupposed by the matrix relation α, over the infinitive.

The question here is not whether verb entailments and presuppositions cluster the way Ladusaw and Dowty say they do. Rather, the question here is whether there are any generalizations to be stated about such clusterings. The fact that Ladusaw and Dowty's OC stories are so much alike suggests that there is indeed a generalization about what is going on in OC cases. How can we express this generalization? I suggest we can state it using the vocabulary of thematic relations.

Why is it that we look for the matrix argument that we assume has Agentive control over the infinitive in OC constructions? I suggest that, because the e to be controlled in OC constructions is a subject argument, in the typical, perhaps universal, syntactic Agent argument position, what we are generally looking for in the matrix is a kind of Agent argument for an antecedent. That is, OC constructions may exhibit a kind of thematic match similar to the Agent′ : Subject :: Patient′ : Object matches exhibited by purpose clauses mentioned above in 4.1.2.1. The difference is that, in OC constructions, the matches involve different notions of Agentivity.

Reconsider (15), repeated here for convenience, in light of possible thematic matches.

(15) a. *Mary asked John$_i$ [e$_i$ to shave himself].*
      b. *Johnny$_i$ asked his mother [e$_i$ to go to the movies].*

In (15a) the thematic sense of the subject of the infinitive is characteristically Agentive, whereas in (15b) the Agentive sense of the subject of the infinitive is eclipsed by some kind of modal qualification, one of permission. In both cases the object of *ask* is the Goal argument, although, as in the case with the controller of the subject of PC mentioned in 4.1.2.2, perhaps the relevant thematic content of the object in both cases is Location′, the most likely "subsequently possible Agent." In (15a), in light of thematic/modal matching, Location′/Agent′ controls Agentive e (exactly as is the case with NOC of the PC subject), and in (15b), a matrix non-Location′/non-Agent′ argument controls a modally eclipsed non-Agent e.

The same kind of thematic/modal matching is exhibited by the most likely (but not obligatory) readings of the examples of pronominal coreference in (18).

(18) a. *Mary asked John$_i$ if he$_i$ could fix the car.*
      b. *John$_i$ asked Mary if he$_i$ could fix the car.*

Just as in (15), the object control sentence in (18a) is about John's ability as an Agent, while the subject control sentence in (18b) strongly suggests that John is asking for permission. So, too, in the famous case of the exceptional control of *promise* illustrated in (19) (assuming, not unintuitively, that the Agent of the *promise* relation ends up as the Location′/Agent′ of the promise),

do the (very rough) facts fall out along the thematic/modal matching lines we
have been considering.

(19)   a. *John$_i$ promised Mary [e$_i$ to leave].*
       b. *John$_i$ was promised t$_i$ [e$_i$ to be allowed to leave].*

The problem of characterizing the controller of subcategorized infinitive
OC complements is notoriously difficult. The thematic/modal-matching- CP
theory of OC sketched above certainly does not straightforwardly account
for all the particulars presented by the data. However, the point of the present
article is not a whole new theory of OC; it is that thematic relations have a
significant part to play in the grammar of control. There is a suggestive correlation between the modal nature of the controlled infinitive and the thematic
nature of the OC controller. A *CP theory abandons the vocabulary, or at
least the theoretical significance of the vocabulary, in which these recurring
clusters of verb entailments and presuppositions can be characterized. In a
*CP theory, there is no way to hypothesize, as we did above, that an argument
which could be characterized as the Location of the Theme in the resultant
state α' of the matrix relation α is the correct characterization of the controller in OC constructions. This characterization of the OC controller as
it stands is perhaps empirically inadequate, but more important, of course, is
that, if it is false, there are ways of demonstrating that it is false. It is not at
all clear how a *CP theory could be falsified. If a likely story is the criterion
for explanation, then, I imagine, as with (16) and (17), there could always be
some story or another for any kind of control fact.

5. THEMATIC RELATIONS IN THE GRAMMAR

I have been arguing that thematic relation can, and do, allow theoretically
interesting and testable generalizations about control to be stated. They do
for PC, and, I think, there is at least the possibility that they can for OC. The
*CP challenge, that thematic relations as such have no place in the workings
of the grammar, is not motivated by all the data that have been considered,
only by some of them. Since the examples that do not seem to allow a straightforward thematic account form a highly restricted class of constructions, IR,
it is reasonable that we allow the *CP point about IR, while rejecting it for
PC, and at least reserving judgment on it for OC.

θCP theories need not offer only inscrutable choices of thematic relations
as appropriate controllers. The thematic-matching theory of PC mentioned
in 4.1.2.1, and the thematic/modal-matching theory of OC sketched above,
put thematic roles to work in theories incorporating the kind of explana-

tion implicit in the *CP accounts of OC. These theories offer explanations in terms of thematic relations, however, and not in terms of likely stories about actions and events.

The conception of thematic roles as verb entailments and presuppositions cuts us loose in a certain way from the Gruber/Jackendoff inventory of thematic relations. Consider, for example, the most invariant case of θCP control mentioned above, the characterization of PC control in 4.1.2.1. The only relevant thematic relations are Theme and some notion of Agent and Patient. To get NOC of the subject of object-gap purpose clauses, the relevant thematic relation is a resultant state notion of Location'/Agent'. It may be that these notions, or aspects of them, are the only thematic notions relevant to control. If so, then the clusters of entailments and presuppositions we refer to as Source or Goal, for instance, would be no less such clusters, and no less aptly named; they would simply be clusters without theoretical significance. The main point of this article is that there remain some such clusters whose theoretical significance is confirmed by how they illuminate certain aspects of control.

ACKNOWLEDGMENTS

Much of the research presented here was supported by the Department of Linguistics of the University of Wisconsin. That support is gratefully acknowledged. Thanks, too, to Wendy Wilkins for enlightening comments and to Bill Ladusaw and David Dowty for generous encouragement.

COMPLEX PREDICATES AND θ-THEORY

K. A. JAYASEELAN

Central Institute of English and Foreign Languages
Hyderabad 500 007, India

1. INTRODUCTION

The "complex predicates" of the title of this article are expressions like *give . . . permission, put . . . blame, make . . . offer*, which alternate with simple predicates like *permit, blame, offer* to produce sentence pairs which have a paraphrase relation with each other. This alternation is illustrated in (1)–(5).

(1) a. *John permitted Mary to leave.*
     b. *John gave permission to Mary to leave.*

(2) a. *John blamed Mary for the accident.*
     b. *John put the blame for the accident on Mary.*

(3) a. *John offered money to Mary.*
     b. *John made an offer of money to Mary.*

(4) a. *John hated Mary.*
     b. *John felt hatred towards Mary.*

(5) a. *John slept well.*
     b. *John had a good sleep.*

The relation between the (a) and (b) sentences here can be characterized as follows: given that (a) has a verb α, (b) has the corresponding deverbal

91

nominal α' as the head of the direct object of a "host" verb; the arguments of
(a) reappear in (b) bearing the same thematic relations to α' as they do to α.
That is, (1a) has *permit* as its verb, and (1b) has *permission* as the head of
the direct object of a host verb *give; John, Mary,* and *to leave* bear the same
thematic relations to *permit* in (1a), and to *permission* in (1b).

The alternation in question is perhaps found in all languages. We illustrate
from Malayalam:

(6)   a. *raajaawə mantRi-ye   pookuwaan anuwadicc-u*
          king-nom minister-acc go-inf   permit-past
          'The king permitted the minister to leave.'
      b. *raajaawə mantRi-kk   pookuwaan anuwaadam   koḍutt-u*
          king-nom minister-dat go-inf   permission-acc give-past
          'The king gave permission to the minister to leave.'

(7)   a. *raajaawə mantRi-ye   sneehikk-unnu*
          king-nom minister-acc love-present
          'The king loves the minister.'
      b. *raajaaw-inə mantRi-yoodə sneeham uṇṭə*
          king-dat minister-2nd dat love-nom have-present
          'The king has love for the minister.'

In Section 2, we present three problems regarding θ-marking in complex
predicate constructions. In Section 3, we briefly glance at some solutions to
these problems offered in the literature, and then present a new solution. In
Section 4, we look at some constraints on one of the processes postulated in
our solution. Section 5 deals with a problem of θ-marking which arises in the
double object construction.

2. θ-MARKING IN COMPLEX PREDICATES:
   THREE PROBLEMS

What makes complex predicates interesting is that the arguments of the
deverbal nominal are not always (or often) realized within the NP of which
it is the head. They may be realized as the subject of the host verb or as
complements in the VP. In (1b), for example, none of the arguments of
permission is realized within the NP of which *permission* is the head. *John* is
obviously the subject of *give*. *Mary* is the indirect object of *give* (even as
permission is the direct object). We argue below that *to leave* is also not a
complement of *permission*.

This illustrates the first problem regarding θ-marking in complex predicate
constructions, namely, how does the nominal θ-mark arguments outside its
maximal projection? Normally, the head of a phrase θ-marks only its com-

plements (Chomsky, 1981). The subject of a sentence is the only recognized exception: The subject appears to be θ-marked by the verb, although it is not a complement of the verb. (Chomsky, 1981, claims that it is only indirectly θ-marked by the verb.)

We said above that some (or all) arguments of the deverbal nominal may be realized outside the NP of which it is the head. We describe this as PROMOTION: the noun's arguments are promoted to argument positions of higher maximal projections.[1] Where the promoted arguments will appear is determined by the thematic structure of the host verb. A general condition on promotion seems to be that a promoted argument which bears the thematic relation θ to the nominal must appear as the θ argument of the host verb. (This naturally imposes a condition of congruence of thematic structure on the host verb and the deverbal nominal.) Thus in (1a), the subject of *permit* (*John*) has (arguably) the θ-role Source, and the object (*Mary*) has the θ-role Goal; therefore in (1b), which has *give* as the host verb, *John* must appear as the subject of *give* (*give*'s Source argument) and *Mary* as the indirect object of *give* (*give*'s Goal argument).[2] We may contrast this with the situation where the host verb is *receive*, which takes a Goal argument in the subject position and a Source argument as a prepositional object (specifically, as the object of *from*); the corresponding complex predicate construction now is (8).

(8)   *Mary received permission from John to leave.*

---

[1] Needless to say, this promotion is different from the promotion in relational grammar. The latter notion corresponds to NP-Movement in the government and binding framework.

[2] About the role assignments: In (1a). *John* is probably both Source and Agent. *Mary* cannot be Theme if we follow Gruber (1965) and Jackendoff (1972, 1976) in maintaining that Theme is the NP which undergoes change of location or whose location is being asserted.

There is some indirect evidence that *Mary* in (1a) is Goal. Růžička (1983) explains the well-formedness of (i) in terms of a thematic identity condition: The (deep) object of *promise* (here, *John*) and the (deep) object of *allow* (here, PRO) have the same θ-role, which Růžička suggests is Receiver.

(i)   *John was promised* [PRO *to be allowed to leave*].

If Růžička's explanation is correct, this tells us what the object of *allow* (or *permit*) is, since it has been fairly widely argued that the object of *promise* is Goal (see Wasow, 1980; Culicover and Wilkins, 1984).

In the last two citations, the infinitival complement of *promise* has been analyzed as Theme. We could extend this role assignment also to the infinitival complement of *permit*.

The required congruence between the thematic roles of the nominal and the host verb may in fact be a weaker relation than identity. See Růžička (1983) for a notion of nondistinctness of thematic roles: Agent and Theme are clearly more distant from each other than, say, Patient and Theme, and a syntactic process may treat the latter pair (in contrast to the former pair) as nondistinct for its purposes. (We illustrate this looser notion of congruence later.)

The contrast between (1b) and (8) should dispel any notion that only the nominal (*permission*, in this case) θ-marks the promoted arguments. Obviously, the host verb also θ-marks them. (Strictly speaking, it θ-marks only some of them; see below for instances of promoted arguments that the host verb cannot θ-mark.) The second problem with complex predicate constructions is in what sense it can be said that both the host verb and the nominal θ-mark these arguments.

A theoretically interesting case is where more arguments are promoted than the host verb's argument structure can accommodate. This situation is best illustrated by the Malayalam data. In (6b), *pookuwaan* 'to leave' is not a complement of *anuwaadam* 'permission.' This can be shown by scrambling *pookuwaan* away from *anuwaadam*:

(6) b'. *raajaawə pookuwaan mantRikkə anuwaadam   koduttu*
          king-nom go-inf   minister-dat permission-acc give-past
     b''. *pookuwaan raajaawə mantRikkə anuwaadam   koduttu*
          go-inf   king-nom minister-dat permission-acc give-past

Malayalam has no rule of syntax which can move a proper subpart of an NP.[3] The fact that (6b') and (6b'') are grammatical shows that *pookuwaan* is not within the NP headed by *anuwaadam*, but has been promoted and made a complement of the host verb *kodutt* 'give'. But *kodutt* is subcategorized only for three arguments: an Agent (or Source), a Theme, and a Beneficiary (which are case-marked nominative, accusative, and dative, respectively). Its typical argument frame is illustrated in (9).

(9) *raajaawə mantRi-kkə oru toppi   kodutt-u*
     king-nom minister-dat one cap-acc give-past
     'The king gave a cap to the minister.'

In (6b), the θ-frame of *kodutt* is saturated: *raajaawə* 'king-nom' is Agent, *anuwaadam* 'permission-acc' is Theme, and *mantRikkə* 'minister-dat' is Beneficiary. *Kodutt* is not subcategorized for a fourth argument, and therefore cannot θ-mark *pookuwaan* in (6b).[4]

Similarly, *mantRi-yoodə* 'toward the minister' in (7b) is not a complement of *sneeham* 'love.' This can be shown first by the scrambling test:

---

[3] Rules such as Extraposition and Extraposition from NP do not apply in Malayalam. The language has no question-word movement in the syntax. Clefting, which is much more widely used in Malayalam than in English, never clefts a subpart of a larger NP. Q-float may move a quantifier expression only to the right of the head noun, not out of the NP. Finally (and in particular), Scrambling may not reorder just a proper subpart of an NP.

[4] In (6a), *pookuwaan* 'to leave' is the Theme of *anuwadikk* 'permit.' (See discussion of the corresponding English verb in footnote 2.) Assuming that it is still Theme in (6b), *kodutt* 'give' cannot accommodate a second Theme (realized here as a proposition).

(7) b'. *mantRiyooḍə   raajaawinə sneeham uṇṭə*
         minister-2nd dat king-dat   love-nom have-present

Also, there is a clinching argument in the fact that a noun in Malayalam may not (in any case) take an NP complement. This is simply a consequence of the fact that a noun may not case-mark; therefore, an NP complement of a noun will be ruled out by the case filter.[5] (A Malayalam noun may not take even a PP complement, for reasons unclear to me.) Genitive case is not assigned by the noun, but by a special rule, and therefore an NP may occur in the genitive position. These facts are illustrated in (10).[6]

(10) a. [NP *raajaaw-inte* (*mantRi-ye   / *mantRi-yooḍə) *sneeham*]
              king-gen   minister-acc   minister-2nd dat love
          'the king's love (*for the minister)'
      b. [NP *raajaaw-inte* (*kavita-ye / *kavita-yeppatti) *wimaRšanam*]
              king-gen   poem-acc   poem-'about'   criticism
          'the king's criticism (*of the poem)'
      c. [NP *dhanatt-inte* (*raajaaw-inaal) *duRwiniyoogam*]
              wealth-gen   king-instr   squandering
          'the wealth's squandering (*by the king)'

Since *mantRiyooḍə* is a case-marked NP, it cannot be a complement of *sneeham* in (7b). It has been promoted and must be a complement of the host verb, *uṇṭə* 'have.' *Uṇṭə*, however, is subcategorized for only two arguments: a Possessor (marked dative), and a Theme (marked nominative). Its argument frame is illustrated in (11).

---

[5] The case filter (Chomsky, 1981) disallows a lexical NP which is not marked for case. Since nouns are not case-assigners, an NP complement of a noun will receive no case and so will be ruled out. English escapes this stricture by inserting a "dummy" preposition *of* in front of such a complement, for example, *the destruction of the city*. Here, *of* assigns case to the complement, so the phrase escapes the case filter. But Malayalam has no similar rule of insertion of an adposition.

[6] Dropping the genitive phrase does not improve the NPs in (10):

(i)   *[NP *mantRi-yooḍə*   *sneeham*]
          minister-2nd dat love
      'love for the minister'

The Malayalam noun escapes its "disability" as regards complements by resorting to a relativization strategy. Thus (ii) is acceptable.

(ii) (*raajaaw-inte*) [S̄ *mantRi-yooḍə uḷḷ-a*   ] *sneeham*
          king-gen   minister-2nd dat is-relativizer love
      '(the king's) love which is for the minister'

Here, *mantRiyooḍə* 'for the minister' is the complement of a verb, and verbs freely take NP and PP complements.

(11)   raaĵaawinə oru ṭoppi   uṇṭə
        king-dat one cap-nom   have-present
        'The king has a cap.'

In (7b), the θ-frame of uṇṭə is saturated: raaĵaawinə 'king-dat' is Possessor, and sneeham 'love-nom' is Theme. Uṇṭə does not subcategorize for a third argument, say, second dative (signifying "for, or toward, NP"); it cannot θ-mark mantRiyooḍə.

In sum, pookuwaan 'to leave' in (6b) and mantRiyooḍə 'for the minister' in (7b) are two arguments which cannot be complements of the nominals anuwaadam 'permission' and sneeham 'love' respectively. They must therefore be complements of the host verbs. But the host verbs cannot θ-mark them, since the verbs' θ-frames are already saturated.

In view of the analysis of the Malayalam data, we might question whether the boldface phrases are complements of their respective deverbal nominals in the English sentences (1b), (3b), and (4b) (repeated below):

(1b)   John gave permission to Mary **to leave**.

(3b)   John made an offer of money **to Mary**.

(4b)   John felt hatred **toward Mary**.

That these phrases are not complements is suggested by familiar tests of constituency. Movement rules do not seem to treat the boldface phrase and the deverbal nominal as a constituent; see (12), (13), and (14) in which the Passive has applied, and (15) and (16) in which Wh-Movement has applied.

(12)   a. Permission was given to Mary **to leave**.
        b. ?Permission **to leave** was given to Mary.

(13)   a. An offer of money was made **to Mary**.
        b. *An offer of money **to Mary** was made.

(14)   a. Hatred was felt toward Mary.
        b. *Hatred **toward Mary** was felt.

(15)   a. This is the person **to whom** John made an offer of money.
        b. *This is the person an offer of money **to whom** John made.

(16)   a. This is the person **toward whom** John felt hatred.
        b. *This is the person hatred **toward whom** John felt.

Further evidence against constituency is that extraneous material (such as an adverb) may be intercalated between the deverbal nominal and the argument in boldface, as in (17)–(19).

(17)   John gave permission to Mary (finally) **to leave**.

(18)   John made an offer of money (incidentally) **to Mary**.

(19)   *John felt only hatred (at that moment)* **toward Mary**.

If the arguments in boldface of (1b), (3b), and (4b) are not complements of the corresponding deverbal nominals, the situation is similar to that in Malayalam. In (1b), *give* is subcategorized for only three arguments, namely a Source, a Theme, and a Goal; these positions are filled respectively by *John, permission,* and *(to)Mary.* It does not have a fourth argument position and therefore cannot θ-mark the promoted argument *to leave.* In (3b), *make* is subcategorized for only two arguments, an Agent and a Theme; these θ-roles are assigned to *John* and *an offer of money* respectively. It is not subcategorized for a Goal argument expressed as a *to*-NP and therefore cannot θ-mark *to Mary.* In (4b), *feel* has only two arguments, an Experiencer and a Theme (cf. *John felt pain*); these positions are taken by *John* and *hatred* respectively. It is not subcategorized for a Goal argument expressed as a *toward*-NP, and therefore cannot θ-mark *toward Mary.*

We see, then, that in the cases of (1b), (3b), and (4b) (English data), and (6b) and (7b) (Malayalam data), we encounter arguments of deverbal nominals which are not their complements. These arguments have been promoted and appear to be complements of the host verbs. Yet the host verbs cannot θ-mark these arguments. Do we (in these cases) have complements which are not θ-marked by the head of the phrase? A claim made by the projection principle is that the head of a phrase θ-marks all its complements.[7] This is the third problem regarding θ-marking in complex predicate constructions.

3. THE PHRASAL NODE θ-FRAME
AND PROMOTION

Previous attempts in the literature to describe how complex predicate constructions are interpreted appeal to diverse types of special mechanisms (Harris, 1957; Cattell, 1969, 1983, 1984; Jackendoff, 1972, 1974; Dixon, 1973; Green, 1974; Higgins, 1974; Oehrle, 1975; Wierzbicka, 1982; and Jayaseelan, 1983, 1984). Jackendoff (1974) appeals to a special rule of interpretation, which he calls the Complex Predicate Rule (CPR). CPR combines the host verb and its direct object (containing the deverbal nominal) into a complex predicate. It produces a subcategorization frame for the complex predicate by

---

[7] The projection principle (Chomsky, 1981) is essentially a bringing together of selection and strict subcategorization: A verb, for example, may not subcategorize for a position which it does not select nor select a position which it does not subcategorize for. For our examples, the prediction of the projection principle is that the "host" verb may not subcategorize for a complement position which it does not select (θ-mark).

eliminating the direct object position of the host verb; for the semantics, it "combines the readings of the main verb and the nominal by superimposing parallel semantic functions" (p. 490). Cattell (1984) creates complex predicates in the lexicon by means of lexical redundancy rules. These rules are triggered by lexical features attached to deverbal nominals, which specify the host verbs with which they may be combined. In contrast to attempts like these, we here try to hold to the thesis that complex predicates are interpreted by the normal mechanisms of θ-marking; in doing this, we are forced to extend θ-theory in several directions.

We have seen that for a theory of θ-marking which says that the head of a phrase θ-marks all (and only) its complements, complex predicate constructions are a prima facie exception. As mentioned above, there is another well-known exception to such a theory, namely the θ-marking of the subject. The verb may θ-mark the subject, even though the subject is not one of its complements. In the *Aspects* model (Chomsky, 1965), this fact was taken care of by saying that selectional restrictions may be nonlocal, whereas strict subcategorization was stipulated to be "strictly local."

In the government-binding theory (Chomsky, 1981), the θ-marking of the subject is claimed to be done by the VP compositionally; the verb is said to only indirectly θ-mark the subject. Let us adopt this solution (see Zubizaretta, 1982; Jayaseelan, 1984; for some arguments in support of this position). But instead of treating compositional θ-marking as a special mechanism that comes into operation only for the θ-marking of the subject, let us take it to be a general property of θ-marking. We propose the following principles:

(20)   A. θ-marking is strictly local. This entails that except at the lowest level (e.g., the level of V and its sister), θ-marking is done by a phrasal node.

   B. The θ-frame of a phrasal node is determined compositionally by its elements.

We also adopt binary branching in phrase structure (see Stowell, 1982; Kayne, 1981; for justification), which ensures that the predicative node (i.e., the node for containing the head of the phrase) will have only one argument to θ-mark, at any level. Suppose binary branching did not obtain. Then for the phrase *give Mary a kiss*, we could have the structure (21):

(21)

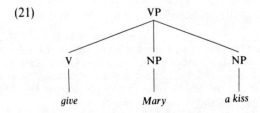

Here *give* may θ-mark both *Mary* and *a kiss* (at the same time). But note that *Mary* is also an argument of *kiss*, and that we have not yet indicated this thematic relation.[8] Given that only the predicative node (i.e., *give* in (21)) may θ-mark, the ternary branching analysis does not allow us to express this thematic relation. Thus the binary branching principle has the desirable consequence that it excludes such analyses. (We reserve our analysis of the double object construction for Section 5.)

Consider how the compositional determination of a phrasal node's θ-frame works in a simple case:

(22)   *John ate an apple.*

First, *eat* marks *an apple* Theme (or Patient). It then promotes its unassigned θ-role, Agent, to VP. The NP, *an apple*, has no argument to promote. Therefore the θ-frame of VP is determined (in this case) by the simple process of promotion of a θ-role from one of its daughter nodes.

Consider next cognate object constructions:

(23)   a. *John danced a dance.*
        b. *John ran a race.*

Although English has only a few instances of these constructions, there are languages in which they are the output of a fully productive process. Thus, Malayalam has a cognate object construction corresponding to every intransitive verb. Let us assume that the verb of a cognate object construction assigns to its sister node the quasi-argument role " # ". Now we come to VP. It is clear (in these cases) that both the verb and the deverbal nominal (e.g., *dance*$_V$ and *dance*$_N$ in (23a)) promote the same θ-roles—and even the same manner markers, in the sense of Jackendoff (1974)—to VP; therefore the two

---

[8] Clearly, *kiss* selects (θ-marks) *Mary*; cf. (i).

(i)   **give the idea a kiss*

If all we can say about (i) is that *give* marks *the idea* Goal, and *a kiss* Theme, we have not accounted for the unacceptability of (i). (Note that *the idea* is a possible Goal of *give*, as in *give the idea little importance*, and *a kiss* is a possible Theme of *give*, as in (21). To account for (i), we must have some way of expressing the selectional restriction between the two NPs of the double object construction.

Oehrle (1975) points out that there is a relation of possession between these two NPs. In a phrase like (ii), *Mary* must have the θ-role of "possessor" with respect to *a book*.

(ii)   *give Mary a book*

But in (21) (or (i)), *Mary* (or *the idea*) is the Goal of *kiss*. Intuitively, too, we know that the same selectional restriction that rules out (i) rules out (iii), namely that the Goal of *kiss* must be a concrete object:

(iii)   **John kissed the idea*

θ-roles are readily superimposed on each other. In these cases, then, the θ-frame of VP is determined by both promotion and superimposition; however, the task of superimposition is very straightforward.

Now consider (4b), a complex predicate construction, where a structure such as (24) is postulated:

(24)

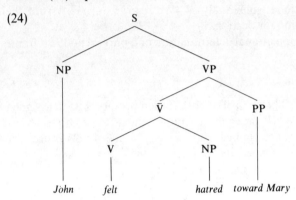

Here, *feel* may assign the θ-roles {Experiencer, Theme}; it marks *hatred* Theme and promotes {Experiencer}. *Hatred* may assign the θ-roles {Experiencer, Goal},[9] both of which are unassigned within the NP and are promoted. Therefore $\bar{V}$ has the θ-frame which is the union of the two sets of promoted roles: {Experiencer} $\cup$ {Experiencer, Goal} = {Experiencer, Goal}. The $\bar{V}$ then assigns Goal to *toward Mary* and promotes {Experiencer} to VP; VP assigns Experiencer to the subject NP, *John*.

Recall that (4b) is an example of all three problems noted in Section 2. The deverbal nominal *hatred* would seem to θ-mark *John* and *toward Mary*, which are outside the maximal projection of which *hatred* is the head (Problem 1). *John* is doubly θ-marked by the host verb and the deverbal nominal (Problem 2). The host verb cannot θ-mark *toward Mary*, although the latter appears to be its complement (Problem 3). The current account resolves all three of these problems. Regarding Problem 1, we can say that *hatred* indirectly θ-marks *John* and (*toward*) *Mary*, both of which are directly θ-marked by a phrasal category. The answer to Problem 2 is that *John* is directly θ-marked only by one category, namely VP. With regard to Problem 3, we can say that (*toward*) *Mary* is not a complement of the host verb, but of the phrasal category, $\bar{V}$; and $\bar{V}$ does θ-mark it. A solution along these lines is applicable to all complex predicate constructions.

---

[9] Emotions such as love, hate, be angry, are directed, hence our analysis of the second argument of *hatred* as Goal. Notice such expressions as *the target of his hatred* and *be angry at John*. The first argument of *hatred* is probably both Experiencer and Source; see also common metaphors like *love flowing from someone*.

One consequence of the current analysis is that it is no longer necessary to distinguish the class of complex predicates, since the interpretation of complex predicates does not appeal to any special rules. This is important, because it may not be possible to demarcate such a class. Consider (25) and (26):

(25)   *John had a headache.*

(26)   *John felt ill will toward Mary.*

(25) and (26) have no corresponding simple predicate constructions with which they have a paraphrase relation, since *headache* and *ill will* are not deverbal. Thus these sentences do not fit our original characterization of complex predicate constructions. Yet *headache* has one argument (like *sleep*, in (5b)) whose θ-role can apparently be identified with the θ-role which *have* assigns to its subject, and which can therefore be promoted. Similarly, *ill will* (like *hatred*, in (4b)) has two arguments, Experiencer and Goal, both of which can be promoted. There is no way we can distinguish between (5b) and (25), or between (4b) and (26), in a principled way and without circularity.

The conclusion of this section seems a good occasion to illustrate the looser notion of CONGRUENCE touched on in footnote 2. Consider the interpretation of the complex predicate illustrated in (27).

(27)   *John harbors feelings of hatred toward Mary.*

We postulate the following structure for this sentence:

(28)

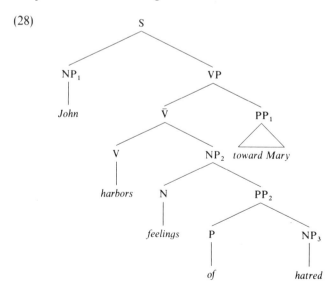

Here *hatred* has the θ-roles {Experiencer, Goal} to assign; neither of these is assigned within NP_3, so they are promoted to PP_2, which promotes them to NP_2. *Feelings* may assign {Experiencer, Theme}; it marks *hatred* Theme (note that *of* is a dummy preposition and does not prevent direct θ-marking of *hatred* by the head noun). It promotes {Experiencer} to NP_2. The θ-frame of NP_2 is the union of the two sets it gets from its daughter nodes: {Experiencer} $\cup$ {Experiencer, Goal} = {Experiencer, Goal}. It promotes this set to $\bar{V}$. The V *harbor* (we postulate) can assign the θ-roles {Location, Theme}. It marks NP_2 Theme and promotes {Location} to $\bar{V}$. Now $\bar{V}$ has the sets {Location} and {Experiencer, Goal}. What happens then?

We suggest that Location and Experiencer are congruent roles and may be superimposed on each other. This is intuitive, since the experiencer of an emotion is also the location of the emotion, a typical case of the metaphorical extension of Location and Motion to predicates of emotion (and *know*-type verbs) that Jackendoff (1972) and Gruber (1965) have described; notice expressions like *the hatred in me*. Let us designate this superimposed function as "Location–Experiencer." We claim that the θ-frame of $\bar{V}$ is now {Location–Experiencer, Goal}. $\bar{V}$ assigns Goal to *toward Mary* and promotes {Location–Experiencer} to VP. VP marks the subject *John* Location–Experiencer.

The point to note is the amalgamation of Experiencer and Location at a certain point along the path of promotion. If such amalgamation of congruent roles were disallowed and absolute identity were insisted on (for superimposition of θ-roles), we would either have to say that the first argument of *hatred* (and of *feelings*) is Location even to begin with, or that the first argument of *harbor* is Experiencer. Neither of these choices seems satisfactory.

4. RESTRICTIONS ON PROMOTION

Our account of complex predicates rests on the claim that the θ-frame of a phrasal node is determined by the promotion of unassigned θ-roles from both its daughter nodes. There are, however, severe restrictions on promotion from the nonpredicative daughter node. We turn now to these restrictions.

Consider (29), which has the structure (30).

(29)   *John did a dance at the inauguration of the conference.*

Here, *do*, which can assign the θ-roles {Agent, Theme}, assigns Theme to *a dance* and promotes {Agent}; *dance*, which assigns just the θ-role {Agent},

(30)

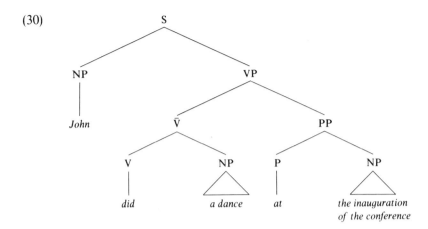

promotes it.[10] The two Agent θ-roles are identified with each other at V̄, whose
θ-frame now is {Agent}. Let us assume that *at* has one θ-role to assign,
{Location}, which it assigns to its object NP. The head of its object NP,
inauguration, has two θ-roles to assign, one of which (Agent) is unassigned
within the NP. Assuming for the moment that the promotion of θ-roles is
completely free, this NP promotes {Agent} to PP. It should then be possible to
identify (at VP) the {Agent} of V̄ and the {Agent} of PP, and the VP should
assign {Agent} to the subject NP. Such a scheme of promotion would yield the
two entailments, "John danced" and "John inaugurated the conference."
Sentence (29) involves the first entailment but not the second. This indicates
that promotion should not be permitted from the prepositional object.
Promotion from a nonpredicative daughter node is possible only from the
direct object position.

   In trying to account for this, let us note that subject and direct object are
the only thematically unrestricted grammatical relations. It is possible to
say that the NP of *to*-NP is a Goal, or that the NP of *on*-NP is a Location,
independently of the context in which it occurs. The θ-role of a direct object
can be determined only with respect to the meaning of the verb, and the θ-role
of a subject can be determined only with respect to the meaning of the VP. Let
us say that the verb θ-marks only the direct object, and that the VP θ-marks
the subject, but that PPs containing thematically restricted prepositions (or, in
wholly case-marking languages, NPs marked with thematically restricted
cases) are not θ-marked. Rather, they are integrated into the thematic frames

---

[10] The second argument of *do* is analyzed as Theme advisedly; its precise thematic content is
not important for our purposes. The single argument of *dance* is both Agent and Theme (see
Jackendoff, 1972).

of their predicative sister nodes by a different mechanism.[11] We indicate direct θ-marking by a lexical category (i.e., "θ-government," in the sense of Chomsky, 1986a), by thematic co-indexing, as suggested in Rouveret and Vergnaud (1980) and Chomsky (1986a). Specifically, an NP or $\bar{S}$ which is governed and directly θ-marked by a lexical category is marked with the superscript of its governor. Thus (30) will be (30′) after thematic co-indexing:

(30′)

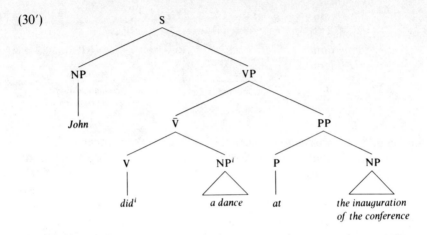

Here *a dance* is cosuperscripted with *did*; *the inauguration of the conference* has no superscript, since it is not θ-marked; and *John* has no superscript because it is not directly θ-marked.

Let us now make thematic co-indexing a condition on promotion. We reformulate Principle B as B′:

B′.   The θ-frame of a phrasal node is the union of the sets of θ-roles promoted from the daughter nodes, where these are thematically co-indexed; otherwise, it is the set of θ-roles promoted from the predicative daughter node.[12]

----

[11] We extend strict locality to this new mechanism (call it R); so that our Principle A should now read:

(A′) θ-marking and R are strictly local.

Note that we leave open the possibility that PPs with thematically unrestricted prepositions—like the transformationally introduced *of* of English, or *a* of French—may be θ-marked by their predicative sister nodes (see discussion of (27).)

[12] It is interesting to note that direct θ-marking of a node by a lexical category also makes that node nonbounding for movement. This idea, first suggested by Cattell (1976) and developed by others (e.g., Kayne, 1983; Pesetsky, 1982), has been incorporated in the definitions of blocking category and barrier in Chomsky (1986a). Obviously, direct θ-marking of Y by X constitutes a very special relation between X and Y, whose nature is only now being understood.

In (30'), *did* and *a dance* are thematically co-indexed, so the θ-frame of $\bar{V}$ will be determined by the promotion of θ-roles from both its daughter nodes (exactly as we described earlier). But $\bar{V}$ and PP are not thematically co-indexed; therefore the θ-frame of VP will contain only the θ-roles promoted from the predicative daughter node, namely $\bar{V}$. $\bar{V}$ promotes only {Agent}, derived from *did* and *dance* (see the above discussion). Therefore, when VP marks the subject NP *John* Agent, we get only the entailments that "John did something" and "John danced," but not the entailment that "John inaugurated the conference." This is the correct result.

A second constraint on promotion is what we expressed in terms of superimposition (identification) of congruent θ-roles (see our discussion of (24) and (28)). That this type of superimposition is a necessary condition is suggested by the following sentences:

(31)   *John witnessed the bombing of the city.*

(32)   *John did the bombing of the city.*

The noun *bombing* can assign two θ-roles, one of which—namely Agent—is unassigned within the NP of which *bombing* is the head. This θ-role is promoted to the VP node in (32), where it is superimposed on the Agent θ-role of the host verb, *do*. This gives us the entailment that "John bombed the city." But in (31), this promotion is apparently blocked because the θ-frame of *witness* does not contain Agent,[13] and therefore (31) does not entail that "John bombed the city." The identification of some of the θ-roles of the deverbal nominal with some of the θ-roles of the host verb is apparently necessary.

But it is not necessary that all the promoted θ-roles of the deverbal nominal should be superimposable on the host verb's θ-roles. We have already examined instances where the nominal promotes θ-roles which are not part of the host verb's θ-frame. The converse is also true: The host verb may promote θ-roles which are not identifiable with the θ-roles promoted by the nominal. This is illustrated by (33).

(33)   *Perfume gives me a headache.*

Here, *headache* has only one θ-role, which it assigns to ⸱*me* (by predication within a small clause, see the next section). *Perfume* is an argument of *give* alone, and not of *headache*.

The constraint therefore cannot be that the sets of θ-roles promoted by the host verb and the nominal should be identical. But apparently they should be

---

[13] Jackendoff (1974) postulates MANNER MARKERS attached to predicates; he claims that a verb and a nominal must be identical with respect to manner markers as well, if they are to form a complex predicate. But we may be able to dispense with manner markers if we have a more refined set of θ-roles.

comparable. (Two sets, A and B, are comparable if either A is a subset of B or B is a subset of A.) We revise our Principle B again, to incorporate this condition:

B″. The θ-frame of a phrasal node is the union of the sets of θ-roles promoted from the daughter nodes, where
    (i) the daughter nodes are thematically co-indexed;
    (ii) the two sets are comparable.
Otherwise, it is the set of θ-roles promoted from the predicative daughter node.

Josef Bayer (personal communication) has pointed out the problem posed by sentences like (34).

(34)   *John condemned the condemnation of capital punishment.*

Here, *condemnation* has two θ-roles, only one of which is assigned within its NP. The unassigned θ-role, which we take to be Agent, should now be available (by our theory) for promotion to the VP node, where it can be identified with the Agent θ-role of the matrix verb *condemn*. This should, however, give us the entailment that "John condemned capital punishment," which is obviously the wrong result.

What prevents promotion of the deverbal noun's θ-role in this case? Note that we have no escape via "a more refined set of θ-roles" here, since the deverbal nominal and the matrix verb are the same lexical item modulo category.

Apparently, the semantics of the host verb is relevant for promotion in some way which we have not yet understood. Verbs that have Source or Goal or Location in their θ-grids (such as *give* or *have*; also a nonbasic verb like *harbor* in (27)) and abstract verbs which signify simply a schema (such as *do*, which applies to all actions) appear to readily act as host verbs in complex predicate constructions. Verbs of perception (*witness, observe, see,* etc.) or verbs of "saying" (*condemn, report,* etc.) never seem to function as host verbs. Action verbs (*jump, kick, dance,* etc.) occur as host verbs only in cognate object constructions. Tentatively, let us say that a host verb must be a "primary" verb of motion or location, i.e., a verb which has Source, Goal, or Location in its θ-grid in its primary sense, without a metaphorical extension. [This would exclude, e.g., *know*, which has Location in its θ-grid by virtue of a metaphorical extension of Location (Jackendoff, 1972).] Or it must be an "abstract" verb of action, like *do*, or of "bringing into existence," like *make*. The idea behind this stipulation is that promotion of θ-roles from a direct object is done by reinterpretation of its θ-roles in terms of primary concepts like GO, BE, DO or MAKE; apparently this reinterpretation cannot be done by a host verb which can itself fit these concepts only by virtue of a metaphorical extension of these concepts.

This stipulation takes care of most host verbs. But we still have problems, e.g., *feel* in (4b). In the worst case we may have to lexically mark verbs as "holes" or "plugs" for θ-role promotion. But it may not be too much to emphasize that such lexical markings do not also mean a return to a completely lexical treatment of complex predicates and the abandonment of the notions of θ-role promotion and compositional θ-marking. There is a parallel here with the passive construction: The passive is lexically governed, yet is an instance of "Move α." A completely general process may be operative in a construction, which is otherwise subject to ill-understood factors of the lexicon.

5. DOUBLE OBJECT CONSTRUCTIONS

In this section we suggest a solution to a problem in θ-marking which arises in double object constructions under a "small clause" analysis of them. Under the small clause analysis, sentence (35) has the structure (36), where α is a small clause.

(35)   *John gave Mary a kiss.*

(36)

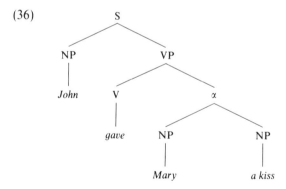

The two NPs of the small clause are interpreted as standing in the relation "NP_1 have NP_2," the θ-role of NP_1 being determined by the semantics of NP_2.[14] (See footnote 8.)

---

[14] To illustrate the relation of possession between the two NPs of the double object construction, consider sentences (i) and (ii).

(i)   *John bought a kimono for his wife.*

(ii)   *John bought his wife a kimono.*

In (36), then, *a kiss* (which is the predicative node) may θ-mark *Mary* without any problem (unlike in the ternary branching structure discussed in Section 3). The question is: How does *give* θ-mark *Mary* and *a kiss*? We do not want *give* to θ-mark into a complement.

As a preliminary to presenting our solution, we suggest that English has a rule—call it the SMALL CLAUSE RULE—which (a) introduces a small clause into the complement position of a verb; (b) suppresses all the verb's VP-internal arguments (or, more precisely, substitutes the small clause for those arguments); and (c) gives the verb a causative meaning. The small clause has an abstract verb, which is BE, HAVE, or GO.

The operation of the small clause rule is seen in the following sentences:[15]

(37) a. *He laughed [$_\alpha$ himself sick].*
      b. *She laughed [$_\alpha$ him out of patience].*
      c. *We talked [$_\alpha$ her out of her crazy scheme].*
      d. *They danced [$_\alpha$ their days away].*

(38) a. *He washed [$_\alpha$ the soap out of his eyes].*
      b. *He shaved [$_\alpha$ his hair off].*
      c. *They wrung [$_\alpha$ a confession from him].*
      d. *He rubbed [$_\alpha$ the tiredness out of his eyes].*
      e. *We kept [$_\alpha$ him out of trouble with the police].*
      f. *They ate [$_\alpha$ us out of house and home].*

(39) a. *They painted [$_\alpha$ the door green].*
      b. *They cooked [$_\alpha$ the chicken dry].*
      c. *They pushed [$_\alpha$ him into a well].*
      d. *They wiped [$_\alpha$ the table clean].*
      e. *He ate [$_\alpha$ it all up].*
      f. *He made [$_\alpha$ the dress too large].*

Sentence (ii) entails that John's wife got the kimono. Thus one can continue sentence (i) as in (iii), but (iv) is a contradiction.

(iii)   *John bought a kimono for his wife, but finally gave it to his mistress.*

(iv)   *John bought his wife a kimono, but finally gave it to his mistress.*

   How this relation of possession comes about can be explained if we assume that a clause that has no overt verb may be interpreted as having an abstract BE or HAVE in certain syntactic contexts. (This is attested in some other languages, e.g., Russian, Tamil.)

   Incidentally, observe that we cannot appeal to this explanation if we do not postulate a clausal structure here. The clausal structure also accounts for the subjectlike properties of the first NP, noticed, e.g., by Herslund (1986) in Scandinavian. Also see Kayne (1981, 1985) for the original arguments for the small clause analysis and binary branching.

   [15] Many of these sentences have figured in the literature under the name of RESULTATIVES; see, e.g., Rothstein (1983).

(40) a. *They permitted [$_\alpha$ John visitors].*
      b. *They sanctioned [$_\alpha$ John some money].*
      c. *John bought [$_\alpha$ his wife a kimono].*
      d. *John gave [$_\alpha$ Mary a kiss].* ($=$(35))

In the sentences of (37), the verb is intransitive, so the small clause rule suppresses no VP-internal argument.[16] But note that the verb gets a causative meaning which it normally does not possess. The sentences of (38) have transitive verbs whose second argument is not allowed to surface. Thus (38a) does not mean that "he washed the soap." In (38b), *he* shaved some unspecified surface, but not his hair. Similar observations apply to all the other sentences in (38). Note again that the verbs acquire a new causative meaning. In the type of sentences illustrated in (39), it is not entirely obvious that the verb's second argument is suppressed. Thus, if one *paints the door green*, it might be argued that one also *paints the door*. But we suggest that this seeming implication is a matter of pragmatics.[17] In the sentences of (40), we have verbs with two internal arguments, both of which (we suggest) are suppressed. In the special case, (40d), which is the sentence we are interested in, the internal arguments of *give* are suppressed.

The answer, then, to the question of how *give* θ-marks *Mary* and *a kiss* in (36) is that it does not. The internal arguments of *give* are not assigned at all, owing to the operation of the small clause rule. Now only one point remains to be

---

[16] Probal Dasgupta (personal communication) has pointed out that ergative verbs (in the sense of Burzio, 1981) do not seem to undergo the small clause rule:

(i) **The people died [$_\alpha$ the town empty].*

This can be explained if *the people* is in the object position in the underlying structure (Burzio, 1981). The small clause rule, which suppresses all the VP-internal arguments of the verb, would suppress this argument too, and (i) will not be generated. What will be generated is the subjectless sentence: *"Δ *died* [$_\alpha$ *the town empty*].

[17] Thus, consider (i) and (ii):

(i)   *They kicked his guts out.*

(ii) *They kicked the ball in.*

It is plausible to say that (ii) also means that "they kicked the ball"; but it is not so plausible to say that (i) means that "they kicked his guts."

An alternative to our account would be along the lines of Rothstein (1983). Rothstein would treat *green* in (39a) as a secondary predication; *the door* would be θ-marked twice, both by *paint* and by *green*. This requires a weakening of the θ-criterion (Chomsky, 1981), which stipulates that an argument may bear only one θ-role. Another problem is that this fails to treat all the resultative data uniformly. In (39a), *the door* is θ-marked twice; but in (37a), *himself* is θ-marked only once (by *sick*). Nor is this difference due to the fact that *paint* in (39a) is transitive and *laugh* in (37a) is intransitive; because (38a) has a transitive verb, and yet *the soap* is θ-marked only by *out of his eyes* and not by *wash*. These differences will require an explanation in the predication analysis.

explained about (36), namely how *John* is interpreted as the kisser. In other words, how does our interpretation mechanism account for the indirect θ-marking of *John* by *kiss*? This presents no problems: (a) *kiss* assigns the θ-role of Goal to *Mary* and promotes its Source to α. The θ-frame of α now is {Source}. *Give*'s sole VP-internal argument (after the operation of the small clause rule) is the small clause, which it θ-marks. (The θ-role assigned is Theme, or whatever is the θ-role assigned by a causative verb to the caused event.) *Give* then promotes {Source}, which is the θ-role of its external argument. By Principle B″, the θ-role(s) of α can be promoted to VP, since α is thematically co-indexed with *give* and the sets of θ-roles promoted by α and *give* are comparable (in fact, identical). The θ-frame of VP then is {Source} ∪ {Source} = {Source}. And VP assigns this θ-role to the subject.

We are now in a position to explain a fairly well-known fact about *give*, namely that in certain sentences containing this verb, the double object construction is judged to have greater acceptability than the construction involving *to*-NP:

(41) a. ?*John gave a kiss to Mary.*
      b. *John gave Mary a kiss.*

(42) a. ??*John gave a kick to the table.*
      b. *John gave the table a kick.*

(43) a. **Perfume gives a headache to me.*
      b. *Perfume gives me a headache.*

If Dative Shift were simply an operation on grammatical relations which left the verb's assignment of θ-roles unaffected, we should be puzzled by these data. However, our analysis claims that in the double object construction, the internal θ-roles of *give* are not assigned. In particular, its θ-role of Goal (encoded in English as *to*-NP) is not assigned. The varying degrees of unacceptability of the (a) sentences of (41)–(43) can be attributed to the varying degrees of inappropriateness of the θ-role of Goal for the argument appearing as the object of *to*. In the (b) sentences, this inappropriateness does not obtain, since Goal is not assigned. Thus the differences in acceptability of the sentences in (41)–(43) constitute an argument for our analysis of the double object construction, and of resultative constructions in general.

The main argument of this article is that the θ-roles of a lexical category may be promoted from its own maximal projection to a higher maximal projection. We use this promotion mechanism to explain how complex predicate constructions are interpreted. We treat promotion as a fully general process (like, say, movement), but subject (like movement) to constraints. Numerous problems remain for this approach, but a profitable research strategy would be to maintain the generality of this process and to investigate the nature of the constraints which limit its application in particular cases.

ACKNOWLEDGMENTS

A paper on which this article is based was presented at the 1984 GLOW colloquium in Copenhagen. I wish to thank K. P. Mohanan, Probal Dasgupta, and Richard Kayne for comments on an earlier version (Jayaseelan, 1984), and the participants of the GLOW colloquium, especially Joseph Bayer, for comments on the present version. I am grateful to Wendy Wilkins for excellent editorial advice. Finally, a special word of thanks to Ray Cattell; interacting with him has been a pleasure during my attempts to analyze complex predicates.

MULTIPLE θ-ROLE ASSIGNMENT IN CHOCTAW

GEORGE AARON BROADWELL

Department of Linguistics
University of California
Los Angeles, California 90024

1. INTRODUCTION

In this article I argue that arguments may be assigned more than one θ-role, based on evidence from the verbal morphology of Choctaw, a Muskogean language spoken in Oklahoma and Mississippi. I argue that a system of lexical decomposition like that of Jackendoff (1972) must be incorporated into grammatical theory and show how the θ-criterion (Chomsky, 1981) can be revised to accommodate this conception of θ-structure.

In Section 2 I show that verbal agreement is sensitive to the θ-role that an argument bears and allows us to identify arguments as Agents, Themes, and so on. In Sections 3 and 4 I explore two additional processes—number suppletion and auxiliary selection—and show that they identify the argument bearing the Theme role. However, there is a class of intransitive verbs in which the single argument is identified as an Agent by the verbal agreement test but as a Theme by the tests of number suppletion and auxiliary selection. I argue that these arguments bear both Agent and Theme roles. In Section 5 I show how the θ-criterion can be modified to accommodate these data, and come to a conclusion in Section 6.

Syntax and Semantics, Volume 21
Thematic Relations

2. THE CHOCTAW AGREEMENT SYSTEM

Choctaw has a complex system of verbal agreement which indexes the subject, object, dative, and certain oblique arguments.[1] A partial table of the agreement morphology is shown in (1), where the labeling of the sets follows Munro and Gordon (1982).

(1)		I	II	III
	1s	*-li*	*sa-*	*am-*
	2s	*ish-*	*chi-*	*chim-*
	3	∅	∅	*im-*
	1p	*il/ii-*	*pi-*	*pim-*
	2p	*hash-*	*hachi-*	*hachim-*[2]

Affixes from Set I agree with the subjects of most transitive verbs and some intransitives, as shown in (2).

(2) *Chi-sso-lih.*
2sII-hit-1sI
'I hit you.'
Chi-ahpali-lih.
2sII-kiss-1sI
'I kissed you.'
Baliili-lih.
run-1sI
'I ran.'

In addition to agreeing with the objects of most transitive verbs, as shown in (2), affixes from Set II also agree with the subjects of some intransitive verbs.

(3) *Sa-chaahah.*
1sII-tall
'I'm tall.'
Chi-kayyah.
2sII-pregnant
'You're pregnant.'
Sa-habishkoh.
1sII-sneeze
'I sneezed.'

---

[1] Oblique morphology has the effect of adding an internal argument to the subcategorization frame of a verb. The role of the argument indexed by the oblique marker may include

Though several of the examples in (3) are translated by predicate adjectives in English, there is clear evidence that they are verbs in Choctaw. The adjectival predicates may occur with the full array of verbal morphology, including person and number agreement and tense marking.

Affixes from Set III generally agree with dative arguments and with the subject of a small number of mostly psychological predicates.

(4)   *Im-aa-li-tok.*
        3III-give-1sI-past
        'I gave it to him/her.'
        I-chopa-li-tok.
        3III-buy-1sI-past
        'I bought it for/from him.'
        A-takoobih.
        1sIII-lazy
        'I'm lazy.'

Although the treatment of III agreement will ultimately be important to the theory of θ-roles, I disregard it in this article and focus on I and II agreement exclusively.

Verbs may have subject agreement from either set I or II. This is a lexical property of individual verbs, and in general a verb's subject may take either I agreement or II agreement, but not both.[3] The distribution of I and II agreement is far from random, and there are several semantic generalizations over these classes of verbs.

Most transitive verbs with agentive subjects take I subject agreement, as do verbs of perception and cognition and verbs of volitional motion. Examples of these types are shown in (5).

---

instrumental, benefactive, comitative, locative, and others, as discussed by Ulrich (1986). I have nothing further to say about oblique morphology in this article.

I do not address the difficult issue of whether the verbal morphology functions as a pronominal argument of the verb or whether it is in fact agreement with some empty category. Both positions are compatible with the account proposed here.

[2] The following orthographic conventions are in use: $\langle$sh$\rangle = /\int/$, $\langle$ch$\rangle = /t\int/$, $\langle$lh$\rangle = /\ell/$. Underlining indicates vowel nasalization. The affixes in Column III surface as Vm- before stems beginning with a vowel, and as *V* before stems beginning with a consonant. Verbs in Choctaw end in an unglossed *h*, as the examples illustrate (see Ulrich, 1986, for details).

[3] There are a few verbs which may take both I and II agreement. These include *habishkoh* 'to sneeze,' *hotilhkoh* 'to cough.' For some speakers, I and II marking are in free variation, while others use I affixes with volitional subjects, and II affixes with nonvolitional subjects.

There are also other verbs which displays I/II alternations under certain syntactic conditions, such as the addition of a dative. These effects seem somewhat variable from speaker to speaker (see Davies, 1981, for a full discussion of this subject).

(5) Sample verbs with I subjects
   a. Agentive transitive verbs
      kobaffih   'break'   *kalashlih*   'cut'
      awashlih   'fry'   *achiifah*   'wash'
   b. Verbs of perception and cognition
      hakloh   'hear'   *pisah*   'see'
      ikhanah   'know'   *ahnih*   'think'
   c. Verbs of volitional motion
      baliilih   'run'   *toloblih*   'jump'
      hilhah   'dance'   *nowah*   'walk'

To delineate the semantic types of verbs which take I subject agreement,
I appeal to the lexical decomposition analyses of Jackendoff (1972, 1976,
1983, 1987) and Dowty (1979), the latter as modified by Foley and Van Valin
(1984). These analyses assume that individual lexical items can be decomposed into a small number of abstract generalized predicates. Furthermore,
the θ-roles borne by various arguments can be defined by their positions
within these predicates. In Jackendoff's system, for example, verbs of motion
have the decomposition GO(x, PATH (y, z)), where the argument x bears
the θ-role Theme; y, Source; and z, Goal. The present analysis generally
follows the proposals of Jackendoff (1972, 1976, 1983, 1987), occasionally
adopting some modifications from Foley and Van Valin (1984) where this
seems more perspicuous.

Turning to the verbs listed in (5), let us examine the lexical decompositions
of each class. I assume the structures given in (6).

(6) a. Agentive transitive verbs
        CAUSE (x, GO (y)), where x = Agent, y = Theme
     b. Verbs of perception
        pred' (x, y), where x = Experiencer, y = Percept
     c. Verbs of volitional motion
        CAUSE (x, GO (x)), where x = Agent and Theme

In addition to the classes of verbs described above, two other types of
verbs take I subjects. The first is the class of verbs with nonvolitional agents,
as in (7).

(7) *Okkisa ish-kooli-tok!*
     window 2sI-break-pt
     'You broke it!'

This sentence can be uttered even when the addressee's unconscious body
fell through the window. Following Foley and Van Valin (1984), I call this
role Effector, and I assume that it is the same role assigned to the causee in a
causative construction.

A final type of verb is exemplified by the verb *receive,* which has a Goal subject that receives I agreement.[4]

(8)   *Habiina-li-tok.*
        receive-1sI-pt
        'I received it.'

Subjects which take I agreement thus include those bearing Agent, Effector, Experiencer, and Goal θ-roles. This range of roles recalls the θ-role hierarchies suggested by Jackendoff (1972) and Foley and Van Valin (1984). Consider the following hierarchy, which incorporates aspects of both the preceding analyses.[5]

(9)   θ-role hierarchy

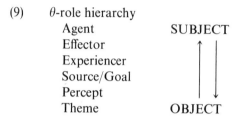

Foley and Van Valin suggest that Theme (in Jackendoff's sense) be divided into two θ-roles, Theme and Patient. The single argument of a stative predicate is assigned the θ-role Patient, while the thing which undergoes motion or whose location is specified literally or figuratively is the Theme. This revision is motivated largely by a desire to simplify the semantics associated with Theme.

However, the Choctaw data do not support this distinction. As is shown in Section 3, number suppletion is tied to both Patients and Themes,

---

[4] There are, of course, other verbs in which the subject takes Goal in addition to some other role (usually Agent), as in the verbs *chopah* 'to buy,' *hokopah* 'to steal,' etc. So far as I know, there are no verbs where the subject bears the Source role alone, though there are many where the subject bears both Source and Agent roles, e.g., *imah* 'to give', *kachih* 'to sell.'

[5] In Foley and Van Valin (1984), this hierarchy is used for the selection of the macroroles actor and undergoer, rather than subject and object. I reject the notions actor and undergoer as relevant for Choctaw grammar, since I believe they are not distinct from subject and object.

The establishment of actor as a notion distinct from subject depends on finding situations in which the two are different. Foley and Van Valin suggest passive as an example of this sort in English. The subject of a active verb is an actor, while the subject of the corresponding passive is an undergoer. Yet this argument has little force in a framework that recognizes multiple levels of grammatical structure. We may say that ACTOR is defined as d-structure subject, and thus the effects attributed to ACTOR can be restated in terms of subject.

At any rate, there is not even a weak argument of this sort in Choctaw, since the language has no rule of passivization which could "demote" an actor from subject position. In Choctaw, all actors are subjects.

As for undergoers, I argue above that undergoer subjects are d-structure objects and undergo movement to subject position. Thus undergoer and d-structure object are not distinct in Choctaw.

suggesting that a unified notion is necessary. In a system of the sort proposed by Foley and Van Valin, number suppletion might alternately be linked to the UNDERGOER macrorole. However, to be consistent, a Foley and Van Valin-style analysis must also link I agreement to the macrorole ACTOR. In this case, the intransitive verbs of volitional motion which both supplete for number and take I verbal agreement (discussed in Section 3) present a logical contradiction for the Foley and Van Valin system, since the same argument must bear both the actor and undergoer macroroles. Hence, number suppletion shows that there must be a unified notion Theme of the sort proposed by Jackendoff (1972).

Recall from (2) and (3) that II agreement is associated with the objects of transitive verbs and the subjects of stative intransitive verbs. In the examples given, the argument bears the Theme role. Davies (1981, 1986) presents a range of arguments within a relational grammar framework for an analysis in which the subjects of stative verbs originate as initial objects and become subjects through the rule of unaccusative advancement (Perlmutter, 1978) or ergative movement (Burzio, 1981). I briefly restate two of Davies's, arguments for unaccusative movement within a government–binding framework.

First, and perhaps most convincingly, the verbal agreement for the subject of an unaccusative is the same as that for the object of a transitive verb, as discussed above. If unaccusative subjects originate as d-structure objects, then we may simply say that arguments in d-structure object position receive II agreement. A desirable consequence is that inflectional rules are not allowed direct access to the content of θ-roles (see Martin, 1986; Broadwell, 1986b, for conflicting positions on the desirability of this consequence).

Second, there is some evidence from switch reference (SR) that supports the unaccusative analysis. The interpretation of these results requires some background in the theoretical treatment of SR in government-binding theory (Finer, 1984; Broadwell, 1986a).

SR is a system in which the complementizer of an embedded clause indicates whether the subject of the clause it occurs on is the same as the subject of the superordinate clause. Typically, there are two distinct types of SR markers: same subject (SS) and different subject (DS). The SS marker is treated as an anaphor and the DS marker as a pronominal (Finer, 1984) or as an obviative anaphor (Broadwell, 1986a). These markers are co-indexed with the subject of the clause in which they appear. So in (10), the SS marker is co-indexed with the subject of its clause *John*. By principle A of the binding theory (Chomsky, 1981), anaphors must be c-commanded by some co-indexed element within their governing category. Thus the SS marker must be c-commanded by some element with the index *i*. In (10a), the SS marker is co-indexed with and c-commanded by the INFL (inflection node) of the second clause, so it satisfies the binding theory, and the sentence is grammatical. But in (10b), the INFL of the second clause bears the index *j*, so the SS marker fails to be bound, and the sentence is ungrammatical.

(10) a. *John-at   taloowa-chah hilha-tok.*
       John-nom sing-ss   dance-pt
       'John$_i$ sang and (he$_i$) danced.'
   b.**John-at   taloowa-chah Pam-at   hilha-tok.*
       John-nom sing-ss   Pam-nom dance-pt
       'John$_i$ sang and Pam$_j$ danced.'

Although these sentences are translated with 'and,' they actually involve subordination, as shown by Linker (1987). The first clause is adjoined to the second in a structure like that shown in (11).

(11)

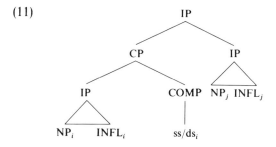

The relevant notion of c-command, drawing on May (1985) and Chomsky (1986b) is given in (12).

(12)   X c-command Y iff X does not dominate Y and every maximal
        projection that dominates X also dominates Y.

MAXIMAL PROJECTION is defined in such a way that the nodes created by adjunction are not distinct maximal projections. Thus IP is the only maximal projection dominating INFL$_j$, and this maximal projection also dominates the COMP containing the SR markers. Thus INFL$_j$ c-commands COMP.

The phenomenon of interest for unaccusative advancement is as follows. For some speakers, a verb which receives II subject marking may be marked as either same subject (SS) or different subject (DS) with respect to a higher verb with a coreferential subject.

(13)   *Sa-hohchafo-{chah/nah} tobi   nonaachi-li-tok.*
        1sII-hungry-ss/ds   beans cook-1sI-past
        'I got hungry and cooked some beans.'

For these speakers, it seems that inserting an expletive in the subject position is an alternative to moving the object into subject position (recall the analogous English pattern *There arrived a package*). The SR marker is then co-indexed with the expletive. The lower clause then has the structure shown in (14).

(14) $[_{S'} [_S e_i [_{VP} NP_k V]] SR_i]$

Therefore DS marking is possible, since the expletive is not coreferent with the matrix subject. It must be noted, however, that the vast majority of speakers accept only the SS version of this sentence. This may be accounted for by saying that unaccusative movement is obligatory for most speakers.

These two arguments suggest that Choctaw does have a process of unaccusative movement, and thus the class of arguments which trigger II verbal agreement may be identified with the class of d-structure objects.

Verbs which show causative morphology may have arguments bearing the roles Goal, Experiencer, and Effector which trigger II agreement on the verb, as shown in (15).

(15)   a. *Sa-habiina-chih.*
          1sII-receive-caus
          'He gave me (something).'[6]
       b. *Holisso sa-pisaa-chih.*
          book   1sII-see-caus
          'He showed me the book.'
       c. *Sa-fohaa-chih.*
          1sII-rest-caus
          'He made me rest / he fired me.'[7]
          (contrast *Fohaa-lih* 'I rested')

In (15a), the object of the verb bears the θ-role Goal; in (15b), it bears the role Experiencer; in (15c), it bears the roles Effector (since it is a causee) and Theme.

I propose that the range of data presented for I and II agreement are best accounted for by interpreting the θ-role hierarchy in (9) as selecting d-structure subject and object. I agreement is then associated with d-structure subject, and II agreement with d-structure object.

Finally, note that although the range of θ-roles borne by subjects and objects overlap, there are certain θ-roles which are unambiguously linked to one or the other. Agents are d-structure subjects, and thus trigger I agree-

---

[6] The semantics of *habiinachih* are somewhat like those of *present* in English, in that the direct object of the verb is the recipient.

[7] I deal here with the literal sense "cause to rest," rather than the idiomatic sense "fire." It seems to me that the analysis of *fire* would be CAUSE $(x, GO(y, z, w))$, where the goal "unemployment" is inherent in the specific lexical semantics of the verb and is thus unexpressed syntactically.

ment. Conversely, Themes are d-structure objects and thus trigger II agreement.[8]

The type of verbal agreement that an argument triggers is indicative of the θ-role it bears. Having established verbal agreement as one criterion for identifying θ-roles, in Sections 3 and 4 I identify two more processes, verbal suppletion and auxilliary selection, which also allow us to identify θ-roles.

3. VERBAL SUPPLETION

Choctaw does not obligatorily mark the number of third person arguments, either on nouns or through verbal agreement.[9] However, there are several verbs which have suppletive stems that indicate the number of some argument, most typically the subject of a intransitive verb or the object of an transitive. Suppletion may be either partial or full. Many of the examples show partial suppletion and certain regularities occur. However, pluralization is not a productive process for Choctaw, and thus synchronically the forms given are monomorphemic. Examples are given in (16).

(16) a. Transitives

kobaffih	'break (1) long object'
kobahlichih	'break (2+) long objects'
palhallih	'split (1) thing'
palhahlichih	'split (2+) things'

  b. Intransitives

takạlih	'be hanging up (sg.)'
takọhlih	'be hanging up (du.)'
takohmạyah	'be hanging up (pl.)'
talạyah	'be right-side up (sg.)'
talọhlih	'be right-side up (du.)'
talohmạyah	'be right-side up (pl.)'

---

[8] However, it must be noted that although this approach to subject agreement has greater generality than previous approaches (Payne, 1981; Heath, 1977), there are still a few exceptional verbs. Munro and Gordon (1982) explore a range of verbs with problematic agreement types. Predominant among these are verbs whose semantics seem stative but which nevertheless take I subject agreement. Examples are quantifiers and certain psychological predicates like *careful*, *proud*, and *jealous*.

[9] There are a number of optional elements that indicate plurality. These include the plural preverb *oklah*, the dual postverb *toklah*, and the auxiliary verb *tahah* 'completive' (discussed in Section 4; see Broadwell, 1983, for more details on *tahah*).

Note that in all these cases, the suppletion is tied to the argument that bears the Theme role.[10] An alternative account might claim that verbal suppletion is tied to some notion like 'absolutive,' which for our purposes we may define as the object of a transitive verb and the subject of an intransitive.[11] However, there is evidence against this position in Chickasaw, a closely related language.

In Chickasaw there are a few transitive verbs in which the subject, rather than the object, controls the verbal suppletion. In these cases, the subject bears the Theme role, thus showing that the generalization concerning suppletion makes reference to θ-roles rather than to relationally based notions like absolutive. An example is given in (17).[12]

(17)   achoshsho'wa   'follow around (sg. subj.)'
        achoshkayya'chi   'follow around (du. subj.)'
        achoshkachit maa   'follow around (pl. subj.)'

Given that suppletion is tied to Themes in Choctaw, consider verbs like those shown in (18).

(18)   onah   'arrive there (1)'
        ittonaachih   'arrive there (2)'
        aayonah   'arrive there (3 +)'
        hikiiyah   'stand up (1)'
        hiilih   'stand up (2)'
        hiyohlih   'stand up (3)'

These verbs supplete for the number of their single argument, but they also trigger I subject agreement. I assume that they have the lexical decomposition shown in (19).[13]

(19) $CAUSE(x, GO(x))$, where x = Agent, Theme

[10] Though this is observationally true for Choctaw, there is cross-linguistic evidence that verbal suppletion tends to be related to Themes. S. Anderson (class lectures) has proposed this analysis for Georgian, and similar facts hold for all the Muskogean languages. It seems that verbs are cross-linguistically sensitive to properties of their Themes, for reasons that are not entirely clear.

[11] A more sophisticated notion of absolutive might be formulated within other theories which would account for (17). For a definition along these lines see Postal (1977).

[12] I thank Pamela Munro for bringing these examples to my attention.

[13] The analysis of 'arrive' differs from that proposed by Burzio (1981) for Italian, where it is claimed that 'arrive' has a nonagentive subject. I claim that 'arrive' is agentive in Choctaw, based on the agreement facts. In general I would argue that languages may differ from each other in this respect. Both the Choctaw and the Italian lexical decompositions are in some sense compatible with our real-world knowledge of the meaning of arrive. Animate arrival is typically a volitional activity, while inanimate arrival is not.

A generalization specific to Choctaw is that any verb whose semantics may be construed as either agentive or nonagentive will always take agentive-type agreement. In this respect Choctaw differs from Tsova Tush, as described by Van Valin (1986).

I have argued above that I agreement is tied to the θ-roles Agent, Effector, Experiencer, and Source/Goal. Since the Choctaw verb 'arrive' triggers I agreement, its subject must bear one of these θ-roles. But I have also argued that suppletion is tied to the Theme, and so the subject must bear the role Theme. We thus have a strong argument for the the type of lexical decomposition shown in (19), where a single argument may bear more than one θ-role.

4. AUXILIARY SELECTION

Additional evidence for the claim that the subject of a verb of volitional motion bears both Agent and Theme roles may be found in the system of auxiliary selection.

In Choctaw, several auxiliary verbs have alternate forms which depend on the choice of main verb. Auxiliaries with alternate forms include *ishahlih/ishahlichih* 'to exceed' (used in the formation of the comparative), *aatapah/aatablih* 'to be/do too much,' and *tahah/tahlih* 'to complete.' The distribution of *tahah/tahlih* is of particular interest.

Tahah/tahlih may be used to indicate both a completed action and a completely affected action. In general, the latter use of the auxiliary is translated into English by pluralizing some argument of the verb, as is shown in (20).

(20) a. *Kobaffi-t tahli-lih.*
         break-t   complete-1sI
         'I finished breaking it/them.' or
         'I broke them all.'
      b. *Taloowa-t tahli-lih.*
         sing-t   complete-1sI
         'I finished singing.'
      c. *Kobaafa-t tahah.*
         broken-t complete
         'It's completely broken up.'

The choice of *tahah/tahlih* is dependent on the θ-role of the subject of the main verb and not on simple transitivity (as the contrast between (20b) and (20c) shows). Verbs with Agent subjects, such as 'sing' and 'break,' select *tahlih*. Verbs with Theme subjects, such as 'be broken,' select *tahah*.

When the θ-role of the subject is other than Theme, the auxiliary is *tahlih*, as the following examples show.

(21) a. *Habiina-t tahli-lih.*
         receive-t complete-1sI
         'I received them all.'
      b. *Pisa-t tahli-lih.*
         see-t complete-1sI
         'I saw them all.'

The subject of 'receive' bears the Goal θ-role, and the subject of 'see' bears the Experiencer θ-role, and both select *tahlih*.[14] The following generalization about the distribution of *tahah/tahlih* is indicated:

(22)   A verb whose subject bears the θ-role Theme selects the auxiliary
         tahah; other verbs select *tahlih*.

Having established this generalization, let us now turn to verbs of volitional motion. As (23) shows, they select the auxiliary *tahah*.

(23) a. *Iya-t ii-tahah.*
         go-t 1pI-complete
         'We all went.'
      b. *Nowa-t tahah.*
         walk-t complete
         'They all walked.'

According to the generalization in (22), only verbs whose subject bears the θ-role Theme select *tahah*. Thus we are led to conclude that the subject of a verb of volitional motion bears the θ-role Theme. But by the test of verbal agreement described in Section 2, the subject bears the θ-role Agent. Again we are led to conclude that the subject bears two θ-roles—Agent and Theme.

The evidence from both this section and the previous section indicate that arguments may bear more than one θ-role. This is inconsistent with the θ-criterion of government-binding theory as it is often formulated.

5. MULTIPLE θ-ROLES AND THE θ-CRITERION

Chomsky (1981, p. 36) first states the θ-criterion as follows:

Each argument bears one and only one θ-role, and each θ-role is assigned to one and only one argument.

As noted, the evidence presented in Sections 3 and 4 is inconsistent with this formulation. In this section, I suggest a reformulation of the θ-criterion to

[14] *Tahah* may also occur as a verbal suffix in the meaning 'finally,' in which case it is not restricted to verbs whose subject bears the θ-role Theme. I consider this a separate construction.

allow arguments to bear more than one θ-role and compare this reformulation to Chomsky's second statement of the θ-criterion and to a similar proposal made by Culicover and Wilkins (1986).

I propose the following revision. At the lexical level, verbs have the type of decomposition illustrated throughout the article (see also Rappaport and Levin, this volume). A process then applies to merge all θ-roles assigned to a single variable into a complex θ-role. The θ-criterion is restated in terms of complex θ-roles:[15]

> Each argument bears one and only one complex θ-role, and each complex θ-role is assigned to one and only one argument.

This formulation allows us to claim that arguments bear more than one θ-role, while still obtaining the desired biunique relation between arguments and complex θ-roles.

Given this process of θ-role merger, we may ask what constraints apply to it, since it does not seem descriptively true that any two θ-roles can be merged. Given our lexical decomposition analysis, however, there is a natural restriction on θ-role merger. Two (or more) θ-roles may be merged only if each component θ-role is assigned by a different abstract predicate. This produces exactly the right descriptive results. The following complex θ-roles are attested, and each meets the well-formedness condition defined: Agent–Theme (*run, jump*), Agent–Source (*give*), Agent–Goal (*receive, take*), and Effector–Theme (*the cane hit the wall*). On the other hand, the following θ-roles are unattested, and would seem to be impossible: Theme–Source, Theme–Goal, Source–Goal.[16]

The revision of the θ-criterion recalls Chomsky's second definition of θ-criterion in Chomsky (1981) and the statement given in Chomsky (1986). Both relativize the θ-criterion to chains, thus allowing an argument to receive more than one θ-role so long as each is assigned by a different predicate (Chomsky, 1986, p. 97). Chomsky's revision allows for multiple θ-role assignment in the syntax, while the proposal here extends multiple θ-role assignment to the level of lexical decomposition.

The statement in (26) and the proposed restriction on the composition of complex θ-roles are also quite similar to the proposal of Culicover and Wilkins (1986), which recognizes two classes of θ-roles—intensional (including θ-roles such as Agent, Patient, and Instrument) and extensional (including

---

[15] I am endebted to Tim Stowell for discussion on this point. My formulation owes much to a proposed revision of the θ-criterion in Stowell (1981), which was motivated by rather different data.

[16] However, Jackendoff (1983) argues convincingly that the Source and Goal roles are assigned by a separate predicate PATH. If his proposal is correct, it is unclear why Theme cannot combine with these θ-roles.

Source, Theme, and Goal). Arguments may be assigned at most one role from both the intensional and extensional classes by a single verb (Culicover and Wilkins 1986, p. 123).

The evidence presented in this article in general supports the Culicover and Wilkins conception of θ-roles, but there is one difference between their account and the restriction on complex θ-roles proposed here. The Culicover and Wilkins system allows at most two θ-roles from any particular verb, while the account here allows an indefinite number, so long as each is assigned by a different predicate in lexical decomposition.

There are a few cases of verbs that may bear more than two θ-roles, though the evidence is far from conclusive. Jackendoff (1987) suggests that the object of *chase* bears three θ-roles, roughly Theme, Patient, and Goal. Another verb sometimes cited as bearing three θ-roles is intransitive *shave* (Schachter, personal communication), where the subject seems to be Agent, Patient, and Goal. These examples may provide some evidence for my proposal over that of Culicover and Wilkins.

6. CONCLUSION

Recent grammatical theory has become increasingly involved in trying to predict syntactic behavior from the lexical properties of words. To succeed, this project needs sharpened conceptions of what lexical properties are important and how they are represented in the theory. In particular, a coherent theory of θ-role content is essential.

An attractive feature of all theories that allow multiple θ-role assignment is that restrictive notions of θ-role content can be maintained, and arguments that have properties of more than one θ-role need not be arbitrarily assigned only one θ-role. This article has shown that not only is such a position desirable on conceptual grounds, it is also necessary for the description of the lexical properties of Choctaw.

ACKNOWLEDGMENTS

I thank Joseph Aoun, Ken Hale, Beth Levin, Pamela Munro, Paul Schachter, Tim Stowell, and Wendy Wilkins for discussion of the issues raised here. Thanks are also due to my fellow students Vicki Carstens, David Cline, Feng-hsi Liu, Jack Martin, and Charles Ulrich. Special thanks are due to Josephine Wade and Gus Comby, who provided most of the data discussed here. My research on Choctaw has been funded by the American Philosophical Society; the Department of Linguistics, UCLA; the UCLA American Indian Studies Center; a National Science Foundation Graduate Fellowship; and the Bilingual Education Program of the Mississippi Band of Choctaw Indians.

Earlier versions of this article were presented at NELS 17 in Cambridge, MA, and at the 25th Conference on American Indian Languages in Philadelphia, PA.

INHERITANCE

JANET H. RANDALL

Department of English and Linguistics Program
Northeastern University
Boston, Massachusetts 02115

1. INTRODUCTION

The distinction between the syntax and the lexicon has been studied since work on the lexicon began. In characterizing the difference between these two components, research has focused on the properties of their rules. The PROJECTION PRINCIPLE, (1), points to one property in particular, the ability to alter argument structure.

(1)   PROJECTION PRINCIPLE: Argument structure is preserved at all
       syntactic levels of a derivation.   (Chomsky, 1981)

Lexical rules, but not syntactic rules, have the privilege of changing the lexical specifications of the forms, they apply to; thus rules that alter argument structure are lexical.

The implication does not hold in the reverse, however. Lexical rules are not obliged to change argument structure. In fact, if we look at morphological rules in terms of the traditional inflectional/derivational classification, we find that argument structure is preserved by the inflectional class. So the locus of argument structure effects is narrow, restricted to the set of derivational rules.

129

My question concerns the systematicity of argument alterations: Exactly how do lexical rules affect argument structure? As a research strategy we pose the question in a bottom-up way. For each rule we ask: When a nonderived form is changed into a derived form, which arguments are "inherited" (i.e., maintained in the argument structure)? The goal is to find the systematicity in inheritance effects and to identify the principles that govern them.

One potential answer to the question of principles lies in the system known as LEVEL-ORDERING, developed to account for other facts about the lexicon (interactions among affixation rules, possible and impossible words, and so on). I begin the investigation here, since level-ordering allows a convenient way to survey the data, and if the level-ordering hypothesis turns out to account for the facts of inheritance, then our search for independent principles would happily be over. We will see that unfortunately, the shoe does not fit— level-ordering cannot explain argument alterations. The alternative that I offer in Section 3 is based not on where in the lexicon a rule applies, but on what it does. I argue that lexical rules obey an INHERITANCE PRINCIPLE, which predicts a rule's inheritance behavior from two features of that rule: whether it changes category and whether it blocks the assignment of a θ-role.[1]

Following this, in Section 4 I show that the inheritance principle is compatible with another principle of the lexicon, the UNIFORMITY PRINCIPLE. In Section 5 I demonstrate that the inheritance principle makes further correct predictions, for cases of θ-role absorption. Finally, in Section 6 there are some speculations.

2. LEXICAL LEVELS: AN INADEQUATE SOLUTION

The basic insight of the level-ordering hypothesis is that lexical rules occur at different levels of lexical structure (see Kiparsky, 1982, for an outline of this

---

[1] There are differing assumptions about argument structure and θ-roles in the current literature. I assume a model which takes as primitive both a level of argument structure (or thematic structure, or lexicosyntactic structure) and a set of θ-roles. Additionally, there are linking principles for assigning θ-roles to arguments. Models along these basic lines are assumed by Pesetsky (1985), Stowell (1981), Marantz (1984), Williams (1981, 1983), Roeper (1987), Zubizaretta (1987), Culicover and Wilkins (1984), and Wilkins (1987a). For rather distinct views on, in particular, the centrality of conceptual structure, see Jackendoff (1983), Levin and Rappaport (1986), and Hale and Keyser (1987).

My claims can be translated into other models, with slight modifications. For example, in a model without explicit θ-roles, we would need to assume that arguments in argument structure are hierarchically ranked: internal direct argument, external argument, internal indirect arguments. The choice of framework in no way dismisses the question of what the primitives are, but simply allows the issue not to dominate this discussion.

approach). The three-level model is sketched roughly in (2):[2]

(2)	3	inflectional rules	$-ing_V$ $-e\,N_V$		
	2	#-boundary rules	$-ing_N$	$-er_N$	$-able_A$
	1	+-boundary rules	$-ing_A$	$-al_N$	$-tion_N$
			$-ment_N$	$-y_N$	$-e\,N_A$

At Level 1 we find +-boundary affixes (Aronoff, 1976; Siegel, 1979; Allen, 1987), which have been shown to be phonologically sensitive; that is, they "count" from the point of view of segmental rules and stress rules. Level 1 outputs, therefore, may be phonologically distinct from their bases. At Level 2 are #-boundary affixes, and at Level 3 are inflectional affixes. The outputs of rules at both of these levels are phonologically insensitive because they are ordered after the phonological operations take place.[3]

If this breakdown is the right one for predicting inheritance, then the degree of inheritance allowed by a rule should depend on the level where it occurs. The simplest hypothesis is that the three-level system correlates with a three-way distinction in argument operations, with rules at each level behaving alike, and differently from rules at other levels.

Consider the inheritance properties of the Level 2 rules: "process" $-ing_N$, $-able_A$, and $-er_N$. Are they consistent with each other? In some ways they are. All three allow the direct argument of their underlying verb to be inherited. Process $-ing$ forms are given in (3); $-able$ forms, whose argument occurs in surface subject position, in (4) (see Randall, 1985; Finer and Roeper, 1987); and $-er$ agent forms in (5):

(3)   a. *the herding of Holsteins*
      b. *the autographing of programs*
      c. *the healing of the sick*
      d. *the writing of speeches*
      e. *the photographing of insects*

(4)   a. *Calculus is learnable.*
      b. *These bolts are removable.*
      c. *This furniture is arrangeable.*
      d. *This disease is curable.*
      e. *That car is not drivable.*

---

[2] I have simplified the picture somewhat in leaving off the arrows that loop back to earlier levels. They are not essential to this discussion.

[3] The simplified picture in (2) gives the impression that each affix is strictly tied to a particular level. In general, this is so, although there are instances of reanalysis (either by looping or bracketing erasure) in which certain late affixations appear in earlier levels. Pairs such as *cómparable/compárable* illustrate this. Here, the Level 2-*able* affix appears in a form with a Level 1 stress pattern and, as I show below, Level 1 inheritance properties.

(5) a. *a flier of rockets*
     b. *a herder of Holsteins*
     c. *a healer of the sick*
     d. *a dancer of pas de deux*

Notice that nonderived (but semantically parallel) agent nouns, in (6), do not allow an argument:

(6) a.**an astronaut of rockets*
     b.**a cowherd of Holsteins*
     c.**a doctor of the sick*
     d.**a ballerina of pas de deux*

Although minimal pairs are difficult to find, it is clear that the Level 2 productive forms also contrast with Level 1 forms, like the stress-shifted -*y* and -*er* forms, which do not allow objects to be inherited.[4] The examples in (7a), parallel to those in (3), differ from (7b) and (7c).

(7) a. *the phótographing of insects*
        the spéctroscoping of stars
        the sténographing of rapid conversations
        the démographing of rural areas
        the télescoping of time

     b. *the photógraphy (*of insects)*
        the spectróscopy (*of stars)
        the stenógraphy (*of rapid conversations)
        the demógraphy (*of rural areas)
        the teléscopy (*of time)

     c. *the photógrapher (*of insects)*
        the spectróscoper (*of stars)
        the stenógrapher (*of rapid conversations)
        the demógrapher (*of rural areas)
        the teléscoper (*of time)

My claim here is not that *of*-phrases (or any other PP complements, for that matter) are blocked from appearing with forms like (7b) or (7c), only that when they do occur they are not understood the same way as the PPs in the (7a) cases. (This point has been made in the literature, but because of its importance to the present discussion it is worth clarifying here.)

---

[4] Thus Level 1 -*er* affixation is distinguished from level 2 -*er* affixation. Whether it is one affix applying at both levels or two different affixes is not relevant here.

The difference between inherited PPs and noninherited PPs can be seen in the minimal pairs in (8).

(8) a. *a phótographer of insects*
         the writer of the document
     b. *the photógrapher (*of insects)*
         the author of the document

As in the other Level 2 cases, (3–5) and (7a), each of the NPs in (8a), *insects* and *document*, is understood as the object of its head noun *phótographer* and *writer*, and the head is understood as grammatically related to the verbs *phótograph* and *write*. In (8b), however, no derivational relationship holds, but *document* (though not *insects*) can be interpreted as an optional complement of its head noun. Many nonderived nouns allow PP complements—for example, *a portrait by Rembrandt, a letter to Bill, a present for Susan* (Wasow, 1980)—but they are not mentioned by their head nouns in their argument structures.

The contrast becomes even clearer when we compare the (7c) forms with newly created -*er* forms where a derivational relationship holds. (9) shows how such forms are derived.

(9)   N   V   N
     a phótograph → *to phótograph* → *a phótographer of insects*
     a démograph   *to démograph*   *a démographer of rural areas*
     a télescope   *to télescope*   *a télescoper of time*
     a spéctroscope   *to spéctroscope* *a spéctroscoper of stars*

A combination of two rules applies: (1) The Level 2 N → V rule (Clark and Clark, 1979) changes a noun into a verb. At Level 2, the operation is opaque to stress rules, and so the derived verbs have the stress pattern of their base nouns; (2) the verbs undergo -*er* affixation, again retaining the original stress pattern.[5] The resulting forms, distinguishable from the (7c) cases by stress, also differ in allowing inheritance.

To summarize: The three Level 2 affixes we have looked at act alike in that they allow inheritance of the argument which serves as object of their base verb. And the affixes act differently from forms produced at Level 1 or below (i.e., unaffixed forms), where no inheritance is possible. So the level-ordering hypothesis explains the inheritance facts we have seen so far.

But there are three kinds of data which refute level-ordering as an inheritance theory. First, certain Level 1 derived forms allow the same kind of

---

[5] Since English contains not only a N → V rule but also a V → N rule, it is not always clear which member of noun/verb pairs is the base form and which is the derived form. Kiparsky (1982) provides tests.

inheritance we have seen for Level 2 forms:

(10)   *the discussion of the issues*
        the displacement of the water
        the discovery of America
        the disavowal of the evidence

Second, Level 2 "result" -*ing* nominals, which should allow inheritance, do not:

(11)   *The cooking (*of Indian food) was starchy.*
        The typing (*of the manuscript) is on the desk.
        Their finding (*of the fossils) appeared in Science.

The third refutation comes from the fact that different affixes at the same level differ in the degree of inheritance that they allow. Consider again the Level 2 operations, process -ing_N, -er_N, and -$able_A$. Both -*er* and -*able* allow an inheritance maximum of one argument. When more arguments are present (whether obligatory or optional), the rules cannot apply, as (12) and (13) show.[6] However process -*ing* allows inheritance of an unlimited number of complements, as (14) demonstrates.

(12)   *-er*   a. OBLIGATORY ARGUMENTS
        *America is a putter of men on the moon.
        *A zoologist is more than just a comparer of African elephants with Indian elephants.
        *A surgical nurse is more than just a hander of scalpels to surgeons.
        *The volunteer office needs a paster of stamps onto envelopes.

[6] When PPs occur as adjuncts and not arguments, however, they may appear:

(i)   *Calculus is learnable (with the right kind of instruction).*
        These bolts are removable (under certain conditions).
        This furniture is arrangeable (for a price).
        Sick children are not curable (without medicine).
        This semi will be drivable (in a week).

Arguments can be distinguished from adjuncts in that only the latter can prepose:

(ii)   {**With difficulty* / *With the right kind of instruction*} *calculus is learnable.*
        {**With a crescent wrench* / *Under certain conditions*} *these bolts are removable.*

b. OPTIONAL ARGUMENTS
He is a learner of poems (*by heart).
This mechanic is an ace remover of nuts (*from sticky bolts).
He is a marvelous arranger of furniture (*into pleasing formats).
She is a healer of sick children (*of their diseases).
She is training to be a driver of semis (*around corners).

(13) **-able** a. OBLIGATORY ARGUMENTS
*Men are puttable on the moon.
*African elephants are comparable with Indian elephants.
*The new scalpels are not as handable to the surgeons as the old ones were.
*These stamps are not pastable onto envelopes.

b. OPTIONAL ARGUMENTS
This poem is learnable (*by heart).
These nuts are not removable (*from their bolts).
This furniture is arrangeable (*into a pleasing format).
Sick children are not healable (*of uncommon diseases).
Those semis are not drivable (*around corners).

(14) **-ing** a. OBLIGATORY ARGUMENTS
the putting of men on the moon
the comparing of African elephants with Indian elephants
the handing of scalpels to surgeons
the pasting of stamps onto envelopes

b. OPTIONAL ARGUMENTS
the learning of poems (by heart)
the removing of nuts (from sticky bolts)
the arranging of furniture (into pleasing formats)
the healing of sick children (of their diseases)
the driving of semis (around corners)

In sum, inheritance under affixation cannot be predicted based on level ordering. A different distinction is necessary.

{ **Into pleasing formats* / For a price } *this furniture is arrangeable.*
{ **Of uncommon diseases* / Without medicine } *these children are not curable.*
{ **Around corners* / In a week } *this semi should be drivable.*

3. THE θ-HIERARCHY AND THE INHERITANCE PRINCIPLE

So far, I have characterized lexical rules in terms of the level at which they apply. But another way to characterize them is in terms of what they do. Most of the affixation rules discussed above function to change the argument structures of their bases. For instance, they may prevent a θ-role assigned in the base form from being assigned in the derived form. One such role is Agent. In (15) and (16) the rules are grouped into those that block the assignment of Agent and those that do not.[7]

(15)   *Rules that block the assignment of Agent*
    a. -*able*$_A$ *The kite is fly**able** (*by experts).*
    b. -*er*$_N$ *the fly**er** of the kite (*by experts)*
    c. -*ing*$_A$ *the fly**ing** kite (*by experts)*
    d. -*eN*$_A$ *The kite was unflow**n** (*by experts).*
    e. $-t/th$$_N$ *the flight of the kite (*by experts)*

(16)   *Rules that permit the assignment of Agent*
    a. verbal passive   *The kite was flow**n** by experts.*
    b. process -*ing*$_N$ *the fly**ing** of kites by experts*

This distinction with respect to Agent may at first seem arbitrary; however, it turns out to be relevant to inheritance behavior. The rules that block Agent, (15), block the inheritance of all indirect arguments; those that assign Agent, (16), allow inheritance. Contrast (17) with (18).[8]

---

[7] In (15d) (and below in (17d)), the *un-* prefix is added to ensure that the adjectival and not the verbal passive reading is understood.

In (15e), the interpretation under consideration is the one in which someone is flying the kite, not the one in which the kite is flying, parallel to *the sight of rainbows.* The *-t/-th* affixation rule is one of a set of nominalization rules that all behave alike with respect to the present discussion. The others are: *-ion, -ment, -y, -al,* and *-ance.* Some of these forms may be marginally grammatical; the important point is that, despite this, they are substantially worse than their "process" *-ing* counterparts.

(i)   *the direct***ion**/-**ing** of traffic *by policemen*
    *the replace***ment**/-**ing** of footlights *by nonunion electricians*
    *the discover***y**/-**ing** of new stars *by amateur astronomers*
    *the apprais***al**/-**ing** of antiques *by experts*
    *the disturb***ance**/-**ing** of the peace *by any citizen*

[8] The possibility of adjuncts here may cloud judgments on certain cases. As pointed out in footnote 6, any PPs which are not preposable should be disallowed here.

Both (17c) and (17d) are also impossible with a prenominal adjective, but for an independent reason. An adjective phrase does not permit intrusion of a noun between its adjectival head and the complements of that head. This holds regardless of whether the adjective is deverbal (ia) or not (ib).

(17) a. *the plane is flyable (*into the wind/*to Paris/*by computer/. . .)*
      b. *the flyer of the plane (*into the wind/*to Paris/*by computer/. . .)*
      c. *the flying plane (*into the wind/*to Paris/*by computer/. . .)*
      d. *the plane was unflown (*into the wind/*to Paris/*by computer/. . .)*
      e. *the flight of the plane (*into the wind/*to Paris/*by computer/. . .)*

(18) a. *the plane was flown (into the wind) (from London) (to Paris)*
         (by a pilot with a death wish) . . .
      b. *the flying of planes (into the wind) (from London) (to Paris)*
         (by pilots with death wishes) . . .

The correlation can be expressed as an implication.

(19) *Agent ⇒ *Instrument, *Goal, *Source, *Location,. . .

Notice that Theme[9] is not among the θ-roles mentioned by this rule (and it must also be excluded from occurring in ". . ."). All of the examples above which block Agent inherit Theme. But we have seen cases in which Theme is blocked. The examples in (20) come from (7b) and (11).

(20) a. *the photógraphy (*of insects)*
      b. *The cooking (*of Indian food) was starchy.*

When we test these nominals for inheritance of other arguments, we find that all inheritance is blocked. The sentences in (21) are ungrammatical when the parenthetical material is included.

(i)   a. **the unflown plane into the wind*
         *the flying plane by computer
         *the torn picture around the edges
      b. **the fond boy of ice cream*
         *the happy lawyer with her job

Futher, unless head plus complement(s) is analyzable as a lexical item (a phrasal adjective), the combination may not appear prenominally:

(ii) a. **the unflown into the wind plane*
         *the flying by computer plane
         *the torn around the edges picture
      b. **the fond of ice cream boy*
         *the happy with her job lawyer

[9] Until more precise definitions of Theme are developed, I adopt an extension of the standard one, from Gruber (1976). The theme is, with verbs of motion, the thing moved; with verbs of location, the thing located. To handle cases like *typing*, we must additionally say that the Theme is, with verbs of creation or destruction, the thing created or destroyed. This definition is a broad one. Other investigators have tightened the definition, identifying the excluded cases with additional roles, such as Patient or Percept.

(21)   a. *the photógraphy (*of insects) (*with special lenses)*
       b. *The cooking (*of Indian food) (*with special techniques)*
           (*in authentic ovens) was starchy.

Again, there is a sharp contrast between these nominals and the process *-ing*
and verbal passive forms, which do not block any θ-role assignment and which
can inherit all arguments:

(22)   a. *The phótographing of insects (with special lenses) can be done only*
           by experts . . . .
           These insects were phótographed (with special lenses).
       b. *the cooking (of Indian food) (with special techniques)*
           (in authentic ovens) takes place . . . .

The generalization for these cases, then, is similar to (19), but even more
restrictive: Rules which block the assignment of Theme block the assignment
of all other θ-roles. In other words,

(23)   *Theme $\Rightarrow$ *Agent, *Instrument, *Goal, *Source, *Location, . . .

   The two relationships in (19) and (23) suggest that a hierarchy underlies the
effects that lexical rules may have on argument structures. A principle which
would explain these effects is given in (25); it is based on the θ-hierarchy
in (24).[10]

(24) θ-HIERARCHY: Theme
                          Agent
                          Instrument, Source, Goal, Path, Location, . . .

(25)   INHERITANCE PRINCIPLE (preliminary version)[11]
       An operation which blocks the assignment of a θ-role blocks the
       assignment of all θ-roles lower on the θ-hierarchy.

For the data discussed thus far, the inheritance principle makes correct
predictions. However, it is necessary to consider one additional set of data.

---

[10] A hierarchy of θ-roles has been proposed by various investigators, among them Jackendoff
(1972), Ostler (1979), Carrier-Duncan (1985), and Wilkins (this volume). Although they are all
alike in that they contain minimally three levels, they all differ in how the levels are arranged.
Although at first pass this may seem surprising, it should not be. It is quite plausible that different
hierarchies of θ-roles operate in different arenas of the grammar. Certain semantic concepts (and
not others) are relevant to particular grammatical structures, so we have no reason to expect that a
hierarchy relevant to one domain would be applicable to another.
   [11] This is a revision of the inheritance principle proposed in Randall (1985) which does not
assume a θ-hierarchy.

The verbs in (26a), known as ERGATIVE verbs (Burzio, 1981; Keyser and Roeper, 1984; also called UNACCUSATIVE, Perlmutter, 1978) are claimed to be related by a lexical rule to the verbs in (26b).

(26) a. *The Renault drove slowly down the road.*
          Clothes are hanging on the line.
      b. *Mary drove the Renault slowly down the road.*
          John is hanging clothes on the line.

The ergative forms in (26a), just like the cases of (15) above, block the assignment of Agent, as shown in (27).

(27)   *The Renault drove slowly down the road (*by Mary).*
          Clothes are hanging on the line (*by John).

These cases seem at odds with the inheritance principle, (25), though. While they resemble (15) in blocking Agent, they do not block the inheritance of θ-roles lower on the hierarchy. The PPs *down the road* and *on the line* are allowed, among others:

(28)   *The Renault drove (from Vancouver) (to Boston) (in third gear).*
          Clothes are hanging (in the attic) (from the rafters).

Ergatives, then, seem to be counterexamples. But notice that these cases differ significantly from all of the cases we have seen so far. Here the ergative verb formed by the lexical ergative rule bears the same category as the rule's input. A verb has been changed into another verb. In the cases above, verbs were changed into either nouns or adjectives.

This fact can be incorporated into the inheritance principle with a slight revision, namely, (25) applies only to rules which change an item's category. The new formulation is given in (29).

(29)   INHERITANCE PRINCIPLE (final version)
          A category-changing operation which blocks the assignment of a
          θ-role blocks the assignment of all θ-roles lower on the
          hierarchy.

How will the inheritance principle operate now for rules which allow full inheritance—verbal passive and *-ing* process nominals? Their outputs are repeated here from (18).

(30) a. *The plane was flow**n** (into the wind) (from London) (to Paris)*
          (by a pilot with a death wish) ...
      b. *the fly**ing** of planes (into the wind) (from London) (to Paris)*
          (by pilots with death wishes) ...

For verbal passives like (30a), (29) says nothing. Since these forms, unlike adjectival passives, remain verbs, they are not formed by a category-changing operation and therefore are not affected by the principle. And although *-ing* process nominals like (30b) are formed by a category-changing operation, it is one which does not block the assignment of a θ-role. Again, (29) is not applicable.

To summarize at this point, we can think of lexical rules as falling into four classes, based on how they affect their inputs. The table in (31) shows the distribution:

(31)

	+Changes category	−Changes category
+Blocks θ-role	$-able_A$, $-ing_A$, $-eN_A$, $-er_N$, result $-ing_N$, $-t/th_N$, $-ion_N$, $-al_N$,	Ergatives
−Blocks θ-role	$-y_N$, $-ment_N$, $-ance_N$,	
	Process $-ing_N$	Inflectional rules

Rules that change category are in the two cells on the left; rules that keep category intact are on the right. In the top two cells are rules which block one or another θ-role from being assigned; in the bottom two, no θ-roles are blocked. The inheritance principle, (29), will apply, then, only to the lexical operations that fall in the cell at the top left. This is exactly the result needed to handle the data.[12]

The statement of the inheritance principle is based on a particular formulation of the projection principle (that of Chomsky, 1981), which stipulates that argument structure must be preserved throughout the syntactic levels of a derivation. Another version of the projection principle has been proposed by Borer (1983):

(32)   PROJECTION PRINCIPLE
        Lexical features must be preserved at every syntactic level, where
        lexical features include features of
        a. θ-role assignment
        b. case assignment

---

[12] In the present framework, whether or not a rule blocks the assignment of a θ-role is not predictable from other features of the rule, but must be stipulated. It is likely, however, that this property can be shown to follow from semantic facts; process *-ing*, seems to preserve meaning in a way that the rules in the top two cells do not. In fact, an earlier version of the inheritance principle and a theory of the acquisition of inheritance (Randall, 1985) are based on this observation. Formally developing the theory in this direction would move it closer to accounting for learnability, since the obligatory absence of arguments is not something that can be learned directly.

    c. subcategorization
    d. category
    e. meaning

Borer's restatement is quite interesting, as it means that particular rules do not have to be assigned to specific components of the grammar (i.e., the lexicon or the syntax). They may apply freely, with the projection principle acting essentially as a well-formedness condition to rule out overgeneralizations in which lexical features have been altered somewhere in the syntax.

We could easily adopt this reformulation, since it is lexical features (32a–e) that determine at which level a particular rule operates. For example, rules which alter category, as rules of word formation, must occur in the lexicon because it is in the lexicon that their new-word outputs are registered. Under (32), the inheritance principle would apply to operations in both the lexical and syntactic components, but would still affect only those operations which both changed category and blocked θ-role assignment. Given this specificity of application, no syntactic rule would ever be affected.

Under either formulation of the projection principle it is assumed that rules of the lexicon are permitted—though not required—to change argument structure. This perspective directly contrasts with other frameworks in which argument structures are assumed to be represented not only at every syntactic level, but at every lexical level as well, essentially the view that argument structures are preserved in the lexicon (see Roeper, 1987; Finer and Roeper, 1987).

4. UNIFORMITY

Other principles have been proposed which constrain how rules can affect argument structures (see, for example, Rozwadowska, this volume). Particularly relevant to the present approach is Chomsky's (1981) UNIFORMITY PRINCIPLE. The question arises as to how compatible this principle is with the inheritance principle.

The uniformity principle, given in (33), prevents a rule from having different effects in different instances of application.

(33)   UNIFORMITY PRINCIPLE
        Each morphological process either
          (i) transmits θ-role uniformly,
         (ii) blocks θ-role uniformly, or
        (iii) assigns a new θ-role uniformly.

This principle has consequences for determining which morphological processes are instances of the same rule. For example, it requires that the process which creates the two -*er* agent forms *dancer* and *dreamer* be the same one but a different process from the one that creates -*er* instrument forms like *blender* or *grater*. As such, it requires that there be two lexical items *poacher* (one a person, one a kitchen utensil), one resulting from each process.

It would also distinguish two classes of -*ing* forms. We have seen that some -*ing* forms are process nominals while others are result nominals, and I have argued that the two types differ, crucially, in their inheritance behavior. Process -*ing* nouns completely inherit the θ-roles from their underlying verb's argument structure, while result -*ing* nouns block the assignment of Theme and, in turn, all θ-roles lower on the θ-hierarchy. Given (33), process -*ing* and result -*ing* forms must arise from two different morphological processes, since the uniformity principle requires that where inheritance effects differ, morphological processes must also differ.

There is a third class of -*ing* forms which we have also encountered, adjectival -*ing* forms. As well as *flying* (from (15c)), the class includes a productive range of cases. Those that undergo adjectival *un*- affixation, a rule which applies only to adjectives, form a class whose adjectival status is guaranteed, e.g., *uncompelling, unrejoicing, unchanging, unrepenting, unrelenting*.[13] But as stated, the uniformity principle would not attribute these forms to a third -*ing* rule, since it says nothing about category. It would group the adjectival -*ing* cases with one or the other of the verbal -*ing* processes unless it could be shown that their θ-assignment properties were different.

The uniformity principle, in this regard, misses a generalization. The fact is that morphological processes have as uniform an effect on category as they do on θ-roles. Each output of a particular rule belongs to the same category as other outputs of the same rule, and the inheritance principle depends on this consistency for its effects. Of course, like θ-role effects, effects of category differ across different morphological processes. Sometimes category is inherited (as with the rules that create ergative verbs and verbs prefixed in *out*- from other verbs); often it is not. Like options (33i–iii) of the uniformity principle, this choice is open.

We can revise the uniformity principle to state the constraints on category in a straightforward manner:

(34)   UNIFORMITY PRINCIPLE (revised):
        Each morphological process either
        a.   (i) transmits θ-role uniformly,
             (ii) blocks θ-role uniformly, or

---

[13] These forms could not have been produced by -*ing* attaching to verb forms like **uncompel, *unrejoice, *unchange, *unrepent, *unrelent*.

  (iii) assigns a new θ-role uniformly
  and
 b. (i) transmits category uniformly or
  (ii) blocks category uniformly.

Returning to θ-role effects for a moment, the analysis proposed here was concerned only with cases that fall under (34a,i) and (34a,ii), operations which either transmit or block θ-roles. But operations which assign new θ-roles could be incorporated as well, with two cells added to the bottom of the chart in (31).[14] Exactly what adjustments in the inheritance principle would be required for these cases is an open question, but the framework allows for the possibility to be considered.

In sum, we have considered the inheritance principle alongside another principle of the lexicon, Chomsky's uniformity principle. This principle, often tacitly assumed in the literature, is what guarantees the "integrity" of distinct morphological processes, requiring that the same operation have the same effect whenever it applies. Considering the two together allowed us to see that the uniformity principle was inadequate and to propose a revised uniformity principle, (33). In addition to ensuring uniform θ-role effects, it ensures uniform category effects for each morphological process. If rules operated in an arbitrary manner with respect to either θ-role or category effects, the inheritance principle would be useless. But with this emendation to the uniformity principle, the inheritance principle can now be guaranteed to predict the inheritance behavior of derived forms.

5. ABSORPTION

One issue which we have not discussed at all, but which is clearly relevant to the total picture, is θ-role absorption. It appears that when certain affixes are attached, the output assumes a θ-role itself: -er in its productive form denotes Agent; -ing result nominals take on the role of Theme.[15]

---

[14] Cases like out- prefixation (Bresnan, 1980) and the lexical resultative rule (Randall, 1983; Carrier-Duncan and Randall, 1987) are two such examples:

(i)   Mary can sing.
       Susan can **out**sing Mary.
(ii)   The king laughed.
       The king laughed himself sick.

[15] The idea of absorption is a relative one and depends on the relationship of an output to its underlying verb. In other words, baker is an Agent with respect to bake; typing, a Theme with respect to type.

Absorbing a θ-role cannot be directly tied to blocking, since many affixes block the assignment of a θ-role but do not absorb one. For example, -er and -able both block the assignment of Agent, but only -er absorbs the Agent role. However, there is an indirect relationship between absorption and blocking. It follows from the θ-criterion that, in each output, only one instance of each θ-role will appear.[16] What this means is that a θ-role can only be absorbed by the output of a rule if the rule itself blocks it. Suppose that a rule does not block the assignment of a θ-role, but rather inherits it. Absorbing it in addition would cause the θ-role to appear twice, a violation of the θ-criterion.

The sketches in (35) illustrate two situations: (a), a rule which blocks Agent; (b), a rule which blocks Theme. By the inheritance principle, all θ-roles below the blocked θ-role are also blocked, while any θ-roles above it are inherited. Any blocked θ-role is available to be absorbed. So the possibilities for a lexical rule to stipulate the absorption of a particular θ-role are limited to those θ-roles that it blocks. In (35a), any θ-role from Agent down may be absorbed; in (35b), since all θ-roles are blocked, any θ-role may be absorbed.

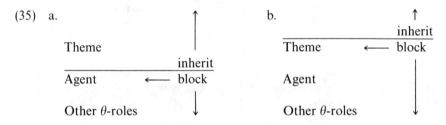

To state it the other way around, for all cases where absorption of a θ-role, R, occurs, blocking of R also occurs, and thus all θ-roles lower than R on the θ-hierarchy will be blocked as well.

The -er agent forms and the -ing result nominals discussed above illustrate situations (35a) and (35b). The -er Agent rule blocks Agent and all θ-roles lower on the hierarchy and absorbs Agent. As predicted, verbs which require such θ-roles, like those in (36a) (= 12a), have no grammatical -er agent form. Verbs which optionally permit these θ-roles, (36b) (= 12b), permit only -er agent forms without them.

(36)   a.   OBLIGATORY ARGUMENTS
          *America is a putter of men on the moon.
          *A zoologist is more than just a comparer of African elephants
             with Indian elephants.

---

[16] I rely on the basic premise of the θ-criterion which stipulates a one-to-one relationship between θ-roles and arguments. The revisions of the θ-criterion (Williams, 1983; and others), which take as its domain the argument complex, is not relevant, since the cases here involve only one argument complex.

*A surgical nurse is more than just a *hander* of scalpels to surgeons.
*The volunteer office needs a *paster* of stamps onto envelopes.

b. OPTIONAL ARGUMENTS

He is a *learner* of poems (*by heart).
This mechanic is an ace *remover* of nuts (*from sticky bolts).
He is a marvelous *arranger* of furniture (*into pleasing formats).
She is a *healer* of sick children (*of their diseases).
She is training to be a *driver* of semis (*around corners).

The *-ing* result nominals are derived by a rule which blocks Theme. As predicted, the outputs disallow, in addition to the Theme role, all lower θ-roles.

(37)   The *cooking* (*of Indian food) (*with special techniques) (*in authentic ovens) was starchy. (=(21))
        The *typing* (*of the manuscript) (*from a dictaphone) is on the desk.
        Their *finding* (*of the fossils) (*in newly opened caves) appeared in *Science.*

One additional case which provides support for this model is instrumental *-er*. It is well known that the *-er* affix may correspond to Instrument as well as Agent. We find *blender* and *toaster* (instruments which blend and toast) and a host of others, since the rule is highly productive. In our terms, this rule of *-er* affixation absorbs Instrument. According to the above discussion, a rule may absorb any θ-role on the hierarchy that it blocks, or any lower θ-role. (36) suggests that the Instrument *-er* rule blocks Agent and may, in fact, block Theme.[17]

(38)   a *crusher* (?of ice) (*by Bill)
        a *dryer* (?of clothes) (*by the laundress)
        a *dryer* (?of hair) (*by the stylist)

Instrument falls below Agent (and also Theme) on the θ-hierarchy; therefore, it is available to be absorbed.

6. SUMMARY

In this article I have argued that lexical operations are systematically constrained with respect to the degree of argument inheritance that they allow from base forms to derived forms. The degree of inheritance depends on the

---

[17] It is not clear that these Themes are blocked, since they appear in instrumental compounds in which *-er* affixation is involved: *ice crusher, clothes dryer, hair dryer.* See Roeper (1987), where the agentive/instrumental interpretations of *-er* compounds and nominalizations are discussed from a structural perspective.

changes in argument structure and category that a lexical rule invokes. The relationship is captured simply with one principle, the inheritance principle, and one assumption about how θ-roles are organized, the θ-role hierarchy. I have demonstrated that this system works in conjunction with other principles of the lexicon: the uniformity principle (under a slight revision), the projection principle, and the θ-criterion. Though not developed with this in mind, the current proposal also handles facts of θ-role absorption and makes predictions about further examples of absorption we might expect to find.

This account has been too brief to address the entire set of rules operating in the lexicon; for example, I have not considered at all rules which add θ-roles, nor have I addressed the question of sentential complements, for which a syntactic account along the lines of Stowell (1981) may be appropriate. But the systematicity that I have found in the rules so far suggests that this framework is one into which further research on lexical operations can be integrated.

ACKNOWLEDGMENTS

I am grateful to Joe Emonds, Tom Roeper, and Wendy Wilkins for their suggestions. Jill Carrier-Duncan contributed significantly to my thinking on these issues, and I regret that I could not incorporate more of her suggestions. The participants in the MIT Morphology Workshop, January 1984, provided valuable comments on an earlier version of this work, presented there and distributed as Randall (1984a). See also Randall (1984b, 1984c, 1985) for additional data and discussion of some of these issues.

THEMATIC RESTRICTIONS ON DERIVED NOMINALS

BOŻENA ROZWADOWSKA

Department of Linguistics
University of Massachusetts
Amherst, Massachusetts 01003

The Institute of English
University of Wrocław
Wrocław, Poland

1. INTRODUCTION

In this article I present arguments for the relevance of thematic restrictions on the distribution of arguments in derived nominals. Evidence from English and Polish suggests that accounts based on syntactic parallelisms do not explain the full range of data when we consider verbs from various semantic classes. I argue against the application of NP movement in accounting for passive nominalizations. Instead, I formulate empirically adequate restrictions based on thematic relations. In so doing I ultimately introduce a feature system and show that the restrictions for both languages exhibit a great deal of similarity, which is interesting from the point of view of language universals and argues in favor of the importance of thematic relations in linguistic theory.

147

Syntax and Semantics, Volume 21
Thematic Relations

2. ENGLISH TRANSITIVE NOMINALS

2.1. Constraint on Movement in NPs

Consider the following derived nominals (the (a) and (b) examples) as compared with the corresponding verbal constructions (the (c) examples):

(1) a. *the enemy's destruction of the city*
     b. *the city's destruction by the enemy*
     c. *The city was destroyed by the enemy.*

(2) a. *John's enjoyment of the film*
     b.*the film's enjoyment (by/of John)*
     c. *The film was enjoyed by John.*

(3) a. *the public's delight in the book*
     b.*the book's delight of the public*
     c. *The book delights the public.*

(4) a. *Mary's disgust at his rude behavior*
     b.*his rude behavior's disgust of Mary*
     c. *His rude behavior disgusts Mary.*

(5) a. *the people's disillusionment with the president*
     b.*the president's disillusionment of the people*
     c. *The president disillusioned the people.*

(6) a. *John's amusement at the books*
     b.*the book's amusement of John*
     c. *The books amused John.*

(7) a. *children's amusement at John's stories*
     b.*John's amusement of the children with his stories*
     c. *John amused the children with his stories.*

The asymmetry in the distribution of arguments between (1) and (2) (that is, the contrast in grammaticality between *the city's destruction by the enemy* and *the film's enjoyment by John*) is accounted for by Anderson (1979) by means of a constraint on movement of "nonaffected" objects inside NPs. She adopts the lexicalist hypothesis (Chomsky, 1970) with its null hypothesis of subcategorizational and selectional correspondences between verbs and derivationally related nominals.[1] Within this approach, the specifier position of

---

[1] In fact, Chomsky (1970, p. 38) notices that "only in the simplest case will exactly the same contextual (and other) features be associated with an item as a verb and as a noun." The basic claim of the lexicalist hypothesis, however, is that "a great many items appear in the lexicon with fixed selectional and strict subcategorization features, but with a choice as to the features associated with the lexical categories noun, verb, adjective" (Chomsky, 1970, pp. 21–22).

a nominal is the subject and the *of*-prepositional phrase is the object. Anderson (1979, p. 23) distinguishes between bare NP complements and prepositional complements and suggests that "NP Preposing will apply regularly whenever a noun has an empty NP in its determiner and an NP not mediated by a preposition in its complement. The only preposition that appears to allow preposing of its object is *of*" (cf. *destruction of the city* and *the city's destruction*).

However, as Anderson recognizes, there exist nominals such as (2) which take *of* as a preposition but still do not allow preposing (*enjoyment of the film* but not **the film's enjoyment*). Here Anderson has to make direct reference to the semantic notion of AFFECTEDNESS and suggests as a further stipulation that only affected NPs count as bare NP-complements; nonaffected NP objects are marked with a LEXICAL preposition *of*, which blocks their movement to the specifier position. The object of *destruction* is not preceded by *of* in D-structure; here the preposition is inserted transformationally. The object of *enjoyment* has a base-generated preposition *of*.

2.2. Adjectival Derivation?

To account for the data in (3)–(7) in Anderson's framework, it is necessary to deny that the nominals in the (a) examples of (3)–(7) are derived from the corresponding verbs in the (c) examples.[2] One might argue, as did Wasow (1977), that the nominals here are derived from adjectival passives, not from verbs. Thus, the base structure for a nominal such as *amusement* would be as in (8):

(8)   *be amused* [*at* NP]

As indicated, (8) contains a prepositional complement, and NP movement to the specifier position is blocked. There are good arguments, however, against this proposal.

First, as was convincingly argued by Amritavalli (1980), such an approach presents serious problems when we try to apply it cross-categorially. It rests on the assumption that there is a parallelism in subcategorizational frame between an NP and that S whose predicate is the morphological base of the head noun (or vice versa). As Amritavalli notices, we can rule out **the walk's tiredness of Mary* by saying that it relates to the passive sentence *Mary was*

---

[2] As was rightly noticed by an anonymous reader, it is not imperative in the lexicalist framework that the base structure for the nominal constructions should be the one in the (c) examples of (3)–(7). However, if we have morphological arguments (see the subsequent discussion) that the nominals here are derived from verbs, the choice of the (c) examples as the subcategorizational frame is in full accord with the lexicalist hypothesis, and the ungrammaticality of the (b) examples needs an explanation.

tired by the walk, and not to the active one *The walk tired Mary*. However, the
paradigm presented in (9) remains unexplained.

(9) a. *The news terrified (horrified) Mary.*
     b.*the news' terror (horror) of Mary*
     c. *Mary was terrified (horrified) at the sight of blood.*
     d. *Mary's terror (horror) at the sight of blood*

In (9) the predicted parallelism does not obtain. The verb in (9a) is
morphologically related to the noun in (9d), yet the subject of the nominal
corresponds to the object of the verb.

Second, we cannot predict when the nominal should be derived from an
adjectival passive and when from a verb. Thus, as Amritavalli points out,
collection and *exploration* are derived from verbs, although there exist
adjectival passives (e.g., *uncollected, unexplored*), but *amusement* must be derived from an adjectival passive by virtue of an ad hoc fact, expressed in the
lexicon. Returning to our examples, we could ask why *enjoyment* is derived
from a verb along with *destruction*, and not from an adjectival passive. There is
no way to tell which direction the morphological derivation goes other than by
accepting it as an arbitrary fact about individual lexical items. But then we
miss the regularity of the data.

Third, Amritavalli offers yet another argument, this time purely morphological, against deriving the relevant nominals from adjectival passives. Any
morphological theory (e.g., Aronoff, 1976) can conceivably allow the morphological derivation of *amusement, annoyance, irritation*, etc., from the
corresponding past participles. We might postulate word formation rules
producing $[[[X]_V ed]_A ment]_N$, and truncate the participial inflection or postulate nasal assimilation. It would be much more difficult to find independent motivation for deadjectival *-ance*, or *-(at)ion*. There are well-motivated
suffixes *-ment, -ance*, and *-ation*, which attach to verbs. Hypothetical deadjectival *-ment, -ance, -(at)ion* could not attach to any other adjectival
bases such as $[Xable]_A$, $[Xive]_A$, $[Xing]_A$. Also, such forms as **unXment,
*unXance, *unXation* are impossible. All these facts constitute evidence
against an adjectival base for these nouns. Especially odd would be to
claim that *irritation* or *exhaustion* are not derived from verbs, *-ion* being a
widely recognized typically deverbal suffix. Yet within an approach appealing to subcategorizational parallelism between NPs and Ss this would be a
necessary step.

In short, the only motivation for not deriving the starred nominals in (3)–(7)
from the related verbs is the fact that the movement analysis then has nothing
to say about their ungrammaticality.

2.3. Thematic Constraint on Specifier

The solution which I propose is in the form of one simple and straightforward thematic principle. Before formulating it, however, let me introduce the thematic relation that would be assigned to *film* in both *John enjoys the film* and *The film amuses John,* and which at the same time would be distinct from affected objects of agentive verbs. Within the Gruber–Jackendoff system, affected objects of agentive verbs are THEMES (e.g., the object of *destroy*) as well as objects of emotive verbs such as *enjoy, hate,* or *like,* or subjects of verbs such as *amuse, irritate,* or *please.* The definition of Theme as "the NP understood as undergoing the motion or whose location is being asserted" (Jackendoff, 1972, p. 29) is extended by analogy to abstract motion or location. Thus Jackendoff (1972, p. 150) treats subjects of psychological predicates of the *amuse* type as themes. As a result, the notion of Theme becomes vague and too broad to reflect finer distinctions. The insufficiency of Theme has led some linguists to introduce various more-specific thematic notions, such as Patient (affected object of agentive verbs), Experienced, or Percept (Jackendoff, 1987). The thematic relation I am introducing covers what Rappaport (1983) calls the Experienced role with emotive verbs (whether it be in subject or in object position) as well as all other nonaffected objects discussed by Anderson (1979). For this relation I suggest the label NEUTRAL and define it as follows:[3]

NEUTRAL: An entity X holds a thematic relation NEUTRAL (N-role) with respect to a predicate Y if

(i) X is in no way affected by the action, process, or state described by Y,
(ii) X does not have any control over the action, process, or state described by Y.

So, the subjects in the (c) examples of (3)–(7) bear the Neutral thematic relation to their respective verbs, as do the objects of the following verbs: *like, enjoy, dislike, hate, admire, respect,* etc., and also *know, see, recollect, perceive, observe, understand,* etc. Neutral is contrasted here with Patient (e.g., an object of *destroy*), both of which were understood as Theme in Jackendoff (1972). The reason I am giving up Theme altogether for the purposes of the present consideration is its inability to distinguish affected objects from nonaffected ones, which distinction is crucial in the account of nominals.[4]

[3] This definition is a slightly modified version of the semantic case Neutral defined by Platt (1977) as a nonaffected entity. Note that the notion Neutral was also used in another sense in Stockwell *et al.* (1973). There it means the same as does Theme in the Gruber–Jackendoff system of thematic relations.

[4] Furthermore, as suggested in Culicover and Wilkins (1984, p. 212), Theme belongs to the class of extensional roles (together with, e.g., Source, Goal, Location), and it seems inappropriate to mix

Crucial in the definition are the negative conditions: no affectedness and no control, the latter necessary to distinguish Neutral from Agent. By affectedness I understand any kind of change, either physical or psychological/emotional. By control I mean conscious physical action performed by volitional Agents, conscious control over feelings by psychological Agents (i.e., Experiencers), as well as mechanical manipulation by Instruments (something like agency projected onto Instruments).

Let me now formulate a simple principle appealing to thematic relations which I call the N-rule:

N-RULE: Neutral cannot appear in specifier position of a nominal.

2.4. Rappaport's Thematic Constancy Principle

The above restriction is similar to the restriction which Rappaport (1983) independently formulates, within lexical–functional grammar, for the assignment of the Poss function in derived nominals. She labels the arguments of emotive verbs as Experiencer, Experienced and says that Experienced is restricted from being assigned the Poss function. Then, quite separately, she mentions other nominals, repeated here in (10):

(10)   a. *history's knowledge
        b. *John's sight by Mary
        c. *the event's recollection
        d. *the problem's perception
        e. *the picture's observation
        f. *the novel's understanding

She says that "Whether or not an argument of a derived nominal may bear the POSS function depends on as of yet poorly understood thematic relations" (p. 133) and refers to Anderson's constraint against the movement of non-affected objects in order to explain the ungrammaticality of the nominals in (10). It seems, however, that Rappaport's restriction and Anderson's constraint are instances of the same phenomenon. They can be reformulated in thematic terms as the one restriction in the N-rule.

---

it with intensional roles, such as Agent, Patient, Instrument. Extensional roles categorize objects as physical entities in terms of their perceived properties, while intensional roles categorize objects according to their status as actors in an action or an emotional situation. The thematic relation Neutral belongs to the class of intensional roles in Culicover and Wilkins's understanding and fills the gap that was filled by Theme before the distinction between the two classes of roles was recognized.

In discussing the restrictions on nominals, Rappaport attributes the lack of syntactic correspondence with the relevant verbs to what is called THEMATIC CONSTANCY in the lexical–functional framework. This means that a given semantically restricted grammatical function (all grammatical functions in nominals are semantically restricted in Rappaport's analysis) can be assigned only to an argument bearing a particular thematic relation. However, the thematic constancy principle does not work consistently, as I show below.

Rappaport assumes that only Themes are assigned the OBL$_{Theme}$ function in nominals and therefore only Themes can be realized as objects of the preposition *of*. She uses this thematically based linking convention to explain the ungrammaticality of nominals such as those in (11), which correspond to the respective sentences in (12).

(11) a. *Herbie's gift of Louise of a bouquet*
      b. *The general's command of the troops to evacuate*
      c. *John's flight of the city*
      d. *John's writing of the British Museum*
      e. *The soldiers' entry of the city*

(12) a. Herbie gave Louise a bouquet.
      b. The general commanded the troops to evacuate.
      c. John fled the city.
      d. John wrote the British Museum.
      e. The soldiers entered the city.

The object NPs in (12) are not Themes. They can be assigned the grammatical function of an object in these cases because it is semantically unrestricted. However, they cannot be assigned the OBL$_{Theme}$ function in nominals because of thematic incompatibility.

If we follow this reasoning, there is no account of the contrast between (13) and (14).

(13) a.   Experiencer   Experienced
             John's love of Mary
      b.   Experiencer   Experienced
             People's hatred of the enemy
      c.   Experiencer   Experienced
             Children's fear of the devil

(14) a. *   Experiencer   Experienced
             John's amazement of the film*
      b. *   Experiencer   Experienced
             People's disgust of cats*

> **Experiencer**   **Experienced**
> c.* *Children's surprise of the presents*

Rappaport assumes that the nominals both in (13) and (14) as well as the corresponding verbs share the argument structure Experiencer, Experienced. Thus, the NPs taking the preposition *of* in (13) bear the same thematic relation of Experienced as do the NPs in the ungrammatical nominals in (14). Recognizing the difference, and hence the incompatibility between Experienced and Theme (which is otherwise implicit in Rappaport's analysis), we could account for the ungrammaticality of the nominals in (14) by saying that Experienced is incompatible with the OBL_{Theme} function and cannot take the preposition *of*. Instead, it must take an idiosyncratic preposition compatible with Experienced, as in (15), which preposition also appears in the passive verbal constructions in (16).

(15)   a. *John's amazement at the film*
       b. *People's disgust with cats*
       c. *The children's surprise at the presents*

(16)   a. *John was amazed at the film*
       b. *People were disgusted with cats*
       c. *The children were surprised at the presents*

But then the grammaticality of (13) is a counterexample to the thematic constancy principle: Experienced should not take the preposition *of* in nominals.

2.5. N-Rule versus Previous Accounts

Since the thematic constancy does not work, I suggest that the thematic restriction in the N-rule be an independent constraint on specifier, and not a fact derivative from the thematic constancy principle governing the assignment of grammatical functions in nominals, as proposed by Rappaport.

Notice that my principle is independent of morphology and works also for basic, nonderived nouns like *terror*:

(17)   a. **Experiencer**   **Neutral**
           Mary's   terror / horror at the news
       b.* **Neutral**   **Experiencer**
           the news' terror / horror of   Mary
       c. **Neutral**   **Experiencer**
           The news terrified / horrified   Mary

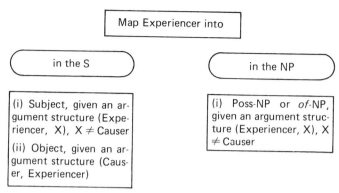

Figure 1. Amritavalli's experiencer hypothesis.

The N-rule is similar to Amritavalli's experiencer hypothesis (presented in Figure 1) in that it refers to thematic roles and not to grammatical relations.

Observe, however, that the experiencer hypothesis implies that the argument structure of a nominal is different from that of a verb: Subject of a verb such as *amuse* is interpreted as Causer (see (ii)), while the argument of the *at*-prepositional phrase in *amusement* (or in the adjectival passive *amused at*) is not a Causer (see (i)), which undermines any attempt to relate the two constructions in the first place. Moreover, the presence of Experiencer in the argument structure is made responsible for the pattern and we have to allow some exceptions, as noted by Amritavalli and repeated in (18).

(18)   a. *John's disappointment of his audience*
           Agent   Experiencer

           Agent   Experiencer
      b. *John's embarrassment of   Mary*

(18a) corresponds to the sentence *John disappoints his audience*; (18b), to the sentence *John embarrases Mary*. Both *his audience* and *Mary* are Experiencers, but they are not mapped to the specifier position of related nominals.

On my account, the acceptability of the above nominals is attributed to the possible agentive readings for *disappoint* and *embarrass*. Similarly, we can make (7b) and (5b) acceptable by forcing an agentive reading.

           Agent   Experiencer
(19)   a. *John's deliberate amusement of the children with his stories*
            Agent   Experiencer
      b. *the president's deliberate disillusionment of the people*

The object remains an Experiencer even on the agentive reading in (19) (why should it be otherwise?). The total unacceptability of (20) is straightforward:

Because there is no possibility of an agentive reading, the specifier NP can only be Neutral, and the examples are ruled out by the N-rule.

(20) a.*Neutral *the news'/results'/performance's* disappointment *of the audience* Experiencer

    b.*Neutral *the disclosure's* embarrassment *of* Mary Experiencer

With the N-rule, we now can preserve one morphological rule deriving *amusement, disappointment,* and so on from their respective verbs *amuse, disappoint,* independent of the thematic interpretation. Both Anderson's and Wasow's theories would require two different types of nominals with different derivations.

Let us return briefly to Rappaport's analysis. She specifically claims that there are no nouns which inherit the argument structure Agent, Experiencer from their related verbs, and this is supposed to account for the ungrammaticality of the nominals in (21) and (22).

(21) a.* *The miracle's* amazement *of the people* (Experienced / Experiencer)

    b.* *The movie's* shock *of the audience* (Experienced / Experiencer)

(22) a.* Amy's fright *by the scarecrow* (Experiencer / Agent)

    b.* *The class's* boredom *by the lecturer* (Experiencer / Agent)

    c.* *Deborah's* amusement *by Randy* (Experiencer / Agent)

    d.* Sam's annoyance *by Dave* (Experiencer / Agent)

First, this single generalization cannot rule out (21), the argument structure in (21) being Experiencer, Experienced and not Experiencer, Agent. Second, my claim is that it is precisely the argument structure Agent, Experiencer, when inherited from the related verb, that explains the contrast between (18) and (20). A dual interpretation of experiential nominals (as in (18)) is not always possible, but where it is, my constraint predicts the correct results.

Evidence presented in this section supports the claim that the distribution of arguments in derived nominals, and specifically the impossibility of certain arguments in specifier position, can be explained in terms of thematic restrictions and is independent of the morphological relation between nominals and verbs. I have thus far shown that both Amritavalli's experiencer hypothesis and Anderson's movement analysis fail to account for all of the data that the thematic account explains. Additionally, because the behavior of derived nominals is taken by Anderson as crucial evidence for NP Movement in the NP domain, the existence of a thematic, nonmovement theory of derived nominals calls into question the application of Move NP within NP. Since an explanation appealing to subcategorization fails, I claim that a verb–noun pair shares an argument structure but not a subcategorization frame. In this respect my approach is similar to that of Rappaport (1983). However, instead of a thematic constancy principle, I postulate an independent linking constraint on Specifier.

3. SINGLE-ARGUMENT TRANSITIVE NOMINALS

Consider now the class of nominal constructions such as (23), discussed in Chomsky (1981, p. 104):

(23) a. *the barbarians' destruction of Rome*
      b. *Rome's destruction (by the barbarians)*
      c. *the destruction of Rome (by the barbarians)*
      d.*the barbarians' destruction* (where *barbarians* = Agent)

Chomsky says that (23a) is the nominal expected given *The barbarians destroyed Rome* and the assumptions of $\bar{\text{X}}$ theory. (23d) is ungrammatical because *destroy* requires an object (cf. **The barbarians destroyed*). The generalization is that θ-role assignment to the subject is determined compositionally by the VP. Thus, a verb subcategorized for an object cannot assign a θ-role to the subject position if the object is not expressed. Similarly, a nominalized construction cannot take a subject argument unless the object is expressed. On this view, then, subcategorization and the compositional assignment of the subject θ-role account for the ungrammaticality of (d). Hence (d) is grammatical only on the interpretation in which *the barbarians* is understood as Patient of *destruction*, or, in other words, where the nominalization is passive.

If we adopt this syntax-based account of single-argument transitive nominals, there is an inconsistency with respect to experiential nominals. These transitive nominals can evidently assign a subject θ-role even in the absence of an object:

(24) a. *John's love*
      b. *Mary's hatred*

Here, in contrast to (23), the argument expressed in a derived nominal corresponds to the subject of the related transitive verb. However, we can appeal to thematic relations in order to avoid inconsistency. Observe that with

Agent–Patient verbs, the corresponding single argument nominal takes the
Patient, while with experiential verbs, this single argument must be the
Experiencer.

4. FEATURE APPROACH TO THEMATIC RELATIONS

At this point it would be helpful to introduce feature notation into the
discussion. Let us assume that both Patients and Experiencers share a
thematic feature [+change] (i.e., are affected physically or psychologically in
the course of action, process, or state). The following generalization then
holds:

PRINCIPLE A: If one of the two arguments of a transitive nominal is
[+change] (or, alternatively, if it is a Patient or an Experiencer), then this
argument must be expressed in a single argument nominal.

Now the ungrammaticality of (23d) follows: On the intended ungrammatical reading *the barbarians* is Agent (i.e., [−change]). Therefore it contradicts
Principle A. By virtue of A, the only available interpretation is with *the
barbarians* understood as Patient (i.e., [+change]). Principle A works consistently, as we can see in (25).

(25)   a. *John's amusement*
       b. *John's pleasure*
       c. *John's surprise*
       d. *John's embarrassment*
       e. *John's dislike*
       f. *John's fear*
       g. *John's hatred*

In all the examples in (25), the specifier position is occupied by an
Experiencer, corresponding either to the subject or to the object of the related
verb. So far, no account appealing strictly to syntactic positions or grammatical relations has been able to explain the facts in (23)–(25).

Recall now the generalization about Neutral, which I defined as a relation involving the absence of both affectedness and conscious control. Let
[+sentient] be the label standing for conscious involvement in the action or
state. With the feature notation, I can now reformulate the N-rule as the
N*-rule:

N*RULE: A [−change, −sentient] argument cannot appear in specifier position of a nominal.

The feature approach makes it possible to capture the overlap among
thematic relations. In the discussion of nominals I argue for the overlap of

TABLE I

INTERPRETATION OF THEMATIC RELATIONS IN TERMS OF FEATURES

Feature			
Sentient	Cause	Change	Thematic relation
+	+	+	Affected Agent (e.g., Agents of monotransitive verbs that undergo some change; traditionally referred to as Agents and Themes at the same time: *John rolled down the hill.*)
+	+	−	Agent (Agents of prototypical Agent–Patient verbs: *destroy, beat, kill, hit, write*, etc.)
+	−	+	Experiencer, possibly Recipient and Possessor
?	+	−	Instruments
−	+	−	Object–Cause of emotion (i.e., Neutral, Rappaport's Experienced, Jackendoff's Percept)
−	−	+	Patient (i.e., affected objects of agentive verbs)
−	−	−	Neutral viewed as a mere object rather than a cause; also object of the verb *enter* (in *John entered the room.*)

Patient and Experiencer. There exist other grammatical phenomena (e.g., binding facts concerning anaphors in English, or impersonal constructions in Polish, discussed in detail in Rozwadowska (1986)) which suggest that there is a thematic similarity between Agents and Experiencers. The feature approach allows cross-classification of various types of arguments into different, overlapping natural classes. This is not available in thematic systems where thematic relations are treated as atomic wholes. In the case at hand, Patient and Experiencer form a natural class with respect to the feature [+change]. In addition to the features [+change] and [+sentient], I suggest the feature [+cause]. Sample interpretations of traditional thematic labels within the feature system are given in Table I.[5]

---

[5] We lack a relation [+sentient, −cause, −change]. This combination appears to correspond to conscious experiencers of states that do not imply any affectedness. The problem seems to be that it is not clear whether there exist perceptual or experiential states which are not understood in terms of change or comparison with another state. Also, I think that all perceptual or experiential states affect our internal or psychological life. Maybe a possible candidate for this combination would be something like "permanent possessor," though even possession seems to imply something like entering into a certain relation with another entity, hence [+change].

A second dubious combination is [−sentient, +cause, +change]. This in turn would imply an unconscious causation directed toward itself. In other words, this would denote an individual that is a Patient and a Causer at the same time, and which is not an Agent. Again, this seems very difficult to imagine. Maybe we could classify instances of spontaneous action as belonging here, but it seems that we attribute the cause of such actions to some unknown force rather than to the unconscious Patient itself.

Instruments seem to have an intermediate status between Agents and Neutrals. A possible explanation could be that although they lack conscious involvement, they still possess some mechanical or physical control.[6] They could be viewed as an anthropomorphic projection of Agents' qualities. This would mean an intermediate or undefined status of Instruments with respect to the feature [+sentient], which finds its reflection in the intermediate acceptability of the nominals in (26b–d) as compared with the perfect (26a) and the ungrammatical (26e).

(26)
    Agent   **Patient**
  a. *the enemy's destruction of the city*
    Instrument   **Patient**
  b. ?*the rocket's destruction of the city*
    Instrument   **Patient**
  c. ?*the key's opening of the door*
    Instrument   **Patient**
  d.??*the knife's damage of the table*
    Neutral   **Experiencer**
  e. **the book's amusement of the children*

Notice also that the formulation of the constraint on specifier in terms of features (the N* rule) works for such nominals as **the city's entry by the soldiers*. Whatever label we decide to assign to *the city* here, it is evidently a [−sentient, −change] argument.

To finish the discussion of English nominals, consider the nominals in (27).

(27)
    Neutral   **Neutral**
  a. *John resembles Bill.*
    Neutral   **Neutral**
  b. *John's resemblance to Bill*
    Neutral   **Neutral**
  c. *Bill's resemblance to John*

Either the examples in (27b–c) have to be treated as exceptions to the N* rule, or we can speculate a little and suggest that the thematic restrictions postulated in this article hold for asymmetric predicates only because a thematic restriction determines which of the two competing arguments, different thematically, appears in a given position. With the symmetric predicates such as *resemble* there is no thematic competition and thus either

---

[6] Comrie (1983, p. 53) suggests that thematic relations form a continuum, the labels representing different points along this continuum. According to him, the continuum as a whole can be regarded as a continuum of control. Like Comrie, I recognize the relevance of control, but unlike him, I propose feature decomposition instead of a continuum.

argument can appear in specifier position. This seemingly exceptional acceptability of the nominals in (27b–c) can be explained on thematic grounds within the feature system if we assume that the value $+/-$ has real significance only if there is another argument with the opposite value. Otherwise, the value $+/-$ does not really matter. If we accept this explanation for *resemblance*, we have another argument for preferring a thematic account to syntax-based approaches. Syntactically, the two arguments in (27) are asymmetrical (i.e., they appear in two different structural positions or bear two distinct grammatical relations), so there is nothing special about the predicate *resemble* as compared with other transitive predicates.

5. POLISH DERIVED NOMINALS

In the previous sections I discussed the English specifier position in nominals. In Polish, the prenominal position is extremely limited (it exists only for pronouns and for some denominal adjectives derived from proper names). Instead, all the functions that specifier position performs in English nominals are taken over by the genitive position following the head noun. The simplest parallel is illustrated by the possessive phrases:

(28)   *książka   Jana*
        book-nom John-gen
        'John's book'

With this parallel in mind, it is interesting to observe the sensitivity of Polish derived nominals to thematic relations. Consider the following examples:

(29) a. *Wróg   zgładził miasto.*
         enemy-nom ruined   city-acc
         'The enemy destroyed the city.'
      b. *Zagłada   miasta (przez wroga)*
         destruction-nom city-gen (by enemy)
         'The city's destruction (by the enemy)'
      c. **Zagłada   wroga   miasta.*
         destruction-nom enemy-gen city-gen
         'The enemy's destruction of the city'

(30) a. *Jan   podziwia Marię.*
         John-nom admires   Mary-acc
         'John admires Mary.'

b. *Podziw   Jana   dla Marii*
admiration-nom John-gen for Mary-gen
'John's admiration for Mary'

c.*Podziw   Marii   przez Jana*
admiration-nom Mary-gen by John-gen
*'Mary's admiration by John'

(31) a. *Andrzej   gardzi   pieniędzmi.*
Andrew-nom feels contempt money-instr
'Andrew feels contempt for money.'

b. *Pogarda   Andrzeja   dla pieniędzy*
contempt-nom Andrew-gen for money-gen
'Andrew's contempt for money'

c.*Pogarda   pieniędzy   przez Jana*
contempt-nom money-gen by John-gen
*'Money's contempt by John'

(32) a. *Marek   szanuje swoich rodziców.*
Mark-nom respects his parents-acc
'Mark respects his parents.'

b. *Szacunek   Marka   dla swoich rodziców*
respect-nom Mark-gen for his parents-gen
'Mark's respect for his parents'

c.*Szacunek   rodziców   przez Marka*
respect-nom parents-gen by Mark-gen
*'Parents' respect by Mark'

(33) a. *Dzieci   zdumiewają rodziców.*
children-nom amaze   parents-acc
'Children amaze parents'.

b. *Zdumienie   rodziców   dziećmi.*
amazement-nom parents-gen children-instr
'Parents' amazement at the children'

c.*Zdumienie   dzieci   rodziców*
amazement-nom children-gen parents-gen
*'Children's amazement of the parents'

At first sight, agentive nominals, illustrated in (29b), suggest that the genitive position in nominals is the object and that a parallel with the related verbs can be established: Objects of verbs appear as genitive complements of related nominals. Since with Agent–Patient verbs it is always Patient that is the object, syntactic and thematic accounts are equivalent. It is only experiential nominals that present evidence for a thematic rather than a syntactic account: It is the Experiencer, corresponding either to the subject, (30–32), or to the object, (33), of the related verb which appears in the genitive complement position. The generalization is thus exactly like Principle A for English single-argument transitive nominals. I formulate it as principle B:

PRINCIPLE B: Only [+change] arguments (i.e., Patient or Experiencers) can be expressed as genitive complements of Polish transitive nominals.

At this point, let me take a closer look at Polish nominals related to object Experiencer verbs, which provide further evidence for preferring a thematic account to a syntactic one. This class of verbs patterns in Polish as follows:

(34)   a. *Nowy film   Wajdy   zaszokował publiczność.*
          new film-nom Wajda-gen shocked   audience-acc
          'A new film by Wajda shocked the audience.'
       b. *Publiczność   zaszokowała się nowym filmem Wajdy.*
          audience-nom shocked Refl   new film-instr Wajda-gen
          'The audience was shocked at a new film by Wajda.'
       c. *Publiczność   była zaszokowana nowym filmem Wajdy.*
          audience-nom was shocked   new film-instr Wajda-gen
          'The audience was shocked at a new film by Wajda.'

The above alternation, which I call the nonreflexive versus reflexive alternation (the sole reason being the presence of the reflexive clitic *się*) is a productive process in the domain of object Experiencer verbs. There are two synonymous nominals, one with the reflexive clitic *się*, the other one without it:

(35)   a. *Zaszokowanie publiczności   nowym filmem Wajdy.*
          shocking-nom audience-gen new film-instr Wajda-gen
          'The audience's shock at a new film by Wajda'
       b. *Zaszokowanie się publiczności   nowym filmem Wajdy.*
          shocking Refl   audience-gen new film-instr Wajda-gen
          'The audience's shock at a new film by Wajda'

By the same type of morphological argument as is relevant for English, I claim that these nominals are related to verbs and not to adjectival passives: The nominals are derived by the attachment of a typical deverbal nominal suffix -*nie* and not through the attachment of the deadjectival suffix -*ość* (cf. **zdumioność*). This means that (35a) is related to (34a) and not to the passive construction (34c), and that (35b) is related to (34b). But then the two synonymous nominals in (35) are related to verbs with different syntactic structure. The fact that they are both grammatical is due to their thematic characteristics. In both cases an Experiencer (i.e., a [+change] argument) occupies the genitive position.

Given the lack of a double genitive construction in Polish, the identity of Principles A and B is interesting and in fact not surprising. In Polish, apart from oblique prepositional phrases, there is only one slot for an argument of a nominal. With experiential nominals, the other (i.e., [−change], or in other words, Neutral) argument may show up only in prepositional phrase, the (b) examples of (30)–(32), or in an oblique case, (33b); with agentive nominals (29b), Agent can appear in an optional *przez-* 'by' phrase. Notice that the same is true of English single-argument nominals: They become two-argument transitive nominals by taking an appropriate prepositional phrase optionally. Thus, the nominals presented in (24)–(25) become the nominals with which I started the present considerations (e.g., *John's amusement at the movie, John's dislike of cats, John's love of music, John's fear of darkness*). This observation suggests that the basic, more universal generalization is Principle B or its English equivalent A rather than the N* rule. It is possible that the latter simply follows from the former and that it is agentive active nominals like *enemy's destruction of the city* that have to be explained rather than the passive ones. This, however, I leave for future research.

6. CONCLUSIONS

The discussion of two-argument experiential nominals along with Agent–Patient nominals argues against a purely syntactic account of the relation between nominals and verbs. An appeal to subcategorization and movement between structural positions cannot provide consistent predictions about the argument structure of the nominals related to both of these classes of verbs. The use of thematic relations, in contrast, provides two simple, adequate generalizations.

First, an argument bearing the thematic relation Neutral (i.e., [−change, −sentient]) may not appear either as the genitive complement of a Polish nominal or in the specifier position of an English nominal.

Second, when only one of two arguments is expressed in a nominal construction, it must be either a Patient or an Experiencer. It must be an argument which bears the thematic feature [+change]. This fact is independent of the subcategorization facts for the corresponding verbal constructions and holds true for both English and Polish. The two languages differ only in the grammatical configuration in which the [+change] argument occurs: specifier in English, genitive complement in Polish.

These generalizations provide some evidence that thematic restrictions on the distribution of arguments in derived nominals might hold universally. They also show that there is an overlap between specifier position in English nominals and genitive position in Polish nominals. The difference between the two stems from the availability in English of a second genitive position, a postnominal *of*-phrase. This makes it possible in English, with agentive constructions, to express an Agent argument in specifier position once the Patient is already expressed in an *of*-phrase. Importantly, despite the availability of two genitive positions in English, there is nevertheless a restriction on the Neutral argument. This fact further motivates the thematic restriction on Neutral in derived nominals and supports the existence of some such thematic relation itself.

ACKNOWLEDGMENTS

This research was supported in part by the System Development Foundation, grant SDF #650: "Research on the Formal Foundation of Semantics." An earlier version of the article was written with the support of an international fellowship from the AAUW and was presented at the LSA Annual Meeting in Seattle, December 1985. I am especially grateful to David Pesetsky for fruitful discussion, help, and encouragement, without which this article would have never been written. I am also greatly indebted to Barbara Partee, Tom Roeper, Anne Vainikka, and Edwin Williams for their valuable comments. Last but not least, I would like to acknowledge my indebtness to Wendy Wilkins, whose suggestions, both substantial and stylistic, have contributed a great deal to the final shape of this work.

THEMATIC RELATIONS AND CASE LINKING IN RUSSIAN

LINDA SCHWARTZ

Department of Linguistics
Indiana University
Bloomington, Indiana 47405

1. INTRODUCTION

The question has often been raised as to whether or not the sentences of natural languages can be adequately accounted for on the basis of a single set of invariant grammatical (and semantic) relations among constituents. Any theory of grammatical structure that assumes such invariance of relations is referred to as a MONOSTRATAL theory, as opposed to all other theories, which are MULTISTRATAL in the sense that certain constituents of sentences may bear one relation at one stratum of analysis (such as initial or d-structure subject) and another different (and incompatible) relation at another stratum of analysis (such as final or s-structure subject). It is important to distinguish here the notion of STRATUM from the notion of LEVEL. I adopt the distinction given in Ladusaw (1985), where different strata are described using the same theoretical vocabulary, while different levels have different theoretical vocabulary.[1]

---

[1] See Ladusaw (1985) for arguments that both relational grammar and government–binding are multistratal in the sense intended here.

Syntax and Semantics, Volume 21
Thematic Relations

Some recent analyses of lexical (*sebja*) and morphological (*-sja*) reflexives and related constructions in Russian either argue for or assume the existence of multiple strata of grammatical relations to capture certain generalizations about these phenomena. Schwartz (1986) shows that certain facts about controllers of lexical reflexives in Russian can be accounted for in a grammatical model using a monostratal syntax. In this article, I expand this account to consider *-sja* constructions, which encode a number of superficially different relations, among them reflexive and reciprocal relations, and which have previously been analyzed as requiring a multistratal syntax. I argue that generalizations of the type captured in the multistratal accounts of these phenomena can be represented in a monostratal model by reference to the level of thematic relations (TRs) (which includes in its vocabulary labels for thematic relations such as Agent, Experiencer, Location, Source, Theme) and the level of case (which includes in its vocabulary, among other things, case features such as nominative, accusative, dative, instrumental), and to principles which specify the co-occurrence restrictions, or "linkings," which hold between entities from these levels as they are associated with noun phrases in a monostratal syntactic representation. In Section 2, I summarize the analysis presented in Schwartz (1986); in Section 3, I present the relevant data regarding *-sja* constructions and some multistratal analyses of the generalizations holding over these constructions; and in Section 4, I present a monostratal analysis of these constructions and show how this analysis can make generalizations quite similar to those made within the multistratal accounts. Section 5 summarizes the important points of this investigation.

2. RUSSIAN REFLEXIVE CONTROLLERS

In Russian, any of the following can be controllers of reflexive pronouns: a nominative NP as in (1) and (2), an instrumental NP of a passive sentence as in (3), a dative NP of an experiential predicate as in (4), a genitive NP in a possessive predication as in (5), and sometimes other dative and genitive NPs as in (6).[2] Examples in this section are adapted from Perlmutter (1980, 1982, 1984) unless otherwise noted.

(1)   *Anna   otpravila Borisa k svoim roditeljam.*
        A-nom sent   B-acc to self's parents.
        'Anna$_i$ sent Boris$_j$ to her$_i$/*his$_j$ parents.'

---

[2] Issues regarding when reflexive as opposed to nonreflexive pronouns appear are not considered here. See Timberlake (1979) and references cited there regarding this issue.

(2)   *Boris   byl otpravlen k svoim roditeljam.*
       B-nom was sent   to self's parents
       'Boris$_i$ was sent to his$_i$ parents.'

(3)   *Èta kniga   byla kuplena Borisom dlja sebja.*
       this book-nom was bought B-inst   for self-gen
       'This book was bought by Boris for himself.'

(4)   *Ej   žal' sebja.*
       she-dat sorry self-acc
       'She feels sorry for herself.'

(5)   *U Ivana byli den'gi   s soboj.*
       at I-gen was money-nom with self
       'Ivan had money with/on him.'   (Chvany, 1975, p. 99)

(6)   *U nego*
       at him-gen
       Emu   *ne   ostavalos' vremeni na sebja.*
       him-dat   neg remained time   for self
       dlja nego
       for him-gen
       'He had no time left for himself.'   (Timberlake, 1980, p. 248)

Not all NPs can be reflexive controllers. For example, the accusative NP in (1) cannot control the reflexive, nor can the dative NPs in (7) and (8).

(7)   *Ja   emu   skazal vse o sebe.*
       I-nom he-dat told   all about self
       'I told him all about myself/*himself.'   (Timberlake 1979, p. 115)

(8)   **Emu bylo skazano o sebe.*
       he-dat was told   about self
       'He was told about himself.'

Thus, in (7), the only interpretation of the Russian sentence is with the nominative first person controller and not with the dative third person controller. In (8), there is no permissible controller. The dative NP is the only overt NP and a dative in this type of structure cannot control reflexivization; there is no well-formed semantic interpretation for the sentence.

A multistratal syntactic analysis of some of these facts is presented in Perlmutter (1980, 1982, 1984), where it is claimed that only NPs which are subjects at some syntactic stratum can control reflexives. For example, in (1) the controller is initial and final subject, in (2) it is final subject, and in (3) and (4) it is initial subject (the latter of an inversion construction). The lack of reflexive control of the accusative NP in (1) and of the dative NP in (7) and (8) follows from this account, because these NPs are not subjects in any stratum. The oblique control in (5) and (6) is not discussed in the sources cited above.

2.1. A Monostratal Account of Reflexive Control

In Schwartz (1986), I present an alternative, monostratal, analysis. There are conventions for linking thematic relations associated with a given predicate to NPs specified with case features[3] in syntactic representations (see Anderson, 1982, for a discussion of how these representations arise). These linking devices are here interpreted as specifying permissible co-occurrences between a given thematic role and an NP specified with a given case feature or with a PP which governs an NP with a given case feature. Two notions are relevant to this account of reflexive control: the notion of MORPHOLOGICAL SUBJECT, defined in (9); and the notion of MACROROLE, taken from the thematic role hierarchy in Foley and Van Valin (1984), given in (10), and used for the principle of default morphological subject selection given in (11).

(9)   MORPHOLOGICAL SUBJECT (MS): nominative inflected argument of a
        predicate; controller of verb agreement.[4]

(10)   ACTOR/UNDERGOER HIERARCHY (Foley and Van Valin, 1984 p. 59):
        Agent   Effector   Locative   Theme   Patient
        actor   ⇆   undergoer

(11)   DEFAULT MORPHOLOGICAL SUBJECT SELECTION HIERARCHY FOR
        RUSSIAN:
        actor > undergoer

---

[3] It is important to distinguish case features from case morphology, since some NPs may not have distinct case morphology, even though their case features are distinct. For example, in sentences like (i) and (ii), *mát'* does not vary in form depending on whether it is nominative or accusative case. If, however, it is modified by an adjective, the adjective will agree in case feature, rather than morphological case, so that the adjective inflection will not be the same, as shown in the corresponding sentences in (iii) and (iv).

(i)   *Mát'   zaščiščáet Víktora.*
        mother-nom defends   V-acc
        'Mother defends Victor.'   (Comrie, 1979, p. 107)

(ii)   *Víktor zaščiščáet mát'.*
        V-nom defends   mother-acc
        'Victor defends mother.'   (Comrie, 1979, p. 107)

(iii)   *Stáraja mát'   zaščiščáet Víktora.*
        old-nom mother-nom defends   V-acc
        'The old mother defends Victor.'   (adapted from Comrie, 1979)

(iv)   *Víktor zaščiščáet stáruju mát'.*
        V-nom defends   old-acc mother-acc
        'Victor defends the old mother.'   (adapted from Comrie, 1979)

All references to 'case' in this article are to be understood as references to case features; this is also true of the interpretation of all glosses.

[4] Nominative case is a necessary but not sufficient condition for verb agreement in Russian (see Corbett, 1983, for a detailed account of factors involved in Russian agreement phonomena).

The hierarchy in (10) is intended to be universal. It is to be interpreted as follows: the actor hierarchy is read from left to right, with Agent taking precedence over other TRs; the undergoer hierarchy is read from right to left, with Patient taking precedence over other TRs. The hierarchy in (11) is to be interpreted as follows: if an actor is available for linking to MS, then it will be MS; if not, then undergoer, if available, will be MS.

In addition to the default-permissible co-occurrence of TR and MS as in (1), the grammar will contain other statements of the permissible co-occurrence of TR and MS. One of these will be a statement that the default linking of undergoer will be to an NP with accusative case when not selected by (11) as MS. Another will be a statement of the correspondence between active and passive morphosyntax. I assume that passive morphology has the effect of preventing the actor from being linked to MS, in the spirit of Kiparsky (1985b). For example, the verb in (1) and (2) will have the thematic structure given in (12).

(12)   _____ Agent/Source, Theme, Receiver/Goal

According to the actor/undergoer hierarchy, Agent will be actor and Theme will be undergoer. In the absence of passive morphology, the default morphological-subject-selection hierarchy in (11) will specify the permissible co-occurrence of actor and MS. With passive morphology, as in (2) and (3), actor cannot be linked to MS, so the next choice down on the subject-selection hierarchy, undergoer, becomes MS. In (2), *Boris* is Theme, and in (3), *èta kniga* is Theme; these both will be selected as undergoer by the hierarchy in (10). Principle (11) then links undergoer and MS, by default, because actor is unavailable. Actor, if present, is realized as an instrumental NP. This is also accomplished by a default co-occurrence (see Section 4).[5]

---

[5] It follows from this characterization that Russian will have no passives in which the dative (or other oblique) NP of a corresponding active sentence is subject, because with a ditransitive verb there will always be choices higher than Locative (including Goal) on the hierarchy for both actor and undergoer. This is correct. For example, an active sentence like (i) can have a passive in which the accusative NP of the active sentence appears as subject of the passive sentence as in (ii), but it cannot have a corresponding passive in which the dative NP of the active sentence is subject of the passive sentence as in (iii).

(i)   *Mal'čik dal mne   knigi.*
       boy-nom gave me-DAT books-acc
       'The boy gave me the books.'   (Schaarschmidt, 1968, p. 88)

(ii)   *Mne byli dany   knigi   mal'čikom.*
       me-dat was given + pl books-nom boy-inst
       'The books were given to me by the boy.'

(iii) **Ja   byl dan knigu   mal'čikom.*
       I-nom was given books-acc boy-inst
       'I was given the books by the boy.'

So-called impersonal dative constructions of the type given in (4) are characterized as having no MS. A lexical entry for a predicate appearing in an impersonal dative "inversion" construction such as that in (4) will have the form given in (13), where both TRs are lexically specified as co-occurring with NPs with nonnominative cases, indicated in the notation by vertical lines linking these levels. I assume that the Experiencer of a predicate of this type is thematically a kind of Location, following Anderson (1971).[6]

(13)   _____ Location,   Theme
                        | |
                       NP   NP
                   [dative] [accusative]

Since both arguments are lexically linked, neither TR is candidate for default MS linking (see Schwartz (1986) for an account of dative inversion constructions with a morphological subject).

A lexical entry for possessive predicates is given in (14).

(14)   _____ Location, Theme
                        |
                       PP
                      [+u]

The Possessor of a possessive predicate is lexically linked, as in the dative inversion constructions, in this case to the locative prepositional phrase expressing 'location at, near.' Nothing more need be stipulated about the case of the Possessor NP, since the preposition u will be specified to govern an NP with genitive case in all its uses, as seen, for example, in its concrete locative use in a sentence like (15).

(15)   *Ona stojala   u okna.*
         she was standing near window-gen
         'She was standing near the window.'   (Maltzoff 1984, p. 57)

It will have the lexical specification given in (16).

(16)   *u:* _____   NP
                    [genitive]

Nothing more need be stipulated about the case of the Theme, either, which, by default, is specified to co-occur with MS. Other lexically specified

---

[6] This is a relatively traditional analysis of affective verbs which take dative Experiencer, as discussed in Vendryes (1931), for example. Kurylowicz (1964) claims that the origin of the IE dative is from a concrete locative inflection.

co-occurrence restrictions between TRs and oblique cases are handled in a similar manner, as in Schwartz (1986).

Returning to the issue of reflexive control, we see that the potential antecedent must be either actor or MS. These two relations coincide in some cases, as is the case with the antecedent in (1) and (7). In other instances, only one or the other relation is present: in (2), only MS; in (4), (5), or (6), where there is no nominative, only actor. This second situation arises when all overt arguments of the verb are lexically specified as co-occurring with NPs with oblique cases features. Both actor and MS are present in (3), but only actor is a plausible controller, since only the animate actor, but not the inanimate MS, is compatible with the benefactive interpretation of the *dlja* phrase. In (8), there is neither an actor nor an MS, hence the ungrammaticality.[7]

The question naturally arises of what will happen when both actor and MS are present and both are plausible controllers of the reflexive (i.e., both are animate). This is the situation, for example, in sentence (17).

(17)   *Boris   byl otpravlen Annoj k svoim roditeljam.*
       B-nom was sent   A-inst to self's parents
       'Boris$_i$ was sent by Anna$_j$ to his$_i$/?*her$_j$ parents.'

Perlmutter (1982) reports that in sentences like (17), in relational grammar terms, either only the final subject controls reflexivization, or, for some speakers, either the initial or final subject controls. In the current analysis, this is expressed in terms of actor and MS.

The multistratal analysis thus requires a statement giving precedence to the final subject for speakers who interpret control as by the final subject only (no restriction is necessary for speakers who allow both interpretations). The monostratal analysis also incorporates such a statement, by giving precedence to the MS. (See Rappaport, 1986, and Timberlake, 1979, for a discussion of other instances where both MS and actor are present.)

In the present account of Russian reflexives, the surface case variation in controllers is attributed to the permissible co-occurrence of TRs and NP case features, while the range of controllers is actually restricted to MS and actor. That the monostratal model still incorporates more than one level allows it to capture multilevel generalizations in terms of statements of co-occurrence without the further assumption of strata within levels.

---

[7] Although the dative NP is the only overt NP present in (8), it cannot be undergoer because the thematic structure of the verb will contain the roles Agent (i.e., the teller), Theme (i.e., that which is told), and Locative (i.e., the receiver of the information), and, following the actor/undergoer hierarchy in (10), Agent will be selected as actor and Theme as undergoer. This brings out a crucial feature of the analysis: actor/undergoer linking is to thematic relations in the thematic structure of the lexical entry of a verb; it is independent of whether these relations are overtly manifested.

3. -*SJA* CONSTRUCTIONS

In this section I examine constructions in which the morpheme -*sja* is attached to a verbal stem. These constructions include reflexives and reciprocals, but their full range of functions is wider than this and is similar, though not identical, to that of the Romance reflexive clitics, as noted in B. Levin (1985). These constructions are discussed by Babby (1975) and B. Levin (1985), both of whom refer crucially to two syntactic strata, so these constructions are of particular interest to proponents of a monostratal syntax. The data presented in this section are taken from their accounts, unless otherwise noted.

3.1. Distribution of -*sja*

The morpheme -*sja* attaches to verbs in a number of different constructions. It takes the form of either -*sja* or -*s'*.

We first consider -*sja* in active/passive pairs with imperfective verbs, as in (18) and (19).[8] The accusative NP in the active sentences alternates with a nominative NP in the passives, and the active nominative NP alternates with an instrumental NP in the passive.[9] In the -*sja* construction in the (b) sentences, the cases are nominative and instrumental, while in the (a) sentences

---

[8] Although Babby (1975) and Schaarschmidt (1968) both cite-*sja* passives with agent phrases, some native speakers of Russian find these sentences acceptable only as agentless passives: I have thus represented them with the agent phrases in parentheses.

[9] Schaarschmidt (1968) reports that the imperfective (− *sja*) passive is restricted to constructions in which the MS is inanimate, as demonstrated in the contrastive pair of sentences in (i) and (ii), where (ib) is claimed to be unacceptable because the MS *rebenok* 'child' is animate, but (iib) is claimed to be acceptable because the MS *avtomobil'* 'car' is inanimate.

(i) a. *Njanja   umyvaet   rebenka.*
        nanny-nom wash-imperf child-acc
        'The nanny washes the child.'   (Schaarschmidt, 1968, p. 31)
     b.*Rebenok   umyvaetsja   njanej.*
        child-nom wash-imperf-*sja* nanny-inst
        'The child is being washed by the nanny.'

(ii) a. *Nanja   umyvaet   avtomobil'.*
        nanny-nom wash-imperf car-acc
        'The nanny washes the car.'   (Schaarschmidt, 1968, p. 31)
     b. *avtomobil' umyvaetsja   njanej.*
        car-nom   wash-imperf-*sja* nanny- inst
        'The car is being washed by the nanny.'

Native speakers were less clear on this point, however, in part, apparently, because of the choice of the verb *umyvaetsja*, which they did not accept with an inanimate Theme. If this restriction does hold, it may be because, with an animate subject, the reflexive interpretation of − *sja* overrides the passive interpretation, a possibility suggested to me by Ronald Feldstein.

the cases are nominative and accusative. Note that (19c) demonstrates that the nominative NP controls verb agreement.

(18) a. *My   zakryvali   ètu dver'.*
          we-nom close-imperf this door-acc
          'We were closing this door.'
      b. *Èta dver' zakryvalas'   (nami).*
          door-nom close-imperf-*sja* (us-inst)
          'This door was being closed by us.'

(19) a. *Rabočie   stroili   dom.*
          workers-nom built-imperf house-acc
          'The workers were building the house.'
                                        (Schaarschmidt, 1968, pp. 84–85)
      b. *Dom   stroilsja   (rabočimi).*
          house-nom built-imperf-*sja* (workers-inst)
          'The house was being built by the workers.'
      c. *Domá   stroilis'.*
          house-nom-pl built-imperf-pl-*sja*
          'The houses were being built.'

This construction is limited to imperfective verbs.[10] There is, for example, no perfective equivalent of (18b), as shown in (20). Rather, the periphrastic passive, (21), is used in the perfective.

(20) **Èta dver'   zakrylas'   (nami).*
      this door-nom was-closed-*sja* (us-inst)
      'This door was closed by us.'

(21) *Èta dver'   byla zakryta nami.*
      this door-nom was closed   us-inst
      'This door was closed by us.'

-*sja* also participates in FLIP CONSTRUCTIONS (Schaarschmidt, 1968; Babby, 1975), as illustrated in (22) and (23). The accusative NP in the (a) sentences alternates with the nominative NP in the (b) sentences, and the nominative NP in the (a) sentences alternates with the instrumental NP in the (b) sentences. -*sja* appears in (22b) and (23b), where the cases are nominative and instrumental, but not in (22a) and (23a), where the cases are nominative and accusative.

(22) a. *Menja očen' ogorčila ego neudača.*
          1-acc very upset   his failure-nom
          'His failure upset me very much.'

---

[10] The perfective or periphrastic passive is formed with the addition of a form of the copula verb and the participial inflection -*en*. See examples (2) and (3).

176 LINDA SCHWARTZ

b. *Ja   očen' ogorčilsja ego neudačej.*
   l-nom very upset-*sja* his failure-inst
   'I was very upset by/with his failure.'

(23) a. *Ego otvet   utešal   mat'.*
        his answer-nom comforted mother-acc
        'His answer comforted the mother.'

(Schaarschmidt, 1968, p. 103)

   b. *Mat'   utešsalas'   ego otvetom.*
      mother-nom comforted-*sja* his answer-inst
      'The mother was comforted by/with his answer.'

Although the flip constructions look quite similar to the imperfective passives given in (18) and (19), they do not share the same restrictions. First, flip constructions are not limited to imperfective aspect. They may occur in perfective aspect as well:

(24) a. *Naši knigi   zainteresujut soldat.*
        our books-nom will interest soldiers-acc
        'Our books will interest the soldiers.'

(Schaarschmidt, 1968, p. 103)

   b. *Soldaty   zainteresujutsja našimi knigami.*
      soldiers-nom will be interested our books-inst
      'The soldiers will be interested in our books.'

Second, the imperfective passives are formed from base verbs which have an associated Agent, while flip constructions are restricted to verbs whose base forms have an associated Experiencer (Locative). Affective verbs in flip constructions will have animate MSs, where the Experiencer appears in nominative case and controls verb agreement. Third, the Agent of an imperfective passive, if overt, is invariantly in the instrumental case. Although for the most part the Effector appears in the instrumental case in flip constructions, (25) and (26) show that this is not the only pattern. In (25b), dative case is required, and in (26b), the preposition *na* is required and governs an NP with locative case.

(25) a. *Strannyj eë kostjum   udivil   menja.*
        strange her costume-nom surprised me-acc
        'Her strange outfit surprised me.'   (Schaarschmidt, 1968, p. 114)

   b. *Ja   udivilsja   strannomu eë kostjumu.*
      l-nom surprised-*sja* stranger   her costume-dat
      'I was surprised at her strange outfit.'

(26) a. *Eë povedenie   ego   rasserdilo.*
        her behavior-nom him-acc angered
        'Her behavior angered him.'   (Schaarschmidt, 1968, p. 114)

b. *On   rasserdilsja   na eë povedenie.*
he-nom was angered-*sja* at her behavior-loc
'He was angry at her behavior.'

The morpheme -*sja* also occurs in a number of constructions in which it alternates with the object of a verb. It may alternate with a reflexive or reciprocal object, as in (27) and (28) respectively, or with an unspecified object, as in (29).[11] Babby observes that verbs of the object-deletable set are interpreted as involving habitual action and an implied animate accusative object.

(27) a. *Rebenok   umyl   sebja.*
         child-nom washed self-acc
         'The child washed himself.'
      b. *Rebenok   umylsja.*
         child-nom washed-*sja*
         'The child washed.'

(28) a. *Oni   vstretili drug druga.*
         they-nom met   each other-acc
         'They met each other.'
      b. *Oni   vstretilis'.*
         they-nom met-*sja*
         'They met.'

(29) a. *Naša sobaka   ne kusaet detej.*
         Our dog-nom neg bite   children-acc
         'Our dog doesn't bite children.'
      b. *Naša sobaka   ne kusaetsja.*
         our dog-nom neg bite-*sja*
         'Our dog doesn't bite.'

In another construction involving transitive verbs in which -*sja* is present in the inchoative/causative alternation, -*sja* appears in the inchoative. The nominative NP in the causatives in (30a) and (31a) is obligatorily absent in the corresponding inchoatives in (30b) and (31b), and the accusative NP in (30a) and (31a) corresponds to the nominative NP in (30b) and (31b).

[11] Babby (1975) claims that a certain class of verbs allows deletion of a specific object. Some verbs which belong to this class are *smorkat'/vysmorkat'* 'to blow (one's nose)' and *nesti/snesti jajca* 'to lay (eggs).' It is unclear whether these should be treated as members of the object-deletable set or as derived verbs. However, it would seem that these verbs, if members of the object-deletable set, are really no different from verbs which allow the deletion of unspecified objects, since it is the meaning of the verb itself which restricts the interpretation of an omitted object.

(30) a. *Rebenok   razbil   rjumku.*
          child-M-nom shattered-M wineglass-F-acc
          'The child shattered the wineglass.'
      b. *Rjumka   razbilas'   pri perevozke.*
          wineglass-F-nom shattered-F-*sja* during move
          'The wineglass shattered during the move.'

(31) a. *Anton   zakryl dver'.*
          Anton-nom closed door-acc
          'Anton closed the door'.
      b. *Dver'   zakrylas' (*Antonom)*
          door-nom closed   (Anton-inst)
          'The door closed (*by Anton).'

The last alternation involving transitive verbs that we consider has to do with word formation processes in which one of a number of prefixes is added to a transitive verb stem and -*sja* is added as a suffix to the stem. The example in (32) below involves $o(b'') + V + sja$ and is interpreted as 'excessive action.'

(32) a. *Rebenok   el bliny*
          child-nom ate blini-acc
          'The child ate blini.'
      b. *Rebenok   ob''elsja   (blinami).*
          child-nom overate-*sja* blini-inst
          'The child overate/gorged (on blini).'

Again, note that the form in which -*sja* occurs has the case pattern {nominative, instrumental} rather than {nominative, accusative}. These forms are termed DERIVED ANTIPASSIVES here, as the effect of the prefix + *sja* combination is to make the MS of a transitive verb into the MS of an intransitive verb and the accusative object of a transitive verb into an oblique object.

In addition to alternations involving transitive verbs, -*sja* also appears with some intransitives. These INHERENT REFLEXIVES have no alternative intransitive forms without -*sja*. The inherent reflexives include unaccusative verbs like *pojavit'sja* 'to appear,' *slučit'sja* 'to happen,' and *ostat'sja* 'to remain,' as well as unergative verbs like *ulibat'sja* 'to smile,' *smejat'sja* 'to laugh,' and *nadejat'sja* 'to hope.' These two classes of verbs pattern differently in terms of whether they allow the genitive of negation construction and other diagnostic tests for unaccusativity (see Pesetsky, 1982, for details). The sentences in (33) and (34) exemplify unaccusative and unergative, respectively.

(33) a. *Zvezdočka   pojavilas' na nebe.*
          little star-nom appeared in sky
          'A little star appeared in the sky.'   (adapted from Pesetsky, 1982)

  b. *Ni odnoj zvezdočki ne pojavilos' na nebe.*
  not one little star-gen neg appeared in sky
  'Not one little star appeared in the sky.'

(34) a. *Ljudi   v poezde ne ulibalis'.*
   people-nom in train neg smile-*sja*
   'People in the train don't smile.'
  b.**Ni odnogo čeloveka ne ulibalos' v poezde.*
   Not one man-gen neg smiled-*sja* in train
   'Not one man smiled in the train.'

Example (33) shows that unaccusative inherent reflexives pattern like other unaccusatives in allowing the genitive of negation, while (34) shows that unergative inherent reflexives pattern like other unergatives in disallowing it. The same is true for other unaccusative diagnostics.

 In summary, -*sja* occurs in the following constructions: imperfective passives, flip constructions, reflexive or reciprocal constructions, unspecified object constructions, derived inchoatives, derived antipassives, and inherent reflexives.

3.2. Multistratal Analyses

 Babby (1975) considers transitive sentences which alternate with -*sja* constructions but does not discuss either derived antipassives or intransitives. Babby's conclusion is that -*sja* is added to transitive verb stems in sentences from which the direct object NP has been either moved or deleted. Imperfective passives, as in (18) and (19), are derived by movement of the underlying object NP into a subject position that has been vacated by Agent Postposing. This triggers insertion of -*sja*. A similar analysis is given of inchoatives, as in (30) and (31), where subject position is assumed to be empty, and the underlying object again is moved into subject position. In flip constructions like (22) and (23), the analysis is that the subject position is empty in underlying structure and that either the underlying direct object or instrumental object may move into surface subject position. If the direct object moves, -*sja* insertion occurs.

 In examples where -*sja* sentences alternate with sentences with overt objects, as in (27)–(29), Babby assumes that the objects are deletable. The interpretation, or range of interpretations, of a specific objectless structure then depends on the type of verb (i.e., whether this interpretation will be reflexive, reciprocal, or unspecified).

 Although Babby does not treat intransitive sentences containing -*sja* in his analysis, sentences containing unaccusative verbs like those in (33) would initially seem to fall nicely into his analysis as well, under the assumption that these derive from underlying structures in which the single argument of the verb is an object rather than a subject. There are two problems with attempting to include them in this analysis, however. First, this would account only for unaccusative intransitives with -*sja* like (33), but would not account for the occurrence of -*sja* with unergative intransitives like (34), since the single argument for an unergative verb is assumed to be underlying subject as well as surface subject; in other words, there would be no object movement to trigger -*sja* insertion. Second, in Babby's analysis, -*sja* insertion should occur whenever an object is moved or deleted.[12] Therefore, if unaccusative intransitives fell under this analysis, we should expect that all unaccusative verbs should trigger -*sja* insertion, which is not the case, as shown in the examples in (35).

(35)   a.   *griby*   *zdes' ne rastut.*
            mushrooms-nom here neg grow-3pl   (Pesetsky, 1982, p. 43)
       b.   *Ni odnogo   gryba zdes'*   *ne rastet.*
            neg one-gen mushroom-gen here neg grow-3sg
            'Not one mushroom grows here.'   (adapted from Pesetsky, 1982)

The verb in (35) is demonstrably unaccusative in that it is acceptable with such unaccusative diagnostics as the genitive of negation, as shown in (35b); nonetheless, -*sja* does not occur here. However, Babby assumes that some instances of -*sja* should not be introduced transformationally; he cites, for example, nonalternating transitive verbs with -*sja* which can occur with accusative objects, such as *slušat'sja* 'obey' and *bojat'sja* 'fear.' Although he does not explicitly discuss the intransitive inherent reflexives, they might easily be handled in the same way as the transitive inherent reflexives in Babby's analysis, presumably with -*sja* as part of the lexical entry for these verbs.

B. Levin (1985), working in a government–binding framework, analyzes the morpheme -*sja* as being [− A], that is, blocking the assignment of accusative case by the verb to which it is attached. Thus, in any transitive d-structure containing an overt object, the presence of -*sja* will require that the object must move to a position where it can receive case—in these instances, subject position. Her analysis of examples like (18)–(19), (22)–(23), and (30)–(31) is then essentially the same as Babby's. In the case of transitive -*sja* structures without overt objects such as (27)–(29), the presence of an object is excluded because the verb assigns a θ-role to its subject. Therefore, the subject has to be present in d-structure, which prevents an overt object from moving into an empty subject position and receiving case. This renders such structures ill formed according to the Case Filter if an object occurs, but well formed if there is no overt object. Levin does include in her discussion the intransitive verbs

---

[12] -*sja* insertion presumably does not occur in the derivation of perfective passives in this analysis because of the insertion of the passive marker. This point is not discussed in Babby (1975).

which invariantly take -*sja*, as in (33) and (34). This presents no problem for her account, since the presence of -*sja* is not triggered by object movement, as in Babby's account, but rather only entails that no overt accusative object may appear. This is consistent with the pattern for all intransitive verbs. However, Levin does not address the issue of word formation and why -*sja* attaches to intransitive verbs which are already [− A], such as (33).

Babby's and Levin's analyses are both multistratal, in that they make crucial reference to at least two strata of syntactic structure, and both involve movement of NPs from an underlying object position into subject position so that grammatical relations across strata are not invariant.

3.3. A Monostratal Analysis of -*sja*

It is possible to translate into a monostratal framework the spirit of the generalizations made in these multistratal accounts regarding the distribution of -*sja*. To show how this is done with transitive verbs requires a further elaboration of the type of lexical information and lexical processes available. It also requires some revision of assumptions stated in Section 2.

I assume that all transitive verbs have the TR structure given in (36), where TRx and TRy are linked to actor and undergoer by default principles referring to the hierarchy in (10), unless the specific lexical entry for a verb contains its own linkings.

(36)   _____ TRx TRy

I first present a preliminary analysis of the individual verb classes to highlight their similarities and differences. A more general revised analysis is then given.

We begin with an examination of the object deletable verbs like those in (27)–(29), repeated here as (37)–(39).

(37) a. *Rebenok   umyl   sebja.*
         child-nom washed self-acc
         'The child washed himself.'
      b. *Rebenok   umylsja.*
         child-nom washed-*sja*
         'The child washed.'

(38) a. *Oni   vstretili drug druga.*
         they-nom met   each other-acc
         'They met each other.'
      b. *Oni   vstretilis'*
         they-nom met-*sja*
         'They met.'

(39) a. *Naša sobaka ne kusaet detej.*
      our dog-nom neg bite children-acc
      'Our dog doesn't bite children.'
   b. *Naša sobaka ne kusaetsja.*
      our dog-nom neg bite-*sja*
      'Our dog doesn't bite.'

These verbs constitute a class, called V_D, that can tentatively be assumed to undergo the lexical process of object deletion. This has the effect on their TR structure given in (40).

(40)   OBJECT DELETION I: TR: undergoer = $\varnothing$
                          Morphology: V_D + *sja*

The notation used for this lexical operation is adapted from that used in lexical functional accounts, e.g., Bresnan (1982a). It differs significantly from the principles of LFG in referring to TRs rather than to the functional relations associated with verbs. The part of the process labeled MORPHOLOGY specifies the input verb class and the affix which is attached. The lexical process of Object Deletion thus specifies that the undergoer TR associated with the verb stem is not linked to any NP in the morphosyntax. Nothing more needs to be said about these structures. The actor will be linked by default to the MS, in conformance with (11).

In the case of derived antipassive verbs, we noted a pattern: The accusative NP in the nonderived form corresponds to an optional instrumental NP in the derived (der) form, as shown in example (32), repeated here as (41).

(41) a. *Rebenok   el bliny.*
      child-nom ate blini-acc
      'The child ate blini.'
   b. *Rebenok ob"elsja   (blinami).*
      child-nom overate-*sja* blini-inst
      'The child overate/gorged (on blini).'

I tentatively assume a class of rules having the schema in (42) to which a set of verbs V_{der} are subject.

(42)   ANTIPASSIVE I: TR: undergoer =   (undergoer)
                                              |
                                             NP
                                        [instrumental]
                          Morphology: PRE + V_{der} + *sja*

Here, the TR change is that the undergoer is specified as optional and linked to an instrumental NP in the morphosyntactic structure. The actor will be linked to MS by default and the undergoer, if present, can be linked to the NP with instrumental case.

A rule of "inchoativization" is assumed to operate on a class of verbs which is here symbolized as V_C—verbs whose basic form is causative, as illustrated in (30) and (31), repeated here as (43) and (44).

(43) a. *Rebenok   razbil   rjumku.*
      child-m-nom shattered-m wineglass-f-acc
      'The child shattered the wineglass.'
    b. *Rjumka   razbilas'   pri perevozke.*
      wineglass-f-nom shattered-f-*sja* during move
      'The wineglass shattered during the move.'

(44) a. *Anton   zakryl dver'.*
      Anton-nom closed door-acc
      'Anton closed the door.'
    b. *Dver'   zakrylas' (*Antonom).*
      door-nom closed   (Anton-inst)
      'The door closed (*by Anton).'

Example (45) is a first approximation of the effect this rule will have on TR structure.

(45) INCHOATIVIZATION I: TR: actor $= \varnothing$
                    Morphology: $V_C + sja$

These derived inchoative verbs, then, will be specified as having no overt actor. The undergoer will be MS by default.

Other transitive alternations to be accounted for are imperfective passives and flip constructions. Separate rules need to be specified for these classes of verbs, however, because of the different conditions on their occurrence in -*sja* constructions.

We first examine the flip verbs such as those in (22) and (23), (25) and (26), repeated here as (46)–(49).

(46) a. *Menja očen' ogorčila ego neudača.*
      1-acc   very upset   his failure-nom
      'His failure upset me very much.'
    b. *Ja   očen' ogorčilsja ego neudačej.*
      1-nom very upset-*sja* his failure-inst
      'I was very upset by/with his failure.'

(47) a. *Ego otvet   utešal mat'.*
      his answer-nom comforted mother-acc
      'His answer comforted the mother.'

    b. *Mat'*   *utešalas'*   *ego otvetom.*
       mother-acc comforted-*sja* his answer-inst
       'The mother was comforted by/with his answer.'

(48)   a. *Strannyj eë kostjum*   *udivil*   *menja.*
       strange her costume-nom surprised me-acc
       'Her strange outfit surprised me.'

    b. *Ja*   *udivilsja*   *strannomu eë kostjumu.*
       l-nom surprised-*sja* strange   her costume-dat
       'I was surprised at her strange outfit.'

(49)   a. *Eë povedenie*   *ego*   *rasserdilo.*
       her behavior-nom him-acc angered
       'Her behavior angered him.'

    b. *On*   *rasserdilsja*   *na eë povedenie.*
       he-nom was angered-*sja* at her behavior-loc
       'He was angry at her behavior.'

This class can be identified by the TR structure given in (50); it will be represented as V_F.

(50)   ____ Effector Experiencer

The Effector is identified by the actor/undergoer hierarchy in (10) as actor, and Experiencer (Locative) is identified as undergoer. The rule in (51) is a first approximation of Flip.

(51)   FLIP I: TR Level: actor =   (actor)
                                  |
                               NP
                          [Oblique]
           Morphology: V_F + *sja*

For verbs which require a case other than instrumental for the actor, or require the presence of a specific preposition in this construction, that information is included in the lexical entry for the verb. Thus a verb like that in (46), which has actor in instrumental case, will have a lexical entry of the type shown in (52), with instrumental being specified by default, while a verb like that in (48), which governs dative case on the actor, will have a lexical entry like that in (53), where dative is specified in the lexical entry.

(52)   ____ (actor)   undergoer
                     |
                  NP
              [oblique]

(53) _____ (actor) undergoer
              |
             NP
          [dative]

The imperfective passives differ from the flip verbs in appearing only in the imperfective aspect. These are illustrated in (18) and (19), repeated here as (54) and (55).

(54) a. *My   zakryvali   ètu dver'*
        we-nom close-imperf this door-acc
        'We were closing this door.'
     b. *Èta dver'   zakryvalas'   (nami)*
        this door-nom close-imperf-*sja* 'us-inst)
        'This door was being closed by us.'

(55) a. *Rabočie   stroili   dom.*
        workers-nom built-imperf house-acc
        'The workers were building the house.'
     b. *Dom   stroilsja   (rabočimi).*
        house-nom built-imperf-*sja* (workers-inst)
        'The house was being built by the workers.'

The lexical process of passivization is given its first approximation in (56).

(56)   IMPERFECTIVE PASSIVE I: TR: Agent = (Agent)[13]
                                             |
                                            NP
                                         [oblique]
                          Morphology: V_{IMP} + *sja*

The Agent, if present, is specified to co-occur with oblique case (instrumental by default), and undergoer will then be MS.

Having now discussed all cases: object deletable verbs, derived antipassives, inchoatives, imperfective passives, and flip constructions, we can see strong similarities among them. The object-deletable verbs and the derived anti-passive verbs undergo processes which remove the undergoer as an obligatory syntactic argument. They differ in whether it can appear syntactically at all: The object-deletable verbs do not allow it, while the derived antipassives allow it to appear as an oblique. The relation between the inchoatives and the viewpoint-shift constructions of imperfective passive and flip is exactly

---

[13] Schaarschmidt claims that all Russian passives are restricted to verbs with an Agent. The restriction can be easily represented, as it is in (56) and (62), but is not crucial here. If it is not represented, Agent can be replaced by actor.

parallel, in that they both undergo processes which remove the actor as an obligatory syntactic argument. Again, they differ in whether it can appear syntactically at all: Inchoatives do not allow it, while the viewpoint-shift constructions allow it to appear as an oblique. All of these processes, then, share the property of "demoting" one of the core macroroles associated with a transitive verb. I would claim, then, that -*sja* marks precisely this. This can be specified as a correspondence between the thematic structure of the base verb and thematic structure of the derived verb, as in (57).

(57) $V: \_\_ TR_1, \ldots TR_n = [[V]\ sja_V]: \_\_ TR_1, \ldots TR_{n-1}$, where $n > 1$

This statement is to be interpreted as follows: a base verb with TRs linked to default-specified arguments can have a corresponding -*sja* form where one less TR is linked to a default-specified argument. The number of default-specified TR-to-argument linkings is required to be greater than one because -*sja* does not combine with intransitive verbs to produce impersonal verbs. The default-specified core arguments are nominative and accusative (for actor and undergoer respectively; instrumental is a default only for oblique). Thus, -*sja* affixation results in blocking the linking by default of a TR to a nominative or accusative NP. In the rest of this section, I explore some of the implications of this claim.

First, the lexical rules given in (40), (42), (45), (51), and (56) are no longer necessary. It is necessary, however, to include in the lexicon for each individual class of verbs information about (a) which macrorole cannot be linked by default, and (b) whether that macrorole can have an alternative manifestation as an oblique-case-marked NP (and if so, which oblique case feature can co-occur with the macrorole). The information in (a) is equivalent to the kind of information which would be encoded into the d-structure in a GB analysis of the kind used by Levin. For example, in the case of the object-deletable verbs, the d-structure would have no overt object, while in the case of in-choativization, the d-structure would have no overt subject. The information in (b) would also be necessary lexical information within a GB framework in order to distinguish, for example, object-deletable verbs (where the TR assigned to an object in the base verb can never appear in the derived verb associated with an oblique NP) from antipassives (where the TR assigned to an object in the base verb may appear in an oblique case NP); recall that a parallel correspondence occurs for inchoatives as compared to flip verbs or imperfective passives. For my analysis, I assume that this kind of information is represented in the lexicon in the form of statements of the type given in (58)–(62). For the sake of parallelism with the previous lexical rules, I re-tain the same terminology. However, these statements should not be taken as rules, but rather as statements of generalizations about thematic structure, ranging over classes of lexical items.

(58) OBJECT DELETION II: $[[V_D] sja_V]$: __ undergoer $= \varnothing$

(59) ANTIPASSIVE II: $[[PRE[V]_V] sja_V]$: __ undergoer
$$|$$
NP
[oblique)

(60) INCHOATIVIZATION II: $[[V_C] sja_V]$: __ undergoer $= \varnothing$

(61) FLIP II: $[[V_F] sja_V]$: __ (actor)
$$|$$
NP
[oblique]

(62) IMPERFECTIVE PASSIVE II: $[[V_{IMP}] sja_V]$: (Agent)
$$|$$
NP
[oblique]

Another implication of this characterization of *-sja* is that it precludes the possibility of incorporating the inherent reflexives into the analysis, because the presence of *-sja* prevents the default linking of a core argument, and that is not what happens with the intransitive verbs which are inherent reflexives. Rather, their single core argument is still syntactically present, and default linked to nominative case. This is not an undesirable result, as the inherent reflexives differ from the other verb classes examined here in that they are the only ones which do not exhibit an alternation between a base verb and a *-sja* inflected verb (i.e., only the *-sja* form exists). Because of this difference, there is no reason to assume that an analysis of the other classes should extend to them.

Turning now from the issue of *-sja*, we consider the formulation of the lexical specification of perfective passives, parallel to the lexical specifications for verbs with *-sja* inflection:

(63) PERFECTIVE PASSIVE: $[[V_{PER}] EN_V]$: __ (Agent)
$$|$$
NP
[oblique]

The Agent is lexically specified to co-occur with oblique case. Nothing more needs to be specified for Agent, as the default for oblique case is instrumental. Comparing the lexical specification for the perfective passive in (63) to that of the imperfective passive in (62), we see that they differ only in the class of verbs (perfective vs. imperfective) and their morphology (-*en* vs. -*sja*).

Some further clarification is required concerning the operation of the default-linking rules as they are used in this model. Thus far the discussion implicitly assumes that these rules operate obligatorily. To derive the obligatory effect, it is possible to incorporate a case filter, something like (64), similar in spirit to that used in GB:

(64)   CASE FILTER: All overt, nonpleonastic NPs must be assigned a case
            feature.

Even with some kind of case filter, however, an additional specification is necessary to derive the correct application of the default-linking rules. This can be seen, for example, in a sentence like (30), repeated here as (65), where there is no actor, so the undergoer can be linked by default to nominative case if selected as morphological subject.

(65)   a. *Rebenok   razbil   rjumku.*
            child-m-nom shattered-M wineglass-f-acc
            'The child shattered the wineglass.'
        b. *Rjumka   razbilas'   pri perevozka.*
            wineglass-f-nom shattered-f-*sja* during move
            'The wineglass shattered during the move.'

If this default linking (i.e., specifically MS linking) is not obligatory, however, nothing would prevent the undergoer from being linked to accusative case by default, thereby satisfying the case filter but producing the ungrammatical sentence in (66).

(66)   **rjumku   razbilosja*
            wineglass-f-acc shattered-n-sg

To prevent this situation, we could establish a precedence among the default linkings. This is the approach taken in Section 2.2, which states that the default linking for undergoer is to accusative case only when undergoer is not selected as MS. The resultant effect is of first linking a core macrorole with MS (nominative case) and then linking any unlinked undergoer to accusative case. An alternative, which would not require such a precedence statement, is to assume, following Levin, that -*sja* is [− A], which would prevent the default linking of any TR to an accusative NP. Then the presence of -*sja* in an example like (64) requires that undergoer can only be linked to MS.[14] I have no reason at this point to favor either alternative.

----

[14] At least some nonalternating transitive verbs with − *sja* would have to be assumed to not have this feature, because Babby (1975) cites cases of some verbs with − *sja* which do have accusative objects, such as *slušat'sja* 'obey' (colloquial) and *bojat'sja* 'fear' (nonstandard).

4. CONCLUSION

In this article I have tried to show that a monostratal syntactic account which specifies linkings between thematic relations and NPs with case features in a syntactic representation can accommodate certain generalizations which in other frameworks have seemed to provide support for the assumption of a multistratal syntax. In particlar, I have presented a unified account of the distribution in Russian of the affix-*sja* when it attaches to alternating transitive verbs. I have provided a general characterization of the effect of the presence of this affix on the thematic structure of such verbs; specifically, the presence of -*sja* prevents the default linking of a core argument to a case-marked NP. Differences in the manifestation and interpretation of individual verb classes are then claimed to be properties of those classes rather than properties of -*sja*. The significance of this is that the theoretical vocabularies which I have used here (thematic relations, case features, syntactic representations) are also necessarily included in the multistratal frameworks, but the additional multistratal assumption is not included in the monostratal account which I have presented here. This raises the question of the necessity and desirability of assuming a multistratal syntax. While the analyses of other natural language phenomena besides those examined here have claimed or assumed to require a multistratal syntax, it seems reasonable to investigate these multistratal analyses further to determine whether a multilevel framework with a monostratal syntax can account for these phenomena in an equally general way.

ACKNOWLEDGMENTS

I am grateful to Valdimir Aptekar, Yuri Bregel, Grev Corbett, Ronald Feldstein, and Louise Hammer for helping me with points of grammar and orthography; to Grev Corbett and Wendy Wilkins for providing me with some helpful references; to Stan Dubinsky, Steven Lapointe, Gerald Sanders, and Wendy Wilkins for their very valuable comments on an earlier draft; and to Louise Hammer and Steve Franks for a very close reading of the manuscript.

THEMATIC STRUCTURE AND REFLEXIVIZATION

WENDY WILKINS

Department of English
Arizona State University
Tempe, Arizona 85287

1. INTRODUCTION

In this article I suggest that the linguistic function of thematic relations is broader than often realized in generative studies.[1] I mention specifically the linguistic function of thematic relations because, following Culicover and Wilkins (1984), I assume that thematic roles have a dual status. They form an integral part of the definition of particular acts and states and as such are components of the mental representation of objects and concepts. This is the defining function of the thematic roles; it crucially involves the content and definition of the role labels. This defining function of roles, involved in the definition of concepts, is independent of the theory of grammar, as is the cognitive capacity for individuating acts or states.

---

[1] The analysis presented here is meant to be compatible with the locality theory of my joint work with Peter Culicover. The definition of r-structure and the conditions of completeness and distributedness were originally proposed in Culicover and Wilkins (1984) and used in Culicover and Wilkins (1986). This is not meant to implicate Culicover in what is presented here, although some of the issues addressed have naturally come up in our conversations and his input has been valuable in shaping my own thinking in a number of relevant areas.

Syntax and Semantics, Volume 21
Thematic Relations

In their linguistic capacity, thematic roles are components of a level of grammatical interpretation. Both the specific semantic content of particular roles and the domain in which the roles are represented turn out to be relevant for the explanation of certain strictly linguistic phenomena. The distribution of the reflexive anaphor is one such phenomenon.[2]

The theory of reflexivization I pursue here adheres to a strong version of the autonomy thesis (see particularly Hale *et al.*, 1977; Culicover and Rochemont, 1983; and Culicover, this volume). On this view, because reflexivization necessarily involves semantic interpretation (often discussed as "coreference"), an explanation in terms of semantic notions would be more parsimonious, and thus more highly valued, than one that relies on the syntactic order or hierarchical arrangement of constituents. Thematic structure is the aspect of semantic interpretation that is relevant to the distribution of reflexives.

2. R-STRUCTURE

I postulate, without argument, a level of thematic structure. For the purposes of the analysis, it is irrelevant whether thematic structure exists as an autonomous level, or whether it forms part of some broader aspect of semantic interpretation, say logical form. It is also irrelevant to the issues at hand whether it is formed by its own independent rules of combination or by a mapping from some other level, e.g., lexical or syntactic structure. Finally, thematic structure might be derivable from either conceptual structure (see Jackendoff, 1983, 1987) or from verb entailments (Ladusaw and Dowty, this volume). The important point is that, in a derivation, there will be a representation of the assignment of roles to individuals within the domain of each role-assigning entity;[3] and the rules of grammar will be able to refer to this representation.

Let us take thematic structure to have the basic characteristics of r(ole)-structure.

---

[2] Much of what is said here is also directly relevant for the reciprocal anaphor (*each other*) in English. I assume, however, that each lexical iterm has its own distributional characteristics, and in fact must be learned independently. (See relevant discussion of the lexical learning hypothesis in Borer, 1984, 1985; Wexler and Chien, 1985; Wexler and Manzini, 1987; and Manzini and Wexler 1987.) Therefore it is not surprising that distributional differences are found among anaphors even in the same language.

[3] More accurately, roles are assigned to representations of individuals. Thematic structure is a linguistic construct, not an aspect of the real world.

(1)   The R-STRUCTURE is a set of triples $\langle i, T, k \rangle$ where for each triple, i is the index of an NP, T is the set of thematic roles $\{t, t', \ldots\}$ assigned to i, and k is the index of the domain on which T is defined.

As indicated in the definition, r-structures are comprised of triples containing an index, a set of roles, and a domain label. The triples are unordered and there is no indication of hierarchical constituent structure. R-structure is not defined in terms of syntactic primitives; it is not a syntactic level.

Example r-structures, simplified somewhat for the sake of illustration, are given in (2).[4] For the sake of expository convenience, a lexical item with a subscript is used to indicate a thematic domain, and a name is used to indicate a referential index.[5]

(2)   a. *John fell.*
          John, {Theme}, $fall_k$
       b. *Mary sold John a car.*
          Mary, {Source, Agent}, $sell_k$,
          John, {Goal}, $sell_k$,
          a car, {Theme, Patient}, $sell_k$
       c. *Sara ate the carrot raw.*
          Sara, {Agent}, eat_k,
          the carrot, {Patient}, eat_k,
          the carrot, {Theme}, raw_l

As the r-structures in (2) show, not only verbs assign thematic roles. Adjectives and event-related nouns are members of the class of role-assigners.[6] Each role assigner defines a thematic domain (a set of triples) at r-structure.

---

[4] There is ample evidence that verbs must be lexically decomposed for an adequate semantic representation. (See especially Jackendoff 1972, 1983, 1987, and Rappaport and Levin, this volume.) Because this lexical decomposition is not directly relevant to the account of reflexivization, r-structures are simplified, with the role assigners treated as single units.

[5] Notice that, as (2b) illustrates, there are cases where an index has more than a single role in a given domain. This is permitted when each is from a different set of roles (see Culicover and Wilkins, 1984, 1986; Wilkins, 1987a). There are minimally two sets. The first contains the perceptual roles (earlier called EXTENSIONAL) of Source, Goal, Location, and Theme. The event roles, the second set (INTENSIONAL), include Agent, Patient, Instrument, etc.

[6] Hellan (1986) adopts Jespersen's (1968) term NEXAL HEAD to indicate the class of role assigners. Nexal heads are verbs, adjectives, and nouns with verbal or adjectival stems. This definition needs to be expanded somewhat to include role-assigning nouns that do not happen to have related verbs or adjectives. *Messages*, as in (4), is such a noun.

In order to make the case for r-structure as the appropriate level for the account of reflexivization, I take the following examples as representative of the core phenomena to be explained.

(3) a. *Ben$_i$ saw a snake near {him$_i$/ *himself$_i$}.*
     b. *Ben$_i$ sent a letter to {*him$_i$/ himself$_i$}.*
     c. *Ben$_i$ put the blanket over {?him$_i$/ himself$_i$}.*

(4) *Jill puts messages to {a. herself/ b. her} in the drawer.*

Most syntactic theories of anaphora, such as many within government–binding theory, predict complementarity in the syntactic distribution of anaphors and pronouns. It is not obvious, however, that the syntactic relation between the antecedent and the NP contained in the PP in (3a) differs from that in (3b). Perhaps a structural distinction could be drawn to distinguish adjunct PPs, as in (3a), from argument PPs, as in (3b). This argument/adjunct distinction, while often difficult to determine (viz., optional arguments), might be sufficient to distinguish these cases in terms of the height of attachment of the PP. Or perhaps certain prepositions, but not others, define small clauses, so that this is the structural difference between (3a) and (3b). Either of these sorts of account, however, would run into difficulties in cases like (3c), where either the anaphor or the pronoun is apparently well formed. A configuration-based syntactic account of (3c) would have to maintain that it is structurally ambiguous, just to account for the reflexivization and pronominalization facts.

Sentences like (4), originally used by Bach and Partee (1980) to argue for the insufficiency of configurational theories of anaphora, present a different sort of problem for a syntax-based theory. Notice that (4a) involves "messages from Jill to herself" whereas (4b) could mean "messages from anyone to Jill." In (4) (as compared to (3c)) the choice of anaphor or pronoun is keyed to a meaning difference. The semantic interpretation must take into account the source of *messages*. Importantly, this source is not represented overtly in the syntax. Of course the syntax could be "enriched" in this case so as to include a nonovert PRO specifier (subject) of the NP which could be interpreted as the Source. Such an analysis would be problematic, however, where NPs have overt specifiers, as in *Jill put yesterday's messages to {herself/her} in the drawer* (see Williams, 1985, for arguments against PRO in NP). The analysis that follows makes no use of PRO in NP (see Culicover and Wilkins, 1984, for arguments against PRO in S).

Aside from the theoretical issue of the status and interpretation of the autonomy thesis, a strictly syntactic account of reflexivization would seem to be artificial in light of data such as (3) and (4).[7] The extent to which an r-

---

[7] This is not meant to say that a syntactic account could not be devised. See Culicover (this volume) on notational devices to encode information from one component into another.

structure account of these data is descriptively well motivated makes the a priori case for a strict interpretation of the autonomy thesis that much stronger.

3. ROLE ASSIGNMENT AND CONDITIONS ON R-STRUCTURE

Let us assume, then, that the distribution of the reflexive anaphor is defined over the thematic domain. The correct generalization can be stated as a locality condition on r-structure, as in (5).

(5)   A reflexive anaphor and its antecedent must occur in the same thematic domain.[8]

Recall that in r-structure each triple contains a k, an indication of the thematic domain. Where the anaphor and the antecedent have the same k (indicated by a lexical item with a subscript), they are in the same domain. Assuming that reflexives are inherently (i.e., lexically) nonreferential, the assignment of a thematic role to a reflexive would result in an r-structure triple for domain k containing a T (a set of thematic roles), but lacking an i (a referential index). All things being equal, a triple lacking i or T for some k would be incomplete and, hence, ungrammatical. This follows from the completeness condition:

The r-structure associated with a predicate and each individual element of it must be COMPLETE. Every required role must be assigned, each role must be assigned to a set of individuatable entities (individuals or identifiable acts), and each set of individuatable entities must have a role.[9]

The reflexive anaphor serves the special function of passing its role onto a referential phrase and thus preventing a completeness condition violation.

On this view, reflexivization is not explained in terms of coreferentiality per se. Instead, reflexivization affects the distribution of thematic roles, permitting

---

[8] I use the terms ANTECEDENT and ANAPHOR here because they are generally understood as relevant in discussions of reflexivization. Strictly speaking, however, these are terms that have no correlates in the thematic domain. As is shown below, the reflexive is not an anaphor with an antecedent, but rather is a term devoid of either thematic role or index that licenses multiple role assignment to some other term.

[9] This particular version of the completeness condition is from Wilkins (1986). It can be seen as a θ-criterion that holds between lexical and thematic structure.

two distinct roles (from the same set) to be associated with a particular referential index. This is exemplified by the r-structures in (6).

(6)   a. *Bill kicked himself.*
          Bill, {Agent}, *kick$_k$*,
          (∗)SELF, {Patient}, *kick$_k$*,
          ────────────────────────
          Bill, {Agent, Patient}, *kick$_k$*,
          SELF, {⌀}, *kick$_k$*
      b. *Bill kicked Fred.*
          Bill, {Agent}, *kick$_k$*,
          Fred, {Patient}, *kick$_k$*,
          ────────────────────────
          Bill, {Agent, Patient}, *kick$_k$*,
          *Fred, {⌀}, *kick$_k$*
      c. *Bill kicked him.*
          Bill, {Agent}, *kick$_k$*,
          him, {Patient}, *kick$_k$*,
          ────────────────────────
          Bill, {Agent, Patient}, *kick$_k$*,
          *him, {⌀}, *kick$_k$*

In (6a) the role which would normally be assigned to the object of *kick* is assigned to the nonreferring SELF. This role is then rewritten onto the triple associated with the referring expression *Bill*. The bottom lines in (6a) are the result of this reassignment of the Patient role. The horizontal line is simply meant to distinguish the algorithmic role assignment from the rewriting of the r-structure, taking into account the effect of SELF. The result of the rewriting in (6a) is grammatical because since SELF has no referential index (does not refer), it may have no thematic role. Compare this situation to (6b). Here, if both Agent and Patient are associated with *Bill*, there is a triple with an index (*Fred*) but without a set of roles (*T*). This results in a completeness violation. The same is true for (6c), assuming that pronouns, like names, have referential indices.

Another way in which ungrammaticality would result in examples like (6) is if the role assigned to SELF remained associated with it. This would mean a triple with a set of roles (*T*) but without a referential index (*i*). This again would be a completeness violation and is indicated by the (∗) in (6a).

As the grammatical (6a) illustrates, reflexivization is a special case of thematic role assignment, allowing two roles from the same class (see footnote 5) to be associated with a single referential index. In such a case the second role is linked (as indicated by the arrow) to the triple containing SELF. In the absence of such linking, two roles (such as Agent and Patient) associated with the same index would violate the distributedness condition:

The r-structure associated with a sentence must be DISTRIBUTED. A thematic role relative to a particular act or state cannot be assigned to more than one set of individuals and more than one thematic role of the same type cannot be assigned to the same individual or set of individuals.

SELF in r-structure licenses dual, or multiple,[10] role assignment. This is expressed as (7).

(7)   A thematic role t linked to SELF is rewritten $t\hat{\,}$.

What (7) then assures is than an r-structure such as (6a) is not filtered out by the distributedness condition. A linked role is considered to be distinct from all others for the purposes of distributedness. Example (6a) is thus correctly expressed as (6a'):

(6)   a'. Bill, {Agent, Patient$\hat{\,}$}, $kick_k$,
            SELF, {$\varnothing$}, $kick_k$.

This view of reflexivization, as a particular type of thematic role assignment, makes it natural that the relevant domain for determining the distribution of the anaphor is the thematic domain. The generalization in (5), to the effect that the reflexive and its antecedent have to be in the same domain, is actually an instantiation of the general case that thematic roles must be locally expressed, a basic premise of the locality theory (the theory within which the present analysis is couched). The scope of thematic role assignment (the local thematic domain) is determined by predicational structure (as in Culicover and Wilkins, 1986; Hellan, 1986; Maling, 1986; see also Rappaport and Levin, this volume; and Section 4). The distribution of reflexives is also influenced by predicational structure. The examples of (3), repeated here, illustrate.

(3)   a. *Ben$_i$ saw a snake near {him$_i$ / *himself$_i$}.*
       b. *Ben$_i$ sent a letter to {*him$_i$ / himself$_i$}.*
       c. *Ben$_i$ put the blanket over {?him$_i$ / himself$_i$}.*

In (3a) the PP *near him* is predicated of *a snake* and therefore *a snake* is Theme of *near*. At the same time *a snake* bears a role (Percept) in the domain of *see*. The important point here is that *Ben* and *him* do not bear roles in the same domain. That is, *see* assigns no role to the PP; the PP is a predicate and a separate thematic domain. In such cases a pronoun, but not an anaphor, may

---

[10] In principle, sentences are not limited to a single reflexive. P. Culicover (personal communication) points out cases like *John introduced himself to himself*.

be used.[11] In r-structure a reflexive in the *near* domain could not "transmit" its role (Location) onto the index associated with *Ben* in the *see* domain and, hence, **Ben saw a snake near himself.* The relevant r-structure is shown in (8).

(8)   *Ben,* {Experiencer}, *see$_k$*,
        a snake, {Percept}, *see$_k$*,
        a snake, {Theme}, *near$_l$*,
        *SELF, {Location}, *near$_l$*

The reflexive in (3a) and (8) would only be grammatical if the Location role assigned to it could be transmitted to some referring expression in the same thematic domain. (3b) is a case where reflexivization is grammatical. R-structure (9) illustrates.

(9)   *Ben,* {Source, Goal^}, *send$_k$*,
        a letter, {Theme}, *send$_k$*,
        SELF, {∅}, *send$_k$*

Example (3c) is particularly interesting. In the version with the reflexive, *put* is analogous to *send.* The curious fact is that the pronoun *him* under the coreferential reading is so much better in (3c) than in (3b). Assuming that this again has something to do with the thematic domain in r-structure, the right results can be obtained if in (3c) predication may optionally apply.

Exploring this possibility, let us make the reasonable assumption that all the (major) constituents in a sentence must participate some way in thematic interpretation. This would mean that a constituent would either be assigned a role or would itself be a role assigner. In a case like (3a), *near him* can be assigned no role because *see* is only a two-place predicate. If *near him* were not treated as a predicate, it would have no interpretation whatsoever. In a case like this, let us say that predication is obligatory; *near him* must be predicated of something.

This situation involving *see* is to be contrasted with (3c) with the verb *put.* Because *put* assigns three roles, its PP will have a thematic interpretation. It therefore need not be treated as a predicate. Any PP in the verb phrase, however, may be a predicate and this PP could be predicated of *the blanket.* The predication in this case is optional. For (3c) the result of this optional predication taking place is that *the blanket* is the Theme of *over.*[12] The PP is

---

[11] As in most recent work on pronouns and anaphora, the assumption here is that pronouns may have independent referential indices. Therefore thematic roles can be assigned to them without producing a completeness violation.

[12] In all cases, for the result of predication to be grammatical, there must be a plausible interpretation of the predication. In (3b) the *to*-PP could, in principle, be predicated of the object *a letter* if there were some semantic interpretation possible of a directional PP predicated of such an NP object.

both the Location of *put* and a predicator that assigns a role. Taking into account the thematic domain created by the optional predication, *Ben* and the object of *over* (*him*) would be in different domains, and hence the use of the pronoun instead of the reflexive anaphor.

The theory, as it now stands, would predict an alternation between the reflexive and the pronoun, with no difference in interpretation, wherever predication is optional. This situation arises in the well-known case of picture nouns. Consider (10).

(10) a. *Ben found* $\left\{\begin{array}{l} a\ picture\ of\ Max \\ a\ book\ about\ Max \end{array}\right\}$.

 b. $\left\{\begin{array}{l} A\ picture\ of\ Max \\ A\ book\ about\ Max \end{array}\right\}$ *was found.*

 c. $\left\{\begin{array}{l} A\ picture \\ A\ book \end{array}\right\}$ *was found* $\left\{\begin{array}{l} of\ Max \\ about\ Max \end{array}\right\}$.

 d. Ben_i *found* $\left\{\begin{array}{l} a\ picture\ of \\ a\ book\ about \end{array}\right\} \left\{\begin{array}{l} himself_i \\ him_i \end{array}\right\}$.

What the examples in (10b) and (10c) are meant to show is that an example like (10a) is structurally ambiguous. *Found* is a verb that allows an NP complement optionally followed by a PP. The PP [{*of*/*about*} *Max*] in (10a) either forms part of the NP object or is a PP dominated by the VP. The movement possibilities reflect these two alternatives. The coreference facts in (10d) also reflect these two alternatives. If *found* simply has an NP object, then there is only one thematic domain and *Ben* is the antecedent of *himself* within that domain. If the PP is a sister to the NP object, it must be predicated of that NP in order to be interpreted (as in *The picture is of Ben*). This means that there are two thematic domains and the appropriate form is *him* (there being no antecedent for *himself* in the second domain).

As support for the analysis in (10), compare (11).

(11) a. *Ben destroyed* $\left\{\begin{array}{l} a\ picture\ of\ Max \\ a\ book\ about\ Max \end{array}\right\}$.

 b. $\left\{\begin{array}{l} A\ picture\ of\ Max \\ A\ book\ about\ Max \end{array}\right\}$ *was destroyed.*

 c. *$\left\{\begin{array}{l} A\ picture \\ A\ book \end{array}\right\}$ *was destroyed* $\left\{\begin{array}{l} of\ Max \\ about\ Max \end{array}\right\}$.

 d. Ben_i *destroyed* $\left\{\begin{array}{l} a\ picture\ of \\ a\ book\ about \end{array}\right\} \left\{\begin{array}{l} himself_i \\ *him_i \end{array}\right\}$.

As is well known (see, e.g., Radford, 1981), *destroy* does not permit the NP versus NP PP alternation in its complement structure. The ungrammaticality of (11c) is due to the fact that only part of the NP constituent was moved. The fact that *destroy* does not permit a PP predicate in its VP correlates with the ungrammaticality of the coreferential pronoun in (11d). There is only one thematic domain and the reflexive must be used.[13]

This brings us to a discussion of thematically real, but syntactically null, arguments and their effect on reflexives. The examples in (12) illustrate ((12a) is a repetition of (4)).

(12) a. *Jill puts messages to {herself / her} in the drawer.*
      b. *Jill thinks messages to oneself should be kept in the drawer.*
      c. **Jill puts Fred's messages to herself in the drawer.*

Sentence (12a) is thematically complex, as discussed briefly in Section 2. The noun *messages*, as must be indicated in its lexical entry, defines a thematic domain (along the lines of Jackendoff's (1972) analysis of nominals) within which there is a Source and a Goal. The Source in this case is unspecified and indicated in r-structure by a variable:

(13) x, {Source}, *message$_k$*

This variable x is essentially the thematic (semantic) counterpart to PRO. Its presence in r-structure is necessitated by the completeness condition; *message* assigns Source and Goal and each must be assigned to some individuatable entity. The reflexive in (12a) is assigned Goal and the variable is assigned Source. Recall that the reflexive is grammatical only if it can transmit its role onto some referring expression (some index). In this case both Source and Goal will be associated with x, and ultimately with whatever set of individuals x is interpreted as referring to.

In (12a) x is controlled by *Jill* (there being no other relevant NP in the sentence). As (12b) shows, x can also have an arbitrary interpretation under certain circumstances, where it refers to an unspecified set of individuals.[14] In either case the result is the same for the reflexive: It transmits its role onto an index (even if that index is arbitrary). As (12a) and (12b) also indicate, there is a requirement (at least in English) of gender and number matching between the reflexive and the NP associated with the index that receives the multiple role assignment. The r-structures in this article abstract away from this issue of agreement by using the neutral term SELF.

[13] Evidently some speakers find (11c) grammatical. The prediction would then be that *him* may be coreferential in (11d) as well. Notice that no explanation is given here for why *destroy* (for some speakers) has such limited complement structure. It is simply the case that there is a correlation between this and the coreference possibilities. I also offer no explanation for why *him* is better when there is a longer VP: ?*Ben$_i$ destroyed a picture of him$_i$ that was on the dining room table.*

[14] The reflexive cannot simply pass its role onto an uncontrolled x, that is, there is no interpretation such as "$\emptyset$ sent messages to $\emptyset$." This is prevented by the completeness condition, because roles can only be associated with indices. In other words, x must be either controlled or assigned an *arb* interpretation.

Finally, the case of (12c) shows the result where the Source of *messages* is overt. In this situation the reflexive could only transmit its role onto the thematically local index and therefore *Jill puts Fred's messages to himself in the drawer* is grammatical. It is interesting to note that, as (12c) exemplifies, this approach to reflexives obviates the need for (any version of) the specified subject condition.

The analysis presented for the examples of (12) is required because *messages* must involve role assignment. If it is changed to some noun that does not necessarily define a thematic domain, then the interpretation of the reflexive is rather different:[15]

(14)   a. *Jill puts pictures of {herself / her} in the top drawer.*
       b. *Jill puts Fred's pictures of {*herself / himself} in the drawer.*

Picture, in the (14a) case, does not impose any thematic structure. The use of *herself* or *her* is determined just as in (10d), and the interpretation is the same for both. In (14b) the NP in the Specifier bears the Possessor (or Location) role (in the most usual interpretation). In this case *picture* does have a thematic domain and the reflexive functions accordingly (as for (12c)).

Along with (12) and (14) it is important to include examples like (15).

(15)   a. *Ben took a picture of himself.*
       b. *Ben took a picture of him.*
       c. *Ben wrote a book about himself.*
       d. *Ben wrote a book about him.*

In the examples of (15), both the pronoun and the anaphor are grammatical, but they cannot be used interchangeably. As Williams (1985) notices, when *picture* is used with the verb *take* (or *book* with *write*), a certain thematic structure is imposed on the representation of the NP. For *take a picture*, the Agent of *take* "is associated with the maker of the event" (Williams, 1985, p. 300). In these terms, the r-structure of (15a) would be as in (16).

(16)   *Ben*, {Agent}, *take$_k$*,
       a picture of SELF, {Theme}, *take$_k$*,
       Ben, {Agent, Patient^}, *picture$_l$*,
       SELF, {∅}, *picture$_l$*

For examples like (15), the Agent of the verb and the Agent of the nominal event must be identical. It is the verb that somehow imposes this thematic structure and therefore (15) is significantly different from (10d). Whether or not the PP in (15) is predicated of the NP *a picture*, the result for reflexivization is

[15] Here I am assuming that *picture* need not define a thematic domain. Alternatively, it might be that it defines a domain which may be empty. This distinction between *message* and *picture* is simply a lexical fact.

the same. *Him* versus *himself* will be determined by the Agent in the domain of *picture*, in this case, *Ben*. *Himself* can transmit its role, as shown in (16), to *Ben* in the domain of *picture*. *Him* may not do so (it is not a reflexive) and hence the Patient is distinct from the Agent for (15b). This analysis given in (16) captures the fact that semantically *take a picture* is interpreted as a unit (as with the verb *photograph*) and the reflexive facts work accordingly: *Ben photographed himself*, **Ben$_i$ photographed him$_i$.*[16]

As additional motivation for considering reflexivization in terms of thematic structure, consider the following examples (from Jackendoff, 1987).

(17)   *The box has books in it (*self).*

(18)   *Bill {brought / carried} some books with him (*self).*

(19)   *The list includes my name on it (*self).*

On first glance these sentences appear to be similar to (3a), where the PP is predicated of some NP other than the subject. If this were the case, then the impossibility of the reflexive would be due simply to the fact that the anaphor and the intended antecedent are in separate thematic domains. However, as Jackendoff correctly points out, the PPs in these examples cannot be interpreted as simple predications; they do not behave like ordinary predicates:

(20)   a. **What does the box have books in?*
        b. **Where does the box have books?*
        (Compare: *Who did Ben see the snake near?*
        Where did Ben see the snake?)

(21)   **Bill {brought / carried} some books with Tom.*
        (Compare: *Ben saw a snake near Tom.*)

(22)   *The list includes my name.* (= (19))
        (Compare: *Ben saw a snake. ≠ Ben saw a snake near him.*)

The PPs in sentences like (17)–(19) cannot be questioned, and therefore examples like (20a,b) are ungrammatical. Predicates can readily undergo *Wh*-Movement (but cf. Chomsky, 1981, p. 82). The ungrammaticality of (21) shows that the pronoun within the PPs in (17)–(19) cannot be replaced by any other NP. Finally, (22) illustrates that this type of sentence means essentially the same thing with or without the PP constituent.

---

[16] It is not really clear where a requirement such as that imposed by *take* on *picture* is to be represented in the grammar. Perhaps it can somehow be incorporated into the relevant lexical entries, or perhaps it is part of the entailments of the verb. This second alternative could have interesting consequences for the nature of r-structures. Perhaps they are to be derived, at least partially, from entailments. (See Ladusaw and Dowty, and the discussion by Jones, both in this volume.)

In these cases the PPs, rather than introducing a new predication, simply repeat part of the meaning of the main predication. In other words, the prepositional meaning is entailed by the verb. For instance, the verb *include* involves a Theme (*my name* in (19)) and a Location (*the list* in (19)). The PP *on it* repeats the Location role. It is this fact that is important for the account of reflexivization. SELF is not appropriate because there is no dual role assignment. Either the PP is not involved at all at r-structure, or it is represented but only repeats the assignment of a role. In either case, *the list* in (19) has only a single role (Location) and therefore no reflexive is involved.[17]

4. EXTERNAL ARGUMENTS

The importance of the thematic domain to reflexivization, discussed in terms of predication, has been recognized by grammarians working on Scandinavian languages. Predicational structure plays a prominent role in Hellan's analysis of Norwegian (Hellan, 1986, and earlier work) and Maling's of Icelandic (Maling, 1986), and this point of view can evidently be traced back to Diderichsen (1939) (see Introduction to Hellan and Christensen, 1986). Predicational structure distinguishes (23a) from (23b) in Norwegian.

(23)   a. *Vi gjorde Jon glad i   seg selv.*
           we made Jon fond of him self
           'We made Jon fond of himself.'
        b.**Vi fortalte Jon om   seg selv.*
           we told   Jon about him self
           'We told Jon about himself.'

The relevant generalization (from Hellan and Christensen, 1986, p. 7 is (24).

(24)   "*Sig* [*seg* in the Norwegian examples] is admitted only if it is
        contained in a constituent understood as PREDICATED of the
        antecedent."

By (24), the reflexive in (23a) can have *Jon* as its antecedent because it is contained in the constituent *glad i seg selv*, which is predicated of *Jon*. Since (23b) involves no predicational relationship between *Jon* and the PP, no reflexivization is possible.

The current analysis readily accounts for (23a) because *Jon* and the anaphor are both assigned roles in the domain of *glad*. Example (23b) is somewhat

---

[17] This does not explain why these "extra constituents" are permitted with these particular verbs. It is only meant to account for the reflexive facts.

more complicated. Clearly if no predication is involved, *Jon* and the anaphor
are not both assigned roles in the domain of *om*. If the PP headed by *om* is not
a predicate, then it must be interpreted as bearing some role in the main
predicational domain of *fortalte*. *Jon* also bears a role in that domain. In other
words, the reflexive and *Jon* both are assigned roles in the thematic domain of
fortalte. By (24), reflexivization is disallowed because *Jon* is not the antecedent
of a predication. But nothing so far in the current account precludes the
transmission of a role by a reflexive onto a referential index associated with an
object in syntactic structure. The only constraint is that the two entities occur
in the same thematic domain. And, in fact, the English equivalent of (23b) is
grammatical:

(25)   *We told John about himself.*

John and SELF must both be in the domain of *tell* for (25). Along with (25),
English also, of course, permits (26).[18]

(26)   *We told John about ourselves.*

What this difference between Norwegian and English points to is the need
for an enrichment of r-structure so that it indicates basic functional structure.
It must indicate which referential index (i in a triple) is to be associated with the
argument of each function, that is, the external argument of each predicate (as
in Williams, 1981). Following general conventions, external arguments are
indicated by underlining. The r-structure (27) is relevant for sentence (26).

(27)   <u>we</u>, {Source, Agent, Theme^}, *tell*$_k$
         John, {Goal}, *tell*$_k$,
         SELF, {$\emptyset$}, *tell*$_k$

In (27), *we* is the external argument. It also happens to correspond to the
subject NP in syntactic structure. "External argument" is not a syntactic
notion, however, and often is not a subject in the syntactic sense. In (23a), *Jon* is
the external argument of the predicate headed by *glad*, and the r-structure
indicates this fact. External arguments necessarily play a special role in
semantic interpretation because their role often must be determined compositionally by the whole VP, rather than by the verb itself (see Chomsky,
1981; Culicover, this volume; Jayaseelan, this volume).

The distinction between Norwegian and English, exemplified by the
difference in grammaticality between (23b) and (25), can be captured by
exploiting this enrichment of r-structure. For English, the transmission of
thematic role via the reflexive element is unconstrained (except, of course, that

[18] Presumably the Norwegian equivalent of (26) is also grammatical since *we* is the prediction
subject of the clause.

it must respect the thematic domain). For Norwegian, by contrast, there is a constraint on r-structure to the effect that the reflexive may pass its thematic role only onto an external argument. (28) for English is well formed, but the Norwegian equivalent would be ungrammatical because *John* is not an external argument.[19]

(28)   *we*, {Source, Agent}, *tell$_k$*,
         John, {Goal, Theme^}, *tell$_k$*,
         SELF, ($\emptyset$}, *tell$_k$*

While much more can, of course, be said about language-dependent differences in the distribution of anaphors (see footnotes 2 and 19), the important point here is that in accord with the autonomy thesis, these distinctions should be drawn without reference to syntactic configuration. The suggested enrichment of r-structure exemplified in (27) makes it possible to distinguish certain reflexivization facts for English and Norwegian without the syntactic notions "subject" and "object."

There is another apparently syntactic condition on reflexivization which can also be resolved in terms of r-structure. Recall well-known examples such as (29).

(29)   *Herself saw Jill.*

The fact that reflexives cannot appear in syntactic subject position is generally discussed in configurational terms such as PRECEDE and/or (C-)COMMAND. Actually, this is a syntactic reflex of a certain property of functional structure as discussed by Keenan (1974). An external argument cannot depend on some property of its associated function (= predicate) for its reference. Keenan states this as a functional principle:[20]

(30)   The reference of the argument expression must be determinable
         INDEPENDENTLY of the meaning or reference of the function
         symbol. (1974, p. 298)

I assume that functional principles, or their equivalent, come into play in the construction of a complete semantic representation. For our purposes here,

---

[19] This difference between English and Norwegian is discussed in Wilkins (1987b) in terms of the learnability of the parameters necessary for reflexivization. For learnability, and arguments from the subset principle (Berwick, 1985; Manzini and Wexler, 1987; Wilkins, 1987b), it must be that Norwegian represents the unmarked case. In the absence of evidence to the contrary, reflexives are associated only with external arguments. Wilkins (1987b) discusses this without use of the constructs "internal" and "external." I use the terms here because they are the ones familiar to most readers.

[20] Keenan proposes this (and another related principle) not only to account for examples like (29), but also to explain certain facts about possessive constructions, restrictive relative clauses, quantified NPs, etc., in a number of different languages.

principle (30) is readily expressed as a constraint on r-structure:

(31)   *<u>SELF</u>

In other words, SELF, being nonreferential, may not be an external argument, or in Keenan's terms, may not be the argument of an associated function. SELF's reference is not independently determinable (in fact, in the terms of the current analysis, it has no referent at all).[21] The ungrammaticality of (29) can be accounted for without recourse to syntactic structure.

5. THE THEMATIC HIERARCHY

Let us return now to examples like (25) and other cases where a nonexternal argument is the antecedent of a reflexive.

(32)   a. *The therapist introduced the new Mary to herself.*
        b. *We left the child {to / by} herself.*
        c. *With that new kind of kryptonite lock, you have to lock the bike to itself.*[22]
        d. *By using a mirror, we pointed the gun at itself.*
        e. *We sold the slave to himself.*[23]

Notice that there are again apparently syntactic conditions on the placement of the reflexive:

(33)   a.*We told himself about John.*
        b.*We locked itself to the bike.*
        c.*We left herself by the child.*

Examples such as (33) could be ruled out simply in the syntax by a prohibition against a reflexive c-commanding its antecedent. This option is unavailable in the present theory on the strictest interpretation of the autonomy thesis. The functional principle (30) is not relevant because in these cases both the reflexive and the antecedent are contained within the predicate. A possible way to account for (33) might be to further enrich r-structure to indicate thematic role assignment directly by the verb versus indirect

---

[21] An unexplained counterexample to (31) would be a reflexive in raised-to-object position; for example, *Ron believes himself to be honest*, if the reflexive is taken simply to be the antecedent (external argument) of the infinitive.

[22] Thanks to M. Olsen (personal communication) for mentioning this example.

[23] Postal (1971) and Jackendoff (1972) both consider this example ungrammatical. Many other speakers, including me, find it good.

assignment via a preposition. In indirect role assignment, a role determined by the verb would be assigned indirectly by a governing preposition. The r-structure for (33a) would then be something like (34).

(34) $\underline{we}$, {Source, Agent}, $tell_k$,
        $John$, {Goal^, Theme$_{about}$}, $tell_k$
        SELF, {$\varnothing$}, $tell_k$

An indication of role assignment via particular prepositions is probably necessary for proper semantic interpretation, and an indication of direct-versus-indirect role assignment might be necessary at thematic structure (see Rappaport and Levin, this volume).[24] If it is, reflexivization could exploit this by requiring that SELF not be directly assigned a role if its antecedent is indirectly assigned its role.

This could be expressed as in (35), understood as a hierarchy, where the reflexive cannot be higher on the hierarchy than its antecedent.

(35) $\underline{i}$, {T}, $k > i$, {T}, $k > i$, {T$_p$}, k

In (35) the first triple indicates the external argument, where thematic role is compositionally assigned (that is, determined by characteristics of the whole VP, rather than just the V); the second one is a triple where {T} is assigned directly by the predicator; and the third triple is the case where {T} is assigned via a preposition. With respect to this hierarchy, then, the triple containing SELF would have to be lower than the one containing the referential index of the intended antecedent. The examples in (33) would be violations of this condition.

An account incorporating (35) would work up to this point, but there are reasons to reject it. First of all, although the first part of the ordering of the triples in (35) has independent motivation as (31) in terms of (30) (and Keenan's various reasons for adopting it), the second part of the hierarchy, incorporating direct and indirect role assignment, is unmotivated except for the requirements of reflexivization. In fact, what (35) allows is the encoding of certain syntactic facts into thematic structure. This is a violation of the spirit, if not the letter, of the autonomy thesis.

While an indication of direct-versus-indirect role assignment might turn out to be necessary in thematic structure for accurate interpretation of the semantic contribution of prepositions, it actually is not sufficient for explaining the reflexivization data. The distinction would not provide an account of the examples in (36).

---

[24] Notice that the assignment of a role via a preposition is distinct from role assignment by a preposition. In a case like (34), *about* assigns Theme of *tell*; it does not define its own thematic domain.

(36)   a. *We talked to John about himself.*
       b.**We talked to himself about John.*
       c.**We talked about John to himself.*

In all three examples of (36) the predicate-internal arguments are assigned
their roles indirectly. But only the reflexive in (36a) is grammatical. In discussing cases like (36), Jackendoff (1972) proposes a hierarchy based on the content
of thematic roles and a thematic hierarchy condition for reflexivization:

(37)   Jackendoff's hierarchy: Agent
                                          Location, Source, Goal
                                          Theme

(38)   Condition: A reflexive may not be higher on the thematic hierarchy
          than its antecedent.

In accord with (38), (36b) and (36c) are both ungrammatical, because in both
cases the reflexive (Goal) is higher on the hierarchy than the antecedent
(Theme). (36a) and (25) are grammatical because the reflexive is lower than the
antecedent. While condition (38) gives the right results for (25) and (36) (and for
many other cases discussed by Jackendoff), it would seem to make the wrong
prediction about examples such as (32). In all of these cases the reflexive is a
Location or Goal (as indicated by the various prepositions) and the antecedent
is apparently the Theme. What is required here is the recognition that the
Themes in cases such as (32) are also Patients. The Patient role often co-occurs
with Theme (also sometimes with Goal), but only when the Theme is directly
affected (see Lebeaux, this volume) and there is an Agent or Instrument (see
Culicover and Wilkins, 1984; Wilkins, 1987a). In all the cases of (32) the
Themes are affected objects in the environment of an Agent and are
Patients.[25] This would suggest that for the purposes of reflexivization, Patient
is higher on the hierarchy than Location or Goal. Where the role transmitted
by the reflexive is Location, the antecedent's role may be Patient:

(39)   we, {Agent}, $lock_k$,
          the bike, {Theme, Patient, $Location_{to}$}, $lock_k$
          SELF, {$\emptyset$}, $lock_k$

The thematic hierarchy must be revised to incorporate not only the role
of Patient, but also the fact that r-structure indices may be associated with
roles from more than a single set. As mentioned in footnote 5, thematic roles
fall into at least two distinct classes. There are those associated with motion
and location in perceptual space: Source, Goal, Location, Theme. And there

---

[25] Jackendoff (1987) suggests that a test for Patient is *X* in *What happened to X is Y* or *What Y
did to X is . . . .*

are those associated with the structure of events: Agent, Patient, Instrument, etc.[26]

This recognition of different classes of roles is important for reflexivization because, as noted in the discussion prior to (39), a Theme that is also a Patient is higher on the hierarchy than a simple Theme. A Goal, whether or not it is also a Patient, is higher than Theme. This turns out to be relevant where the order of complements in the VP is variable. The complement next to the verb is the Patient, and this accounts for an interpretation difference. Consider the double object construction in (41) (see relevant discussion by Oehrle (1975) and Herslund (1986), among others).

(41) a. *We sold   the slave   to Bill.*
                 [Theme, Patient] [Goal]
      b. *We sold   Bill   the slave.*
                 [Goal, Patient] [Theme]
      c. *What we did to the slave was sell him to Bill.*
      d. *What we did to Bill was sell him the slave.*
      e.* *What we did to Bill was sell a slave to him.*

The (c) and (d) examples show that a Theme or a Goal can also be Patient when it is the first object following the verb (see relevant discussion in Rappaport and Levin, this volume). This correlates well with both the passivization and reflexivization facts:

(42) a. *The slave was sold to Bill.*
      b. *Bill was sold the slave.*

(43) a. *We sold   the slave   to himself.* (= (32e))
                 [Theme, Patient] [Goal]
      b. *We sold   the slave   himself.*
                 [Goal, Patient] [Theme]
      c.* *We sold   himself   the slave.*
                 [Goal, Patient] [Theme]

Passivization is permitted in (42) where in each case a Patient is in surface subject position. Reflexivization is permitted in (43a) and (43b) because Patient is placed higher on the hierarchy than simple Goal or Theme.

Consider next the case of PPs in the VP, as in (44).

(44) a. *We talked   about John   to Mary*
                 [Theme, Affected] [Goal]
      b. *We talked   to Mary   about John.*
                 [Goal, Affected] [Theme]

---

[26] The roles Experiencer and Percept might well comprise a third class of roles.

Let us assume, following the logic of the discussion of the double object construction, that a PP immediately following the verb may be an affected object. This option will be possible where the verb plus the following preposition may be considered a SEMANTIC UNIT. Formally speaking, there is a difference in thematic role assignment that correlates with this undefined, but intuitively plausible, notion of semantic unit. Compare (45a) and (45b).

(45)   a. *John slept in New York.*
                    [Location]
          b. *John slept   in the bed.*
                    [Location, Affected]

The interpretation distinction (adapted from Culicover and Wilkins, 1984) between the prepositional object in (45a) and that in (45b) has to do with how affected it is. *The bed* is affected by the sleeping; *New York* is not. This distinction is highlighted by the possibilities for passivization:

(46)   a. **New York was slept in.*
          b. *The bed was slept in.*

Returning to examples like (44), we see from the passivization possibilities that it is plausible to treat a prepositional object immediately following the verb as affected.

(47)   a. *Mary was talked {to / about}.*
          b. *Mary was talked* $\begin{Bmatrix} to\ about\ Fred \\ *about\ Fred\ to \end{Bmatrix}$.
          c. *Mary was talked* $\begin{Bmatrix} about\ to\ Fred \\ *to\ Fred\ about \end{Bmatrix}$.

Affected prepositional objects are not interpreted in the same way as Patients. Note the strangeness of (48).

(48)   a. *?What happened to Mary is that we talked to her.*
          b. *?What we did to Mary was talk about her.*

A prepositional object immediately following the verb may be understood to be affected by the verb, but it is not affected to the same extent that a Patient is. As Wilkins (1987a) argues, Affected and Patient are two distinct roles.[27] This is relevant for prepositional objects and reflexivization. (49) illustrates.

---

[27] This distinction shows up clearly in the following examples:

(i)   a. *We saw the book.*
                    [Percept]
         b. *We read the book.*
                    [Affected]

(49) a. *We talked   to John   about himself.* (=(36a))
                  [Goal, Affected]   [Theme]
      b.* *We talked   to himself   about John.* (=(36b))
                  [Goal, Affected]   [Theme]
      c.* *We talked   about himself   to John.*
                  [Theme, Affected]   [Goal]
      d.* *We talked   about John   to himself.* (=(36c))
                  [Theme, Affected]   [Goal]

What (49b) and (49c) show is that a reflexive may not be Affected if its antecedent is a simple Theme or Goal. (49d) shows, as Jackendoff correctly said, that the reflexive cannot be Goal where the antecedent is the (lower) Theme. All the data we have examined thus far can be accommodated by incorporating Patient and Affected into the hierarchy as in (50), where the top line contains the Event roles and the botton line has the Perceptual roles.

$$(50) \quad \text{Agent} > \text{Patient} > \begin{Bmatrix} \text{Affected} \\ \text{Location, Source, Goal} \end{Bmatrix} > \text{Theme}$$

With respect to (50), the antecedent must be higher than the reflexive. (49b) fails because either Goal or Affected is higher than Theme; (49c) fails because while Theme is lower than Goal, Affected is not (they are at the same level, as indicated by the curly braces). (49d) is ungrammatical because Affected, on the antecedent, is at the same level as Goal, rather than higher.

The thematic condition for reflexives in the vocabulary of the present theory would be as in (51).

(51)   THEMATIC CONDITION ON REFLEXIVES: Within the set of thematic
        roles {T} associated with an index i, t must be higher on the
        hierarchy than $t\hat{}$.

In other words, the thematic role assigned to the antecedent in the normal course of role assignment, that is t, must be higher on the hierarchy than the role transmitted from SELF to the antecedent, that is $t\hat{}$.

---

      c. *We burned the book.*
              [Patient]
(ii) a.* *What we did to the book was see it.*
      b.? *What we did to the book was read it.*
      c. *What we did to the book was burn it.*

The distinction between Affected and Patient is used in Wilkins (1987a) to account for certain morphological processes, such as resultative formation, and middle vs. ergative formation.

The advantage that this account has over Jackendoff's original one is that it correctly characterizes the grammatical examples in (32) and (43) as well as properly excluding the ungrammatical (49b–d).

6. CONCLUSION

Most recent accounts of the distribution of anaphoric elements have paid little or no attention to the type of data originally discussed by Jackendoff in terms of the hierarchy of thematic relations. This is understandable in strictly syntactic theories of anaphora because the content of semantic roles is not generally addressed in syntactic theories. In the present theory, where thematic structure is the determining factor in the occurrence of reflexives, a hierarchy that makes reference to thematic roles would seem to be directly relevant.

The advantage of working out further details of the thematic account of reflexives is that it provides for a theory of anaphora in accord with a strict interpretation of the autonomy thesis.[28] The adherence to strict autonomy is an advantage, all things being equal, because it constrains the class of possible grammars.

In this case, all things are not strictly equal. A purely syntactic treatment of reflexivization is necessarily descriptively inadequate. As Bach and Partee's examples of nonovert arguments, Jackendoff's examples of the thematic hierarchy condition, and Hellan's Norwegian examples show, configuration is not sufficient to distinguish the distribution of anaphors from that of pronouns. Thematic and predicational information is crucial to the account. Attempts to explain these semantic facts in the syntax lead to unnecessary and unmotivated complications of the syntax, complications such as a PRO subject in NP and syntactically unjustifiable small clauses.

---

[28] This article has not touched on the issue of reflexives embedded within subjects:

(i)   *A picture of {him/himself} on a Wanted poster would bother Ronald.*

(ii)   a. *Inaccurate descriptions of him bother Ronald.*
       b. *Inaccurate descriptions of himself (don't) bother Ronald.*

The theory of reflexivization here, as elsewhere, is intertwined with the theory of control. Kiparsky (1985, 1987) notices that anaphora in these constructions must be bound by Experiencers, and he provides an interesting discussion of them as a particular aspect of a broad class of Experiencer constructions. An analysis involving the Experiencer role would naturally be constrained by the autonomy thesis to be formulated in terms of strictly thematic primitives, and in the present theory, to be expressed at r-structure.

A much more natural theory explains these semantic facts at a semantic level. It is difficult to show, however, that some syntactic account is necessarily inadequate because semantic details can always be encoded into the syntax. This has been the case both with the use of θ-roles to incorporate some aspects of thematic structure into the syntax, and the use of indices (and co-indices) to build reference (and coreference) into the syntax. Continued incorporation of semantic facts into the syntax can only lead to a hopelessly involuted syntactic component. The more modular approach, which adheres to a strict interpretation of the autonomy thesis, excludes the syntactic encoding of semantic facts. On this view, both theoretical and descriptive criteria favor a thematic explanation of the distribution of reflexives.

TOWARD A LEXICAL REPRESENTATION
OF WARLPIRI VERBS

MARY LAUGHREN

Department of Education
Northern Territory of Australia
Yuendumu, NT 5751, Australia

1. INTRODUCTION

Verbs in Warlpiri, an Australian language, typically participate in a number of constructions which differ from each other with respect to the meaning of the verb, the case marking of the noun phrase (NP) bearing the object grammatical function (GF), and, in a tensed clause, the choice of the auxiliary (AUX) person–number clitic construed with the object NP.[1] In this article

[1] Only one verb manifests an alternation involving the subject NP and that is *janka-mi* 'to burn, cook, heat, ripen' as shown in the contrasting pair of sentences (i) and (ii).

(i)   *Miyi ka   jankami.*
      food impf cook
      'The food is cooking.'

(ii)   *Miyi ka   jankami warlu-ngku.*
      food impf cook   fire-erg
      'The fire is cooking the food.'

Note, however, that the NP subject of the transitive variant as in (ii) can only refer to a source of heat, as it does in (ii). The verb does not admit a (free) agent subject, as seen in (iii).

Syntax and Semantics, Volume 21
Thematic Relations

I examine two sets of contrasting constructions, both of which exhibit a contrast between a nonsubject NP in the unmarked (phonologically null) absolutive case, and one in the marked dative (dat) case *-ku*.[2] What distinguishes one set from the other, as far as the surface form is concerned, is the form of the AUX clitic which is construed with the dat case-marked NP bearing the object GF.

The order of nominal and verbal words in a finite clause is free in Warlpiri. One constraint on word order is the requirement that the AUX morphemes, which form a complex templatelike unit, form part of the first phonological phrase of a larger phonological unit, the phonological clause (see Nash, 1986, for a detailed description and analysis of the Warlpiri AUX).

Let us look at examples of the relevant constructions.[3]

(1) a. *Jurlarda-rna paka-rnu ngajulu-rlu (watiya-rla).* (obtain)
         honey-1sg   chop-past 1sg-erg   (tree-loc)
         'I chopped out the honey (in the tree).'
     b. *Jurlarda-ku-rna-rla paka-rnu ngajulu-rlu (watiya-rla).* (goal dative)
         honey-dat-1sg-3dat chop-past 1sg-erg   (tree-loc)
         'I chopped for the honey (in a tree).'

(2) a. *Watiya-rna paka-rnu ngajulu-rlu (jurlarda-ku).* (effect)
         tree-1sg   chop-past 1sg-erg   (honey-dat)
         'I chopped a tree (for honey).'

(iii)   **Miyi ka-rna   jankami ngajulu-rlu.*
        food impf-1sg cook   1sg-erg
        'I am cooking food.'

To express the English translation of (iii), the verb *purra-mi* 'to burn, cook, ripen' is required as illustrated in (iv).

(iv)   *Miyi ka-rna   purrami ngajulu-rlu.*
        food impf-1sg cook   1sg-erg
        'I am cooking food.'

Purra-mi cannot be substituted for *janka-mi* in (i) and (ii).

[2] In our glosses, the absolutive case is not overtly indicated. Any noun phrase not overtly case marked is to be interpreted as being in the absolutive case, unless otherwise explicitly indicated.

[3] The following abbreviations are used in the morpheme-by-morpheme English glosses: impf, imperfective aspect; imp, imperative mood; inf, infinitive mood; 1, first person; 2, second person; 12, first person inclusive; 3, third person; sg, singular; d, dual; pl, plural; dat, dative case; dd, double dative; erg, ergative case; loc, locative case; 3 dat, third person singular dative case; neg, negative.

b. *Watiya-ku-rna-rla-jinta paka-rnu.* (conative)
tree-dat-1sg-3dat-dd   chop-past
'I chopped at the tree.'

The subject NP, *ngajulu-rlu* '1sg-erg' is marked by the ergative case *-rlu* in each of the sentences in (1) and (2). The first person singular subject clitic *-rna* is also found in each of these sentences, and is construed with the ergative case-marked NP. However, the nonsubject clitics differ. In the (a) sentences in (1) and (2), the nonsubject NP, *jurlarda* 'honey' in (1) and *watiya* 'tree' in (2), is in the absolutive case; in the (b) sentences, the nonsubject NP is in the dative case, *jurlarda-ku* 'honey-dat' in (1) and *watiya-ku* 'tree-dat' in (2). In (1a) and in (2a) there is no phonologically overt nonsubject clitic since there is no phonologically nonnull clitic form corresponding to third person singular construed with an NP in the ergative or absolutive case. If the number value were changed to plural, then the clitic *-jana* would be employed as in the sentences in (3), which parallel those in (1).

(3) a. *Janganpa-rna-jana paka-rnu   ngajulu-rlu.*
     possum-1sg-3pl   chop-past 1sg-erg
     'I chopped out the possums.'
  b. *Janganpa-ku-rna-jana paka-rnu   ngajulu-rlu.*
     possum dat-1sg-3pl   chop-past 1sg-erg
     'I chopped for possums.'

The AUX person–number clitic construed with the dative case-marked NP *janganpa-ku* 'possum-dat' in (3b) is *-jana* '3pl.' This clitic is construed with the absolutive case-marked NP *janganpa* 'possum' in (3a). Thus the only formal reflex of the semantic difference between (3a) and (3b) is the contrast in case marking on the object NP, absolutive in (3a) and dative in (3b). The only overt contrast between clitics construed with an absolutive case-marked nonsubject NP and a dative case-marked nonsubject NP is in the third person singular where the contrast, as is shown in (1), is between phonologically null $/\emptyset/$ and *-rla*.

In (1b), the nonsubject clitic form is *-rla*, which is construed with the dative case-marked NP *jurlarda-ku* 'honey-dat.' In (2b), however, the dative–double dative clitic complex *-rla-jinta*, which includes *-rla*, is coreferent with the dative case-marked NP *watiya-ku* 'tree-dat.' One of the aims of this article is to account for this difference in the form of the nonsubject clitic construed with the dative case-marked NP in the goal dative and conative constructions. In pursuing the investigation of what gives rise to the double dative construction as opposed to the "simple" dative clitic construction, other cases in which the double dative construction is used are compared. For example, if we add the double dative clitic -*jinta* to the AUX clitics in (1b), we obtain (4), in which the interpretation of the clitics is quite different, apparently, from that of (2b).

(4)   *Jurlarda-ku-rna-rla-jinta paka-rnu ngajulu-rlu.*
       honey-dat-1sg-3dat-dd chop-past 1sg-erg
       'I chopped for honey for him/her.'

In (4), the double dative clitic -*jinta* signals the presence of an additional adjoined "purposive" or "benefactive" dative argument which could be further identified by an overt dative case-marked NP such as *Jakamarra-ku* 'Jakamarra-dat' in (5).

(5)   *Jurlarda-ku-rna-rla-jinta paka-rnu ngajulu-rlu Jakamarra-ku.*
       honey-dat-1sg-3dat-dd chop-past 1sg-erg   J-dat
       'I chopped for the honey for Jakamarra.'

Four uses of *paka-rni* 'to chop' are exhibited in (1) and (2). The (a) variants present ergative–absolutive case marking of their subject and object NPs respectively and present identical AUX clitics, while the (b) variants present ergative–dative case marking of their subject and object NPs respectively but show a difference in their person–number AUX clitics. These morphosyntactic differences correspond to semantic contrasts. These meaning–form correlations are not random, nor are they unique to this verb. Rather, they characterize an important class of verbs of which *paka-rni* is a member, along with verbs like *jarnti-rni* 'to carve,' *luwa-rni* 'to hit with missile,' *paji-rni* 'to cut,' *panti-rni* 'to pierce,' *pangi-rni* 'to dig,' *yurrpa-rni* 'to grind, file.' These verbs will be called IMPACT VERBS.

The ability of a given verb to enter into one or both of the pairs of constructions exemplified in (1) and (2) depends not on its structural or syntactic properties—what we will refer to as its PREDICATE ARGUMENT STRUCTURE (PAS)—but rather on its lexicosemantic properties, which will be referred to as its LEXICAL CONCEPTUAL STRUCTURE (LCS). A verb's PAS, I argue, is derived from its LCS. The morphological reflexes (case marking of NP arguments, form of AUX person–number clitics) of the different "meanings" of *paka-rni* in (1) and (2) result from differences in the PAS of the verb which are in turn derived from different LCSs, as well as from independent principles of case theory.

Given the correlations, observable in (1) and (2), between differences in the meaning and differences in the morphosyntactic properties of the sentences, I attempt to identify the relevant components of meaning, which are to be represented in the verb's LCS. I discuss the mechanisms by which the PAS, conceived not as a level of semantic representation but rather as the interface between the LCS and the syntactic component proper, is derived from the LCS. The PAS encodes deep structural relations between a verb and its arguments. In Warlpiri, the correspondence between the arguments of a verb as represented in its PAS and the syntactic categories such as NP and the AUX person–number clitics which are associated with them, is far from straightforward.

2. GRAMMATICAL FUNCTIONS

In comparing the syntactic constructions in (1) and (2), we have seen that, superficially at least, the (a) sentences are equivalent with respect to AUX clitics and the case marking of the NPs bearing the same GF. A comparison of the (b) sentences reveals identical case marking on the NPs associated with identical GFs, identical clitics construed with the ergative case-marked NP, but nonidentical AUX clitics construed with the dative case-marked NPs.

Let us examine some additional facts about these Warlpiri sentences. In (1) and (2), the 1sg clitic -rna and the ergative case-marked independent 1sg pronoun *ngajulu-rlu* are associated with the subject grammatical function. This can be formally shown by the addition to each of these sentences of a predicate headed by the complementizer -karra 'subjcomp'. The subject of this nonfinite predicate is obligatorily controlled by the subject of the matrix clause. (See Hale, 1982, Nash, 1986, Simpson, 1983, and Simpson and Bresnan, 1983, for a detailed discussion of subjcomps and objcomps.)

(6) a. *Janganpa-rna paka-rnu   ngajulu-rlu yunpa-rninja-karra-rlu.*
         possum-1sg   chop-past 1sg-erg   sing-inf-subjcomp-erg
         'I chopped out a possum while (I was) singing.'

     b. *Janganpa-ku-rna-rla paka-rnu   ngajulu-rlu yunpa-rninja-karra-rlu.*
         possum-dat-1sg-3dat chop-past 1sg-erg   sing-inf-subjcomp-erg
         'I chopped for a possum while (I was) singing.'

(7) a. *Watiya-rna paka-rnu   ngajulu-rlu yunpa-rninja-karra-rlu.*
         tree-1sg   chop-past 1sg-erg   sing-inf-subjcomp-erg
         'I chopped a tree while (I was) singing.'

     b. *Watiya-ku-rna-rla-jinta paka-rnu   ngajulu-rlu yunpa-rninja-karra-rlu.*
         tree-dat-1sg-3dat-dd   chop-past 1sg-erg   sing-inf-subjcomp-erg
         'I chopped at a tree while (I was) singing.'

Note that the obligatory addition of the ergative case marker -rlu to the subjcomp -karra acts as an additional index relating this predicate to the subject NP of the main clause, itself marked by the ergative case.

In each of the sentences in (1) and (2), the nonsubject clitics and the absolutive case-marked NPs in (1a) and (2a) bear the object GF since they can control the subject of a nonfinite predicate headed by the complementizer *-kurra* 'objcomp.' The subject of this predicate is obligatorily controlled by the object of the main finite clause. The dative case-marked NPs in (1b) and (2b) also bear the object grammatical function and can control the subject of a predicate headed by the complementizer *-kurra* 'objcomp.'

(8)   a. *Janganpa-rna paka-rnu   ngajulu-rlu nguna-nja-kurra.*
           possum-1sg   chop-past 1sg-erg   lie-inf-objcomp
           'I chopped out a possum while (it was) sleeping.'
     b. *Janganpa-ku-rna-rla paka-rnu   ngajulu-rlu nguna-nja-kurra-(ku).*
           possum-dat-1sg-3dat chop-past 1sg-erg   lie-inf-objcomp-(dat)
           'I chopped for a possum while (it was) sleeping.'

(9)   a. *Watiya-rna paka-rnu   ngajulu-rlu nguna-nja-kurra.*
           tree-1sg   chop-past 1sg-erg   lie-inf-objcomp
           'I chopped the tree while (it was) lying down.'
     b. *Watiya-ku-rna-rla-jinta paka-rnu   wanti-nja-kurra-(ku).*
           tree-dat-1sg-3dat-dd   chop-past fall-inf-objcomp-(dat)
           'I chopped at the tree while (it was) falling.'

Note that the dative case agreement between the dative case-marked controller NP and the *-kurra*-headed predicate in (8b) and (9b) is not obligatory, especially in the speech of older Warlpiri speakers.[4]

The relation between the subject of the main predicator of a tensed sentence and a predicate headed by the subjcomp *-karra* is constant whether the object of a sentence is in the absolutive ((1a), (2a), (6a), and (7a)) or dative ((1b), (2b), (6b), and (7b)) case. Furthermore, it is not affected by whether the AUX clitic construed with the object NP is the simple dative clitic as in (1b) or the double dative of (2b). More striking, perhaps, is the fact that the object GF in Warlpiri may be borne by an NP in the absolutive case, as in the (a) sentences in (1) and (2), or by the dative case, as in the (b) sentences—and this despite the different AUX clitics with which the dative NPs are construed. The object status of both the absolutive and dative NPs in (1) and (2) is borne out by the control relation which holds between the logical subject of the *-kurra* 'objcomp'-headed predicate and the absolutive NP in the (a) sentences in (8) and (9), and between the logical subject of the same predicate and the dative NP in the (b) sentences in (8) and (9).

---

[4] In the contemporary Warlpiri of many speakers under 30 years of age, *-kurra* is used to head both subject- and object-controlled predicates in which the time of the event in the main finite clause and in the adjoined nonfinite clause headed by COMP is simultaneous (time of the matrix clause binds or controls the time of the subordinate clause). For these speakers, case agreement appears to be obligatory for both subject and object GFs.

3. CASE MARKING: NPs AND PERSON–NUMBER AUX CLITICS

Warlpiri has been called a morphologically ergative language in terms of the typology established by Comrie (1978).[5] The NP bearing the object GF is governed by either the absolutive or dative case, as illustrated by the pairs of sentences in (1) and (2) and in (6)–(9). The NP which bears the subject GF to a tensed verb is either governed by the absolutive or the ergative case, depending on the transitivity of the verb. Roughly speaking, transitive verbs have ergative case-marked NP subjects while intransitive verbs have absolutive case-marked subjects, as illustrated by the contrast between (10) and (11).

(10)   *Wati-ngki turaki rdilyki-pu-ngu.*
       man-erg   truck broken-hit-past
       'The man broke the truck.'

(11)   *Turaki rdilyki-ya-nu.*
       truck   broken-go-past
       'The truck broke.'

In (10), the subject NP *wati-ngki* 'man-erg' is case marked by ergative case, while the object NP *turaki* 'truck' is in the absolutive case. In (11), which contains an intransitive verb—the inchoative counterpart of the verb in (10), the subject NP *turaki* 'truck' is in the absolutive case. An absolutive case-marked subject NP is not compatible with an absolutive case-marked object NP. The attested case frames are the following:

Subject	Object
abs	
abs	dat
erg	
erg	abs
erg	dat

All logical possibilities are attested in Warlpiri. Ditransitive verbs such as *yinyi* 'give,' and *punta-rni* 'remove from' exhibit the following case array:

Subject	Object	Object2
erg	dat	abs

---

[5] The status of Warlpiri in a typology of ergative languages is discussed in detail in Levin (1983).

In this article only sentences which feature ergative-absolutive and ergative-dative NP subject–object case arrays like those illustrated in (1) and (2) are considered.

In Warlpiri, the arguments of a predicator, such as a verb or predicative nominal, are not obligatorily expressed by an overt NP.[6] The arguments of a verb in a tensed clause are obligatorily expressed by phonologically nonnull AUX person–number clitics, except where the argument is evaluated by the features 3sg. In (12) and (13), there are no NPs, the arguments of the verb *paka-rni* 'to chop' being associated only with AUX clitics. These sentences parallel those in (1) and (2).

(12) a. *Paka-rnu-rna.*
         chop-past-1sg
         'I chopped it out.'
      b. *Paka-rnu-rna-rla.*
         chop-past-1sg-3dat
         'I chopped for it.'

(13) a. *Paka-rnu-rna.*
         chop-past-1sg
         'I chopped it.'
      b. *Paka-rnu-rna-rla-jinta.*
         chop-past-1sg-3dat-dd
         'I chopped at it.'

Since the arguments of a predicator in a main clause are not obligatorily expressed by the syntactic category NP (or KP, see note 6) in Warlpiri, it has been argued, principally by Jelinek (1984), that the NPs associated with these arguments do not occupy the argument positions in the syntactic projection containing the predicator, but that they behave syntactically like adjuncts to the structure which contains the real argument positions. These positions, it has been further argued, are filled by the person–number clitics. The relation between a clitic and an NP, which Jelinek claims to be one of predication, would be sanctioned by case.[7]

---

[6] What is referred to here as an NP should more properly be called a CASE PHRASE (KP), since it is a maximal projection of the category case (K), and not of the category N. The complement of K is NP, giving the structure [$_{KP}$ NP K]. Included in the phrasal category KP are NPs in the phonologically unmarked absolutive case, since their surface-syntactic distribution is like that of other KPs and not like that of bare NPs.

[7] A full and adequate discussion of the respective roles of the person–number clitics and KPs is beyond the scope of this article, since it must include a consideration of many other syntactic phenomena characteristic of Warlpiri (see Hale, 1973, 1982; Nash, 1986; Simpson, 1983). Both Jelinek (1984) and Speas (1986) offer insightful analyses of the relative status of NPs and clitics in both Warlpiri and Navaho.

	Clitics			NPs		
One-argument verbs:	subject			subject		
	nom			abs		
	nom			erg		
Two-argument verbs:	subject	object		subject	object	
	nom	acc		erg	abs	
	nom	dat		abs	dat	
	nom	dat		erg	dat	
	nom	dat-dd		erg	dat	
Three-argument verbs:	subject	object	object2	subject	object	object2
	nom	dat	—	erg	dat	abs

In Warlpiri, all NPs are governed by overt case markers, except for the NP said to be in the absolutive case. If we assume, as does Jelinek (1984), that the phonological contrast between the AUX clitics having the same person–number features is a reflex of different cases, as well as of different GFs, the case marking of the person–number clitics diverges from that of the NPs semantically linked to the same logical argument. The AUX person–number clitics appear to be characterized by a nominative (nom)–accusative (acc) system of case marking in contrast with the ergative–absolutive case marking on NPs, including the nonbound pronominals.[8] The clitic case arrays and the corresponding NP case arrays are given in Table I.

As Table I shows, a nominative case clitic may be construed with either an absolutive or ergative case-marked NP depending on the verb type. An accusative clitic may also be construed with an absolutive case-marked NP, whereas a dative clitic is always construed with a dative case-marked NP. Only with the dative is there a one-to-one correspondence between the case of the clitic and that of the NP. We must note also that the only surface morphological distinction between accusative and dative case in the relevant paradigm of nonsubject person–number clitics occurs in the third person singular: /∅/ 'acc,' /-rla/ 'DAT.' A clitic construed with a dative case-marked NP may be followed by the additional double dative construed with a dative case-marked NP, whereas a nonsubject clitic construed with an absolutive case-marked NP cannot be followed by the double dative clitic. For example,

[8] This divergence in case marking is very common in the Pama–Nyungan languages of Australia, which include Warlpiri (see Blake, 1977; Dixon, 1980).

the clitic in (14a), *-ngalingki* '12,' could be construed with a dative case-marked nonbound pronominal *ngali-ki* '12d-dat' and/or a dative case-marked NP such as *yarnunjuku-ku* 'hungry (ones)-dat' as in (14b). The double dative *-rla* which is construed with the dative case-marked NP *kuyu-ku* 'meat-dat' is thus permitted in the AUX complex.

(14)   a. ***Kuyu-ku*-ngalingki-*rla* *nya-nja-ya-nta!***
          meat-dat-12d-dd   see-inf-go-imp
          'Be looking for some meat for us as you go along!'
       b. *Kuyu-ku-**ngalingki**-rla nya-nja-ya-nta **ngali-ki yarnunjuku-ku!***
          meat-dat-**12d**-dd   see-inf-go-imp *12d-dat hungry-dat*
          'Be looking for meat for us hungry ones as you go along!'

The double dative AUX complex which consists of two dative nonsubject clitics as shown in (14) does not extend to (15) which contains the triadic verb *yi-nyi* 'to give' which has an ergative–absolutive–dative case-array. (15) is not acceptable on the interpretation where the clitic *-ngalingki* '12d' is construed with the absolutive case-marked nonbound pronominal *ngali* '12d' which bears the theme semantic role, that is, the entity given.

(15)   **Jakamarra-ku-**ngalingki**-rla yu-ngu   **ngali**.*
         J-dat-12d-dd   give-past 12d
         'He gave us to Jakamarra.'

   Clearly, the relation between a clitic and the NP with which it is construed is sensitive to the case governing the NP. The behavior of the nonsubject clitics in the double dative construction points to a distinction between dative case, on the one hand, and accusative and absolutive cases, on the other. Dative case is an "inherent" case (see Chomsky, 1981) assigned to an argument of a predicator represented in the PAS of that predicator. It is a lexical property of the verb. Absolutive and accusative cases are "structural" cases (see Chomsky, 1981) in the sense that they are assigned to an NP or nonsubject clitic respectively by virtue of the syntactic or structural relation which holds between the NP or clitic and the syntactic category which assigns the case.
   Simpson (1983), following Hale (1973), argues that the AUX person–number clitics reflect the GFs attributed to the arguments (or thematic roles) of a predicator in the lexicon, but that they do not bear case. In the parlance of the government and binding (GB) framework (Chomsky, 1981), they would neither "absorb" case nor would they be "assigned" case, the latter being reserved for syntactic categories with the feature [+N], such as the nominal (N). Like Simpson, I assume that the AUX person–number clitics reflect, in a direct manner, information encoded in the lexical entry of the main predicator, the semantic head of a finite clause, without denying that they absorb case in some way.

Structurally, the obtain and effect uses of *paka-rni* 'to chop,' as illustrated in (1a) and (2a) respectively, have identical properties: GFs (subject and object), syntactic categories associated with these GFs, and the case marking of the syntactic categories. These properties are set out schematically in (16).

(16)   GF:

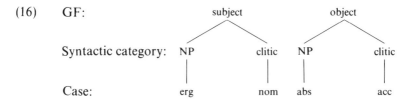

The semantic contrast between the obtain (1a) and effect (2a) uses of the verb are clearly not attributable to differences in their structural or syntactic properties, since these are identical. The differences in meaning derive from differences in the LCSs associated with the two uses of the verb. The relation between the obtain and effect uses must be captured at that level of representation, as we discuss in detail in the following section.

The structural properties of the obtain and effect uses, set out in (16), contrast with those of the goal dative and conative uses, exemplified in (1b) and (2b), respectively, which in turn present some structural differences which are shown in (17) and (18).

(17)   GF:

(18)   GF:

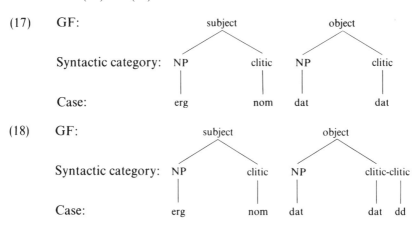

The different structural properties of (16) (obtain and effect uses), (17) (goal dative use), and (18) (conative use) derive from differences in the lexical properties associated with each use. These are represented at two distinct, but related, levels of lexical representation: the LCS and the PAS. The differences in meaning do not result from the different structural properties associated with the verb. Rather these properties derive from the differences in meaning.

Furthermore, it is shown below that the ability of a verb to participate in the range of construction types exemplified in (1) and (2), or to be associated with the structural properties shown in (16)–(18), is constrained by the verb's lexical-semantic properties, which are represented in its LCS.

4. SEMANTIC DECOMPOSITION AND LEXICAL CONCEPTUAL STRUCTURE

The LCS of the verb *paka-rni* 'chop' as it is used in (1a) consists of two main predicates: an OBTAIN[9] predicate which takes two arguments, an obtainer and an obtainee, and an EFFECT predicate which also takes two arguments, an effecter and an effectee. The EFFECT predicate of *paka-rni* might be defined as "x produce separation in y, by sharp-edged entity forcefully coming into contact with y." This definition contains a number of subpredicates such as "x produce separation in y," "sharp-edged entity forcefully come into contact with y." The EFFECT predicate component is examined in more detail in the context of the LCSs underlying the effect and conative uses of *paka-rni* shown in (2a,b). For the sake of simplicity and clarity at this stage of the discussion, the relevant EFFECT predicate is abbreviated as CHOP (chopper, choppee).

The two predicates, OBTAIN and CHOP, are related to each other by a means relation, in that the EFFECT (or CHOP) predicate is the means by which the result of obtaining is brought about. We represent the means relation by the preposition *by*. It is a function which takes two arguments: means, result.

The LCS underpinning the obtain use of *paka-rni* illustrated in (1a) links the obtainer argument of the OBTAIN predicate with the chopper argument of the CHOP (EFFECT) predicate. The choppee argument is related to the obtainee argument as the material source or location of the obtainee. By using variables $x, y, \ldots$) to denote the argument of the OBTAIN and CHOP functions, these relations of identity can be captured in the LCS as in (19).

(19)   (x OBTAIN y) *by* (x CHOP material source/location of y)
         result   means

The LCS underlying the goal dative use of *paka-rni* as in (1b) is minimally different from that of the obtain use. The goal dative LCS contains the same two predicates, OBTAIN and CHOP, but the relation between them is different.

---

[9] While the notion of "obtaining" can be analyzed or decomposed into a number of simpler notions including that of control (see Langacker, 1983; Hale and Laughren, 1983), for the sake of convenience, these notions will be simply represented by OBTAIN.

Instead of the means relation which characterizes the obtain use, there is a purpose relation expressed as *in order that*. The proposed LCS is shown in (20).

(20)   (x CHOP material source/location of y) *in order that* (x OBTAIN y)
        means   result

The difference in meaning between the obtain and goal dative uses of *paka-rni* can be characterized in terms of a difference in truth conditions with respect to the predicate OBTAIN. (1a) is true iff *I obtained honey*, whereas (1b) is true irrespective of whether *I obtained honey*. This difference in meaning is captured in the LCS we have proposed in (19) and (20) by the different roles of the OBTAIN predicate with respect to the CHOP predicate. In (19), it is the result argument of the *by* function, whereas in (20) it is the result argument of the IN ORDER THAT function, more properly a purpose or goal.

The PAS associated with each use is also different. This is reflected in the contrasting syntactic realizations described in the preceding sections. In both the obtain and goal dative constructions, the syntactic category associated with the obtainer argument, or thematic role, bears the subject GF, while the syntactic category associated with the obtainee argument bears the object GF. The formal difference lies in the case marking of the object syntactic categories (NP and person–number clitic). In the obtain construction which implies that the act of obtaining is fully realized, the object NP is in the absolutive case and the clitic with which it is construed is in the accusative case.

On the assumption that it is the verb which assigns accusative case to the syntactic category it directly governs, we can assume that the obtainee argument, identified as the variable y in the LCS in (19), combines with the syntactic category V to form the structure shown in (21).

(21) $[_{V'} \; y \; V]$

The obtainer argument, represented in the LCS as x, composes with the nonminimal category V' in the following manner:[10]

(22) $[_{V''} \; x \; [_{V'} \; y \; V]]$

This is the basic PAS of the obtain use of *paka-rni*. The GFs borne by the syntactic categories (NPs and person–number clitics) which are associated with the x and y arguments are determined by the PAS in conjunction with general principles of grammar which are not discussed here. The cases as-signed to these categories are not indicated in the PAS since they are struc-tural cases (ergative, absolutive (NPs), and nominative, accusative (clitics)) assigned in function of the structural relations which obtain between the

---

[10] Hale and Laughren (1983) propose that in Warlpiri the subject is in fact internal to the VP (= V''). This position is assumed, but not argued for, in this article.

case-assigning categories and the case-bearing categories (NP and clitic), in
the syntactic component of the grammar.

The goal dative construction reflects a PAS in which the inherent dative
case is explicitly represented as the direct governor of the y argument. Thus
the PAS of the goal dative use of *paka-rni* is (23).

(23) $[_{V''} x [_{V'} [_{KP} y \text{ dat}] V]]$

This formal difference between (22) and (23) reflects the semantic difference
between the obtain and goal dative constructions. In the former, the obtainee
argument, y, of the OBTAIN predicate represents an achieved goal, whereas in
the latter, it is only a potentially achieved goal.

The correlation between the dative case and the semantic concept of "goal"
is very regular in Warlpiri. The dative case has a very broad range of uses in
Warlpiri, and this meaning correspondence is only one of those uses.

That the relation between the obtain and goal dative uses of a verb must
be represented at the level of LCS and not simply at that of the PAS, or at
some other level of syntactic structure, can be argued for convincingly if we
consider the possible uses of the verb *ma-ni* 'to obtain, get, pick up, gather.'
This verb does not participate in the goal dative construction, as shown
by (24b).

(24)   a. *Karnta-ngku-lu yarla ma-nu.*
          woman-erg-3pl yam get-past
          'The women got yams.'
        b.*Karnta-ngku-lu-rla   yarla-ku ma-nu.*
          woman-erg-3pl-3dat get-past
          'The women got for yams.'

What distinguishes *ma-ni* (and other verbs like it such as *kardi-rni* 'to fetch
water') from the verbs which do participate in the obtain–goal dative alternation is the absence of a means component in its LCS. The LCS of *ma-ni* consists simply of an OBTAIN predicate as in (25).

(25) x OBTAIN y

Apart from the "impact" verbs such as *paka-rni*, the "perception" verbs also
exhibit both the obtain and goal dative uses. These are shown in (26).[11]

(26)   a. *Janganpa-rna nya-ngu ngajulu-rlu (wilypiri-rla).* (obtain)
          possum-1sg see-past 1sg-erg   (hollow-loc)
          'I saw the possum (in a hollow).' or 'I looked at the possum...'

---

[11] In addition to the monomorphemic verb *nya-nyi* 'see, watch, look at,' compound verbs
containing the same root *nya-* also belong to the class of perception verbs which exhibit the same
range of meaning alternations, e.g., *purda-nya-nyi* 'to hear, listen to,' *parnti-nya-nyi* 'to smell.'

b. *Janganpa-ku-rna-rla nya-ngu ngajulu-rlu (wilypiri-rla).*
   (goal dative)
   possum-dat-1sg-3dat see-past 1sg-erg   (hollow-loc)
   'I looked for the possum(in a hollow).'

(26a) implies that I obtained an image of a possum (by means of eyes). Thus the implication that I did not see the possum in (27a) would be contradictory. In (27b), related to (26b) this implication does not result in a contradiction.

(27) a.**Janganpa-rna nya-ngu, kala kula-rna nya-ngu.*
         possum-1sg see-past but neg-1sg see-past
         'I saw the possum, but didn't see it.'
         'I looked at the possum, but didn't see it.'
         'I saw the possum, but didn't look at it.'
         'I looked at the possum, but didn't look at it.'
      b. *Janganpa-ku-rna-rla nya-ngu, kala kula-rna nya-ngu.*
         Possum-dat-1sg-3dat see-past but neg-1sg see-past
         'I looked for the possum, but did not see it.'

There exists in Warlpiri a verb *warri-rni* which has a more abstract meaning akin to that of English 'seek' or 'search for.' The LCS of this verb would be something like (28).

(28)   *x* do something, in order to obtain image/knowledge of *y*.

The PAS of this verb is like that of the goal dative impact and perception verbs given in (23).

The LCS given in (28) is the only one associated with *warri-rni*, thus it only admits one PAS. This provides further evidence that there is no general rule which operates in Warlpiri on the level of representation we have called the PAS which would convert one PAS into an alternate one for a given verb. In other words, no redundancy rule of the form of (29) exists in Warlpiri.

(29) $[_{V''} x[_{V'} y \text{ V}]] \begin{Bmatrix} \rightarrow \\ \leftarrow \\ \leftrightarrow \end{Bmatrix} [_{V''} x[_{V'} [_{KP} y \text{ dat}] \text{ V}]]$

That the ability of a verb to participate in the alternations examined depends on the form of its LCS is thus further borne out. (29) would lead to the wrong results for *ma-ni* 'to get' (see (24b)) (and for thousands of other verbs with the PAS of (22)) and also for *warri-rni*.

All verbs which have a LCS of the form *by* (result, means) where result = "*x* obtain *y*" and means = "*x* produce effect on location/material source of *y*" or where result = "*x* obtain sensory perception (image, sound, smell) of *y*" and means = "*x* use body-part" participate in both the obtain use and the goal dative use. Verbs whose LCS lacks a means component, while having the OBTAIN predicate, fail to participate in the goal dative construction. Conversely, verbs with the LCS corresponding to the goal dative do not necessarily also display an obtain use, as *warri-rni* shows. This would seem to indicate then that the lexical organization involved in the obtain–goal dative alternation contains an asymmetrical implication of the form

> If a verb has a LCS of the form *by* (result [= x OBTAIN y], means)
> then it also has the LCS of the form *in order that* (means, result
> [x OBTAIN y])

but that the converse implication is not true. Rules with double-headed arrows do not operate on LCSs. The lexical rule which does operate on the lexicon of Warlpiri verbs to license the obtain-goal dative alternation can be formulated in terms of a goal dative-forming rule which takes as its input the LCS corresponding to the obtain construction and transforms that LCS into the LCS corresponding to the goal dative construction. This rule is given in (30).

(30)   *by* (result [x OBTAIN y], means) → *in order that* (means, result)

The PAS which corresponds to both the obtain and goal dative LCSs is derived from each of these by virtue of general principles having to do with the projection of arguments identified in the LCS onto structural positions in the maximal projection of the verbal category, V (see footnote 10).

To summarize, then, verbs whose LCS contains an OBTAIN predicate modified by a means component are subject to the goal dative lexical rule which operates on the LCS. Two classes of verbs, the perception verbs and the impact verbs, participate in the obtain–goal dative alternation.

Let us now turn to the other pair of constructions involving the impact verb *paka-rni* given in (2). While the impact verbs participate in both pairs of constructions, the perception verbs only participate in the obtain–goal dative pair. We consider the nature of the relation between the effect and conative uses of impact verbs and also the relation between the effect and obtain uses of impact verbs.

The differences in logical entailments between (2a) (effect use) and (2b) (conative use) are somewhat similar to the differences in meaning displayed by the obtain and goal dative pair described above.

The effect use of *paka-rni* in (2a) implies that *I chopped the tree*, that is, that the designated agent (speaker) produced the effect (i.e., *chopped*) described by the verb on the designated patient (i.e., *tree*). By contrast, the sentence containing the conative construction, (2b), does not share the same entailments, since (2b) may be true, whether or not I chopped the tree. These entailment facts are illustrated in (31).

(31) a.*Watiya-rna paka-rnu, kala kula-rna paka-rnu.
        tree-1sg   chop-past but neg-1sg chop-past
        *'I chopped the tree, but I didn't chop it.'
      b. Watiya-ku-rna-rla paka-rnu, kala kula-rna paka-rnu.
        tree-dat-1sg-3dat chop-past but neg-1sg chop-past
        'I chopped at the tree, but I didn't chop it.'

The LCS corresponding to the effect use of *paka-rni*, (2a), contains a main predicate, the EFFECT predicate: *x* produce separation in *y*. It also has a means component which modifies the EFFECT predicate. The means component is, in itself, complex, as it is made up of two related subpredicates: (sharp-edged entity come forcefully into contact with *y*) by (*x* manipulate sharp-edged entity).

The difference in logical entailments between the effect and conative uses also extends to these subpredicates of the means component, namely the CONTACT predicate which is modified by the means clause "*by x* manipulate entity." The effect use of an impact verb, as in (2a), implies that the relevant entity (a sharp-edged entity, in the particular case of the verb *paka-rni*) comes into contact with an entity representing the *y* variable in the LCS of the verb. In (2a), this entity is a tree (*watiya*). Thus the effect construction has two related entailments: (a) that *x* produce effect on *y*, and (b) that entity come into contact with *y*. Both these entailments involve the *y* argument, the one associated with the syntactic categories bearing the object GF. Neither of these entailments holds for the conative construction.

Thus the conative rule, which takes as its input the LCS corresponding to the effect use, produces, as its output, an LCS in which the relation between the result and means predicates is converted from *by* to *in order that*, and, furthermore, the relation between the two subpredicates which constitute the means component of the LCS is similarly converted from *by* to *in order that*. The *y* argument of the conative LCS bears a potential or unachieved goal semantic role with respect to both the effect predicate and the contact predicate. The conative rule is given in (32).

(32)   (*x* produce effect on *y*) by ((entity come into contact with *y*) by
        (*x* manipulate entity)) → ((*x* manipulate entity) in order that (entity
        come into contact with *y*)) in order that (*x* produce effect on *y*).

The reflex, in the syntactic component, of the semantic role of the *y* argument defined by the conative LCS is the dative–double dative person–number clitic complex as in (2b). This AUX construction reflects the PAS derived from the conative LCS. The PAS of the conative verb is given in (33).

(33) $[_{V''} x [_{V'} [_{KP} [_{KP} y \text{ dat}] \text{ dat}] V]]$

The PAS derived from the LCS corresponding to the effect use of the verb is identical to that of the obtain construction as given in (22) and repeated here.

(22) $[_{V''} x[_{V'} y\ V]]$

That the generalizations about the relation between the effect and conative constructions do not obtain at the level of the verb's PAS is further borne out by the fact that perception verbs (and many others) with the PAS given in (22) do not participate in the conative construction and hence do not display the PAS given in (33).

All verbs which participate in the effect–conative alternation, i.e., the impact verbs, also participate in the obtain–goal dative alternation. The converse does not hold, as we noted in respect of the perception verbs which only participate in the obtain–goal dative alternation. Warlpiri has two verbs which we might gloss as 'dig,' *pangi-rni* and *karla-mi*. The former participates in the full range of constructions, while the latter only participates in the obtain–goal dative pair. These properties of the two verbs are illustrated in (34) and (35).

(34)   a. *Walya-rna pangu-rnu ngajulu-rlu.* (effect)
            earth-1sg dig-past   1sg-erg
            'I dug the earth.'

        b. *Walya-ku-rna-rla-jinta pangu-rnu ngajulu-rlu.* (conative)
            earth-dat-1sg-3dat-dd dig-past   1sg-erg
            'I dug at the earth.'

        c. *Yarla-rna pangu-rnu ngajulu-rlu.* (obtain)
            yam-1sg   dig-past   1sg-erg
            'I dug up yams.'

        d. *Yarla-ku-rna-rla   pangu-rnu ngajulu-rlu.* (goal dative)
            yam-dat-1sg-3dat dig-past   1sg-erg
            'I dug for yams.'

(35)   a.*Walya-rna karla-ja.* (effect)
            earth-1sg   dig-past
            'I dug the earth.'

        b.*Walya-ku-rna-rla-jinta karla-ja.*
            earth-dat-1sg-3dat-dd dig-past
            'I dug at the earth.'

        c. *Yarla-rna karla-ja.* (obtain)
            yam-1sg   dig-past
            'I dug up yams.'

        d. *Yarla-ku-rna-rla   karla-ja.* (goal dative)
            yam-dat-1sg-3dat dig-past
            'I dug for yams.'

Here again we have evidence of an asymmetrical relation between the LCS corresponding to the effect use of a verb and the LCS corresponding to the verb's obtain use. This relation is captured by the lexical rule which we call the OBTAIN RULE. The obtain rule derives an LCS which contains an OBTAIN predicate modified by a means component containing the LCS which is the input to the rule. Thus the obtain rule applies to the LCS of *paka-rni*, which corresponds to the effect use of that verb to produce the LCS, which corresponds to the obtain use of the verb. This rule is summarized in (36).

(36)   (x produce effect on y) *by* ((entity come into contact with y) *by* (x manipulate entity)) → (x OBTAIN y) *by* (x produce effect on material source/location of y)...

The LCS which is the output of (36) satisfies the conditions for the application of the goal dative rule (see (20)), which results in the LCS that corresponds to the goal dative use of the verb as exemplified for *paka-rni* by (1b) and for *pangi-rni* by (34d). The failure of verbs like *karla-mi* 'dig' to participate in the effect and related conative uses shows that the lexical rules are not bidirectional, but rather unidirectional, as represented in this article.

Considerable economy can be realized in the representation of the lexical entries of verbs if instead of listing all the possible meanings of each verb, we represent the sorts of regularities described in this article in the form of productive rules which generate the correct range of meanings. This form of lexical organization is sketched in (37).

$$(37) \quad \text{LCS (effect)} \xrightarrow{\text{conative rule}} \text{LCS (conative)}$$

$$\xrightarrow{\text{obtain rule}} \text{LCS (obtain)}$$

$$\text{LCS (obtain)} \xrightarrow{\text{goal dative rule}} \text{LCS (goal dative)}$$

A verb's lexical entry consists of at least two levels of representation: LCS and PAS.[12] The LCS is the relevant level at which generalizations about the range of uses or meanings which characterize a verb are made. The PAS represents categorical information about the syntactic properties of the verb—the nature of its maximal projection and the organization of the verb's arguments with respect to this projection. This is the relevant level of representation which determines the GFs borne by syntactic categories which are associated with the arguments of a verb.

---

[12] A verb's lexical entry obviously contains other types of information—phonological, morphological, etc.—which are not relevant to the verbal properties discussed in this article.

5. RELATION BETWEEN LCS AND PAS

The LCS represents linguistically relevant components of a verb's meaning. The LCSs proposed for the various uses of the verbs under discussion in the preceding section make no reference to thematic roles, sometimes referred to as θ-ROLES in the government and binding framework literature, or as DEEP CASES following Fillmore (1968). The LCSs we have proposed take the form of related semantic functions. The arguments which these functions take are represented as variables. These are mapped, in nonarbitrary ways, onto structural positions in the maximal projection of V, which we have taken to be V''.[13] The semantic relations which make up the LCSs set out in Section 4 are asymmetric. For example, x obtain y does not imply y obtain x, nor does x produce effect on y imply that y produce effect on x. In each case, there is an argument which we might describe as the ACTIVE argument (x in the examples just cited) while the other argument is, by comparison, PASSIVE (see Hale and Keyser, 1986).

Typically, the syntactic category associated with the active argument bears the subject GF, while the one representing the passive argument bears the object GF. This correlation holds of the four constructions given in (1) and (2). Of course this correlation holds much more generally both in Warlpiri and cross-linguistically.

As was noted previously, the syntactic categories associated with the passive argument exhibit different case marking while bearing the same GF, i.e., object, depending on the nature of the semantic relation defined in the LCS between it and the active argument. Where the LCS defines a function such that the passive argument is an entity on which an effect is actually produced by the active argument or an entity which is obtained by the active entity, represented by the x variable, the passive entity, represented by the y variable, is linked to a structural position in the verb's PAS such that it is directly governed by V. In other words, it is the direct sister of V, or direct object of V.

---

[13] This discussion of the relation between the LCS and the syntactic components of the grammar does not take into account the specification of other lexical or inherent cases which allow the overt syntactic expression of the logical arguments that do not bear the core GFs of subject and object, e.g., the use of locative governing the NP referring to the "location/material source of" entity obtained or searched for in both the obtain and goal dative uses (see *watiya-rla* 'tree-loc' in (1) and *wilypiri-rla* 'hollow-loc' in (26)). Baker (1985) develops an interesting theory of the syntactic structures derived as a function of the thematic relations holding between a predicator and the syntactic categories with which it combines in d-structure. He develops his theory on the basis of a body of data showing a number of important differences in the syntactic behavior of syntactic categories associated with different thematic roles. In particular, the contrast in incorporation behavior between purposive as opposed to instrumental arguments leads him to posit different thematic relations structures between the category V and the syntactic categories, NP and clitics, to which these roles are assigned.

It is not obvious if there exists a coherent semantic notion which defines the general class of semantic roles defined by functions such as obtain, produce effect on, etc. An attempt to formulate very general rules or conventions for the mapping of arguments identified in a verb's LCS onto structural prositions in a verb's PAS in terms of thematic roles like Patient, Theme, Agent, or Goal might prove to be wrongheaded. More research must be done to throw light on this area of lexical organization (see Rappaport and Levin, this volume).

Where the obtain and produce effect functions are defined in a verb's LCS as arguments of the purpose function, *in order that*, the passive argument of those functions is indirectly projected onto a structural position governed by V by means of dative case. The dative case is the reflex of the purpose function—thus the difference between the PAS in (22) corresponding to the obtain construction and the PAS in (23) corresponding to the goal dative construction.

The PAS in (33), which corresponds to the conative use, contains two dative cases, one being adjoined to the maximal projection (KP) of the other. These dative cases are the reflexes of the two purpose functions present in the conative LCS, which is the output of the lexical conative rule in (32). These purpose functions modify the semantic role of the y argument with respect to both the contact and effect functions. That is, y is defined as a POTENTIAL GOAL with respect to each of these functions, not as an ACTUAL or REALIZED GOAL (or Patient) as in the effect LCS formulated as the input to the rule in (32).

If we can define the principles by which the level of representation we have called PAS is derived from the LCS, then considerable economy can be achieved in the amount of explicit information which must be included in a verb's lexical entry. Only the basic LCS would need to be listed, along with morphophonological properties.

6. RELATION BETWEEN PAS AND
   SYNTACTIC COMPONENT

In Warlpiri, two distinct sets of syntactic categories are involved in the identification or evaluation of the arguments which figure in a verb's PAS. These are person–number AUX clitics and NP. Both categories are case marked. Case marks and identifies the relation between a syntactic category and the structural position which the argument with which it is associated occupies in the PAS. The person–number clitics express deictic information about the referent (speaker or addressee) as well as the number of individuals involved in the scope of the reference (one, two, more than two). The NP provides information about non-speech-act-related attributes of the referent. However, this correlation between syntactic category and referential function is not clear-cut, as the syntactic category NP includes the independent pronouns which express person–number features equivalent to that of the corresponding clitics.[14]

Person–number clitics are only associated with arguments of a verb identified in its LCS when the verb is governed by the inflectional syntactic category tense/mood, that is, when the verb is used in a finite clause. In nonfinite clauses, the tense is dependent on the tense of the finite clause to which the nonfinite clause is related. The AUX, which contains morphemes expressing tense and aspect as well as person–number clitics, is only present in finite clauses. In fact, it is obligatory in such clauses.

The syntactic reflex of the inherent dative case which governs the y argument in the PAS derived from the goal dative LCS, repeated here as (38), is the dative AUX clitic-*rla* which evaluates y as third person singular in (1b).

(38) $[_{V''} x[_{V'} [_{KP} y \text{ DAT}] \text{ V}]]$

The y argument is further evaluated by the attribute 'honey,' expressed in (1b) by means of the dative case-marked NP *jurlarda-ku*. The overt presence of the NP is optional, however, as illustrated by comparing (1b) with (12b).

Where the V in (38) is associated with the syntactic category V, governed by the infinitive (inf) mood which has no independent tense, then the only syntactic reflex of the y argument which may be overtly expressed is a dative case-marked NP. This contrasts with the finite constructions in (1a,b) which show two morphosyntactic contrasts that correlate with the semantic contrast between the sentences: difference in case of clitic associated with y argument (accusative in (1a), dative in (1b)), and difference in case marking of NP associated with y argument (absolutive in (1a), dative in (1b)). In the pair of nonfinite clauses contrasted in (39) there is only one morphosyntactic difference, which is realized on the NP associated with the y argument, *jurlarda* 'honey' in (39a) and *jurlarda-ku* 'honey-dat' in (39b).

(39)   a. ...*wati-ki jurlarda paka-rninja-rlarni.* (obtain use)
                man-dat honey chop-inf-obvcomp
          '...while the man (is/was) chopping out honey.'
        b. ...*wati-ki   jurlarda-ku paka-rninja-rlarni.* (goal dative use)
                man-dat honey-dat   chop-inf-obvcomp
          '...while the man (is/was) chopping for honey.'

---

[14] In Warlpiri, the case marking of independent pronouns is like that of other NPs. Important syntactic differences, revealed in constructions not relevant to the present discussion, do, however, exist between independent pronouns and nouns.

Unlike its counterpart in the finite clause in (1a), the non-case-marked noun *jurlarda* in the nonfinite construction in (39a) is not in the absolutive case. Whereas the non-case-marked noun *jurlarda* 'honey' in (1a) may occupy any position in the finite clause relative to the verb *paka-rnu* 'chop-past,' the noun *jurlarda* 'honey' in (39a), forms part of a constituent with the infinitival verb *paka-rninja* 'chop-inf.' The head of this constituent is the obvcomp *-rlarni*. If *jurlarda* occupies any position in the clause other than that immediately preceding the verb, then it must be overtly marked by the obvcomp ending, as in (40), where *jurlarda* is postposed to the infinitive verb.

(40)   ... *wati-ki   paka-rninja-rlarni   jurlarda-rlarni.*
          man-dat chop-inf-obvcomp honey-obvcomp
          '... while the man (is/was/will be) chopping out honey.'

The dative case-marked NP *jurlarda-ku* 'honey-dat' in (39b) does not form a constituent with the verb and the complementizer ending on the verb. The dative case is the head of the constituent of which the noun, *jurlarda*, is the complement. Thus the dative case-marked NP may occupy any position in the clause.

The assignment of absolutive case to an NP is only sanctioned by the presence of an independent tense/mood morpheme which characterizes the finite clause. Absolutive case is assigned to the category NP in the syntactic component of the grammar, by virtue of structural relations. Absolutive case is not specified as part of a verb's lexical properties, as represented in its PAS.[15] It is reserved for the category NP and can only be realized in finite clauses. Dative case, on the other hand, is specified as part of a verb's lexical properties. This specification constrains the case marking of the NP and clitic associated with the argument governed by dative case in the verb's PAS. Dative case, unlike absolutive case, does not depend on an independent case assigner in the syntactic component in order to be realized. It is assigned in both finite and nonfinite clauses, and it marks both clitics and NPs.

The PAS derived from the conative LCS contains two dative cases as shown in (33), an "inner" dative which directly governs the *y* argument, and an "outer" dative adjoined to the KP, the maximal projection of the dative case. The dative–double dative AUX clitic complex in finite clauses is the morphosyntactic reflex of this double dative structure. The NP associated with the *y* argument does not have double dative case marking. The actual realization of case marking is clearly subject to morphosyntactic constraints. For example, no NP may be suffixed by more than one grammatical case, i.e., ergative, dative.

---

[15] Similar principles apply to the assignment of ergative case, but they are not described here.

Unlike the dative nonsubject AUX clitics which express the full range of person–number features, the double dative clitic *-rla* is invariable except for the allomorph *-jinta*, which is used following the 3sg dative clitic *-rla*. Thus the double dative clitic does not evaluate an argument in the manner of the other clitics, that is, it does not express deictic person–number features of the referent. Only the dative clitic has this function.

The double dative clitic performs a number of roles in Warlpiri grammar, one of which is its role in the conative construction. The conative double dative is special in that it is associated with the argument of the verb with which the preceding dative clitic is also associated. In other uses of the dative–double dative construction, the double dative clitic signals the presence of an adjoined purposive or benefactive dative-governed argument in addition to a dative-governed argument of the verb. The adjoined dative argument is represented by z in (41). The dative argument of V is represented by y.

(41) $[_{V''} [_{V''} x [_{V'} [y \text{ dat}] V]] [z \text{ dat}]]$

The syntactic category associated with y in (41) bears the object GF. However, it is the invariant double-dative clitic which is associated with this same argument. The dative clitic, which expresses values for person and number features, is associated with the adjoined z argument. The NPs associated with y and z are marked by dative cases. (14b), repeated here as (42), illustrates this use of the double dative construction.

(42)   *Kuyu-ku-**ngalingki**-rla nya-nja-ya-nta **ngali-ki** yarnunjuku-ku!*
          meat-dat-**12d**-dd   see-inf-go-imp **12d-dat** hungry-dat
          'Be looking for meat for us hungry ones as you go along!'

The first person inclusive dual clitic-*ngalingki* and the independent pronoun *ngali*, marked by dative case, are both associated with the benefactive dative argument, represented as z in (41). The double dative AUX clitic *-rla* is construed with the dative case marked NP *kuyu-ku*, which is associated with the y argument in (41). These latter two syntactic categories bear the object GF to the verb, *nya-nja-ya-nta* 'go along looking for.'

Where a dative-governed argument is adjoined to the PAS of a verb which has no dative governed object argument but only a direct object argument, as in (43), it is the adjoined dative argument that is associated with the nonsubject clitic. There is no clitic reflex of the verb's direct object. This may only be expressed by an NP.

(43) $[_{V''} [_{V''} x [_{V'} y V]] [z \text{ dat}]]$

In (44), *marlu-jarra* 'kangaroo-dual' is associated with the y argument of (43), but there is no clitic construed with it. The dative case-marked NP, *purlka-ku* 'old man-dat' is associated with the adjoined z argument of (43) and is construed with the 3sg dative clitic *-rla.*

(44)   ***Purlka-ku-rna-rla***   *luwa-rnu   marlu-jarra.*
      old man-dat-1sg-**3dat** shoot-past kangaroo-dual
      'I shot two kangaroos for the old man.'

In the absence of an adjoined dative argument, a nonsubject clitic would be associated with the direct object argument of the verb, as in (45), where *marlu-jarra* is construed with *-palangu.*

(45)   ***Marlu-jarra-rna-palangu luwa-rnu.***
      kangaroo-dual-1sg-**3d**   shoot-past
      'I shot two kangaroos.'

The conative construction in (46) differs minimally in its apparent surface form from the sentence in (47), the only surface difference between the two sentences being the presence of the double dative clitic in (46) and its absence from (47). However, the interpretation of the two sentences is quite different. They are the reflexes of different PASs and of different LCSs.

(46)   *Marlu-ku-rna-rla-jinta*   *luwa-rnu.* (conative)
      kangaroo-dat-1sg-3dat-dd shoot-past
      'I shot at the kangaroo.'

(47)   *Marlu-ku-rna-rla*   *luwa-rnu.* (effect + adjoined dative)
      kangaroo-dat-1sg-3dat shoot-past
      'I shot it for/with the kangaroo.'

Unlike (46), which does not imply that anything was actually shot, (47) does imply that something was shot, for example a tree (*watiya*), and that this entity is related in some way to the kangaroo, expressed by the dative case-marked NP *marlu-ku* 'kangaroo-dat' which is construed with the third person dative AUX clitic *-rla*. The entity shot may be overtly referred to by means of an absolutive NP such as *watiya* in (48).

(48)   *Marlu-ku-rna-rla*   *luwa-rnu   watiya.*
      kangaroo-dat-1sg-3dat shoot-past tree
      'I shot the tree for/with the kangaroo.'

(47) and (48) could be uttered in a context where the speaker shoots a tree and then perceives that there is a kangaroo standing near the tree. The PAS underlying (47) and (48) is that given in (43). The dative NP *marlu-ku* and the clitic *-rla* are associated with the adjoined z argument, whereas the absolutive NP *watiya* in (48) is associated with the y argument of (43). There is no surface

reflex of the y argument in (47). In (46), the dative NP *marlu-ku* is construed with the third person dative clitic *-rla*. These categories are associated with the y argument of the conative PAS shown in (33). The double dative clitic in (46) is not associated with an additional adjoined dative argument, but rather it is the reflex of the outer dative in (33), and thus it is indirectly associated with the same y argument. The component of the conative PAS containing the two dative cases, [[y DAT] DAT], reflects the two purposive relations defined in the corresponding LCS which modify the semantic role of the y argument.

In a nonfinite conative construction, the only possible surface reflex of the y argument is a dative case-marked NP as in (49).

(49)   *Wati-rna nya-ngu marlu-ku   luwa-rninja-kurra.*
        man-1sg see-past kangaroo-dat shoot-inf-objcomp
        'I saw a man shooting at a kangaroo.'

Thus the difference between the goal dative and conative uses of a verb are not morphologically marked in non-finite clauses. The interpretation depends on contextual factors. It is an operation which associates a possible PAS and LCS with the syntactic configuration.

Given that the association of an NP with an argument in a verb's PAS is always optional, the four uses of *paka-rni* 'chop' illustrated in (1) and (2) could be realized simply as an infinitive verb governed by a complementizer, thus giving rise to a surface form four-ways ambiguous. Even in finite clauses, there is possible ambiguity between the obtain and effect uses because of the structural identity which derives from the fact that both uses have the same PAS. They only differ with respect to their LCSs.

The ambiguity possible in infinitival constructions is more superficial in the sense that it is attributable to mechanisms proper to the syntactic component which include the association of syntactic categories with entities defined in the PAS. The superficial ambiguity present in nonfinite constructions is dispelled when the verbs are realized in finite constructions.

7. CONCLUSION

This fairly detailed examination of four construction types—effect, conative, obtain, and goal dative—shows that there are at least three autonomous, but related, levels of structure which characterize a verb. In investigating the properties of these four construction types, the lexical properties of a verb, as represented in its LCS and PAS, have been differentiated from the syntactic properties which characterize a construction in which the verb is used.

The ability of a verb to participate in one or more of these constructions depends on its semantic properties, which are captured at a level of representation we have called the LCS. These properties determine the form of the verb's PAS, which contains no semantic information.[16]

The PAS represents structural relations between the category V and the arguments of the verb identified as arguments of semantic functions defined in the corresponding LCS. The structural relation between V and an argument may be mediated by an inherent case, such as dative. The form of the PAS is constrained by the nature of the verbal projection—number of levels to which it projects, nature and number of complement(s), specifier, etc.

In turn, the PAS restricts the possible syntactic configurations in which a verb may be realized, relative to the syntactic categories which are associated with the arguments represented in the verb's PAS. It determines the "deep" GFs, such as subject, object, which nominal and pronominal syntactic categories associated with verbal arguments bear in relation to the verb. The syntactic component is also subject to constraints which are independent of the PAS of any given verb; for example, the interdependence of various categories such as tense, mood, aspect, and case and their relation to the nominal and pronominal syntactic categories.

The relationship between the four constructions studied is shown to be best formulated at the lexicosemantic level called the LCS. These relationships are represented in the form of unidirectional lexical rules which have an LCS as their input and output. These rules are productive in that they do not operate on the fully specified LCS of a particular verb, but rather are formulated such that they operate on LCS types or classes which contain features common to the LCS corresponding to the individual verbs which are members of those verb classes. The rules pick out those components of meaning which are common to the classes of verbs which participate in the relevant construction types.

The morphosyntactic differences between the constructions studied are shown to result from the application of general conventions involved in the mapping of LCS components into PAS. A comparison of the form of finite and nonfinite clauses featuring the four uses of impact verbs under discussion

---

[16] In its absence of semantic content, the PAS, as it is proposed here, resembles Zubizarreta's (1987) LEXICOSEMANTIC STRUCTURE in representing hierarchical structural relations between the arguments of a predicator, represented as variables, conceived as placeholders for lexical content, and the predicator. It also approaches Higginbotham's (1985) θ-grids which simply indicate the number of θ-roles associated with a verb which must be "saturated" in the hierarchically structured syntactic component.

made it clear that the differences in meaning between each of these uses cannot derive from the difference in superficial morphosyntactic properties associated with a given construction, since these differences can fail to be realized concretely in nonfinite constructions. Differences in meaning of the sort examined in this article do not derive from syntactic differences, but rather the converse holds.

ACKNOWLEDGMENTS

In writing this article I have had the benefit of many hours of discussion with Ken Hale, who has generously shared his rich insights into Warlpiri with me, and also with Beth Levin and Malka Rappaport. Extensive critical comments and editorial suggestions from Wendy Wilkins were very helpful in revising the original draft. This discussion also owes much to previous work on Warlpiri grammar by Ken Hale, David Nash, and Jane Simpson. I am, of course, solely responsible for its contents. This article was written as part of the Lexicon Project of the MIT Center for Cognitive Science. Support for the project was provided by a grant from the System Development Foundation. Long-term funding from the Northern Territory Department of Education has allowed me to do extensive fieldwork in Warlpiri communities.

THE FEATURE +AFFECTED AND THE FORMATION OF THE PASSIVE

DAVID LEBEAUX

Department of Linguistics
University of Maryland
College Park, Maryland 20742

1. INTRODUCTION

Accounting for a delay in the acquisition of the so-called nonactional passive over the actional passive is a problem mentioned and dealt with in a number of works (Borer and Wexler, 1987; Berwick and Weinberg, 1984). The basic data in (1) and (2) are taken from Maratsos *et al.* (1979).

(1)   Actional passives
       John was hit.
       The bottle was broken.

(2)   Nonactional passives (delayed in acquisition)
       John was liked.
       John was seen.

Borer and Wexler (1987) refer to a similar finding, citing Maratsos *et al.* (1983). Unlike Borer and Wexler (1987) and Berwick and Weinberg (1984), I

243

argue that the delay in acquisition of (2) as compared to (1) may be derived in the following way:

(3)   A set of primitives P is ANALYTICALLY DEPENDENT on a set of
       primitives Q (equivalently: Q is analytically prior to P), iff Q must
       logically be applied to the input for P to apply.

(4) θ-theoretic primitives used in the acquisition of the passive are
       analytically prior to Case-theoretic primitives.[1]

The thematic analysis in which the s-structure subject is labeled + affected is analytically prior to the case analysis of the passive. This is not to say that the initial passive rule is stated in terms of the movement of a thematic element, as is explained below. Semantic bootstrapping accounts of various sorts (e.g., Pinker, 1984) are subcases of accounts using analytic priority: That is, semantic bootstrapping involves the postulation of a set of semantic (i.e., thematic) primitives which must be applied to the data before the string may be analyzed in terms of grammatical relations. The analysis in terms of grammatical relations in turn precedes a phrase-structural analysis (Pinker, 1984). In the terms above, the set of thematic primitives would be analytically prior to the set of grammatical–functional primitives, and the latter would be analytically prior to the phrase-structural primitives. Stowell's (1981) derivation of phrase structure (PS) configuration from case theory would be another instance of the same type, phrase structure being analytically dependent on case theory. Thus the adjacency of the object to the verb in the PS tree would follow, in Stowell's theory, from the necessary adjacency of case assignment to the accusative-marked element.

2. THE POSSIBILITIES

There are three possibilities for the initial restriction on the formulation of the passive:

(5)   a. A (thematic) restriction on movement or lexical rule application
           (Weinberg, 1981; Pinker, 1982)
       b. A restriction on A-chain formation (Borer and Wexler, 1987)
       c. A restriction on the positing of the trace (in this article: the relation
           of s-structure to the surface; see also Berwick and Weinberg, 1984)

---

[1] I use Case capital with an initial here to mean abstract Case in the government-binding sense. Henceforth, I simply refer to abstract Case as *case*.

These proposals differ essentially in the level at which the constraint in the grammar is placed. Assuming the general T-shaped model of Chomsky and Lasnik (1977) and Chomsky (1981), the rule Move-α maps deep structures (d-structures) into s-structures, and additional rules map s-structure into PF (for our purposes, the surface) or LF (logical form).

(6)   Chomsky–Lasnik T-model

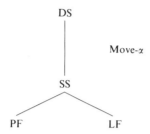

The first of the proposals above, in its GB form (Weinberg, 1981), suggests that there is a thematic restriction on Move-α at the stage discovered by Maratsos *et al.*, namely, that the original form of the rule is not Move-α, but rather Move Theme. A similar proposal is made in the LFG framework by Pinker (1982), namely, that passive as a lexical rule is initially thematically restricted to Agent/Patient relations.

The second sort of approach, advocated in Borer and Wexler (1987), suggests that there is an initial impossibility of A-chain formation. That is, structures of the following sort are barred at s-structure at this stage of language acquisition.

(7)   *John$_i$ was liked e$_i$.*

Since the A-chain (*John$_i$*, e$_i$) is by hypothesis unavailable at this stage, the child can only analyze the input as (8), where there is no trace or unindexed trace.

(8)   *John was liked.*

This means, however, that the lexical argument structure of *like* is not satisfied, or to the extent to which it is satisfied, *John* is treated as an external argument (Borer and Wexler, 1984). This would mean, in turn, that the construction would not be correctly understood.

What about the constructions which are understood appropriately at this stage? According to Wexler and Borer, these are not syntactic passives at all, but lexical passives as in (9).

(9)   *The bottle was broken.* (adjective passive)

Accordingly, there is no movement (and hence no A-chain formation), but the structure is appropriately understood.

In this, article I advocate a third approach, namely, that the constraint is on surface structures, or, more exactly, on the mechanism by which the trace is posited given a particular surface structure and lexical representation. In this way, the approach is similar to that advocated in Berwick and Weinberg (1984). In fact, this involves a change in the role of directionality in the grammar. In (5c), the trace-enriched s-structure is projected from two separate levels, d-structure and the surface, the "external levels" (Chomsky, class lectures) which jointly determine the content of s-structure. The basic structure of the grammar is thus identical to that which Chomsky and Lasnik assume, but with one of the arrows reversed and d-structure and the surface considered in tandem.

(10)

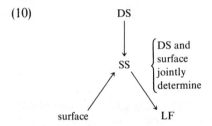

That is, information about the surface—directly available to the child—and about d-structure (or, more exactly, about lexical properties of heads) jointly determine the form of s-structure. The fact that the surface is available to the child is hardly questionable; the other assumption, that d-structure is available as well, is much more so, in spite of its commonness as a necessary assumption to get the acquisition system off the ground (see Wexler and Culicover, 1980, where the availability of d-structure is assumed; a comparable assumption in Pinker, 1984, is the availability of functional structures). In the present approach, the counterintuitiveness of this assumption is considerably lessened in that it is not necessary to assume the accessibility of a full d-structure but rather of the lexical properties of heads, including the external/internal argument division. Insofar as this part of the d-structure representation may be assumed to be available to the child, being predictable from universal constraints on argument structures, the proposal escapes the charge of impracticality.

Note that to the extent to which central constraints should be stated on the d-structure + surface → s-structure mapping, the position and role of directionality becomes more central and an object of research.

Pinker (1982, from 1979) suggests the approach in (5a), in which the passive—treated as a lexical rule—is stated first in the most restrictive domain, and then the restriction is relaxed until the full passive is stated. Lebeaux (1981) amplifies this proposal as in (11) in an early version of the subset principle of Berwick (1982).

(11)   DOMAIN AGGREGATION: Set the passive at the universally most
         restrictive domain. Upon encountering exemplars outside that
         range, expand the domain to the less inclusive set. Continue until
         all passives in the input are accounted for.

This formulation of domain aggregation allows for the cross-linguistic acquisition of passives differing in domain without reference to negative evidence, i.e., without assuming that the child has access to "starred" sentence(s) in the body of data leading to the induction of the final grammar. Proposals of this type are conceptually very nice precisely because negative evidence need not be referred to. Nonetheless, there seems to be empirical grounds for rejecting such an approach, or at least calling it into question. Given a domain-aggregation approach, a particular sort of acquisition pattern would be expected, both individually and cross-linguistically, namely, the initial grammar G1 would be the smallest in a sequence of containing grammars G2, G3, ..., Gn with respect to the parameter at hand as shown in (12).

(12)

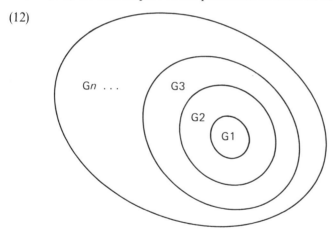

G1 would thematically define the passive at the earliest stage, G2 later, and G3 through Gn later still. The "transformation" in the grammar G1 → G2 would be determined by the child encountering a passive not generated in G1, the domain being in general successively expanded upon the detection of counterexemplifying inputs (i.e., passives outside the current domain).

This model makes two predictions, or at least allows for two potentialities. First, there would be the successive expansion of domain from the smallest to the largest for the acquisition of passive by individuals, as domains are aggregated. (An alternative explanation for the apparent expansion in English is given below.) Second, an array of different domains should be exhibited cross-linguistically, since each domain would be a possible "stopping-off point" for the acquisition of the appropriate domain. While the data are not exactly determinate, this prediction does not seem to be borne out. The restriction cross-linguistically to actional passives in final grammars seems to be virtually unattested. While the restriction to certain other passive types, e.g., adversatives in Japanese, certainly is well attested, there is no apparent gradation in domain as suggested in the model above. Finally, it might be argued that those languages which employ a passive restricted in domain have in fact a different passive than the one which is unrestricted. This would go against the hypothesis that the passive is the same (in the relevant languages) but simply differs in domain, as suggested by the theory above. In fact, two passives may exist alongside each other, one restricted in domain and the other not, as is the case in Japanese. This would not be predicted by the domain aggregation approach above, which would predict instead a distinct, different, single domain from language to language.

3. SEMANTIC BOOTSTRAPPING AND THE FEATURE +AFFECTED

There is one crucial way in which certain problems in language acquisition apparently differ from problems in grammatical theory, that is, with respect to directionality and input to the system. In general, rules in the grammar (or the rule, Move-α) map phrase markers into other phrase markers. The grammar is at least implicitly directional, in the sense that Move-α applies to d-structure to derive s-structure and, in the Chomsky–Lasnik model, to s-structure to derive LF and the surface. The directionality for certain purposes in acquisition is reversed. In particular, in order to determine the grammar of the language, the child must first determine the set of structures being faced. For example, in order to determine whether the verb in the language governs leftward or rightward, an analysis of the string must be undertaken which determines s-structure; from this structure, the setting of various parameters (e.g., directionality of government) may be determined. Let us call the string input N-STRUCTURE (input string structure) for the purpose of analysis. The problem is to determine the s-structure from that.

Let us break this up into two steps: the mapping from n-structure to surface structure, and from surface structure to s-structure. I use the term SURFACE STRUCTURE in a restricted and technical sense, to mean s-structure with all null categories and their dominating nodes eliminated.[2] The mapping is therefore as follows:

(13)   n-structure   →   surface structure   → s-structure
            (string structure)   (s-structure without traces)

For example:

(14)   a. N-STRUCTURE REPRESENTATION

       b. SURFACE STRUCTURE

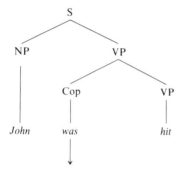

---

[2] That is, neither *wh*-trace nor NP-trace is present. This assumption may be counterfactual, the presence of a *wh*-trace in the phonology is a matter of some debate. For this article, nothing hangs on the existence or nonexistence of the *wh*-trace; what is crucial is the nonexistence of an NP-trace. This assumption is generally accepted.

I note in passing a potential argument against the existence of a *wh*-trace blocking contraction, and hence against the significance of the "wanna" facts, and a potential response. The crucial data are examples like *Who do you believe's left?* Such examples seem to me fine. To the extent that they are generally accepted (and they seem to be), it appears that the case-marked trace in the subject position is not blocking contraction.

There is an interesting, though radical, response. Suppose that ADJACENCY is defined in the following way:

α is adjacent to β iff, α and β are sisters and
   (i) no γ intervenes between them, or
   (ii) α is initial and β final, or β is initial and α final.

In essence, this definition is the standard one, with the difference that the initial and final sisters are defined as adjacent. The conception is that the phrase-marker is joined back over itself at each level, like a cylinder.

Assuming such a definition, the following is a perfectly well-formed d-structure

c. S-STRUCTURE

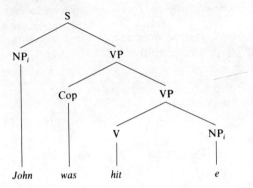

From s-structure, various properties of the system may be determined, for example, the directionality of government.

The first of these rules, mapping n-structure to surface structure, may be considered structure building; it takes strings and maps them into trees. It would appear to have no direct analog with the rule Move-α, nor would mapping from surface structure to s-structure. Nonetheless, the principles which characterize the grammar as a whole—case theory, θ-theory, the projection principle, and so on—are used in determining these mappings. The true representation would then be closer (15) than (14).

(15)

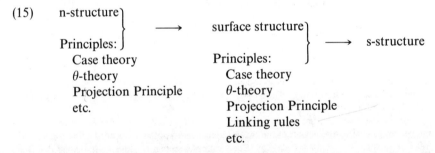

By LINKING RULES I mean the rules linking the modules, in particular, those linking the (abstract) case and thematic systems. In the following, I show how a particular linking rule, characterizing the relation of internal argumenthood to θ-role assignment, plays a central role in the acquisition of the passive. The

---

(AGR VP NP)$_s$. Here, NP is adjacent to AGR. The resulting structure is similar to that given in Pesetsky (1982) for PRO-clauses.

Assuming this as a possible d-structure, extraction may take place from the final position, similar to (though not identical to) the analysis of such data in Italian. There would be no case-marked trace in subject position to block contraction.

relevant portion of the grammar in which it plays a role is in the second mapping in (15), from surface structure plus principles into s-structure. Further, integral properties of the final grammar, in particular, the restriction on passives in nominals but not sentences, follows from the same mapping.

3.1. The Mapping from N-Structure to the Surface

Consider first the problem of the child facing a string consisting of a verb and two arguments. The basic structure of the language, SOV, SVO, VOS, VSO, etc., must be learned. Thus the subject and object must be isolated and labeled. One possibility is the following universal thematic linking principle (Grimshaw, 1979; Pinker, 1984):

(16)   If α is an agent, it is a subject.

Note that the form is an implicational universal rather than a biconditional. The latter would be false. Given a thematically labeled string, the formulation in (16) allows the phrase structure to be constructed, bootstrapping from the canonical structural realization of thematic roles.

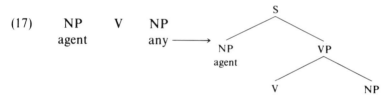

(17)   NP   V   NP
        agent   any

Assuming the invariable existence of a VP—a common assumption in GB—the rule in (16) picks out the subject and the other NP gets grouped with the verb as an internal argument.

While principle (16) both allows for the structure to be determined and gives a close syntax/semantics mesh, there are reasons to think that an alternative formulation would be preferable. First, it is by no means clear that all agents are external (i.e., subjects). For example, in passive constructions the *by* phrase is not external to the verb phrase and does not bind an external trace.[3] Second, we may consider a restriction on so-called unaccusative or ergative-moved constructions (Burzio, 1986). Such constructions exemplified in (18), are commonly assumed to involve a trace of the subject in the object position.

(18)   a. *John is swimming.*
        b. *John$_i$ appeared t$_i$.*

How might this restriction be captured? Let us suppose that the generalization is thematic that is, *John* undergoes a change of state in the sentence in (18b)

---

[3] External in the sense of Williams (1980), meaning external to the VP.

(with respect to the situation), but does not do so in (18a). This means that, thematically, *John* is + affected in (18b) but not in (18a). But how does the child determine that the subject starts off internally in (18b)? If we assume some principle requiring that + affected elements be internal at deep structure, i.e., a constraint on the thematic linking of the internal argument, then this sort of analysis would become viable. Note that a constraint on the linking of the external argument, such as that given in (16), would not do the job.

Let us therefore adopt the following constraint:

(19)   AFFECTED ARGUMENT CONSTRAINT: If α is + affected, it is an object
        (is case-marked by the verb) at d-structure.

The affected argument constraint, then, allows the child to determine the d-structure which underlies surface structures like that in (20a), namely, the d-structure in (20b). Without such a principle, how could the d-structure be determined?

(20)   a. *John appeared.*
       b. appeared John.

Given the principle in (19), there are tree-building principles of the same sort that Pinker and Grimshaw suppose. However, rather than determining the subject-of relationship (via the annotation of an element as an agent) and consigning all the other elements by exclusion to the VP, the tree-building principles determine the object (via the affected argument constraint) and label the leftover NP as a subject. While hardly decisive, this is more in accord with the usual mechanism of tree building in a Montague-type approach (Montague, 1973; Partee, 1979), where the tree is built bottom upward.

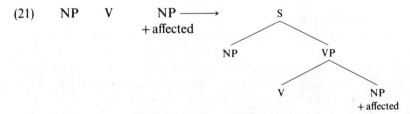

The real benefit, however, has to do with movement constructions, and how they can be analyzed. It is to this that we now turn.

3.2. Trace-Mapping and the Affected Argument Constraint

I suggested in (3) and (4) that a particular set of primitives may be analytically dependent on another set. In particular, the set of grammatical-functional primitives (and ultimately the phrase structure tree itself) is analytically dependent on a thematic analysis. The thematic analysis, in this case, is the labeling of the d-structure object by means of the label + Affected, together with a constraint which holds that all such +affected elements are internal to the VP.

The thematic analysis allows for the basic structure of the language to be determined (e.g., ultimately such primitives as the directionality of government), but the thematic primitives are not those used in the ultimate analysis of the string (Pinker, 1984). Rather, given that the basic structure of the S has been determined, the system is freed from its direct reliance on θ analysis to determine structure. This allows elements with a much freer range of θ roles to appear in the subject and object positions. This is the situation with respect to the initial acquisition situation.

However, the type of analysis above and the affected argument constraint are of greater use than simply allowing the child to determine the basic phrase structure of the grammar. They are also used to determine the passive in the language at a later stage in development.

Consider again the Maratsos sentences: the prior acquisition of sentences like (22) over those like (23).

(22)   a. *John$_i$ was hit t$_i$.*
        b. *John$_i$ was destroyed t$_i$.*

(23)   a. *John$_i$ was liked t$_i$.*
        b. *John$_i$ was seen t$_i$.*

I assume that a more accurate characterization of the difference between them is not in actional versus nonactional passive, but in passives having affected objects versus those which do not. The θ-theory that I assume is an extension of that of Kegl and Gee (undated), in that I assume that θ-roles are actually composites of θ feature sets (see also Rozwadowska, this volume). In particular, I assume that θ-roles have features from three domains: prominence, location, and degree of control, as shown in (24). The first of these is represented with the feature + theme assigned to the most prominent element. The second is represented with the θ-features +Goal, +Source, and so on, giving movement to or from a location. The third is represented with the features + agent and + affected. The θ-feature + agent is equivalent to the logical subject of CAUSE, while the + affected element is that which undergoes a change of state. Note that I assume that it is the + Affected feature, rather than some other feature, which marks the element undergoing a change of state. The Patient θ-role, I would argue, is actually a composite of two θ-features, + Affected and + Theme (25). A principle of θ-feature uniqueness accompanies these assumptions.

(24) θ-role features
   a. Domain 1: Prominence (e.g., +Theme)
   b. Domain 2: Location
         (i) Subtype 1 (movement to or from a location, e.g., +Source, +Goal)
         (ii) Subtype 2 (pure location, e.g., +Loc)
   c. Domain 3: Degree of control (e.g., +Agent, +Affected)

(25)   Reinterpretation of traditional θ-roles as θ-sets, for example,
   a. Patient = (+Theme, +Affected)
   b. Subject of *give* = (+Source, +Agent)

(26) θ-feature uniqueness: An element is assigned only one θ-feature
              from each θ-domain (prominence, location, degree of control)

Consider now how the child may discover chains in the surface input.[4] The child is faced with two identical surface structures in (27) and (28). Recall that the surface structure does not include traces.

(27)   *John sang.*

(28)   *John appeared.*

A thematic analysis of the string, by hypotheses available to the child, allows for the two to be differentiated, where *John* undergoes a change of state with respect to the situation in (28) but not in (27).

(29)   *John   sang.*
              +Theme

(30)   *John   appeared.*
              +Theme
              +Affected

But now, given (30) and the affected argument constraint, a trace must be posited in (30), since +Affected elements must be internal to the VP at d-structure. By the affected argument constraint, the structure of (30) must actually be (31), where the co-indexed trace marks the d-structure position of the element.

(31)   *John$_i$ (appeared t$_i$)*

---

[4] A CHAIN is a sequence of co-indexed nodes, generally left by movement (Chomsky, 1981). The subject in the passive and its trace would form a chain, as would the *wh*-element and its trace. A chain may have length more than two if several movement operations have applied (e.g., NP-movement followed by *wh*-movement).

It is informative to consider the logic used. *John* in *John appeared* is in some sense the element which undergoes a change of state with respect to the situation (namely, he enters the scene). Therefore, the child analyzes it thematically as + Affected. But that analysis, in collaboration with the affected argument constraint, allows for the trace to be correctly posited in (31). As an acquisition problem, what differentiates (29) and (30) is the ability to posit a trace, and this is what the affected argument constraint allows. It is precisely a constraint on the mapping of surface structures into s-structures that the acquisition system requires.

The situation with nominals is similar. The child is faced with the nominals in (32) and (33).

(32)   *the song's singing*
        John's perception

(33)   *the city's destruction*

In (33), the element in subject position in the nominal is read as the LOGICAL OBJECT. In (32), however, no similar reading is possible, in spite of the pragmatic bias in that direction. *The song's singing* cannot mean that someone is singing the song, nor can *John's perception* mean that someone perceives John. Rather, the song must (nonsensically) be doing the singing, and John must be perceiving.

This difference, noted by Fiengo (1980) and Anderson (1979), has been summarized as the + affected constraint in nominals: only + Affected elements may be NP-moved in nominals. The constraint follows from the principles advocated here. Suppose that the child is faced with the two surface structures in (34). A thematic analysis may be given. I have assumed above that the θ-role Patient is really a compound (+ Theme, + Affected), while Theme is simply + Theme. The thematic analysis of these NPs would then be the following:

(34)   a. *the play's performance*
              + theme
        b. *the city's destruction*
              + theme
              + affected

Now, given the affected argument constraint and assuming an internal/ external division of arguments in NP, the affected element in (34b) must come from an internal position. We therefore get the difference in assigned structures in (35).

(35) a. *the play's performance*
          +theme
      b. *the city's$_i$ destruction t$_i$*
          +theme
          +affected

The restriction on NP-movement in nominals is therefore derived as a property of the acquisition device.

To summarize, I have shown how an otherwise inexplicable restriction on movement in NPs and an otherwise problematic difference in surface intransitive structures would both be correctly analyzed by assuming the affected argument constraint. In each case, after thematic analysis, an internal trace must be posited (with respect to the surface structure string), and it is this which allows the correct assignment of s-structure.

Note as well that these syntactic cases decide between the formulations necessary for the semantic bootstrapping part of the problem. It was noted above that the basic structure of the sentence could be picked out either by assuming that agents are external (Pinker's account) or that +Affected elements are internal (this account). Both accounts work for semantic bootstrapping, the first by determining the subject thematically, and the second by determining the object thematically. However, only the latter proposal extends to the full range of syntactic evidence considered here. Thus it is to be preferred.

4. THE GRAMMATICALIZATION OF PASSIVES

I have pursued two goals in the discussion above: to show how thematic primitives are analytically prior in the analysis of the string (and, in particular, in the postulation of NP trace), and to argue that for some acquisition purposes the directionality of the grammar should be reversed, with d-structure and surface structure jointly determining s-structure. In this section, I show how these come together in the analysis of the passive to determine the acquisition sequence noted by Maratsos and others.

There are five logical steps or stages:

1. The passive form is recorded from surface structure.
2. In passives with moved +Affected elements (e.g., that of *hit*), a trace is posited with the aid of the affected argument constraint.
3. A chain composed of the trace and the surface subject is thus formed. Since chains may only be case marked once, the child deduces that the object position is not case marked, since the subject position is.

4. Since the verb associated with the passive normally case marks the object position, the child deduces that there is a productive morphological affix absorbing case attached to the verb. This amounts to learning the passive.
5. Given productive case-absorbing morphology, the passive is "grammaticalized," i.e., extended over the full range of verbs.

The two visible stages in this progression are 2 and 5: 2, where the child postulates a trace on thematic grounds, and 5, where the passive has become fully productive and grammaticalized. Examples of the stages are shown below.

(36)   Stage 1 (no analysis): Child has active form, but no passive.
        John was hit.
        John was liked.

(37)   Stage 2 (trace postulated by affected argument constraint): difference in comprehension.
        John$_i$ was hit t$_i$.
        John was liked.

(38)   Stage 3 (deduction of no case):
        John$_i$ was hit t$_i$
        $\uparrow$
        no case

(39)   Stage 4 (deduction of productive passive morphology):
        John$_i$ was ((hit)) t$_i$.
        $\uparrow$
        Case-absorbing morphology

(40)   Stage 5 (general passive):
        John$_i$ was ((hit)) t$_i$.
        John$_i$ was ((like)ed) t$_i$. Case-absorbing morphology on all verbs

Some general points should be mentioned about the acquisition sequence. The grammaticalization of the passive depends on the decoding of case-absorbing morphology, thus extending the projection of a movement operation to all structures from just a subset. It is just this grammaticalization and movement to full syntactic generality which distinguished the passive movement from the restricted movement in NPs. The crucial part of the passive, as a syntactic operation, involves in this view the introduction of case-absorbing morphology onto the verb. It is this which constitutes the passive. Since this is the crucial operation, once this has been determined by the child (Stage 4), the passive becomes fully general.

Thus the passives in cases of movement within NP are not "real" passives, in the sense that there is no rule of productive inflectional morphology absorbing case. Rather, the trace is introduced, both for nominals and sentences, for thematic reasons, namely, the affected argument constraint. From that point in development, the sentential structure and the nominal structure diverge. The sentential structure does allow, ultimately, the detection of the inflectional, case-absorbing morphology on the verb, and therefore the passive becomes fully general, or "syntactic." This corresponds to Steps 4 and 5 above. The nominal case never goes through Stages 4 and 5, so no general nominal rule is posited. Hence the nominal movement retains, even in the adult grammar, the thematically restricted form. The acquisition sequence provides an explanation for why this is the case: In the nominal there is the (internal) affected argument constraint, and hence the possibility of movement (i.e., trace projection), but there is no grammaticalization of the passive, because there is no introduction of inflectional, case-absorbing morphology.

5. PASSIVES, ANALYTIC PRIORITY, AND THE STRUCTURE OF THE GRAMMAR

I have given an account which draws together, and attempts to explain, the following phenomena:

1. the thematic restriction on passive movement in adult nominals
2. the thematic restriction on unaccusative verbs of appearance
3. the initial thematic restriction in children's passives and the ultimate grammaticalization of the passive

This has required one postulated thematic universal, the affected argument constraint, and at a more general level, a shift in how certain processes are viewed. In particular, for some purposes, the grammar will be looked at in an uncoventional way, with deep structure and surface structure mutually determining s-structure.

There has, indeed, been an approach akin to this in the recent work of Chomsky. Chomsky (class lectures) has suggested that all constraints on the grammar have to do with external levels, deep structure, surface structure, and LF, and that s-structure is in some sense derived. The conception here is somewhat similar, though in this case it is not that constraints are stated only on external levels, but rather that s-structure representations are derived from the two more-external levels.

It is clear how this is so in the positing of the trace in Stage 2 above. In order for the (thematically restricted) chain to be projected onto the structure, it is necessary for the child to simultaneously consider two levels of representation: surface structure and the lexical/thematic properties of the head, roughly, d-structure. The trace is posited by virtue of the comparison and mutual satisfaction of these two levels. While the lexical subcategorization frame of the head requires that there be an object, the actual surface structure shows the relevant element in the subject position. The trace is posited by virtue of the comparison and mutual satisfaction of these levels, as shown in (41).

(41)   D-structure (lexical subcategorization)

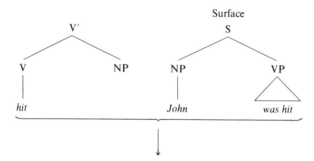

(42)   S-structure

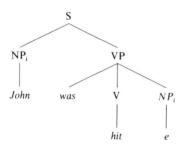

The surface structure (in the sense used here) was originally *John was hit* with no object trace. However, at the same time, the structure must satisfy the subcategorization frame of the head, its selectional properties as represented in pure form at deep structure. This is represented as a subcategorization frame, or, perhaps better (as suggested by T. Roeper, personal communication), as a subtree. For both of these to be satisfied, it is necessary that a trace be posited in the object position. In short, this constitutes a mapping from d-structure and surface structure to s-structure.

It might be supposed that on the basis of (41) and (42) that the mechanism for positing the trace is not thematically restricted, contrary to stage 2 above. In fact it is, as may be seen by considering the case more closely. The child faced with two constructions, *John was hit* and *John was liked*, will automatically thematically label each. However, only *John* in *John was hit* will be labeled +Affected; *John* in *John was liked* is simply a Theme. That means (by the affected argument constraint) that *John was hit* cannot be a direct representation of d-structure relations, because a +Affected element is in subject position. This forces the child to consider the subcategorization frame (or lexical property of the head) along with the surface structure in order to determine the trace-enriched s-structure. Thus the affected argument constraint forms, together with the thematic labeling, the additional analytic step. No such step is forced in the initial analysis of *John was liked*, because *John* there is not +Affected. In this case, it is only possible for the child to analyze the construction as it is, without positing an object trace, thus misconstruing the meaning. The object trace is, for this case of verbs (the nonaffected verbs), only posited at a later point (Stage 5), on purely syntactic grounds, after the general case-absorbing property of the morphology has been decoded.

6. CONCLUSION

I have outlined a particular sort of treatment for the acquisition of the passive. This involves a stagelike deductive structure in acquisition, where the trace is first posited on universal grounds for a subset of the verbs (the internal affected argument constraint) and then generalized over the full set of verbs once the case-absorbing property of the morphology has been deduced. The latter deduction takes place in several steps: (a) the trace is posited by the affected argument constraint, (b) the chain formed by the subject and object is required to have only one case (universal principle on chain formation), (c) the NP-trace must therefore not have case, (d) the verb must therefore not be assigning case, (e) case-absorbing morphology is detected on the verb. At this point, the passive is generalized over the full set of forms.

This sort of deductive reasoning, together with the assumption that θ-theoretic primitives are analytically prior in the analysis of the input to case-theoretic primitives, explains the Maratsos data, and does so in a fashion which also allows certain other properties of the grammar to be deduced—for example, the +Affected constraint in nominals of Fiengo (1980) and Anderson (1979). The analysis above differs from the subset principle-type approach of Pinker (1982, from 1979), and Lebeaux (1981) in that, while it is true that the original domain is more restricted than the final domain (and so the analysis does have a subset property), it is not this nesting of domains per se which is central to the analysis, but rather the notion of analytic priority of one set of primitives over another. Like the analysis of Berwick and Weinberg

(1984), the analysis assumes that there is an initial analysis without a trace, and a final analysis with one, though the principles mediating between the two representations are different in the two analyses.

Finally, I have suggested that an analysis of the acquisition of the passive should reconsider the role that levels of representation play in the grammar. In particular, for some purposes at least, it appears that we should consider the role of directionality in the grammar in a somewhat different way than has been standard since Chomsky and Lasnik (1977) and earlier work. Rather than supposing the existence of a single rule, Move-α, which mediates between d-structure and surface structure, I have suggested that the acquisition facts are best explained by hypothesizing a joint mapping of the surface and d-structure into s-structure. This would mean that the external levels in Chomsky's sense were determining the structure of the internal level, s-structure, a proposal akin to Chomsky's proposal, with, however, the difference that, unlike Chomsky, I assume that the structure of the internal level is determined by the more external levels, and not that no constraints are stated over that level.

ACKNOWLEDGMENT

Much of this work was done while I was a visiting faculty member at the University of Arizona. I thank the faculty and students there.

THEMATIC ROLES AND LANGUAGE COMPREHENSION

GREG N. CARLSON*
MICHAEL K. TANENHAUS†

*Department of Foreign Languages
University of Rochester
Rochester, New York 14627

†Department of Psychology
University of Rochester
Rochester, New York 14627

1. INTRODUCTION

The general idea of thematic roles has played an important part in linguistic theory since the mid-1960s. Since the seminal insights of Gruber (1965), Fillmore (1968), Jackendoff (1972), and others, there has been a flurry of activity from a variety of different points of view (e.g., Verkuyl, 1978; Stowell, 1981; Chomsky, 1981; Jackendoff, 1983, 1985; Culicover and Wilkins, 1984) Nonetheless, fundamental questions about the identification, individuation, and, especially, the theoretical status of thematic roles remain unresolved. For instance, there is not only considerable question about whether thematic roles are syntactic, semantic, or conceptual in nature, but also whether they should be regarded as grammatically significant entities at all (see, e.g., Ladusaw and Dowty, this volume).

While it is not our present purpose to resolve any of these issues, we wish to discuss an alternative perspective which may shed light on some of these questions in the future. The idea we explore, is that thematic roles play a

263

Syntax and Semantics, Volume 21
Thematic Relations

central role in language comprehension. We suggest that thematic roles provide a mechanism whereby the parser can make early semantic commitments, yet quickly recover from the inevitable misassignments that occur as a consequence of these early commitments. Further, we suggest that thematic roles provide a mechanism for interaction among the syntactic processor, the discourse model, and real-world knowledge, and that thematic roles help create coherence in local discourse structure.

Details of our representational and processing assumptions are presented later. Here, we present an outline of the basic ideas. We assume that

1. Lexical access makes available all the senses of an ambiguous verb in parallel and the sets of thematic roles associated with each sense (one set of such roles we call a THEMATIC GRID, following Stowell (1981)).
2. Only the one sense of the verb that is contextually most appropriate (or, in the absence of biasing context, the most frequent sense) remains active, along with its thematic grid(s).
3. Thematic roles are provisionally assigned to arguments of the verb as soon as possible; any active thematic roles incompatible with such an assignment become increasingly inactive.
4. Any active thematic roles not assigned to an argument remain as open thematic roles in the discourse model, appearing as free variables or unspecified "addresses' in the model.

2. BACKGROUND AND MOTIVATION

Our primary motivation for exploring these ideas comes from a confluence of findings from the language comprehension and word recognition literature. First, research on language processing suggests that the processor makes extremely early (and hence often incorrect) decisions, with each word being integrated as fully as possible with preceding context as it is encountered (Marslen-Wilson, 1975). Second, the processor appears to compute structures serially (Frazier, 1978; Ford et al., 1982; Frazier and Rayner, 1982). Evidence comes from studies demonstrating local increases in processing complexity when the parser pursues an analysis that turns out to be inconsistent with the remainder of the sentence or the biasing context. Yet the parser is usually able to rapidly recover from these misassignments, and in the case of biasing context may avoid these local garden paths altogether. This picture suggests that while the parser computes structures serially, it also has ready access to alternative structures.

Frazier and colleagues (Frazier, 1986; Rayner et al., 1984) have argued that thematic relations are the only vocabulary shared by the parser, discourse model, and world knowledge. They have proposed a special thematic processor which provides a channel of communication among these domains. On our view, quite similar in spirit to theirs, thematic roles themselves can do much of this work by virtue of the way they interact with other comprehension mechanisms. If all thematic roles on an active grid remain active in parallel, the parser could pursue a single analysis while much of the time having available the critical information required to revise the parse rapidly and mechanistically. In effect we would have a SERIAL PARSER with LATENT PARALLELISM. (See Cottrell, 1984; and McClelland and Kawamoto, 1986, for computational models in which parallel activation of case roles (roughly, thematic roles) play an important part in resolving lexical and syntactic ambiguities.)

Placing the source of parallelism in the lexicon is attractive because a large body of research on lexical processing demonstrates that multiple codes in a word's lexical entry becomes activated in parallel regardless of context. For instance, multiple senses of ambiguous words are initially accessed even in the presence of biasing context (Onifer and Swinney, 1981; Seidenberg et al., 1982; Swinney, 1979; Tanenhaus et al., 1979). Moreover, a number of lexical and sublexical phenomena, such as the word-superiority effect (i.e., that letters, for instance, are recognized more quickly as parts of words than as parts of nonwords), and effects of spelling–sound and orthographic regularity in visual word recognition can be explained elegantly on the assumption that there is parallel bottom-up activation, with incompatible representations competing with one another (McClelland and Rumelhart, 1981; Seidenberg, 1985). When representations are compatible, on the other hand, all remain active (Seidenberg and Tanenhaus, 1979; Tanenhaus et al., 1980).

There have also been a number of recent demonstrations that verb structure mediates or interacts with structural decisions in parsing. Ford et al. (1982) show that in the absence of biasing context, lexical preference determines the more salient interpretation of sentences with attachment ambiguities (see also Kurtzman, 1984), although it remains an open question whether these lexical preferences can override structural parsing biases (e.g., minimal attachment) in determining the initial parse (Frazier, 1978). Mitchell and Holmes (1985) demonstrate that lexical preference has a greater initial impact on some parsing decisions than purely structural biases. Clifton et al. (1984) demonstrate that verbs which have both transitive and intransitive readings show lexical bias in favor of one over the other, rather than there being some general structural bias applying to all. Clifton et al. (1984), Tanenhaus et al. (1985), and Stowe and Tanenhaus (1987) all report lexical effects in making filler–gap assignments.

Thus, we see two primary issues of interest in this work. The one issue is how language processing proceeds in real time. But an equally important matter is the structure of the lexical entries themselves. We are interested in what the nature of on-line processes can tell us about these lexical structures: What kinds of information are associated with lexical entries, and how and when does that information contribute to the developing representation? In light of the growing evidence for multiple-code activation in lexical processing, for strong lexical effects in parsing, and for on-line serial commitment and rapid local garden-path recovery, it seems reasonable to seek a mechanism whereby lexical structures can help to organize a parse, guide local garden-path recovery, and communicate with the discourse model. Thematic roles provide a promising candidate for such a mechanism.

3. REPRESENTATIONAL ASSUMPTIONS

On our view, thematic roles are semantic or conceptual phenomena, roughly in keeping with the views of Jackendoff (1983), Verkuyl (1978), Parsons (1980), Chierchia (1984), Carlson (1984), and Culicover and Wilkins (1984, 1986), rather than being fundamentally syntactic constructs (Chomsky, 1981; Stowell, 1981). We most closely follow Parsons (1980) and Carlson (1984) in assuming that a main function of thematic roles is to relate "arguments" of a verb to the meaning of the verb in semantic interpretation. This is at variance with the common view that verb meanings are n-ary functions, operating on a sequence of n arguments to yield a proposition. (See Dowty, 1987, for a detailed discussion contrasting the two positions.) Thus, we assume thematic roles to be the elements which, when associated with a verb, are responsible for that verb's ability to "take" semantic arguments. We also assume, in keeping with some common assumptions of psychologists and formal semanticists (e.g., Johnson-Laird, 1983; Kamp, 1979, 1981; Heim, 1982; Partee, 1984; Seuren, 1985), that an integral element of the interpretation of a sentence is a discourse model which represents an ongoing record of the discourse. Thematic roles appear in the discourse model as elements relating the interpretation of a verb to the various entities that play roles in what a verb is taken to denote. Carlson (1984, 1985) generally follows the lead of Davidson (1967) and Bach (1977) in suggesting that verbs denote eventualities, or types of events, processes, and states.

Like many other aspects of semantic interpretation, thematic roles are closely associated with the syntactic/lexical structure of a sentence. Obviously, there must be some means of associating a particular thematic role with a given argument of a verb. While we do not offer a particular mechanism for carrying out this association, we do share with Bresnan (1982c) and many others the following guiding assumptions:

1. Every argument of a given verb is assigned a thematic role.
2. No argument is assigned more than one thematic role.
3. Every argument of a verb is assigned a unique thematic role.

Though none of these can be fully accepted without qualification, we take them as reasonable generalizations which, if properly qualified, may serve as primary guiding assumptions.[1]

We also wish to advance some more-specific hypotheses about the linguistics of thematic roles which may not be so widely shared. First, the set of syntactic arguments of a verb—those constituents whose meanings are assigned thematic roles—are the subject of the sentence, and the subcategorized phrases in the VP, which are sisters of and governed by the verb. The verb, we assume, assigns thematic roles to no constituents beyond these.[2] This places a principled (and empirically determinable) upper limit on how many thematic roles may be associated with a given verb. No adverbial modifiers or adjuncts are assigned thematic roles by the verb. This is probably most controversial in the cases of instrumentals and benefactives (e.g., *sweep the floor **with a broom***; *fix a sandwich **for your mother***). In such cases, we hold that the PPs are not subcategorized phrases (not being sisters of the main verb by standard tests of VP constituency—see Lakoff and Ross, 1966; McCawley, 1982) and hence are not assigned thematic roles by the verbs directly. Instead, the lexical meanings of the prepositions themselves relate the prepositional objects to the meaning of the VP. If a PP is a subcategorized element, on the other hand, we take it that a thematic role is assigned to the PP itself; in some instances the preposition may have no lexical meaning (as, perhaps, in *give the book to **Mary***, or *be complimented **by your host***; see Gazdar *et al.*, 1985), whereas in other cases it might have lexical meaning (*take candy **from a baby***). Either way, a thematic role and not the preposition itself mediates the relation between the PP and the verb meaning for those PPs that are subcategorized. Additionally, we allow thematic roles to be assigned to sentential phrases, both finite and nonfinite.

---

[1] It appears some NPs might not be assigned roles, as in *John pushed **his way** through the crowd* (cf *John pushed his mother through the crowd*). In some cases the same NP may receive two roles, as in reflexively understood constructions like *John dressed*, where *John* may be both Agent and Theme, or two NPs may receive the same role, as in reciprocally understood constructions (e.g., *John and Mary fought*). Further, there might be different types or "tiers" of thematic roles which can be assigned to the same argument; Culicover and Wilkins (1984, 1986) suggest one such distinction.

[2] We speak of verbs assigning roles as a matter of convenience. We certainly wish to allow for general rules of thematic assignment (as in, e.g., Anderson, 1977; or Fillmore, 1968), not associated with lexical entries themselves, to be one possible mechanism.

In a verb's lexical entry, the first major lexical division is into senses (CORE MEANINGS) of the word. Each distinct sense may have a number of different syntactic subcategorizations associated with it. Our assumptions in this respect are quite standard. Once we bring in thematic roles as independent elements, a number of immediate questions arise concerning the relationship between verb subcategorizations and thematic grids. We take the position that while grids and subcategorizations appear to encode very much the same sort of information, they are independent of one another. Let us illustrate some of the linguistic consequences of this claim.

Consider the very productive class of causative/ergative pairs of intransitive and transitive verbs, as in (3).

(3)   a.   *The butter melted / John melted the butter.*
       b.   *The vase broke / Mary broke the vase.*
       c.   *The meat cooked / Sam cooked the meat.*

On the intransitive readings of each, there appears to be no necessary Agent participant implied, whereas an Agent serves as the subject in each of the alternative transitive versions. Our hypothesis is that such examples do not involve a sense ambiguity, but rather involve identical core meanings of the same verb, but associated with different thematic grids. The intransitive examples have the set of thematic roles {Theme}, whereas the transitive versions have {Agent, Theme}. Thus, a verb meaning consists of (at least) two separable components: a core meaning plus a thematic grid.

Or, consider the "middle" construction (Keyser and Roeper, 1984), where there is some intuitive appeal to the claim that the core verb meaning is the same (as in the pairs of examples below) while the difference in meaning resides in the sets of thematic roles associated with the verb.

(4)   a.   *John drives his car well.* {Agent, Theme}
       b.   *This car drives well.* {Theme}

(5)   a.   *Mike plays the trumpet poorly.* {Agent, Theme}
       b.   *This trumpet plays poorly.* {Theme}

If this is correct, then more than one thematic grid may be associated with a single verb sense; in these cases, the grids are associated with individual subcategorizations as well, though this is not always so, as we shall see.

That we are dealing with the same verb sense in such examples as (3)–(5) is plausible, and we leave it thus for now. We do note, though, that verb alternations where we claim there is a shared single core meaning that has alternative thematic grids are often associated with inflectional (as well as derivational) morphology, in a variety of languages. If alternative inflected forms (as opposed to derive forms) never operate on the core meaning of the word, as we suspect, we nonetheless allow for inflectional operations to manipulate thematic roles since roles are not a part of core verb meaning. This suggestion that grid manipulation can be associated with syntactic operations is at variance with the θ-criterion (Chomsky, 1981).

Not all changes of subcategorization entail a change in the associated thematic grid. In many cases, the syntactic elimination of an argument position does not entail a corresponding revision of the roles in a grid, as might be suggested by the causative/inchoative and middle examples of (3–5). Under these circumstances, a thematic role on a grid may be assigned to no constituent. When this occurs, OPEN thematic roles arise.

Consider the well-known example of passive sentences like those below:

(6)   a. *The fire was extinguished by the firemen.*
      b. *The fire was extinguished.*

Assuming the *the fire* is assigned the role Theme and *the firemen* is Agent in (6a),[3] how should (6b) be analyzed on the nonstative verbal reading? Certainly, *the fire* should still be Theme, but should there also be an Agent role associated with this occurrence of the verb as well? We assume that there is an Agent role present in (6b), even if no constituent is actually assigned that role. In part, this decision is based on the intuition that (6b) is understood as having some unstated agentive participant (this is reflected in the formerly common transformational analysis deriving (6b) by Agent deletion from a structure like (6a)). Contrast (6b) with *the fire went out*, in which there is no such understood agentive participant, though the meaning is quite similar in all other respects. But further substantiating these intuitions is the presence of an alternative subcategorization of the same verb, with intuitively the same core meaning, in which an agent is overtly expressed, as in (6a). We take this as an indication that an Agent role is to be associated with the verb in (6b), even if assigned to no constituent. Thus, we assume that there can be unfilled or open thematic roles. Open thematic roles, we suppose, appear in the discourse model as indefinites, "addresses" in need of further identification or elaboration.[4]

---

[3] While we believe our role attributions are plausible, we set aside for the time being questions about their accuracy. For our immediate purposes, it matters little if what are called Themes should instead be called Patients, or our Agents should be Causers.

[4] Our notion of open thematic roles may simply be the verbal counterpart of the implicit arguments studied in nominalizations by Roeper and others. While this work has doubtless influenced our thinking, we have not undertaken a systematic comparison of implicit arguments and what we are here calling "open thematic roles."

Open thematic roles appear in many other constructions besides agentless passives. Consider lexically governed constructions of English reminiscent of "applicative" constructions of a variety of other languages (Baker, 1986; Marantz, 1984), exemplified by the verb *load*. This verb has at least three subcategorizations, exemplified in (7).

(7)   a.   *John loaded the truck.* (_____ NP)
      b.   *John loaded the furniture onto the truck.* (_____ NP $PP_{[+loc]}$)
      c.   *John loaded the truck with furniture.* (_____ NP $PP_{[+with]}$)

In (7a), *load* is a simple transitive; in (7b) it takes an object and a following locative PP; and in (7c) *load* takes an object and a PP headed by the preposition *with*.[5] In the latter two versions, three associated thematic roles appear: the Agent (*John*), the Theme (*the furniture*), and Location (*the truck*). In the case of the simple transitive (7a), we assume that all three thematic roles are available there as well. Here, *John* is Agent, and *the truck* could be either Location or Theme, though the former is more plausible (trucks get other things put into them more often than they are put into or onto other things). Whichever role is assigned the object in (7a), there is the clear understanding that the other role remains, though unspecified (i.e., if Location, then something was put into the truck; if Theme, that the truck was put somewhere—e.g., onto a railroad car). So we conclude that the verb in (7a) has three thematic roles associated with it as well. Some other constructions we assume to give rise to open thematic roles are examples of object deletion or detransitivization (*John ate the cake* vs. *John ate*), and ditransitives used transitively (*John served the meal to his guests* vs. *John served the meal*), in addition to a number of other less-productive classes.

We have seen that it is possible for the same thematic grid to be associated with alternative subcategorizations of a verb. As a result, in any given case of a verb with alternative subcategorizations, there is some uncertainty about whether it retains the same thematic grid or whether the grid is adjusted. Ultimately, we would hope that psycholinguistic results of the sort discussed in the next section would serve as a means of resolving such uncertainties. However, in the interest of making future experimental predictions, we discuss two particularly controversial cases: instrumentals and benefactives.

Benefactives typically can show up as either *for* adjuncts or as (derived) objects, and are optional.

---

[5] This *with* phrase is not an instrumental. It may, for instance, co-occur with a true instrument phrase (*Bill loaded the truck with hay with his new pitchfork*) even though in general two instrumentals may not co-occur (*??John ate the meal with a fork with a spoon*).

(8) a. *John bought a book **for Sally.***
     b. *John bought **Sally** a book.*
     c. *John bought a book.*

As we noted above, the PP in (8a) is not a subcategorized element and hence is not assigned a thematic role by the verb. In (8b), on the other hand, the Beneficiary role is assigned to *Sally* by the verb, as the NP *Sally* is in the thematic domain of the verb. This does not necessarily mean that only the verb in (8b) has a beneficiary role in its grid. It would be possible for the verbs in (8a) and (8c) to have the same grids. However, we believe that the verbs in (8a) and (8c) have no Beneficiary role, for two reasons. First, it is not clear that a Beneficiary is a necessary participant in such actions as described in (8c); it seems one can buy something and then later decide what to do with it, or that one can make a cake without making it for someone, and so on. Second, since contrastive judgments are often more compelling than absolute ones, we detect no striking differences in judgment of necessary Beneficiary participation between those verbs like *buy* or *make* which display the alternation illustrated in (8), and those that do not, as those verbs in (9).

(9) a. *John smiled a broad smile for Mary.* / **John smiled Mary a broad smile.*
     b. *Max gathered the family for his mother.* / **Max gathered his mother the family.*
     c. *Antonio phoned his cousin for his father.* / **Antonio phoned his father his cousin.*
     d. *John performed **Hamlet** for his classmates.* / **John performed his classmates **Hamlet**.*

That is, we do not sense a consistent contrast between the verbs in (9) and those that may take the benefactive as an indirect object that could be characterized in terms of the necessary participation of some role (e.g., *The bomb exploded* vs. *The bomb was exploded*). Furthermore, these alternations appear to be subject to significant individual or dialectal variation. For instance, while we ourselves find *prepare Max a meal* or *confiscate the kids some more weapons* to be unacceptable, others find them acceptable. Given that we find no striking differences in intuition between the two classes of verbs about necessary participants, and given that by our criteria such verbs as those in (9) cannot have a Beneficiary role on their grids since no Beneficiary ever appears as a subcategorized element, we tentatively assume there are no open Beneficiary roles in such examples as *John bought a book*.

Much the same can be said about English instrumentals, which have been occasionally regarded as within the thematic domain of the verb (we construe, for instance, Fillmore (1968) and Bresnan (1982c) as making such a claim). Instrumentals, like benefactives, show an adjunct–argument alternation, illustrated in (10).

(10) a. *John sliced the salami* **with the razor-sharp knife.**
      b. **The razor-sharp knife** *sliced the salami with ease.*

Since *with a knife* in (10a) is not a subcategorized PP, it is only necessary for the verb to assign Agent to *John* and Theme to *salami* for an interpretation, an Instrument role being unnecessary. In (10b), though, the verb must assign an Instrument role to the subject as that argument is in the thematic domain of the verb. The question, then, is whether Instrument is a role in a sentence like (11).

(11)   *John sliced the salami.*

Here, direct intuition is less decisive than in the case of benefactives (e.g., can one slice things without an instrument? If one uses one's hand, is that an instrument?). However, we are going to claim that there is no Instrument role in examples like (11). Cases can be found which allow *with* phrases but not Instrument subjects, as in (12), yet one does not find a striking difference regarding Instrument participation when contrasting such examples to those which do display the alternation, (10).

(12) a. *John ate the salami with a fork.* / **John's fork ate the salami.*
      b. *Max first noticed the galaxy with a radio telescope.* / **A radio telescope first noticed the distant galaxy.* (cf. *detected*)
      c. *Fred read the phone book with a magnifying glass.* / **The magnifying glass read the phone book.*
      d. *Mary addressed the crowd with a bullhorn.* / **A bullhorn addressed the crowd.*

Again, by our criteria, none of these verbs has Instrument on their grids, as Instrument is never assigned to a subcategorized phrase. Thus, we claim that in such cases as *John sliced the salami* there is no open Instrument role. This does not mean, however, that the core meaning of the verb itself does not entail, or strongly imply, the presence of an instrument; entailed participation is a necessary but not a sufficient condition for the presence of a thematic role.

Summing up, we assume that at least two sets of thematic roles are associated with verbs like *buy* and *slice*, though there is no ambiguity of verb sense:

(13) a. *John bought Mary a present* {Agent, Beneficiary, Theme}
      b. *John bought a present for Mary.* {Agent, Theme}

    c. *Seymour sliced the salami with a knife.* {Agent, Theme}
    d. *A sharp knife sliced Seymour's salami.* {Instrument, Theme}

Though the core verb meanings of (13a,b) are the same, in (13b,c) the Beneficiary and Instrument roles are provided by the lexical meanings of the prepositions and do not emanate from the verb itself.

4. EMPIRICAL PREDICTIONS

Our view of thematic roles in processing, coupled with our representational assumptions, make some potentially strong claims about language processing. In this section we present a mix of intuitive and experimental evidence which provides encouragement for the view we are developing. We focus on three areas: differences between proposed components of verb meaning involving thematic ambiguities versus ambiguities of core meaning (sense ambiguities), feedback between thematic assignments and parsing decisions, and how thematic roles may play a part in the creation and integration of local discourse structure.

4.1. Sense and Thematic Role Ambiguities

Our assumptions about lexical access predict processing differences between sentences with verbs displaying sense ambiguities (e.g., *set* meaning 'to place' or 'adjust (as a clock),' and those displaying thematic ambiguities (e.g., *load the truck* where *the truck* is either Theme or Location). Lexical access will make available multiple senses of such a word as *set*, but only the contextually most appropriate (or, in absence of context, most frequent) sense will remain active and the others become unavailable (see Simpson, 1984, for a review of relevant literature). In contrast, in a thematic ambiguity, all the thematic roles on the active grid remain, and all remain available, even if (as we hold) thematic roles are assigned to constituents on-line.

These assumptions have a number of empirical consequences. When a reader or hearer initially selects the wrong sense of an ambiguous verb, reinterpretation would require retrieving the no-longer-available alternative sense. This should take time and processing resources. However, when the wrong thematic assignment is initially made, then thematic reassignment should be relative cost free because (a) the core meaning of the verb remains constant, and hence the verb's lexical entry need not be reopened, (b) the alternative thematic roles on a grid are often already active and available, and

(c) even if they are not, the syntactic–thematic mappings provide explicit information about how roles are to be assigned, so only a limited domain of information needs to be reexamined; this may result in ease of recovery, as well. Thus, thematic roles allow the processor to make early commitments without undue cost. Thematic reassignment may not be completely costfree, of course, but it will be easier, we assume, than reopening lexical entries. The null hypothesis is that both types of ambiguities are really just sense ambiguities and hence are not fundamentally distinct.

A recent experiment conducted in collaboration with Curt Burgess provides initial confirmation of our predictions. We constructed sets of materials similar to those sense ambiguities in (14) and the thematic ambiguities in (15).

(14) a. *Bill set the alarm clock for six in the morning.*
      b. *Bill reset the alarm clock for six in the morning.*
      c. *Bill set the alarm clock onto the shelf.*
      d. *Bill put the alarm clock onto the shelf.*

(15) a. *Bill loaded the truck with bricks.*
      b. *Bill filled the truck with bricks.*
      c. *Bill loaded the truck onto the ship.*
      d. *Bill drove the truck onto the ship.*

In examples (14a) and (14c), different senses of *set* are selected by the final disambiguating phrase; disambiguation does not take place until after presentation of the direct object NP. Examples (14b) and (14d) are control sentences using unambiguous verbs that have core meanings related to the appropriate sense in the ambiguous version of the sentence. The sentences of (15) repeat that same pattern for the thematic ambiguities: (15a) and (15c) involve temporary ambiguity of thematic assignment to the direct object, to be disambiguated by the final constituent; (15b) and (15d) serve as unambiguous controls.

The sentences were displayed on a CRT and the subjects' task was to decide as quickly as possible whether the sentence "made sense" (many of the filler trials were sentences that did not make sense). We assume that subjects will initially select the incorrect verb sense or thematic assignment on approximately half the trials where temporary ambiguity is possible. If incorrect sense selection results in a garden path once disambiguating information to the contrary arrives, this should be reflected in longer reaction times in deciding whether such sentences make sense and should result in fewer of these judged to make sense, all relative to controls. Data from 28 subjects are presented in the following tabulation, which displays mean reaction time (in msec) to the sentences judged to make sense, and percentage of sentences judged to make sense.

	Type of verb	
Type of ambiguity	Ambiguous	Control
Sense	2445 (77%)	2290 (94%)
Thematic	2239 (92%)	2168 (93%)

There is a clear difference between sense and thematic role ambiguities. Sense ambiguities take longer than their controls to comprehend and are less often judged to make sense. In contrast, sentences with thematic ambiguities are not significantly more difficult to comprehend than the unambiguous controls and are fully as often judged to make sense. Using our own intuitions, we divided the ambiguous sentences into those in which preferred and non-preferred initial sense or thematic assignment is correct. The next tabulation presents these results.

	Type of verb	
	Ambiguous	Control
Sense ambiguity		
Preferred sense	2277	2317
Less-preferred sense	2613	2264
Thematic ambiguity		
Preferred assignment	2198	2177
Less-preferred assignment	2268	2158

This tabulation shows that the sense ambiguities are more difficult than their controls only when the less-preferred sense turns out to be correct. This is predicted by our assumptions. In addition, there is a slight (marginally significant) reprocessing cost for selection of the incorrect thematic assignment, though not nearly as high a cost as recovering from an incorrect sense. Thus, this experiment provides support for a processing contrast between sense and thematic ambiguities, as well as some reason to think that provisional thematic assignments are made on-line.

We can also present intuitive evidence for the distinction between sense and thematic ambiguities. One of our key representational assumptions is that the same verb meaning may be associated with different thematic grids [as the transitive and intransitive uses of verbs such as *break* in (3)], the alternative hypothesis being that, different uses of such verbs reflect an ambiguity in the verb's core meaning. Experimental evidence shows that in the absence of biasing context, the dominant reading of an ambiguous word is rapidly selected (Simpson and Burgess, 1985; Hudson and Tanenhaus, 1984). A standard assumption in the word-recognition literature is that frequency is a function of recency. On this account, recent choice of one meaning of an ambiguous word should bias the reader or listener to select the same meaning the next time the word is encountered, making selection of the alternative sense more difficult.

Consider the following short paragraphs, in which either of the first two sentences is taken to immediately precede the third; (16) contains a sense ambiguity, while (17) and (18) contain thematic ambiguities.

(16)   *The general commanded the troops in battle.*
         The general led the troops in battle.
         Afterwards, he commanded their respect.

(17)   *John packed the books in the morning.*
         John crated the books in the morning.
         Then he packed the truck.

(18)   *John hurried the kids off to school.*
         John rushed the kids off to school.
         Then he hurried off to work.

When different senses of an ambiguous verb are used in adjacent sentences, as in (16), the second occurrence seems awkward (*The general commanded the troops in battle. ?Afterwards, he commanded their respect.*). The awkwardness seems to go away, though, when the priming occurrence is replaced by a close synonym (e.g., *The general led the troops in battle. Afterwards, he commanded their respect.*). But thematic ambiguities behave differently. Using the same verb with different thematic assignments, as in examples (17) and (18), does not result in the same sense of awkwardness found in (16) *John hurried the kids off to school. Then he hurried off to work.*) Thus, the ambiguity of a verb like *hurry* is not like a sense ambiguity. This is just what we would predict since we would not attribute the different meanings of *hurry* in (18) or *pack* in (17) to an ambiguity of core meaning.

4.2. Thematic Feedback to the Parser

The assumption that arguments are assigned thematic roles immediately (at least once the verb is encountered) suggests that provisional thematic role assignment may provide a mechanism whereby pragmatic knowledge and processing context influence subsequent syntactic decisions. It seems plausible that the meaning of an argument, the core meaning of the verb, as well as general world knowledge are taken into account in making provisional thematic assignments (e.g., *pack the suitcases* prefers *suitcases* as Location, while *pack the clothes* prefers *clothes* as Theme, because of the nature of suitcases and clothes, but not because of any grammatical properties NPs denoting these things may have). Since thematic assignments often have direct syntactic consequences, the nonsyntactic information used in assigning thematic roles might well have parsing consequences. Some evidence in support of the hypothesis that initial thematic assignments can provide feedback to the parser comes from some studies by Stowe and Holmes (reported in Stowe, 1987).

In one experiment they used causative/ergative verbs such as *stopped*. Used transitively (*Frank stopped the car*), the subject is Agent and the object is Theme; used intransitively (*The car stopped*), the subject is Theme. These verbs were placed in subordinate clauses preceding the main clause, as in *Even before the police stopped the driver was getting nervous*. Frazier (1978) and Frazier and Rayner (1982) have shown that in the absence of punctuation, readers initially assume that the NP following the verb is its object, rather than closing off the subordinate clause and taking the NP to be the subject of the main clause. This results in a garden-path effect in this example. If, however, the subject of the subordinate clause is inanimate, and thus more likely to be a Theme than an Agent, then the reader may "close off" the subordinate clause after the verb, there being no unassigned roles remaining on the grid. To test this prediction, Stowe and Holmes manipulated the animacy of the subject of the subordinate clause, using materials like (19).

(19)   a. *Even before the police stopped the driver was getting nervous.*
       b. *Even before the truck stopped the driver was getting nervous.*
       c. *Even before the police stopped at the light the driver was getting nervous.*
       d. *Even before the truck stopped at the light the driver was getting nervous.*

Subjects read sentences such as these one word at a time, with a secondary task of pressing a button if and when the sentence became ungrammatical. Reading times were recorded, as were judgments of ungrammaticality.

The main finding was that when the subject of the subordinate clause was animate (19a), the reading times for the main clause were longer by more than half a second compared to controls (19c,d). On the other hand, there was no corresponding effect when the subject was inanimate (19b). This provides evidence that at least animacy was playing a role in determining parsing decisions. In the presence of an animate subject, the verb was taken as transitive, leading to a garden path in the main clause. Our account is that animacy, in this case, affects thematic assignment, which in turn has direct consequences for the syntax of the sentence being processed. Whether or not properties other than animacy (a salient and often grammatically important property) can have similar effects has yet to be shown. Under the hypotheses

advanced here, though, similar effects should be found for other semantic
distinctions that may affect thematic assignment.

We caution that this issue remains controversial. It is important to replicate
the Stowe and Holmes results with a task that does not involve an explicit
decision on each word. This is particularly important because Ferreira and
Clifton (1986) report results that appear to be inconsistent with the Stowe–
Holmes results. Ferreira and Clifton examined eye-fixation durations in
sentences such as *The man/car (that was) towed from the parking lot was
parked illegally*. The subject NP was either animate or inanimate. They
reasoned that if thematic assignment could provide feedback to the parser,
then reading times for the postverbal *by* phrase, which unambiguously shows
the verb to be a past participle (in a reduced relative) rather than a simple past
tense, should be shorter when the subject is inanimate (*The car towed...*)
than when it is animate (*The man towed...*). Reading times on the verb were
longer when the subject was inanimate, which would be consistent with a thematically based revision. However, there was no significant animacy effect
at the *by* phrase, suggesting that the parser was not able to use thematic feedback. But this lack of an effect may have been due to the nature of Ferreira
and Clifton's materials. As Susan Garnsey pointed out to us, more than half
the sentences had plausible continuations in which the inanimate subject
could be continued with a simple past (e.g., *The car towed the boat*). Clearly,
further work is necessary to resolve the issue of thematic feedback.

4.3. Open Thematic Roles and the Discourse Model

We have proposed that open thematic roles are represented as unspecified
entities in a discourse model or other conceptual representation of a discourse,
and that they, like anaphors and presuppositions, can help create local
discourse coherence (Grosz, *et al.*, 1983). We now consider several predictions
that follow from this view.

First, definite NPs will be more rapidly integrated into a discourse interpretation if a previous sentence introduces an open role which can plausibly
be filled by the NP. An open role, it appears, represents a point in the discourse
which invites further specification or is otherwise salient. In filling such a
role, one does not have to rely wholly upon general inferential processing
of the type typically required to integrate information into a single scheme.

Consider by way of example a sentence like *John loaded the truck*. In
understanding this sentence, not only are John and a truck introduced into the
discourse, but so is an unspecified entity playing the role of the Theme (i.e.,
whatever got loaded onto the truck). In contrast, a sentence like *John wrote a*

letter introduces just John and the letter, and no entity playing the role of an instrument (such as a pen), even if an instrument is conceptually judged to be a necessary participant in such actions; such entities would have to be introduced inferentially.

In a preliminary experiment conducted in collaboration with Susan Hudson, we demonstrated, that sentences beginning with a definite NP are comprehended more rapidly where preceded by a context sentence introducing an open thematic role the NP can plausibly fill. In (20) are sample materials.

(20)   a. *Bill hurried to catch his plane.*
       a'. *Bill hurried to unload his car.*
       b. ***The suitcases** were very heavy.*

A sentence such as (20b) was preceded by either a sentence like (20a'), which leaves an open thematic role of the sort a suitcase could plausibly fill (here, the Theme), or a sentence like (20a) which introduces no open role but which invites at least as plausible an inference that a suitcase would be a part of the scene (e.g., that Bill while rushing to his plane was lugging suitcases is at least as likely as that while he was unloading his car he was unloading suitcases).[6] The subjects read the context sentence (e.g., (20a,a')) and then judged whether the target sentence (e.g., (20b)) made sense given the context. We found that when the context introduced an open thematic role, mean reading time to the target sentence was 1628 msec, with 97% judged to make sense. When no open role was introduced by the context sentence, reading times rose to 1847 msec, and judged sensibility fell to 84%. In such cases, the open roles did appear to aid discourse integration.

One consequence of the assumption that thematic roles create discourse addresses is that introducing a definite NP should result in more of a perceived topic shift when it can fill no open role and is hence not elaborating on something already introduced. Intuitions suggest that this is the case. Consider the examples of (21).

(21)   a. *Mary put dinner on the table.*
       a'. *Mary served dinner.*
       b. *The guests were complimentary.*
       c. *Dinner was delicious.*
       c'. *It was delicious.*

---

[6] If one replaces the article *the* with a possessive in these examples (e.g., ***His** suitcases were very heavy*), the contrast is much less clear. Since the pronoun makes explicit reference to something already introduced into the discourse model, it may bring into play potentially quite different mechanisms of reference assignment for the whole NP.

(21a) does not introduce an open Goal role, whereas (21a') does (to serve is to serve to someone). In (21b), a definite NP is introduced which can plausibly fill the open Goal role of (21a'), or easily be integrated inferentially with the event described in (21a) (e.g., that guests were seated at the table). A third sentence follows these sequences, one beginning with a full NP and the other with a pronoun referring back to an entity already presented in the discourse (the dinner). If the second sentence introduces a topic shift, the noun version (21c) should be more easily understood than the pronoun version (21c'). This appears to be the case. We find that the sequence beginning with the introduction of an open role and ending with the pronoun (22) is more natural than a very similar sequence which introduces no open role (23):

(22)   *Mary served dinner at the table. The guests were complimentary. It was delicious.*

(23)   *Mary put dinner on the table. The guests were complimentary. It was delicious.*

(22) is, in our opinion, more natural than (23), because there is no introduction of a topic shift in (22). We find similar intuitions when the open role is presented subsequently to the NP that fills it. Consider cases of sentences giving rationale for an action, keeping in mind that rationale is particularly keyed to the role of Goal (Jones, 1985b). If the second sentence contains an open Goal role plausibly filled by an entity already introduced, it is much more easily integrated with the first sentence than when no open role occurs. Consider the contrast found in (24), between the (24b) continuation with an open Goal role, and the (24b') continuation lacking such a role.

(24)   a. *Her nephew's birthday was coming up, so ...*
        b. *Mary sent a book.* (open Goal)
        b'. *Mary bought a book.* (no open Goal)

From a general conceptual point of view, if one knows that someone's birthday is coming up, buying a gift is certainly at least as common as sending a gift; so situational plausibility offers no straightforward account of this contrast. Similar results may be obtained by filling the role in the second sentence, so no open goal occurs, but there is still the inference of some entity involved. For instance, *give away* and *donate* mean roughly the same thing, but we would analyze *give away* as having the Goal role filled (by *away*, it appears):

(25)   a. *The Salvation Army was having a Christmas drive, so ...*
        b. *John donated some toys.* (open Goal)
        b'. *John gave away some toys.* (no open Goal)

We perceive a marked contrast between the (25b,b') continuations in these examples, with (25b') being more difficult to integrate with (25a) than (25b).

We are not suggesting that thematic roles are the only mechanism for discourse integration effects with definite NPs, by any means. It is well known that definite NPs can be used felicitously in part–whole situations, such as, *Bill climbed out of his car*. Then he shut *the door*. Verb core meanings as well may lead to ease of integration, even in the absence of thematic roles. Melissa Bowerman (personel communication) pointed out to the verb *perform*, which on our analysis does not provide a thematic role for an audience. Still, the core meaning of the verb would involve saying something about a performance being intended for an audience (even if one does not show up). Thus, the ease of integrating a discourse like *The schoolboys performed the play.* ***The audience was wildly enthusiastic.*** We see open roles as but one road to discourse integration.

Finally, we find some support for the idea that open roles may play a part in parsing decisions. In particular, they may provide an integral part of an account of ease of recovery from garden paths. Consider the well-studied types of garden paths introduced by reduced-relative clauses beginning with past participles, as in Bever's well-known example, (26).

(26)   *The horse raced past the barn fell.*

Though sentences of similar structure may always result in some degree of garden path, various other factors, including length, semantic plausibility, and existing presuppositions affect the magnitude of the garden-path effect, presumably by influencing speed and ease of recovery (Frazier and Fodor, 1978; Crain and Steedman, 1985; Kurtzman, 1984). The thematic proposal we are pursuing suggests that lexical properties of the verb may also play a role in ease of recovery. Consider momentarily the thematic structure of the verb *raced* in (26), which is ambiguous between a transitive and an intransitive form (we set aside consideration of the directional PP), where the transitive version (the past participle) has two roles associated with it—an Agent and a Theme—while the intransitive version has but a Theme for subject.

Two things are of importance here. First, in the confusion between the transitive passive particle and a simple past tense, the role assigned to the horse is Theme in both cases. Second, on the (mistaken) intransitive analysis, there is no remaining role available. Contrast this situation with a case where there is an open role available on the main verb reading, as in (27).

(27)   a. *The girl sent the flowers.*
        b. *The man served the rare steak.*

In cases such as these an open Goal role remains—the flowers were sent to someone, the steak was served to someone. Our intuition suggests that garden-path recovery is easier when these structures are placed into sentences that invite mistaken main verb analyses, such as (28), in contrast to the more difficult (29), with examples structurally similar to (26).

(28)   a. *The girl sent the flowers didn't appreciate them very much.*
       b. *The man served the burned steak complained to the head waiter.*
       c. *Professors taught German are better than those who know Latin.*
(29)   a. *The child hurried out the front door slipped on the icy steps.*
       b. *The butter melted on the stove dripped onto the kitchen floor.*
       c. *Dogs walked quickly live a lot longer.*

The more difficult examples of (29) represent verbs falling into the causative/ergative pattern, with the same role assigned to subject of the intransitive and (underlying) object of the transitive. In contrast, the open roles in (28) appear to us to facilitate recovery.

An alternative pattern exists for transitive/intransitive pairs, which is traditionally thought of as detransitivization (e.g., *John ate the soup / John ate*). Here, the subject retains the same role in both versions. In *John ate the soup*, for instance, *John* is Agent and *the soup* Theme, while in the intransitive *John ate*, *John* remains Agent and the Theme is either eliminated or quite possibly remains as an open role (whether all such detransitives leave open roles is uncertain). The verbs *sue*, *watch*, and *study* pattern likewise. Now consider the reduced relatives of (30).

(30)   a. *The doctor sued for a million dollars became very upset.*
       b. *The opponents studied very carefully were easily defeated.*
       c. *The spy watched through the mirror saw Sally and ran.*

Our intuitions are that such examples are again substantially easier to comprehend than examples such as those in (26) and (29). The difference appears to correlate with the presence of an open role in the mistaken main verb analysis of the reduced relative, and the fact that the initial NP is assigned different roles on the main verb analysis and the reduced relative analysis.

Presently lacking a fully explicit account, we can nonetheless present a sketch of an explanation along the following lines. Consider the thematic grids associated with the verbs in *The child hurried* and *The girl sent the note*. In the first, the thematic grid consists of $\{Theme_i\}$ (the subscript indicating it has been assigned to NP_i, in this case, *the child*). In the second example, the thematic grid would be $\{Agent_i, Theme_j, Goal\}$ (the Goal without a subscript indicates an open role). These are the available roles present when the garden path is encountered. Presumably, recovery is governed by global strategy rather than by strict rule, but let us assume that one available strategy is to reassociate NPs with alternatively available thematic roles, open roles being the most available. In the case of *The child hurried fell*, this strategy will yield no results as the comprehension mechanism is already considering the child to be Theme: In other words, it is not a new hypothesis to consider. On the other hand, if one tentatively assigns the subject NP to the open Goal upon encountering the garden path in *The girl sent the note didn't respond*, it is a new hypothesis. Its consequences for the grammatical analysis can begin to be worked out. For example, if *the girl* is the Goal, *sent* cannot be an active main verb since it would not take a Goal as subject. There is, however, a homophonous passive version which assigns Goal to its subject, being an underlying object available for passivization; it cannot be a main verb, lacking the copula, and structurally it can only then be, for example, a modifying phrase. We are not suggesting that such consequences are worked out consciously. We are suggesting, however, that tentative reassociation of an NP with an open role forces one to give up hypotheses presently entertained about the structure of the sentence, and this represents a "foot in the door" to getting at the correct analysis. In the absence of the possibility of reassociation, one major strategy for recovery is eliminated, and recovery is correspondingly more difficult.

5. CONCLUDING REMARKS

One of our major hypotheses has been that thematic role assignment is made on-line, and that associating and reassociating thematic roles with arguments of the verb bearing those roles is relatively costfree. We have presented intuitive as well as experimental evidence in support of this claim. In general, it does not appear to be at all difficult to change assignment of thematic roles. This appears to hold even for cases of uncertain thematic assignment to subject NPs, as well as postverbal constituents. Consider as an example a sentence that begins like (31).

(31)   *Charlie Evans rented a very large house...*

At this point, two types of continuations are possible:

(32)   a. *... from his neighbor's friend.*
       b. *... to his neighbor's friend.*

If the continuation is (32a), the subject of the sentence must be assigned the role Goal, while continuation (32b) requires the subject be assigned the role Source. However, in neither case does the continuation appear to make the sentence difficult to comprehend. Our hypothesis is that, in fact, thematic commitments have already been made at the point in the sentence indicated in (31), but that reassociation is so costfree that if the less-expected continuation is encountered, the garden-path effect is slight. So, suppose at the end of (31) the thematic grid under consideration is {Source, Theme$_j$, Goal$_i$}, with Charlie Evans being NP$_i$ and *a very large house* being NP$_j$ (this represents our intuitions about the favored reading). Now, suppose the unequivocal Goal is encountered in continuation (32b), conflicting with the present thematic commitments. If reassociation is quite easy, then the shift to {Source$_i$, Theme$_j$, Goal} from the previous assignment clears the way for the final {Source$_i$, Theme$_j$, Goal$_k$} (*his neighbor's friend* being NP$_k$). A subsequent checking of this hypothesis shows that it is consistent with a possible pattern of assignments for the verb *rent*.

The informal notation presented here treats thematic assignment as a sort of indexing procedure. If we take this just a bit more seriously, a possible account of the ease of thematic reassignment begins to take shape. One common observation about discourse models, in our view a grounding motivation, is that recovery from misconstrual of the reference of a series of phrases can take place *in toto* without unduly taxing computational resources. Consider, for example, a case of a conversation in which two people think they are discussing the same person, but the listener is mistaken about the identity of the person under discussion. Upon finding the error, the listener transforms all the information formerly believed to be about the mistaken individual into information about the actually intended individual (*Oh, so **that's** who said all those nasty things*, etc.) It does not appear one must go back and recompute the meanings individually of all propositions understood incorrectly, since this transformation is achieved so rapidly and easily. Or, more locally, if one hears a sentence like (33) and initially takes *he* as coreferential with *Bob*, a later readjustment necessitated by further context (e.g., (34)) is relatively simple to make, although it does result in a temporary garden path (Hudson, *et al.*, 1986).

(33)   *Bob talked to Charlie after he ...*

(34)   *... threatened to sue Bob for slander.*

Thus, if we view thematic assignment as an indexing and reindexing operation of the same general sort, we can at least reduce the question of why thematic assignment is fairly costfree to the larger question of why indexing or reference-assignment operations in general are relatively costfree. It is true that thematic assignments and reassignments have very strictly laid out syntactic consequences that pronoun reassignments do not generally exhibit; evaluating these consequences may add some cost, but reassociation itself appears quite easy.

This may shed some light on some initially puzzling experimental results that we found in experiments with filler–gap constructions conducted in collaboration with Laurie Stowe (see Tanenhaus *et al.*, 1985, for a preliminary report; for details see Stowe and Tanenhaus (1987)). In these experiments we investigated the comprehension of embedded *wh*-questions which contained an optionally transitive verb (e.g., *asked*). We were primarily interested in testing Janet Fodor's (1978) hypothesis that the preferred subcategorization of the verb, or LEXICAL PREFERENCE, determines whether or not a gap is posited at the verb.

We contrasted two gap locations, one immediately following the main verb (as in (35a)), and the other occurring later in the sentence after a preposition (as in (35b)); these are the "early" and "late" gaps respectively.

(35) a. *The district attorney found out which witness the reporter asked ____ about the meeting.* (early)

   b. *The district attorney found out which witness the reporter asked anxiously about ____.* (late)

There were two groups of verbs. Half favored the expectation of a transitive reading over the corresponding possible intransitive reading, while the other half led to the expectation of the intransitive over the transitive. An example of an early and a late gap sentence with the intransitive expectation verb *raced* is illustrated in (36).

(36) a. *The sheriff wasn't sure which horse the cowboy raced ____ down the hill.*

   b. *The sheriff wasn't sure which horse the cowboy raced desperately past ____.*

Finally, we had plausible and implausible fillers. Plausibility was defined solely with respect to the direct object position of the verb. The plausible and implausible fillers were equally plausible as objects of the preposition. This contrast is illustrated in (37).

(37) a. *The district attorney found out **which witness** the reporter asked ____ about the meeting.* (plausible)

   b. *The district attorney found out **which church** the reporter asked ____ about the meeting.* (implausible)

Altogether then, there were eight conditions, depending on whether the gap was early or late, whether the verb had a transitive or intransitive expectation, and whether filler was plausible or implausible with respect to the object position of the verb.

The logic behind this experiment was the following. When subjects posited and filled a gap with an implausible filler, sentences would become implausible at that point. Thus, plausibility effects could serve as a diagnostic for when gaps are posited and filled. In our first experiment, the sentences were presented one at a time to the subject on a CRT. The subject's task was to decide whether or not the sentence presented was comprehensible. It turned out that sentences with intransitive preference verbs are judged comprehensible significantly more often with late gaps (as in (36b)) than with early gaps (as in (36a)). Moreover, the plausibility of the filler at the possible early position did not affect judgment to late-gap sentences. These results suggest that readers were not initially positing a postverbal gap for the intransitive preference verbs. In contrast, the transitive preference verbs show a preference for the positing of an early gap, suggesting that readers were initially treating the filler as the direct object of the verb. Somewhat surprisingly, the penalty for missing an early gap was larger than the penalty for having to reassign a previously assigned filler. That is, the effect of gap location is greater for the intransitive preference verbs, where our data suggest early gaps are often missed, than for the transitive preference verbs, where late gaps would require the reassignment of an already-assigned filler.

In a second set of experiments, we had the subjects read the sentences one word at a time at their own pace. It turns out that reading times in sentences with transitive preference verbs were slower beginning at the verb for the implausible fillers, demonstrating that subjects were immediately taking the filler to be the object of the verb. For sentences containing intransitive preference verbs, however, there was no effect of plausibility at the verb, demonstrating that readers were not assuming there to be a postverbal gap that the filler could be assigned to.

To summarize, then, gaps are posited and filled at the verb for transitive preference verbs; readers do not wait to identify further structure after the verb before doing this. Reassigning an erroneously assigned filler to a later gap seems to be easier than recovering from a postverbal gap which has been missed and is in need of recovery.

This pattern appears puzzling if one thinks in terms of constructing and repairing syntactic structures. However, if one thinks in terms of thematic assignments, the pattern may make more sense. First, if thematic roles become available upon opening a verb's lexical entry, and if thematic assignments are made on-line as soon as possible to potential fillers as well as to other arguments, then we would expect effects of assignment at the verb, instead of after. On this view, then a preliminary semantic interpretation is defined on an incomplete syntactic representation and is maintained unless inconsistent information arrives; thus the syntax acts more like a filter for proposed interpretations than as the input. A filler is temporarily assigned to a remaining available role, once the subject NP has received its role and before subsequent structure has been identified. But once temporarily assigned, reassignment is quite simple; this is what occurs in examples like (35b). Here, at the end of the sentence when the true gap is identified as the object of the preposition, the reassignment of the filler from the thematic role of the verb to the preposition (in (35b), from the Goal of *ask* to the object of the preposition *about*) is, on our account, a fairly simple matter of reindexing. On the other hand, in early-gap intransitive expectation sentences like (36a), an intransitive misanalysis of the verb leaves no available role (the subject NP takes up the only one available). Thus, when it becomes apparent at the end of the sentence that a gap should have been posited elsewhere, there is no ready thematic reassignment that could guide recovery. One must instead recover an increasingly inactive alternative thematic grid; this ought to be more difficult than working with active and hence readily available information. So not only does the perspective entertained here make sense of why filler–gap assignment takes place at the verb instead of after, but it also promises an account of the asymmetry we found in ease of contructing revised analyses. More work is plainly called for, but this approach seems promising.

One final speculation. We have been assuming that in processing, thematic roles come into play as the result of recovering a verb's lexical entry, and only at that point can thematic assignment begin. So, for instance, in English the subject role would not be assigned until the verb has been encountered. While this seems a fairly palatable state of affairs, matters become more interesting in those many SOV languages which place the verb at the end of the sentence (see Frazier, 1987a). If indeed thematic roles are the means by which arguments are integrated into a proposition, and if thematic reassignment is a fairly costfree computational venture, it is reasonable to speculate that preverbal arguments can be assigned tentative thematic roles, creating a set of mild expectations about which thematic roles the verb, when encountered, will actually assign. This was, for instance, the compelling intuition behind Bever's (1970) proposal that there is an N–V–N, Actor–Action–Object perceptual strategy responsible for patterns found in sentence processing and language acquisition. There is most certainly a persistent "default" pattern of thematic assignment throughout natural language—animate subjects are Agents and objects are Themes, inanimate subjects are Themes (encoded in various proposals for thematic assignment, such as Anderson, 1977). This pattern appears to be reflected in any number of ways, such as case-marking patterns, patterns of preferred animacy, markedness of passives versus actives, and the relative predominance of transitives and intransitives versus other subcategories of verbs, (see Chomsky, 1986b, for some discussion). The notion that thematic roles constitute the primary locus of this general pattern is certainly worth exploring.

In any case, detailed and sophisticated investigation of the on-line representations that are created in the course of language comprehension, as well as very explicit comprehension models, are required to even begin to seriously evaluate many of the hypotheses and speculations advanced here. At present, though, it appears that taking thematic roles seriously as processing entities can lead to a deeper understanding of what it is to know a language.

ACKNOWLEDGMENTS

We thank Melissa Bowerman, Charles Clifton, Gary Dell, Susan Garnsey, Padraig O'Seahgda, and Laurie Stowe for their detailed comments on preliminary drafts of this article; we are also grateful to Tom Bever and Tom Roeper for their help. This research was supported in part by NSF grants BNS-8217378 and BNS-8617738.

REFERENCES

Allen, M. (1987). *Morphological Investigations*. Garland, New York.

Amritavalli, R. (1980). Expressing cross-categorial selectional correspondences: An alternative to the X̄-syntax approach. *Linguistic Analysis* **6**, 305–343.

Anderson, J. (1971). *The Grammar of Case*. Cambridge University Press, London.

Anderson, M. (1979). *Noun Phrase Structure*. Doctoral dissertation, University of Connecticut, Storrs.

Anderson, S. R. (1971). On the role of deep structure in semantic interpretation. *Foundations of Language* **7**, 387–396.

Anderson, S. R. (1977). Comments on the paper by Wasow. In *Formal Syntax* (P. W. Culicover, T. Wasow, and A. Akmajian, eds.). Academic Press, New York.

Anderson, S. R. (1982). Where's morphology? *Linguistic Inquiry* **13**, 571–612.

Aronoff, M. (1976). *Word formation in generative grammar*. Linguistic Inquiry Monograph, No. 1. MIT Press, Cambridge, Mass.

Babby, L. (1975). A transformational analysis of transitive -Sja verbs in Russian. *Lingua* **35**, 297–332.

Bach, E. (1977). Review of P. Postal *On Raising*. *Language* **53**, 621–654.

Bach, E. (1979). Control and Montague grammar. *Linguistic Inquiry* **10**, 515–531.

Bach, E. (1982). Purpose clauses and control. In *The Nature of Syntactic Representation* (P. Jacobson and G. Pullum, eds.). Reidel, Dordrecht.

Bach, E., and Partee, B. (1980). Anaphora and Semantic Structure. *Papers from the Parasession on Pronouns and Anaphora*, Chicago Linguistic Society, 1–28.

Baker, M. (1985). *Incorporation: A Theory of Grammatical Function Changing*. Doctoral dissertation, Massachusetts Institute of Technology, Cambridge.

Baker, M. (1986). *Incorporation and the Syntax of Applicative Constructions*. Unpublished paper, Massachusetts Institute of Technology, Cambridge.

Baker, M. (1987). *Incorporation*. University of Chicago Press, Chicago.

Belletti, A. and Rizzi, L. (1986). Psych-verbs and Th-theory. *Lexicon Project Working Papers*, **13**. Center for Cognitive Science, Massachusetts Institute of Technology, Cambridge.

Berwick, R. (1982). *Locality Principles and the Acquisition of Syntactic Knowledge*. Doctoral dissertation, Massachusetts Institute of Technology, Cambridge.

Berwick, R. (1985). *The Acquisition of Syntactic Knowledge*. MIT Press, Cambridge, Mass.

Berwick, R. and Weinberg, A. (1984). *The Grammatical Basis of Linguistic Performance*. MIT Press, Cambridge, Mass.

Bever, T. G. (1970). The cognitive basis for linguistic structures. In *Cognition and the Development of Language* (J. R. Hayes, ed.). Wiley, New York.

Bhat, D. N. S. (1977). Multiple case roles. *Lingua* **42**, 365–377.

Blake, B. J. (1977). *Case marking in Australian languages. Linguistic Series*, No. 23. Australian Institute of Aboriginal Studies, Canberra.

Boons, J.-P. (1973). Acceptability, interpretation and knowledge of the world: Remarks on the verb PLANTER (to plant). *Cognition* **2**, 183–211.

Borer, H. (1983). The projection principle and the lexicon. *Proceedings of NELS* **14**. *University of Massachusetts, Amherst*.

Borer, H. (1984). *Parametric Syntax*. Foris, Dordrecht.

Borer, H. (1985). *The Lexical Learning Hypothesis and Universal Grammar*. Paper presented at the Tenth Annual Boston University Conference on Language Development.

Borer, H. and Wexler, K. (1987). The maturation of syntax. In *Parameter Setting* (T. Roeper and E. Williams, eds.). Reidel, Dordrecht.

Bresnan, J. (1980). Polyadicity: Part I of a theory of lexical rules and representations. In *Lexical Grammar* (T. Hoekstra, H. van der Hulst, and M. Moortgat, eds.). Foris, Dordrecht.

Bresnan, J., ed. (1982a). *The Mental Representation of Grammatical Relations*. MIT Press, Cambridge, Mass.

Bresnan, J. (1982b). The passive in lexical theory. In *The Mental Representation of Grammatical Relations* (J. Bresnan, ed.). MIT Press, Cambridge, Mass.

Bresnan, J. (1982c). Polyadicity. In *The Mental Representation of Grammatical Relations* (J. Bresnan, ed.). MIT Press, Cambridge, Mass.

Bresnan, J. (1982d). Control and complementation. *Linguistic Inquiry* **13**, 343–434.

Broadwell, G. A. (1983). *The Choctaw Auxiliary Verb taha*. Unpublished paper, University of California, Los Angeles.

Broadwell, G. A. (1986a). *Choctaw Syntax and the Binding Theory of Switch-Reference*. Masters thesis, University of California, Los Angeles.

Broadwell, G. A. (1986b). Multiple Th-Role Assignment. *Proceedings of NELS* **17**, 46–58.

Burzio, L. (1981). *Intransitive Verbs and Italian Auxiliaries*. Doctoral dissertation, Massachusetts Institute of Technology, Cambridge.

Burzio, L. (1986). *Italian Syntax: A Government-Binding Approach*. Reidel, Dordrecht.

Carlson, G. (1984). Thematic roles and their role in semantic interpretation. *Linguistics* **22**, 259–279.

Carlson, G. (1988). The semantics of *Same* and *Different. Linguistics and Philosophy*, in press.

Carrier-Duncan, J. (1985). Linking of thematic arguments in derivational word formation. *Linguistic Inquiry* **16**, 1–34.

Carrier-Duncan, J. and Randall, J. H. (1987). *Derived Argument Structure: Evidence from Resultatives*. Unpublished paper, Harvard University and Northeastern University.

Carter, R. J. (1976a). *Some Linking Regularities*. Unpublished paper, University of Paris VIII, Vincennes.

Carter, R. J. (1976b). Some constraints on possible words. *Semantikos* **1**, 27–66.

Carter, R. J. (1984). *Compositionality and Polysemy*. Unpublished paper, Massachusetts Institute of Technology, Cambridge.

Cattell, R. (1969). *The Role of Give and Some Related Verbs in English Syntax*. Doctoral dissertation, University of Newcastle, New South Wales.

Cattell, R. (1976). Constraints on movement rules. *Language* **52**, 18–50.

Cattell, R. (1983). *θ-Role Assignment in Complex Predicate Constructions*. Unpublished paper, University of Newcastle, New South Wales.

Cattell, R. (1984). *Composite Predicates in English*. Academic Press, New York.

Chierchia, G. (1984). *Topics in the Syntax and Semantics of Infinitives and Gerunds.* Doctoral dissertation, University of Massachusetts, Amherst.

Chomsky, N. (1965). *Aspects of the Theory of Syntax.* MIT Press, Cambridge, Mass.

Chomsky, N. (1970). Remarks on nominalization. In *Readings in English Transformational Grammar* (R. Jacobs and P. Rosenbaum, eds.). Georgetown University Press, Washington, D.C.

Chomsky, N. (1975). Questions of form and interpretation. *Linguistic Analysis* **1,** 75–109.

Chomsky, N. (1980). On binding. *Linguistic Inquiry* **11,** 1–46.

Chomsky, N. (1981). *Lectures on Government and Binding.* Foris, Dordrecht.

Chomsky, N. (1982). *Some Concepts and Consequences of the Theory of Government and Binding.* MIT Press, Cambridge, Mass.

Chomsky, N. (1986a). *Barriers.* MIT Press, Cambridge, Mass.

Chomsky, N. (1986b). *Knowledge of Language: Its Nature, Origin, and Use.* Praeger, New York.

Chomsky, N. and Lasnik, H. (1977). Filters and control. *Linguistic Inquiry* **8,** 425–504.

Chvany, C. (1975). *On the Syntax of BE-Sentences in Russian.* Slavica Publishing, Cambridge, Mass.

Clark, E. V., and Clark, H. H. (1979). When nouns surface as verbs. *Language* **55,** 767–811.

Clifton, C., Frazier, L., and Connine, C. (1984). Lexical expectations in sentence comprehension. *Journal of Verbal Learning and Verbal Behavior* **23,** 696–708.

Comrie, B. (1978). Ergativity. In *Syntactic Typology* (W. P. Lehmann, ed.). University of Texas Press, Austin.

Comrie, B. (1979). Russian. In *Languages and Their Status* (T. Shopen, ed.) Winthrop, Cambridge, Mass.

Comrie, B. (1981). *Language Universals and Linguistic Typology.* University of Chicago Press, Chicago.

Comrie, B. (1985). Reflections on subject and object control. *Journal of Semantics* **4,** 47–65.

Corbett, G. (1983). *Hierarchies, Targets and Controllers.* Croom Helm, London.

Cottrell, G. (1984). *A Connectionist Approach to Word Sense Disambiguation.* Doctrol dissertation, University of Rochester.

Crain, S. and Steedman, M. (1985). On not being led up the garden path: The use of context by the psychological syntax processor. *In Natural Language Parsing* (D. Dowty, L. Karttunen, and A. Zwicky, eds.). Cambridge University Press, London.

Culicover, P. W. (1987). *On Thematic Relations.* MIT Working Papers, in press.

Culicover, P. W., and Rochemont, M. (1983). Stress and focus in English. *Language* **59,** 123–165.

Culicover, P. W., and Wilkins, W. (1984). *Locality in Linguistic Theory.* Academic Press, New York.

Culicover, P. W., and Wilkins, W. (1986). Control, PRO, and the projection principle. *Language* **62,** 120–153.

Davidson, D. (1967). The logical form of action sentences. In *The Logic of Decision and Action* (N. Rescher, ed.). University of Pittsburgh Press, Pittsburgh, Pa.

Davies, W. (1981). *Choctaw Clause Structure.* Doctoral dissertation, University of California, San Diego.

Davies, W. (1986). *Choctaw Verb Agreement and Universal Grammar.* Reidel, Dordrecht.

Diderichsen, P. (1939). Om pronominerne *sig* og *sin, Acta Philologica scandinavica* **13,** 1–95.

Dixon, R. M. W. (1973). The semantics of giving. In *The Formal Analysis of Natural Languages* (M. Gross, M. Halle, and M.-P. Schutzenberger, eds.). Mouton, The Hague.

Dixon, R. M. W. (1980). *The Languages of Australia.* Cambridge Language Surveys, Cambridge University Press, London.

Dowty, D. R. (1979). *Word Meaning and Montague Grammar*, Reidel, Dordrecht.

Dowty, D. R. (1986). Thematic roles and semantics. *Proceedings of the Twelfth Annual Meeting of the Berkeley Linguistics Society*, 340–354.

Dowty, D. R. (1988). On the semantic content of the notion 'thematic role.' In *Property Theory, Type Theory, and Semantics* (G. Chierchia, B. Partee, and R. Turner, eds.). Reidel, Dordrecht, in press.

Dowty, D. R., Wall, R., and Peters, S. (1981). *Introduction to Montague Semantics*. Reidel, Dordrecht.

Faraci, R. (1974). *Aspects of the Grammar of Infinitive and for Phrases*. Doctoral dissertation, Massachusetts Institute of Technology, Cambridge.

Farmer, A. (1987). On 'I held his breath' and other puzzles for binding theory. *Linguistic Inquiry* **18**, 157–163.

Ferreira, F., and Clifton, C. (1986). The independence of syntactic processing. *Journal of Memory and Language* **25**, 348–368.

Fiengo, R. (1980). *Surface Structure*. Harvard University Press, Cambridge, Mass.

Fillmore, C. (1968). The case for case. In *Universals in Linguistic Theory* (E. Bach and R. T. Harms, eds.). Holt, New York.

Finer, D. (1984). *The Formal Grammar of Switch-Reference*. Doctoral dissertation, University of Massachusetts, Amherst.

Finer, D. and Roeper, T. (1987). From cognition to thematic roles: The role of the projection principle in language acquisition. In *Proceedings of the Ontario Conference on Learnability* (R. Matthews and R. May, eds.), in press.

Fodor, J. D. (1978). Parsing strategies and constraints on transformations. *Linguistic Inquiry* **9**, 427–473.

Foley, W., and Van Valin, R., Jr. (1984). *Functional Syntax and Universal Grammar*. Cambridge University Press, London.

Ford, M., Bresnan, J., and Kaplan, R. (1982). A competence-based theory of syntactic closure. In *The Mental Representation of Grammatical Relations* (J. Bresnan, ed.). MIT Press, Cambridge, Mass.

Frazier, L. (1978). *On Comprehending Sentences: Syntactic Parsing Strategies*. Doctoral dissertation, University of Connecticut, distributed by Indiana University Linguistics Club.

Frazier, L. (1987a). Syntactic processing: Evidence from Dutch. *Natural Language & Linguistic Theory* **5**, 519–560.

Frazier, L. (1987b). Theories of sentence processing. In *Modularity in Knowledge Representation and Natural Language Processing* (J. Garfield, ed.). MIT Press, Cambridge, Mass., pp. 291–307.

Frazier, L., and Fodor, J. D. (1978). The sausage machine: A new two-stage parsing model. *Cognition* **6**, 291–325.

Frazier, L., and Rayner, K. (1982). Making and correcting errors during sentence comprehension: Eye movements in the analysis of structurally ambiguous sentences. *Cognitive Psychology* **14**, 178–210.

Fukui, N., Miyagawa, S., and Tenny, C. (1985). Verb classes in English and Japanese: A case study in the interaction of syntax, morphology and semantics. *Lexicon Project Working Papers*, **3**. Center for Cognitive Science, Massachusetts Institute of Technology, Cambridge.

Gazdar, G., Klein, E., Pullum, G., and Sag, I. (1985). *Generalized Phrase Structure Grammar*. Harvard University Press, Cambridge, Mass.

Green, G. M. (1973). A syntactic syncretism in English and French. In *Issues in Linguistics* (B. Kachru et al., eds.). University of Illinois Press, Urbana.

Green, G. M. (1974). *Semantic and Syntactic Regularity*. Indiana University Press, Bloomington.

Grimshaw, J. (1975). *A Note on the Interpretation of Subjects of Infinitival Relatives*. Unpublished paper, University of Massachusetts, Amherst.

Grimshaw, J. (1979). Form, function, and the LAD. In *The Logical Problem of Language Acquisition* (C. L. Baker and J. McCarthy, eds.). MIT Press, Cambridge, Mass.

Grosz, B., Joshi, A., and Weinstein, S. (1983). Providing a unified account of definite noun phrases in discourse. *Proceedings of the 21st Annual Meeting of the Association for Computational Linguistics*. Association for Computational Linguistics.

Gruber, J. (1965). *Studies in Lexical Relations*. Doctoral dissertation, Massachusetts Institute of Technology, distributed by the Indiana University Linguistics Club.

Gruber, J. (1967). Look and See. *Language* **43**, 937–947.

Gruber, J. (1976). *Lexical Structures in Syntax and Semantics*. North-Holland Publ., Amsterdam.

Guerssel, M. (1986). On Berber verbs of change: A study of transitivity alternations. *Lexicon Project Working Papers*, **9**. Center For Cognitive Science. Massachusetts Institute of Technology, Cambridge.

Guerssel, M., Hale, K., Laughren, M., Levin, B., and White Eagle, J. (1985). A cross-linguistic study of transitivity alternations. *Papers from the Parasession on Causatives and Agentivity at the 21st Regional Meeting*, Chicago Linguistic Society.

Hale, K. L. (1973). Person marking in Walbiri. In *A Festschrift for Morris Halle* (S. Anderson and P. Kiparsky, eds.). Holt, New York.

Hale, K. L. (1982). Some essential features of Warlpiri verbal clauses. In *Papers in Warlpiri Grammar in Memory of Lothar Jagst* (S. Swartz, ed.), *Working Papers of SIL-AAB, Series A* **6**.

Hale, K. L. and Keyser, S. J. (1986). Some transitivity alternations in English. *Lexicon Project Working Papers*, **7**. Center for Cognitive Science, Massachusetts Institute of Technology, Cambridge.

Hale, K. L., and Keyser, S. J. (1987). A view from the middle. *Lexicon Project Working Papers*, **10**. Center for Cognitive Science, Massachusetts Institute of Technology, Cambridge.

Hale, K. L., and Laughren, M. (1983). The structure of verbal entries: Preface to dictionary entries of verbs. *Warlpiri Lexicon Project*, Massachusetts Institute of Technology, Cambridge.

Hale, K. L., Masayesva Jeanne, L., and Platero, P. (1977). Three cases of overgeneration. In *Formal Syntax* (P. W. Culicover, T. Wasow, and A. Akmajian, eds.). Academic Press, New York.

Harris, Z. (1957). Co-occurrence and transformation in linguistic structure. *Language* **33**, 283–340.

Heath, J. (1977). Choctaw cases. *Proceedings of the Third Annual Meeting of the Berkeley Linguistic Society*. 204–213.

Heim, I. (1982). *The Semantics of Definite and Indefinite Noun Phrases*. Doctoral dissertation, University of Massachusetts, Amherst.

Hellan, L. (1986). On anaphora and predication in Norwegian. In *Topics in Scandinavian Syntax* (L. Hellan and K. K. Christensen, eds.), pp. 103–124. Reidel, Dordrecht.

Hellan, L., and Christensen, K. K. (1986). Introduction. In *Topics in Scandinavian Syntax* (L. Hellan and K. K. Christensen, eds.), pp.1–29. Reidel, Dordrecht.

Herslund, M. (1986). The double object construction in Danish. In *Topics in Scandinavian Syntax* (L. Hellan and K. K. Christensen, eds.), pp. 125–147. Reidel, Dordrecht.

Higgins, F. R. (1974). *The Pseudo-Cleft Construction in English*. Doctoral dissertation, Massachusetts Institute of Technology, Cambridge.

Higginbotham, J. T. (1985). On semantics. *Linguistic Inquiry* **16**, 547–593.

Hook, P. E. (1983). The English abstrument and rocking case relations. *Papers from the 19th Regional Meeting*, Chicago Linguistic Society, 183–194.

Horn, L. R. (1978). Remarks on neg-raising. In *Syntax and Semantics 9: Pragmatics* (P. Cole, ed.). Academic Press, New York.

Horn, L. R., and Bayer, S. (1984). Short-circuited implicature: A negative contribution. *Linguistics and Philosophy* **7**, 397–414.

Huang, C.-T. J. (1982). *Logical Relations in Chinese and the Theory of Grammar.* Doctoral dissertation, Massachusetts Institute of Technology, Cambridge.

Huang, C.-T. J. (1984). On the distribution and reference of empty pronouns. *Linguistic Inquiry* **15,** 531–574.

Huang, C.-T. J. (1987). Remarks on empty categories in Chinese. *Linguistic Inquiry* **18,** 321–337.

Hudson, S. B., and Tanenhaus, M. K. (1984). Lexical ambiguity resolution in the absence of contextual bias. *Proceedings of the Sixth Annual Cognitive Science Meeting.*

Hudson, S. B., Tanenhaus, M. K., and Dell, G. S. (1986). The effect of discourse center on the local coherence of a discourse. *Proceedings of the Sixth Annual Cognitive Science Meeting.*

Hust, J. R., and Brame, M. K. (1976). Jackendoff on interpretive semantics. *Linguistic Analysis* **2,** 243–277.

Jackendoff, R. S. (1972). *Semantics in Generative Grammar.* MIT Press, Cambridge, Mass.

Jackendoff, R. S. (1974). A deep structure projection rule. *Linguistic Inquiry* **5,** 481–505.

Jackendoff, R. S. (1976). Towards an explanatory semantic representation. *Linguistic Inquiry* **7,** 89–150.

Jackendoff, R. S. (1983). *Semantics and Cognition.* MIT Press, Cambridge, Mass.

Jackendoff, R. S. (1985). Multiple subcategorization and the theta-criterion: The case of *climb.* *Natural Language & Linguistic Theory* **3,** 271–296.

Jackendoff, R. S. (1987). The status of thematic relations in linguistic theory. *Linguistic Inquiry* **18,** 369–411.

Jayaseelan, K. A. (1983). Case-marking and θ-marking in Malayalam: Implications for the projection principle. *Proceedings from the Ninth Annual Meeting of the Berkeley Linguistics Society.*

Jayaseelan, K. A. (1984). Complex predicates and the theory of θ-marking. *CIEFL Working Papers in Linguistics,* **1,** 1. Central Institute of English and Foreign Languages, Hyderabad, India.

Jeffries, L., and Willis, P. (1984). A return to the spray paint issue. *Journal of Pragmatics* **8,** 715–729.

Jelinek, E. (1984). Empty categories, case, and configurationality. *Natural Language & Linguistic Theory* **2,** 39–76.

Jespersen, O. (1968). *The Philosophy of Grammar.* Allen & Unwin, London.

Johnson-Laird, P. (1983). *Mental Models.* Harvard University Press, Cambridge, Mass.

Jones, C. (1984). Under control: Where is the controlled element? *Papers from the 20th Regional Meeting,* Chicago Linguistic Society.

Jones, C. (1985a). Agent, patient, and control into purpose clauses. *Papers from the Parasession on Causatives and Agentivity,* Chicago Linguistic Society, 105–119.

Jones, C. (1985b). *Syntax and Thematics of Infinitival Adjuncts.* Doctoral dissertation, University of Massachusetts, Amherst.

Kamp, H. (1979). Events, instants, and temporal reference. In *Semantics from Different Points of View* (R. Bäuerle, U. Egli, and A. von Stechow, eds.). Springer-Verlag, Berlin.

Kamp, H. (1981). A theory of truth and semantic representation. In *Formal Methods in the Study of Language* (J. Groenendijk, T. Jannsen, and M. Stokhof, eds.). Mathematical Center, Amsterdam.

Kayne, R. S. (1981). Unambiguous paths. In *Levels of Syntactic Representation* (R. May and J. Koster, eds.). Foris, Dordrecht.

Kayne, R. S. (1983). Connectedness. *Linguistic Inquiry* **14,** 223–249.

Kayne, R. S. (1984). *Connectedness and Binary Branching.* Foris, Dordrecht.

Kayne, R. S. (1985). Principles of particle constructions. In *Grammatical Representation*, (J. Gueron, H. G. Obenauer, and J.-Y. Pollock, eds.). Foris, Dordrecht.

Keenan, E. (1974). The functional principle: Generalizing the notion of 'Subject Of.' *Papers from the Tenth Regional Meeting*, Chicago Linguistic Society, 298–309.

Kegl, J., and Gee, J. (undated). *ASL Structure: Toward a Theory of Abstract Case*. Unpublished paper.

Keyser, S. J., and Roeper, T. (1984). On the middle and ergative constructions in English. *Linguistic Inquiry* 15, 381–416.

Kiparsky, P. (1982). Lexical morphology and phonology. In *Linguistics in the Morning Calm* (I.-S. Yang, ed.). Hanshin, Seoul, South Korea.

Kirparsky, P. (1985a). *Morphology and Grammatical Relations*. Unpublished manuscript, Stanford University, Stanford, Calif.

Kiparsky, P. (1985b). Th-structure, lexical structure, and linking. Lectures presented at the Indiana University Linguistics Club Summer Seminar.

Kiparsky, P. (1987). Th-Structure, Lexical Structure, and Linking. University of Arizona Colloquium.

Kirkpatrick, C. (1982). The transitive purpose clause in English. *Texas Linguistic Forum* 19.

Kisala, J. (1985). Review of Chapter 1 of Ostler's thesis, *Case-Linking: A Theory of Case and Verb Diathesis Applied to Classical Sanskrit*. In *Lexical Semantics in Review, Lexicon Project Working Papers* (B. Levin, ed.), 1. Center for Cognitive Science, Massachusetts Institute of Technology, Cambridge.

Koopman, H. (1984). *The Syntax of Verbs*. Foris, Dordrecht.

Koster, J. and May, R. (1982). On the constituency of infinitives. *Language* 58, 116–143.

Kurtzman, H. (1984). *Studies in Syntactic Ambiguity Resolution*. Doctoral dissertation, Massachusetts Institute of Technology, distributed by the Indiana University Linguistics Club.

Kurylowicz, J. (1964). *The Inflectional Categories of Indo-European*. Winter, Heidelberg.

Ladusaw, W. A. (1985). *A proposed distinction between levels and strata*. Paper presented at the 1985 Annual Meeting of the Linguistic Society of America.

Ladusaw, W. A. (1987). Inference patterns from infinitival complements. *Proceedings of the Sixth Annual West Coast Conference on Formal Linguistics*, in press.

Lakoff, G. and Ross, J. (1966). Criteria for verb phrase constituency. *Harvard University Computation Laboratory Report to NSF on Mathematical Linguistics and Automatic Translation*, #NSF-17.

Langacker, R. W. (1983). *Foundations of Cognitive Grammar*. Indiana University Linguistics Club, Bloomington.

Laughren, M. (1986). *Towards a Lexical Representation of Warlpiri Verbs*. Unpublished paper, Massachusetts Institute of Technology, Cambridge.

Lebeaux, D. (1981). *The Acquisition of the Passive*. Masters thesis, Harvard University, Cambridge, Mass.

Levin, B. C. (1983). *On the Nature of Ergativity*. Doctoral dissertation, Massachusetts Institute of Technology, Cambridge.

Levin, B. C. (1985). Case theory and the Russian reflexive affix. *Proceedings of the Fourth West Coast Conference on Formal Linguistics*, 178–189.

Levin, B. and Rappaport, M. (1986). The formation of adjectival passives. *Linguistic Inquiry* 17, 623–661.

Levin, L. (1985). *Operations on Lexical Forms: Unaccusative Rules in Germanic Languages*. Doctoral dissertation, Massachusetts Institute of Technology, Cambridge.

Linker, W. (1987). On the coordinating status of the switch-reference markers -*chah* and -*nah* in Choctaw. In *Muskogean Linguistics* (P. Munro, ed.). *UCLA Occasional Papers in Linguistics* **6**, 96–110.

Maling, J. (1986). Clause-bounded reflexives in modern Icelandic. In *Topics in Scandinavian Syntax* (L. Hellan and K. K. Christensen, eds.), pp. 53–63. Reidel, Dordrecht.

Maltzoff, N. (1984). *Essentials of Russian Grammar*. Passport Books, Lincolnwood, Illinois.

Manzini, R. M., and Wexler, K. (1987). Parameters, binding theory, and learnability. *Linguistic Inquiry* **18**, 413–444.

Marantz, A. (1984). *On the Nature of Grammatical Relations*. MIT Press, Cambridge, Mass.

Maratsos, M., Kuczaj, S., II, Fox, D., and Chalkley, M. (1979). Some empirical studies in the acquisition of transformational relations: Passives, negatives, and the past tense. In *Minnesota Symposium on Child Psychology*, (W. A. Collins, ed.), Vol. 12. Erlbaum, Hillsdale, N.J.

Maratsos, M., Fox, D., Becker, J., and Chalkley, M. (1983). *Semantic Restrictions on Children's Early Passives*. Unpublished paper, University of Minnesota.

Marslen-Wilson, W. D. (1975). Sentence preception as an interactive parallel process. *Science* **189**, 226–228.

Martin, J. (1986). *Agreement in Creek and the theory of inflection*. Paper presented at the Seventeenth Annual Meeting of the Northeastern Linguistic Society.

May, R. (1985). *Logical Form*. MIT Press, Cambridge, Mass.

McCawley, J. (1982). Parentheticals and discontinuous constituents. *Linguistic Inquiry* **13**, 91–106.

McClelland, J. L., and Kawamoto, A. (1986). Mechanisms of sentence processing: Assigning roles to constituents of sentences. In *Parallel Distributed Processing, Part 2: Psychological and Biological Models* (J. McClelland and D. Rumelhart, eds.). MIT Press, Cambridge, Mass.

McClelland, J. L., and Rumelhart, D. (1981). An interactive activation model of context effects in letter perception: Part I. An account of basic findings. *Psychological Review* **88**, 375–405.

McConnell-Ginet, S. (1982). Adverbs and logical form: A linguistically realistic theory. *Language* **58**, 144–184.

Melvold, J. (1985). *Getting PRO Under Control*. Unpublished paper, Massachusetts Institute of Technology, Cambridge.

Mitchell, D. C., and Holmes, V. M. (1985). The role of specific information about the verb in parsing sentences with local structural ambiguity. *Journal of Memory and Language* **24**, 542–559.

Montague, R. (1973). The proper treatment of quantification in English. In *Approaches to Natural Language*, (J. Hintikka, J. M. E. Moravcsik, and P. Suppes eds.). Reidel, Dordrecht.

Moravcsik, E. A. (1978). On the case marking of objects. In *Universals of Human Language, 4: Syntax* (J. H. Greenberg *et al.*, eds.). Stanford University Press, Stanford, Calif.

Munro, P., and Gordon, L. (1982). Syntactic relations in Western Muskogean: A typological perspective. *Language* **58**, 81–115.

Nash, D. G. (1986). *Topics in Warlpiri Grammer*. Garland Press, New York.

Newmeyer, F. (1983). *Linguistic Theory in America*. Academic Press, New York.

Nishigauchi, T. (1984). Control and the thematic domain. *Language* **60**, 215–250.

Oehrle, R. (1975). *The Grammatical Status of the English Dative Alternation*. Doctoral dissertation, Massachusetts Institute of Technology, Cambridge.

Onifer, W., and Swinney, D. A. (1981). Accessing lexical ambiguities during sentence comprehension: Effects of frequency of meaning and contextual bias. *Memory and Cognition* **9**, 222–236.

Ostler, N. D. M. (1979). *Case-Linking: A Theory of Case and Verb Diathesis Applied to Classical Sanskrit.* Doctoral dissertation, Massachusetts Institute of Technology, Cambridge.

Parsons, T. (1980). Modifiers and quantifiers in natural language. *Canadian Journal of Philosophy, Suppl.* **VI**, 29–60.

Partee, B. H. (1979). Constraining transformational montague grammar. In *Linguistics, Philosophy, and Montague Grammar* (S. Davis and M. Mithun, eds.). University of Texas Press, Austin.

Partee, B. H. (1984). Nominal and temporal anaphora. *Linguistics and Philosophy* **7**, 243–286.

Payne, D. (1981). Chickasaw agreement morphology: A functional explanation. In *Studies in Transitivity* (S. Thompson and P. Hopper, eds.). Academic Press, New York.

Perlmutter, D. M. (1978). Impersonal passives and the unaccusative hypothesis. *Proceedings of the Fourth Annual Meeting of the Berkeley Linguistic Society.*

Perlmutter, D. M. (1980). Relational grammar. In *Current Approaches to Syntax* (E. Moravcsik and J. Wirth, eds.). Academic Press, New York.

Perlmutter, D. M. (1982). Syntactic representation, syntactic levels and the notion of subject. In *The Nature of Syntactic Representation* (P. Jacobson and G. Pullum, eds.). Reidel, Dordrecht.

Perlmutter, D. M. (1984). On the inadequacy of some mono-stratal theories of passive. In *Studies in Relational Grammar II* (D. Perlmutter and C. Rosen, eds.). University of Chicago Press, Chicago.

Pesetsky, D. (1982). *Paths and Categories.* Doctoral dissertation, Massachusetts Institute of Technology, Cambridge.

Pesetsky, D. (1985). Morphology and logical form. *Linguistic Inquiry* **16**, 193–246.

Pinker, S. (1979). *A Theory of the Acquisition of Lexical-Interpretive Grammars,* Unpublished paper, Massachusetts Institute of Technology.

Pinker, S. (1982). A theory of the acquisition of lexical-interpretive grammars. In *The Mental Representation of Grammatical Relations* (J. Bresnan, ed.). MIT Press, Cambridge, Mass.

Pinker, S. (1984). *Language Learnability and Language Development.* Harvard University Press, Cambridge, Mass.

Platt, J. (1977). *Grammatical Form and Grammatical Meaning: A Tagmemic View of Fillmore's Deep Structure Case Concepts.* North Holland Publ., Amsterdam.

Postal, P. (1971). *Crossover Phenomena.* Holt, New York.

Postal, P. (1977). Antipassive in French. *Lingvisticae Investigationes* **1**, 333–374.

Radford, A. (1981). *Transformational Syntax.* Cambridge University Press, London.

Randall, J. H. (1983). A lexical approach to causatives. *Journal of Linguistic Research* **2**, 77–105.

Randall, J. H. (1984a). Morphological complementation. *MIT Working Papers in Linguistics* **7**, 70–85.

Randall, J. H. (1984b). Thematic structure and inheritance. *Quaderni di Semantica* **5**, 92–110.

Randall, J. H. (1984c). Grammatical information in word structure. *Quaderni di Semantica* **5**, 313–330.

Randall, J. H. (1985). *Morphological Structure and Language Acquisition.* Garland Press, New York.

Rappaport, G. (1986). On anaphoric binding in Russian. *Natural Language & Linguistic Theory* **4**, 97–119.

Rappaport, M. (1983). On the nature of derived nominals. In *Papers in Lexical-Functional Grammar* (L. Levin, M. Rappaport, and A. Zaenen, eds.). Indiana University Linguistics Club, Bloomington.

Rappaport, M., and Levin, B. (1985). *A Case Study in Lexical Analysis: The Locative Alternation.* Unpublished paper, Massachusetts Institute of Technology, Cambridge.

Rayner, K., Carlson, M., and Frazier, L. (1984). The interaction of syntax and semantics in sentence processing: Eye movements in the analysis of semantically biased sentences. *Journal of Verbal Learning and Verbal Behavior* **22**, 358–374.

Roeper, T. (1987). Implicit arguments. *Linguistic Inquiry* **18**, 267–310.

Rosen, C. (1984). The interface between semantic roles and initial grammatical relations. In *Studies in Relational Grammar 2* (D. Perlmutter and C. Rosen, eds.). University of Chicago Press, Chicago.

Rosenbaum, P. (1967). *The Grammar of English Predicate Complement Constructions*. MIT Press, Cambridge, Mass.

Rothstein, S. (1983). *The Syntactic Forms of Predication*. Doctoral dissertation, Massachusetts Institute of Technology, Cambridge.

Rouveret, A., and Vergnaud, J.-R. (1980). Specifying reference to the subject: French causatives and conditions on representations. *Linguistic Inquiry* **11**, 97–202.

Rozwadowska, B. (1986). *Thematic Relations as Features*. Unpublished paper, University of Massachusetts, Amherst.

Růžička, R. (1983). Remarks on control. *Linguistic Inquiry* **14**, 309–324.

Safir, K. (1985). *Syntactic Chains*. Cambridge University Press, London.

Schaarschmidt, G. (1968). *The Syntax of -sja Verbs in Russian*. Doctoral dissertation, Indiana University, Bloomington.

Schwartz, L. (1986). Levels of grammatical relations and Russian reflexive controllers. *Proceedings of the Tenth Annual Meeting of the Berkeley Linguistic Society*.

Schwartz-Norman, L. (1976). The grammar of 'content' and 'container.' *Journal of Linguistics* **12**, 279–287.

Seidenberg, M. (1985). Constraining models of word recognition. *Cognition* **14**, 169–190.

Seidenberg, M., and Tanenhaus, M. (1979). Orthographic effects in rhyme and monitoring. *Journal of Experimental Psychology: Human Learning and Memory* **5**, 546–554.

Seidenberg, M., Tanenhaus, M., Leiman, J., and Bienkowski, M. (1982). Automatic access of the meanings of ambiguous words in context: Some limitations of knowledge-based processes. *Cognitive Psychology* **14**, 489–537.

Seuren, P. (1985). *Discourse Semantics*. Blackwell, Oxford.

Siegel, D. (1979). *Topics in English Morphology*. Garland Press, New York.

Simpson, G. (1984). Lexical ambiguity and its role in models of word recognition. *Psychological Bulletin* **96**, 316–340.

Simpson, G., and Burgess, C. (1985). Activation and selection processes in the recognition of ambiguous words. *Journal of Experimental Psychology: Human Perception and Performance* **11**, 28–39.

Simpson, J. H. (1983). *Aspects of Warlpiri Morphology and Syntax*. Doctoral dissertation, Massachusetts Institute of Technology, Cambridge.

Simpson, J. H., and Bresnan, J. W. (1983). Control and obviation in Warlpiri. *Natural Language & Linguistic Theory* **1**, 49–64.

Speas, M. J. (1986). *Adjunctions and Projections in Syntax*. Doctoral dissertation, Massachusetts Institute of Technology, Cambridge.

Stockwell, R., Schachter, P., and Partee, B. (1973). *The Major Syntactic Structures of English*. Holt, New York.

Stowe, L. (1987). Thematic structures and sentence comprehension. In *Linguistic Structure in Language Processing* (G. Carlson and M. Tanenhaus, eds.). Reidel, Dordrecht, in press.

Stowe, L., and Tanenhaus, M. (1987). *Models of Filler-Gap Assignment: The Role of Pragmatic and Lexical Information*. Unpublished paper, University of Rochester.

Stowell, T. (1981). *Origins of Phrase Structure*. Doctoral dissertation, Massachusetts Institute of Technology, Cambridge.

Stowell, T. (1982). A formal theory of configurational phenomena. *Proceedings of Northeastern Linguistic Society* **12**.

Swinney, D. A. (1979). Lexical access during sentence comprehension: (Re)consideration of context effects. *Journal of Verbal Learning and Verbal Behavior* **18**, 645–659.

Talmy, L. (1972). *Semantic Structures in English and Atsugewi*. Doctoral dissertation, University of California, Berkeley.

Talmy, L. (1985). Lexicalization patterns: Semantic structure in lexical forms. In *Language Typology and Syntactic Description* (T. Shopen, ed.), Vol. 3. Cambridge University Press, London.

Tanenhaus, M., Leiman, J., and Seidenberg, M. (1979). Evidence for multiple stages in the processing of ambiguous words in syntactic contexts. *Journal of Verbal Learning and Verbal Behavior* **18**, 427–440.

Tanenhaus, M., Flanigan, H., and Seidenberg, M. (1980). Orthographic and phonological code activation in auditory and visual word recognition. *Memory and Cognition* **8**, 513–520.

Tanenhaus, M., Stowe, L., and Carlson, G. (1985). The interaction of lexical expectation and pragmatics in parsing filler-gap constructions. *Proceedings of the Seventh Annual Cognitive Science Society Meetings*.

Timberlake, A. (1979). Reflexivization and the cycle in Russian. *Linguistic Inquiry* **10**, 109–141.

Timberlake, A. (1980). Oblique control of Russian reflexivization. In *Morphosyntax in Slavic* (C. Chvany and R. Brecht, eds.). Slavica, Cambridge, Mass.

Travis, L. (1984). *Parameters and Effects of Word Order Variation*. Doctoral dissertation, Massachusetts Institute of Technology, Cambridge.

Ulrich, C. (1986). *Choctaw Morphophonology*. Doctoral dissertation, University of California, Los Angeles.

Van Valin, R. (1986). The unaccusative hypothesis vs. lexical semantics: Syntactic vs. semantic approaches to verb classification. *Proceedings of Northeastern Linguistic Society* **17**.

Vendryes, J. (1931). *Language*. Knopf, New York.

Verkuyl, H. J. (1978). Thematic relations and the semantic representation of verbs expressing change. *Studies in Language* **2**, 199–233.

Veyrenc, J. (1976). Sur la double diathèse d'object des enonces translocatifs. *Bulletin de la Société de Linguistique de Paris* **72**, 241–273.

Visser, F. T. (1973). *An Historical Syntax of the English Language*. Brill, Leiden.

Wasow, T. (1977). Transformations and the lexicon. In *Formal Syntax* (P. W. Culicover, T. Wasow, and A. Akmajian, eds.). Academic Press, New York.

Wasow, T. (1980). Major and minor rules in lexical grammar. In *Lexical Grammar* (T. Hoekstra, H. van der Hulst, and M. Moortgat, eds.). Foris, Dordrecht.

Weinberg, A. (1981). Abstract. Paper presented at 1981 meeting of Generative Linguists of the Old World (GLOW).

Wexler, K., and Chien, Y.-C. (1985). *The Development of Lexical Anaphors and Pronouns*. Unpublished paper, University of California, Irvine.

Wexler, K., and Culicover, P. W. (1980). *Formal Principles of Language Acquisition*. MIT Press, Cambridge, Mass.

Wexler, K., and Manzini, M. R. (1987). Parameters and learnability in binding theory. In *Parameter Setting* (T. Roeper and E. Williams, eds.). Reidel, Dordrecht.

Wierzbicka, A. (1982). Why can you "have a drink" when you can't "have an eat"? *Language* **58**, 753–799.

Wilkins, W. (1986). *Thematic Structure and Language Learnability*. Unpublished paper, University of Washington, Seattle.

Wilkins, W. (1987a). On the linguistic function of event roles. *Proceedings of the Annual Meeting of the Berkeley Linguistic Society, Parasession on Grammar and Cognition*, 460–472.

Wilkins, W. (1987b). On the learnability of the scope of reflexivization. *Proceedings of the Sixth West Coast Conference on Formal Linguistics*, in press.

Williams, E. (1980). Predication. *Linguistic Inquiry* **11**, 203–238.

Williams, E. (1981). Argument structure and morphology. *The Linguistic Review* **1**, 81–114.

Williams, E. (1983). Against small clauses. *Linguistic Inquiry* **14**, 287–308.

Williams, E. (1985). PRO and the subject of NP. *Natural Language & Linguistic Theory* **3**, 297–315.

Xu, L. (1986). Free empty category. *Linguistic Inquiry* **17**, 75–93.

Zaenen, A., and Maling, J. (1984). Unaccusative, passive and quirky case. *Proceedings of the Third Annual West Coast Conference on Formal Linguistics*, 317–329.

Zubizaretta, M. L. (1982). *On the Relationship of the Lexicon to Syntax*. Doctoral dissertation, Massachusetts Institute of Technology, Cambridge.

Zubizaretta, M. L. (1987). *Levels of Representation in the Lexicon and in the Syntax*. Foris, Dordrecht.

INDEX

A

-able$_A$, 131, 134, 136, 144
Absorption, *see* θ-role, absorption
A-chain formation, 244–246
Acquisition, 4, 243–261, 287
Actor, 117n, 118, 170–171, 171n, 173,
    181–185, 185n, 188
Actor/undergoer hierarchy, 170, 173n, 181,
    184
  actor hierarchy, 171
Adjacency, 249n
Adjectival passive formation, 8, 16, 33–34
Adversative, 248
Affected, 4, 31, 32, 210, 210n, 211, 211n,
    243–261; *see also* Thematic feature;
    Affectedness
Affected argument constraint, 252–256, 258,
    260
Affectedness, 19, 21, 22n, 23, 26, 28, 149,
    151, 152, 159, 208, 210
Agent, 4, 12, 13, 17, 19, 19n, 20, 22–24, 29,
    31, 32, 37, 42, 45, 61, 64, 73, 82, 84,
    87, 89, 93n, 94, 97, 99, 103, 103n, 105,
    106, 113, 117, 117n, 120, 123–126,
    136–139, 143, 143n, 144, 145, 152,
    152n, 156, 158–160, 162, 164, 165, 168,
    170, 171, 173n, 176, 185, 185n, 187,
    193n, 196, 202, 208, 209, 235, 245, 251,
    253, 254, 267–270, 272, 273, 277, 281,
    282, 287
  possible, 81
Agent Postposing, 179
Agentivity, 86, 87
Agreement, 113; *see also* Choctaw,
    agreement

Amalgamation, 102
Analytic dependence, 244, 252
Analytic priority, 244, 256, 258–260
Antipassive, 179, 182, 186, 187; *see also*
    Derived antipassive
APF, *see* Adjectival passive formation
Applicative construction, 270; *see also*
    Locative alternation
Arb, 41, 42, 200, 200n
Arbitrary index, *see* Arb
Argument
  active, 234
  empty subject, 78, 79
  external, 12–15, 17, 20, 31, 33–35, 35n,
    110, 130n, 203–207, 245, 246, 251,
    251n, 255, 256
  implicit, 269n
  infinitival, 69
  inheritance, 129–146
  internal, 12, 14, 15, 33, 34, 109, 110,
    114n, 246, 250–252, 255, 256
    direct, 12–15, 17, 20–22, 25, 28, 31,
      33–35n, 130n, 131
    indirect, 12, 14, 15, 20, 21, 31, 33, 34,
      130n, 136
  obligatory, 134, 135
  optional, 135
  passive, 234, 235
  phonetically empty, 75
  promoted, 93, 94, 97
  structure, 129–165, 246
    alternation, 4, 130
    suppression, 108, 109, 109n
    θ, 93
Argument classification, 15n

Autonomous systems view, 38, 38n
Autonomy, 36–60, 212
  thesis, 3, 38–41, 48, 192, 194, 195,
    205–207, 212, 212n, 213
AUX clitic, 3, 215–227, 235–240
Auxiliary selection, 113, 121, 123, 124

B

Barrier, 104n
Benefactive, 267, 270–272
Beneficiary, 94, 271–273
Berber, 21
Bijacency, 41, 54, 55, 57–60
Binary branching, 59, 59n, 60, 98, 99, 108n
Binding, 159
Binding theory, 118
Blocking category, 104n

C

Case
  inherent, 224, 228, 234n, 236, 241
  lexical, 234n
  structural, 224, 227
Case absorption, 224, 257, 258, 260
Case assignment, 28, 140, 224, 228, 237n,
  260
Case feature, 168, 170, 170n, 188, 189
Case filter, 95, 95n, 180, 188
Case frame, 32
Case linking, 167–189; see also Linking rule
Case marking, 95, 104, 221–226, 235, 236n,
  252, 256, 257, 287
Case theory, 3, 4, 218, 244, 250, 260
Categorial grammar, 39
Causative, 108–110, 116, 120, 177, 183, 268,
  269, 277, 282
[cause], 159
Causer, 155, 159n, 269n
C-command, 14, 44, 83n, 118, 119, 205, 206
  mutual, 14
[change], 158–160, 163, 164
Chickasaw, 122
Choctaw, 4, 113–127
  agreement, 114–112
CHOP predicate, 226, 227
Clefting, 94n

Cognate object construction, 99, 106
Co-index rule, 41, 52, 54, 60
Co-indexing, 47, 48, 79, 104, 120
  thematic, 104–106, 110
Comparable set, 106, 110
Completeness condition, 45n, 191n, 195,
  195n, 196, 198n, 200, 200n
Completive, 121n, 123, 124
Complex predicate, 4, 91–111
Complex Predicate Rule, 97
Composition, 55, 56, 60, 69, 98, 99, 107,
  204, 227; see also θ-role assignment,
  compositional
Comprehension, 4, 263–288
Conative construction, 217–241
Conative rule, 231, 235
Conceptual structure, 24, 39n, 192
Congruence, 93, 93n, 101, 102, 105
CONTACT predicate, 231
Continuum of control, 160n
Control, 3, 5, 8, 38, 40, 42, 46–53, 47n, 54,
  57, 60, 63, 64–73, 75–89, 212n
  nonobligatory, 79–85, 89
  obligatory, 50, 51, 53, 69–73, 79, 85–89
  pragmatic, 48
  thematic, 64–69, 73
Controller problem, 75–89
Core meaning, 268, 269, 272–275, 281
Coreference, 38, 39, 48, 85, 119, 120, 192,
  195, 199
  pronominal, 84, 85n, 87
CP, see Controller problem

D

Dative alternation, 11n; see also Double-
  object construction
Dative construction
  impersonal, 172
  inversion, 172
Dative shift, 110; see also Dative alternation
Dative verb, 21n
Decomposition, 3–5, 9, 17, 18, 24–28,
  31–33, 36, 37n, 113, 116, 122, 122n,
  123, 125, 193n, 226–234
Derivational rule, see Lexical rule
Derived antipassive, 178, 185; see also
  Antipassive
Detransitivization, 270, 282
Deverbal nominal, see Nominal, deverbal

Different subject, 118–120
Discourse model, 4, 264, 266, 278, 288
Discourse structure, 264, 273
Distributedness condition, 191n, 197
Domain aggregation, 247, 248
Double dative construction, 217, 218, 220, 223, 224, 237–240
Double object construction, 4, 21n, 92, 99, 99n, 107–110, 209, 210
DS, *see* Different subject

E

Effect construction, 226–241
EFFECT predicate, 226, 231; *see also* CHOP predicate
Effector, 116, 117, 120, 123, 125, 170, 176, 184
Entailment, 2, 61–73, 76–78, 81, 83–87, 89, 103, 105, 106, 108n, 192, 202n, 203, 230, 231, 272
EQUI, 38
-*er*$_N$, 131–134, 136, 144
    agent, 142–144, 145n
    instrument, 142, 145, 145n
Ergative, 109n, 118, 211n, 268, 277, 282
    movement, 118, 251
    verb, 109n, 139
Evaluation, 13, 235, 236, 238
Event, 37, 37n, 89
Event role, 193n, 211
Experienced, 151, 152, 154, 156
Experiencer, 32, 97, 100–102, 117, 120, 123, 124, 152, 154–156, 158, 159, 162–164, 168, 172, 172n, 176, 184, 209n, 212n
Experiencer hypothesis, 155, 156
Extensional role, 125, 126, 151n, 193n
Extraposition, 94n
Extraposition from NP, 94n

F

Feature system, *see* θ-role, feature
Filler-gap assignment, *see* Filler-gap construction
Filler-gap construction, 265, 284–287
Flip construction, 175, 176, 179, 183–187
For phrase, 47n

French, 21
Functional structure, 204, 205

G

Garden path, 264, 266, 274, 277, 281–284
GB, *see* Government-binding theory
Generalized phrase structure grammar, 39n, 75
Generative semantics, 38
Genetive of negation, 178–180
Georgian, 122
GF, *see* Grammatical function
Goal, 19–24, 26, 28, 31, 32, 34, 41, 52, 53, 61, 64–68, 77, 78, 86, 87, 89, 93, 93n, 97, 99n, 100, 100n, 101–103, 106, 110, 116, 117, 117n, 120, 123–126, 137, 138, 151n, 171, 171n, 193n, 200, 208, 209, 211, 235, 253, 254, 280–284, 287
Goal dative construction, 217–241
Governing category, 118
Government, 14, 43–47, 58, 59n, 60, 104, 234, 235, 267
    directionality, 248, 250, 253
Government-binding theory, 1, 2, 7, 10, 15, 39, 62, 68, 93n, 98, 118, 124, 167n, 180, 186, 188, 194, 224, 234, 244n, 245, 251
Grammatical function, 9, 12, 13, 16, 17, 31n, 41, 154, 215, 216, 219–221, 223–225, 227, 231, 233, 234, 234n, 238, 241; *see also* Grammatical relation
Grammatical relation, 2, 11, 16, 63, 75, 78, 103, 110, 141, 167, 168, 244; *see also* Grammatical function

H

Human action, principles, 61–73, 76, 89
Hungarian, 21

I

Icelandic, 203
Identification, 103, 105, 106, 235
Impact verb, 218, 228–230, 241
Inchoative, 177, 179, 183, 185, 186, 221, 249
Inchoativization, 183, 187

Index, arbitrary, *see* Arb
    referential, 41; *see also* Co-index rule
Infinitival complement, 3, 44, 70, 71, 79, 85
Infinitival indirect question, 64
Infinitival relative, 3, 65–67, 69, 79–85, 88
Infinitive complement, *see* Infinitival
    complement
Infinitive subject, 49–51
-ing$_A$, 136, 142
-ing$_N$
    process, 131, 134–136, 136n, 138–140,
        140n, 142
    result, 134, 142–145
Inherent reflexive, *see* Reflexive, inherent
Inheritance, *see* Argument, inheritance
Inheritance principle, 130, 138–141, 144,
    146; *see also* Argument, inheritance
Instrument, 29, 32, 125, 137, 138, 145, 152,
    152n, 160, 193n, 208, 209, 272, 273
Instrumental, 267, 270–272
Intensional role, 125, 126, 152n, 193n
IR, *see* Infinitival relative
Italian, 122n

J

Japanese, 21, 248

K

Kannada, 21, 29n

L

Latent parallelism, 265
Latin, 29n
LCS, *see* Lexical–conceptual structure
Learnability, 140n, 205n
Level, 167, 173, 189
    external, 246, 258, 261
Level-ordering, 130–136
Lexical feature, 140, 141
Lexical learning hypothesis, 192n
Lexical preference, 258
Lexical redundancy rule, 10
Lexical rule, 129–146
Lexical semantics, 63
Lexical structure, 130, 266

Lexical–conceptual structure, 3, 9–36, 218,
    225–242
Lexical-functional grammar, 15n, 75, 152,
    153, 182, 245
Lexical-government, 43–46, 49, 56, 58
Lexical-semantic representation, 7–36
Lexical-semantic structure, 18n
Lexical-syntactic representation, 7–36
Lexicalist hypothesis, 148, 148n, 149n
Lexicalization patterns, 30
Lexicosemantic structure, 241n
Lexicosyntactic structure, 130n
LF, *see* Logical form
LFG, *see* Lexical-functional grammar
L-government, *see* Lexical-government
Linking principle, *see* Linking rule
Linking rule, 3, 9, 10, 17, 18, 20, 20n, 21,
    21n, 22–25, 25n, 27, 28, 31, 32, 130n,
    168, 170, 171, 186–189
    module, 250
Locality, 40, 41, 53, 55, 57, 98, 104n, 191n,
    195, 197
Location, 12, 13, 32, 65, 67, 69, 82, 84,
    84n, 87, 89, 102, 103, 106, 137, 138,
    151n, 168, 172, 193n, 198, 199, 201,
    203, 208, 254, 270, 276
Locative, 170, 171n, 173, 176, 184
Locative alternation, 3, 9, 18–31; *see also*
    Applicative construction
Locatum, 19–23, 28
Logical form, 44, 192, 245, 248, 258

M

Macro-role, 5, 117n, 118, 170, 188
Malayalam, 4, 92, 94–97, 99
Manner marker, 99, 105n
Mental representation, 37
Middle, 211n, 268, 269
Monostratal syntax, 3, 168, 170–174,
    181–189
Monostratal theory, 167
Montague grammar, 39, 75, 252
Morphological rule, *see* Lexical rule
Morphological subject, 170–173, 174n, 176,
    178, 182, 183, 188
Move-α, 107, 245, 248, 250, 261
Move Theme, 245
MS, *see* Morphological subject
Multiple strata, *see* Multistratal theory

Multistratal syntax, 168, 169, 179–181, 189
Multistratal theory, 167, 167n, 168, 173
Muskogean, 113, 122n

N

N → V rule, 133, 133n
Navaho, 222n
Negative evidence, 247
Neutral, 151, 151n, 152, 152n, 156, 158, 160, 164–165
Nexal head, 193n
NOC, *see* Control, nonobligatory
Nominal, +Affected constraint, 260
Nominal
    derived, 4, 147–165
    deverbal, 91–93, 96–100, 105, 106
    experiential, 156, 157, 162, 164
    passive, 4, 147, 157, 255–256, 258
Nonpredicative node, 102, 103
Norwegian, 203–205, 205n, 212
Noun complement, 66, 67
NP movement, 4, 93n, 147, 149, 157, 164, 181, 254n, 255
    within NP, 157
NP-preposing, *see* NP movement
NP-trace, 4, 244–246, 249n, 251, 254–256, 258–261
N-rule, 152, 154–158
N*-rule, 158, 160, 164
N-structure, 248, 249
Number suppletion, 113, 117, 118

O

Object deletable verb, 181, 185, 186; *see also*
    Unspecified object construction; Object deletion
Object deletion, 182, 187, 270
Obtain construction, 226–241
OBTAIN predicate, 227, 228, 230, 233
Obtain rule, 233
Obviative anaphor, 118
OC, *see* Control, obligatory
Old English, 29n
Open thematic role, *see* θ-role, open
Out-prefixation, 142, 143n

P

Pama-Nyungan, 223n
Parameter, 16, 205n
Parser, serial, 265
Parsing, 4, 5, 264, 273, 277, 278, 281
PAS, *see* Predicate–argument structure
Passive, 4, 5, 59, 71–73, 96, 107, 117n, 136, 136n, 138–140, 154, 163, 164, 168, 171n, 174, 174n, 185n, 209, 210, 243–261, 269, 283, 287
    actional, 243, 253
    adjectival, 8, 136n, 140, 149, 150, 163, 245; *see also* Adjectival passive formation
    agentless, 174n, 270
    grammaticalization, 256–258
    imperfective, 174–176, 179, 183, 185–188
    lexical, 245, 246; *see also* Passive, adjectival
    morphology, 171
    nonactional, 4, 243, 253
    perfective, 175, 175n, 187
    periphrastic, 175, 175n
Passive nominalization, *see* Nominal, passive
PATH, 19n
Patient, 17, 20, 37, 45, 64, 82, 84, 87, 89, 93n, 99, 117, 125, 126, 137n, 151, 152n, 157–159, 159n, 162–165, 170, 193n, 196, 202, 208–211, 211n, 235, 245, 253–255, 269n
    possible, 81
PC, *see* Purpose clause
Percept, 137n, 151, 197, 209n, 210n
Perception verb, 228–230, 232
Perceptual role, 193n, 211
Person–number clitic, *see* AUX clitic
PF, 245
Phonological clause, 216
Picture noun, 199
Polish, 4, 147, 161–164
    impersonal construction, 159
Poss function, 152
Possessor, 95, 96, 99n, 172, 201
Predicate–argument structure, 3, 9–36, 218, 219, 224, 225, 228–242
Predication, 12n, 14, 37–60, 67, 79, 80, 105, 197–199, 201–203, 222; *see also* Predicative node
    nonthematic, 41, 46, 53–60
    secondary, 109n

Predicational domain, *see* Predicational
    structure
Predicational structure, 197, 203, 204; *see
    also* Thematic structure
Predicative node, 98, 99, 104–106, 108
Presupposition, 61–73, 76–78, 81, 83–87, 89,
    278
Primary location hierarchy, 67
PRO, 40, 40n, 43, 44, 48, 64, 67–69, 83,
    194, 200
    arbitrary, 47
    in NP, 194, 212
Processing, 264, 273–288
Processor, 4, 264, 265
PRO-clause, 250n
Projection principle, 5, 10, 16, 34, 97, 97n,
    129, 140, 141, 146, 250
Promotion, 93, 95, 99–107, 110; *see also*
    Argument, promoted
Pronominal coreference, *see* Coreference,
    pronominal
Psychological predicate, 115, 121n, 151
Purpose clause, 3, 63–65, 67, 69, 79–89
    object gap, 64, 79, 79n, 83, 89
    subject gap, 64, 79n
Purpose construction, 65–69; *see also*
    Purpose clause

Q

Q-float, 94n

R

Real-world knowledge, 4, 5, 264, 265, 276
Receiver, 93n, 171
Reciprocal, 168, 174, 177, 179, 192n
Reflexive, 48, 49, 168–174, 174n, 177, 179;
    see also Russian, -*sja*
    inherent, 178–180, 187
Reflexivization, 3, 5, 8, 191–213; *see also*
    Reflexive
Relational grammar, 93n, 118, 167n, 173
Relative clause, 84
    reduced, 281–283
Relativization, 95n
Resultative, 4, 108n, 109n, 110, 143n, 211n
Role assignment, *see* θ-role, assignment
Romance, 174

R-structure, 14n, 37n, 40–47, 48n, 51–55,
    57, 57n, 60, 191n, 192–213
Russian, 3, 21, 29n, 108n, 167–189
    -*sja*, 3, 168, 174–189

S

Same subject, 118–120
Sanskrit, 29n
Saturation, 13, 96, 241n
Scandinavian, 108n, 203
Scrambling, 94, 94n
Segmental rule, 131
Selection, 97n, 98, 99n, 148, 259
Selectional feature, *see* Selection
Semantic bootstrapping, 244, 248–261
Sense ambiguity, 273–276
[sentient], 158–160, 164
-*sja*, *see* Russian, -*sja*
Small clause, 105, 107, 108n, 110, 194, 212
Small clause rule, 108–110
Source, 19n, 23, 41, 52–54, 61, 65–67, 86,
    89, 93, 93n, 94, 97, 100n, 106, 110, 116,
    117n, 123, 125, 125n, 126, 137, 138,
    151n, 168, 171, 193n, 194, 200, 201,
    208, 253, 254, 283, 284
    secondary, 77
SR, *see* Switch reference
SS, *see* Same subject
Stratum, 167
Stress rule, 131
Subcategorization, 10, 11, 15, 43, 58, 69,
    79, 85, 88, 94, 95, 97, 97n, 98, 114n,
    141, 148–150, 157, 164, 259, 260,
    268–272, 285
Subset principle, 205n, 260
Superimposition, 100, 105
Switch reference, 118–119

T

Tamil, 108n
Thematic ambiguity, 273–276
Thematic condition on reflexives, 211
Thematic constancy principle, 152–154
Thematic controller problem, 76–89
Thematic domain, 193, 193n, 195, 195n,
    197–205, 207n, 271
Thematic feature, 4, 24n, 158–161; *see also*
    θ-role, feature

Thematic feedback, 273, 276-278
Thematic grid, *see* θ-grid
Thematic hierarchy, 48, 170, 206-212; *see also* θ-role, hierarchy
Thematic identity condition, 93n
Thematic inheritance principle, 4; *see also* Argument, inheritance; Inheritance principle
Thematic role assignment, *see* θ-role, assignment
Thematic role hierarchy, *see* Thematic hierarchy
Thematic structure, 113, 130n, 173n, 191-213; *see also* Argument, structure
Theme, 4, 12, 13, 16, 17, 20-23, 25, 27-34, 41, 52-54, 61, 65, 67-69, 77, 80, 82, 83, 89, 93n, 94-97, 99, 99n, 100-103n, 110, 113, 116-118, 120, 122-126, 137, 137n, 138, 142, 143, 143n, 145, 145n, 151, 151n, 153, 154, 168, 170-172, 173n, 174n, 193, 197, 198, 203, 208, 209, 211, 224, 235, 253-255, 260, 267n, 268-270, 272, 273, 276-279, 281-284, 287
   displaced, 28, 29
θ-argument, *see* Argument
θ-assignment, *see* θ-role, assignment
θCP, *see* Thematic controller problem
θ-criterion, 1, 4, 5, 10, 13, 16, 16n, 34, 39, 39n, 40, 40n, 62, 109n, 113, 124-126, 144, 144n, 146, 195n, 269
θ-feature, *see* θ-role, feature
θ-feature uniqueness principle, 253-254
θ-frame, 96, 102, 103, 105, 106, 110
   phrasal node, 97-102
θ-government, 104
θ-grid, 7, 12, 13, 62, 106, 241n, 264, 265, 268, 269, 271-273, 275, 282, 283, 287
   manipulation, 269
θ-hierarchy, *see* θ-role, hierarchy
θ-linking, 47, 49, 51-55, 57, 60
θ-marking, 4, 92-112; *see also* θ-role, assignment
   compositional, 107; *see also* Composition
   direct, 100, 102, 104, 104n
   indirect, 4, 93, 98, 100, 110; *see also* θ-role, assignment, compositional
θ-merging, 55-60, 57n, 125
θ-role
   absorption, 130, 143-146
   assignment, 13-16, 33, 42-46, 54, 56-58, 60, 62, 68, 83, 100, 101, 103, 130,

136, 140, 157, 180, 193, 193n, 195-203, 210, 250, 276-278, 283, 284, 287; *see also* θ-marking
   algorithmic, 196
   compositional, 4, 98, 157; *see also* Composition
   direct, 45, 206, 207
   indirect, 45, 206-208
   manner of, 9, 14, 16, 20, 33
   multiple, 113-127
   blocking, 4
   class, 40, 125, 196, 208, 209, 209n; *see also* Tier; θ-role, set
   complex, 125
   defining function, 191
   definition, 25
   diacritic use, 62
   external, 42, 44, 46, 54, 56, 57n
   feature, 18n, 24n, 31, 32, 147, 253, 254; *see also* Thematic feature
   hierarchy, 20n, 25n, 31n, 64, 117, 117n, 120, 138, 138n, 144-146; *see also* Thematic hierarchy
   internal, 110
   label, 8, 9, 13, 16-18, 20, 20n, 24, 25, 27, 33, 191
   linguistic function, 191
   list, 9, 15n, 17-23, 25, 27, 28, 31n, 36, 62
   nondistinctness, 93n
   open, 269, 269n, 270, 272, 278-288
   promotion, 4
   set, 193n, 208; *see also* θ-role, class
   syntactic, 38-40
θ-structure, *see* Thematic structure
θ-theory, 4, 15, 62, 91-111, 244, 250, 260
Tier, 31, 22n, 40n, 267n; *see also* θ-role, class
Trace mapping, 252
Tsova Tush, 122n

U

Unaccusative, 34, 35, 35n, 36, 118, 139, 178, 179, 180, 251, 258
Unaccusative, advancement, 118-120
un-affixation, 142
Undergoer, 117n, 118, 170, 171, 171n, 173n, 181-185, 188
Unergative, 35, 35n, 36, 178, 180

Uniformity principle, 141–143, 146
Unspecified object construction, 177, 177n,
    179; *see also* Object deletable verb

V

V → N rule, 133n
Verb entailment, *see* Entailment
Verbal suppletion, 121–123; *see also* Number
    suppletion
Visser's generalization, 71

W

Warlpiri, 3, 27, 215–242
Wh-movement, 96, 254n
Wh-trace, 249n
With phrase, 28–32
Word recognition, 264, 265, 275

X

X-bar theory, 10, 157

SYNTAX and SEMANTICS

Volume 1
edited by John P. Kimball

Volume 2
edited by John P. Kimball

Volume 3: Speech Acts
edited by Peter Cole and Jerry L. Morgan

Volume 4
edited by John P. Kimball

Volume 5: Japanese Generative Grammar
edited by Masayoshi Shibatani

Volume 6: The Grammar of Causative Constructions
edited by Masayoshi Shibatani

Volume 7: Notes from the Linguistic Underground
edited by James D. McCawley

Volume 8: Grammatical Relations
edited by Peter Cole and Jerrold M. Sadock

Volume 9: Pragmatics
edited by Peter Cole

Volume 10: Selections from the Third Gronigen Round Table
edited by Frank Heny and Helmut S. Schnelle

Volume 11: Presupposition
edited by Choon-Kyu Oh and David S. Dinneen

Volume 12: Discourse and Syntax
edited by Talmy Givón

Volume 13: Current Approaches to Syntax
edited by Edith A. Moravcsik and Jessica R. Wirth

Volume 14: Tense and Aspect
edited by Philip J. Tedeschi and Annie Zaenen

Volume 15: Studies in Transitivity
edited by Paul J. Hopper and Sandra A. Thompson

Volume 16: The Syntax of Native American Languages
edited by Eung-Do Cook and Donna B. Gerdts

Volume 17: Composite Predicates in English
Ray Cattell

Volume 18: Diachronic Syntax: The Kartvelian Case
Alice C. Harris
Volume 19: The Syntax of Pronominal Clitics
edited by Hagit Borer
Volume 20: Discontinuous Constituency
edited by Geoffrey J. Huck and Almerindo E. Ojeda
Volume 21: Thematic Relations
edited by Wendy Wilkins